GAME AUDIO PROGRAMMING

GAME AUDIO PROGRAMMING

James Boer

CHARLES RIVER MEDIA, INC.
Hingham, Massachusetts

Publisher: Jenifer Niles
Production: Publishers' Design and Production Services, Inc.
Cover Design: The Printed Image
Cover Image: James Boer

CHARLES RIVER MEDIA, INC.
20 Downer Avenue, Suite 3
Hingham, Massachusetts 02043
781-740-0400
781-740-8816 (FAX)
info@charlesriver.com
www.charlesriver.com

This book is printed on acid-free paper.

James Boer. *Game Audio Programming*.
ISBN: 1-58450-245-2

Library of Congress Cataloging-in-Publication Data

Boer, James R.
  Game Audio Programming / James Boer.—1st ed.
      p.   cm.
  ISBN 1-58450-245-2
  1. Computer games—Programming.   2. Computer sound processing.   I. Title.
  QA76.76.C672 B64 2002
  794.8'165—dc21
                              2002012582

Printed in the United States of America
02   7 6 5 4 3 2   First Edition

Dedicated to my family, for always reminding me
what is truly important in life.

CONTENTS

Appendices

PREFACE

Sound and music have always had an important place in computer games. From the earliest video-game creations, designers intrinsically felt the need to give players a form of feedback they could not only see, but hear as well. The simple beeps of *Pong*, the menacing rhythms of *Asteroids,* the whimsical arpeggios of *Donkey Kong,* and the relentless crunching of *Pac-Man* all left their marks early on the quarter-dropping kids of the 1980s. As gaming hardware improved technologically, game audio improved right along with everything else. Home computers became viable gaming platforms, albeit modest ones at first. The earliest PC computers, with a simple one-tone speaker, were sorely lacking in audio capabilities; but the free market prevailed, and add-on audio cards eventually became a de facto standard in nearly every PC sold. As audio hardware improved in both home computers and home console systems, developers found new ways to deliver exciting and dynamic sound and music content with their games.

Development of new audio capabilities, however, usually took a back seat to visual enhancements—and frankly, for a good reason. After all, even the name "video game" indicates that the primary communication medium is the graphical image. Hearing is arguably our second-most important sense after sight, and so it stands to reason that visual information in a game is more important than audio. I would venture to submit that if one were to quantify the importance of sight versus hearing in everyday life, it might turn out to approximately reflect the same video-versus-audio priority ratio when it comes to component development effort and cost in modern entertainment hardware and software.

But despite its inevitable second-banana status, the emotional power of sound and music can provide some exciting returns for developers who are willing to make a modest investment in their game's audio development/content budget. Unlike visual content, audio tends to offer a subtle, yet very powerful stimulus, providing auditory clues to a player, which, while seemingly very minor, can help to make a big difference in encouraging suspension of disbelief within the game environment. A simple effect such as the sound of footsteps reverberating off the walls of a large cave can provide spatial perception, almost seeming to improve even the visual quality of the small window through which a player must peer into the game world. Likewise, a dramatic musical score can elicit an emotional response in the player—a response unlikely to be tapped by any other means. A truly outstanding game still requires outstanding audio.

It's with this context and perspective that I'm hoping you will read and utilize this book. While modern game audio programming is turning into a highly complex and technical endeavor, it is important to never lose sight of the fact that sound and music, more than anything else, can so easily evoke such a dramatic range of basic emotions. Conversely, bad audio, whether in content or programming, can similarly have the opposite effect. Lifeless and uninspired sounds will rob your game of emotional impact, and a dull, repetitive musical score will quickly be turned off as it becomes tiresome to the player. It's your job as an audio programmer to create capabilities and tools that will enable your sound designers and composers to seamlessly integrate their content into your game with a minimum of technical fussing or tinkering. With this perspective and focus, new games of the modern era will continue to excite and thrill players with not only fantastic new graphical wizardry, but also with dynamic, pulse-pounding sound and music as well.

Here's to a great future for game audio!

ABOUT THE AUTHOR

James Boer is an audio programmer and a sound designer/composer. A number of best-selling games are credited to his name, including *Deer Hunter, Deer Hunter II,* and *Rocky Mountain Trophy Hunter.* Other programming and audio credits include *Pro Bass Fishing, Microsoft Baseball 2000, Jamoke, Tex Atomic's Big Bot Battles,* and audio components for the Lithtech engine. In addition to writing *Game Audio Programming,* he has also contributed to *Game Programming Gems I & II* (Charles River Media, Inc.), co-authored *DirectX Complete* (McGraw-Hill), and has written several articles for *Game Developer* magazine. He is currently employed at Adrenium Games and can be reached for comments or questions at *james.boer@gte.net.*

SPECIAL THANKS

I'd like to say "thanks" to a number of people for their contributions, direct or indirect, toward the completion of this book. First and foremost, thanks to my family for *everything*. My publisher, Jenifer Niles, was infinitely patient with me as I struggled to ensure this book was as good as I could possibly make it, and I sincerely appreciate the latitude and support I was given in this regard. The editing team at Charles River Media also did a great job on the manuscript. Jack Buser at Dolby Labs was very helpful in teaching me about the latest Dolby technologies, and Peter Clare and the folks at Sensaura were kind enough to make sure I had appropriate hardware for testing the Sensaura-specific property sets. Special thanks, also, to David Yackley, Duncan McKay, and the rest of the Microsoft DirectX Audio team for taking the time to meet with me and for providing some valuable feedback.

PART I

INTRODUCTION AND THEORY

CHAPTER 1

INTRODUCTION

Welcome to *Game Audio Programming*, your comprehensive guide to interactive audio programming for the Microsoft Windows® platform. We will be covering a huge range of topics relevant to today's audio programmers, including DirectX Audio, audio decompression libraries, hardware filters and effects, geometric representation of world data for effects, occlusion and obstruction, and much more.

There are several general-purpose audio-programming books on the market, and there are dozens of game-programming books, many of which cover sound and music programming to some degree. Audio programming, however, has progressed far beyond the simplistic treatment afforded it in most game-programming books, and most general-purpose audio programming books deal in too many irrelevant subjects to be of much help. Thus, *Game Audio Programming* was born.

WHO THIS BOOK IS FOR

Game Audio Programming is designed to provide a comprehensive reference for C++ programmers who are implementing an audio system of any sort for an entertainment or multimedia title on the Win32 platform. While the reader will be shown, in step-by-step instructions, how to implement a DirectX Audio-based system (and given sample code on the accompanying CD-ROM), those readers wishing to use a third-party audio library should understand that this book covers far more than simply describing DirectSound. (We describe the pros and cons of commercially licensed audio libraries later in this chapter.)

PREREQUISITES

Throughout the book, it is assumed that the reader has a working knowledge of C++ and object-oriented programming principles. It is also assumed that the reader possesses at least a basic understanding of Windows programming.

The samples and libraries were compiled with Microsoft Visual C++ 6.0, with Service Pack 5 installed. DirectX 9.0 is used for all DirectX-related applications. The samples were compiled on Windows 2000 and additionally tested on Windows 98, Windows ME, and Windows XP. The audio libraries developed require an installed DirectX-compatible sound card with working DirectX drivers.

PRESENTATION AND ORGANIZATION

While some chapters by necessity build on information presented in previous chapters, an effort has been made to keep topics somewhat independent of each other. This means you should be able to jump to the topic of most interest to you and plunge right in without having to read the book sequentially. If additional information is required that is found in previous sections of the book, a clear reference will tell you where to find this information. Additionally, all figures, tables, and code listings are numbered by chapter, and then order of appearance within the chapter to help you more easily locate cross-references. This book has been divided into six logical parts; they are:

PART I —INTRODUCTION AND THEORY

Basic theory about sound, digital audio, modern hardware, and design theory are presented. You will learn some essential background information relating to digital audio as well as a few pointers on how to design a robust and easy-to-use audio system interface.

PART II—DIRECTX AUDIO

Here we cover both basic and advanced topics on DirectSound and DirectMusic. In this part, the groundwork is laid for the more-advanced topics that follow. If you are an experienced DirectSound or DirectMusic programmer, you might only need to skim the introductory chapters; although the more-advanced chapters might still be of interest to you.

PART III—HIGH-LEVEL AUDIO PROGRAMMING

Using the foundation of a basic audio system, you will be shown how to create high-level audio systems, including script-driven sound templates. You will learn how to build an interactive music system from the ground up.

PART IV—CUSTOM AUDIO FORMATS AND LOADERS

In Part IV, we will examine alternative file formats and the SDKs (Software Developer's Kits) needed to access them, including the Windows Media SDK (for WMA and MP3 files), Ogg Vorbis, and the Windows Audio Compression Manager. We will also show you how to create custom file system loaders using the standard COM IStream interface.

PART V—ADVANCED 3D TECHNIQUES

Here we will discuss a number of cutting-edge 3D audio-related topics. The use of hardware extensions such as EAX, ZoomFX, and MacroFX will be covered in detail. Beyond this, different approaches, both proven and theoretical, for actually getting this information into your game will be covered. For instance, we will examine some preprocessor algorithms that could be used for automatically scanning and processing a 3D environment in order to determine how to choose an appropriate set of EAX parameters, as well as how to dynamically calculate and assign occlusion and obstruction values for audio buffers.

PART VI—MISCELLANEOUS

In Part VI, we discuss how to play Redbook audio from a CD. Numerous other general optimizations and strategies will be covered that you might find useful.

THE SAMPLE AUDIO LIBRARY

Game Audio Programming attempts to cover as much ground as possible, providing you with the information you need to get the job done in as efficient a manner as possible. Most important, these topics are not presented to you in a vacuum or in passing theory. A full-featured, documented, and internally commented audio library (referred to as the *GAP*, or *Game Audio Programming*, library) is available for your use either as a ready-to-use library for your own games or as reference code to help you implement your own audio system. Throughout the book, we will be referencing this library (or at least relevant portions of it) to explain concepts ranging from playing a simple sound to advanced dynamic resource management.

ON THE CD   Conversely, an effort was also made to not needlessly dump pages of irrelevant code for you to wade through. Code is listed, in part or full, where appropriate and necessary; but to understand the material being covered fully, you should also be prepared to browse through both the source code on the CD-ROM and the DirectX SDK documentation when appropriate.

Because of the necessity to demonstrate higher-level concepts, such as built-in scripting support, the *GAP* library tends to provide a bit more high-level functionality than most audio libraries, which has its good and bad points. While the additional functionality might be handy for you, it could, in fact, either conflict with or be redundant with systems your game already uses. For example, you might have your own text file parsing and scripting mechanisms you wish to use instead of the built-in script definition language provided. In this case, it is recommended to simply strip out the unwanted features (the scripting systems are actually a separate library); or you might instead opt to build your own audio system from the ground up, and only refer to the provided system for guidance.

PLATFORM AND API CHOICES

As the title suggests, this is not a book dealing with all aspects of audio programming. Game programming has unique demands of its own, and we will be focusing on those specific aspects of audio programming most useful for that purpose. For instance, we do not cover DirectSound audio capture, as this is not a required feature for most games. This book's choice of platform and API (application programming interface) is Win32 and DirectX because it is the most popular and accessible platform available for game programmers today. There are, of course, many other great platforms and APIs currently available, but it is not realistic to cover in great detail every one of these platform/API combinations.

For professionals developing on and for the Win32 platform, DirectX Audio is by far the most popular choice for audio APIs. As such, we'll be examining DirectSound and DirectMusic in detail, showing how the two systems can integrate seamlessly into a total audio solution. DirectShow also has some interesting possibilities worth investigating for certain situations. But DirectX is not the only API required for a complete audio solution. Others include the Microsoft Audio Compression Manager, Windows MCI functions, Windows Media, Ogg Vorbis, and MP3 playback using the popular X-Audio library.

One new API that might offer a cross-platform audio solution is Open-AL (Open Audio Library), which is modeled in part after OpenGL, the cross-platform 3D graphics library. However, OpenAL, with its narrow focus on 3D-only sound rendering, currently provides a somewhat smaller subset of the features found in DirectX Audio. There is no reason, though, that the lessons learned in this book could not apply equally well to a system based on OpenAL or another API (with the obvious exception of the DirectX-specific chapters).

There are other API choices as well. Some companies prefer the convenience of licensing a third-party audio library. There are many high-quality products on the market. One of the oldest and most popular is the Miles Sound System (*www.radgametools.com*). FMOD (*www.fmod.org*) is another audio library that has enjoyed a growing popularity as well, especially among freeware and demo developers. (By 'demo,' we're referring to the small tech demos created by those in the 'demo scene,' which is especially popular in Europe). More recently, Sensaura, traditionally known for creating the chips used in many PC sound cards, has developed a cross-platform audio library for PC, Xbox, Playstation 2, and Nintendo GameCube.

Why would you consider licensing a third-party audio library when DirectX is free and available to use? Licensing a third-party audio system has both advantages and drawbacks.

If you are developing for multiple platforms supported by one of these libraries, this could be the most compelling reason of all. While creating a custom library using native APIs such as DirectX is not too daunting on a single platform, learning and implementing native sound hardware and APIs on several different platforms could prove to be a formidable task, which would be eased considerably by having to only write to a single API, with only minor adjustments for platform-specific code. Worse, many platforms don't have the high-level functionality provided by DirectX or similar systems, forcing the developers to work directly with the hardware at a very low level, which always translates into greater development costs.

Beyond cross-platform availability, perhaps the biggest attraction is the instant functionality a library provides. DirectSound in particular has a well-earned reputation as being a somewhat difficult library to work with. While this is true to some extent, one reason for this is that DirectSound makes no assumptions about the intended use of the library; it favors mid-level performance and flexibility over ease of use—although it is not as low-level as working directly with hardware.

High-level APIs can afford to encapsulate functionality into a more narrowly defined (but usually more fully developed) set, making it easier to use. For example, most libraries offer simple, one-function audio streaming; whereas DirectSound requires a large amount of coding to perform this same task. (DirectMusic, on the other hand, performs many of these tasks for you automatically.) If you wish to use a specific high-level feature of a library (e.g., MOD playback), buying a solution might be cheaper than attempting to implement your own.

■ THE MOD MUSIC FORMAT

The MOD music format was born on the Amiga platform as a way of playing high-quality music while using very little memory or disk space. A MOD file contains sequenced notes (timed markers containing pitch, duration, and other specific information) along with digital audio samples that produce the actual sounds of the song. The format eventually evolved along with the platform, spawning dozens of subvariants; but the principle of all of these formats remains the same, and all are collectively referred to as MOD files. You may notice that the description of MOD files sounds suspiciously like a MIDI+DLS (discussed in Chapter 3) combination format, and this is exactly what it is. For professional use, MIDI has both better composition tools and is more flexible in its use (due to its more general nature). However, this is not to say that you cannot achieve polished, professional results with MOD files, as hundreds or perhaps even thousands of games over the years have proven.

So why bother using DirectX Audio at all, when these other APIs offer more functionality, are easier to use, and can be more portable? Beyond the fact that DirectX is both free and a standard library on Win32 platforms, here are a few other reasons why DirectX Audio might be the correct choice for you:

- DirectX is a continually evolving product that is enhanced and refined as the Windows/PC platform and related sound hardware evolves. Since most audio libraries are in fact built on top of DirectSound drivers, or even on top of the API itself, there will inevitably be a delay between the release of a new version of DirectX and the time in which a library can make use of these new features. In such a highly competitive market such as game development, touting the latest and greatest features can take on a good deal of importance. As DirectSound and DirectMusic evolve into DirectX Audio, it appears that functionality is growing at an even faster rate. For instance, there are few third-party audio libraries available that take advantage of the functionality provided by DirectMusic, or which come anywhere close to offering equivalent musical capabilities. Many offer competing standards, such as MOD or MIDI+DLS playback, but it's a safe bet to assume that the Microsoft DirectMusic tools and standards will continue to evolve rapidly, making it difficult or impractical for third-party audio library developers to keep up.

- Because DirectSound is a low-level API, it is relatively easy to create a wrapper API that enhances and controls the audio exactly as you want it to. In this case, the low-level nature of DirectSound, while often more difficult to program, provides the flexibility you need to perform just about any audio task and to organize it in a manner of your choosing. While this flexibility can sometimes be achieved with other libraries, you are often stuck with the implementation they provide, which might not be what you need.

  As an example, many commercial APIs are still written in C, since this is considered to be a 'common denominator' language, or perhaps because they are based on older legacy code. It is a good bet that you and your game team are coding in C++ at this point and could use the increased ease of use and natural functionality of an object-oriented audio SDK. With an older C-style library, you will still likely end up having to write some wrapper classes in order to ensure it fits in seamlessly with your game.

- Finally, there is a simple matter of stability and control. While most licensed audio libraries are solid pieces of software engineering and are well tested, the fact of the matter is that almost all pieces of complex software have bugs. Although there is no guarantee that your code will have fewer bugs than a licensed library, you at least have the option of fixing bugs in your code. This is usually not an option with licensed libraries—more often than not, the source does not come with them. And while the argument can be made that DirectX is an external library like others, DirectX is so extensively used that most bugs are quickly uncovered and fixed, resulting in a very stable base from which to build.

The bottom line is that a good case can be made for either using DirectX audio or for licensing a third-party API. It all depends on the features your game needs, and how you plan to implement and integrate the sound system into your game libraries. You'll have to do the research and decide for yourself. There are links to a number of companies that supply commercial audio libraries in Appendix E. Or, you can visit this book's Web site at *http://www.gameaudioprogramming.com* to get an up-to-date list of audio-development resources online.

LICENSING A THIRD-PARTY SOUND LIBRARY

Pros
- Potential for cross-platform availability, saving development time and money.
- Ease of use.
- Instant functionality, such as streaming audio, filters, and compressed format support.

Cons
- Typically requires a licensing fee.
- No control over feature set or underlying operation.
- No control over product quality—difficult to locate and fix bugs.

WRITING YOUR OWN SOUND SYSTEM WITH DIRECTX AUDIO

Pros
- DirectX is free.
- A well-tested library means both a lower risk of bugs and good stability.
- A low-level library means more control over audio system design and more flexibility in building a wrapper API.

Cons

- Can be difficult to work with.
- Requires a lot of wrapper code to create a suitably high-level API.
- Only available on two major platforms.

THE BIGGER PICTURE

An audio system is more than a collection of APIs. As games become increasingly larger in scope and depth, the scale of resources managed by audio systems grows exponentially. In addition, more games are moving to a 'seamless world' paradigm, where the user never sees a loading screen during the course of a game. Dynamic memory and resource management will play a huge role in any future audio system. This book will show you how to implement a robust resource manager that can handle the demands of a changing real-time environment in such a game, and how to build this right into your audio system.

There is also a matter of high-level sound system integration with your game engine. Whether creating a library for a single game or developing a system that will be licensed to dozens of companies with vastly different products, it is important to properly integrate the audio system into your game with an appropriate balance of flexibility and ease of use. For instance, your game engine might provide support for a scripting system. You will likely want to add extensions to support audio functionality. Likewise, your world editor will need some mechanism for placing sound and music objects in the world, and the job of designing these objects and the functionality they provide likely will fall on the shoulders of the audio programmer. If your game takes place in a 3D virtual world, you will need to decide how to best implement and utilize EAX and other hardware extensions, and how to organize your world data to generate and store occlusion and obstruction information. Most games utilize some sort of in-game music. If you require any sort of interactivity and real-time cueing, this again means more integration with existing in-game scripting systems—or perhaps even the design of your own music system, developed in conjunction with your game's composer.

As you can see, there is much more to an audio system than the basic functionality provided by a sound/music API. Much of the audio-related work involves integration of that system so it becomes a seamless part of your game engine.

CONCLUSION

Game audio is a growing field and is becoming more complex all the time. As such, there is a need for reliable information dedicated to the needs of audio programmers, instead of being relegated to a chapter or two in a general game-programming book. *Game Audio Programming*'s goal is to fulfill this need.

In Chapter 2, we will discuss the basic principles of sound and the digital reproduction of audio. While it is not necessary to have a deep understanding of the physics of sound, a basic understanding of it and the way it is reproduced on a computer can be helpful.

THEORY AND PRINCIPLES OF DIGITAL SOUND AND ACOUSTICS

In order to effectively make use of modern audio hardware in today's games and interactive multimedia titles, it is important for developers to understand the underlying fundamental principles of sound and acoustics. The theories, principles, and terminologies discussed here will provide a basic foundation of knowledge that will help any audio programmer while working with higher-level technology and tools.

ANATOMY OF A SOUND

In somewhat simplistic terms, audible noise (sound) is generated by physically vibrating material. The vibrating substance produces equivalent pulses (pressure waves) through a compressible medium, often the air. These atmospheric pressure pulses push a small, thin membrane in our ears, which in turn vibrate a series of small bones. These inner-ear bones translate the pulses into electrical impulses, which are sent to the brain and translated/perceived as sound. The physical characteristics of these pulses (vibrations) is what defines the aural properties of each sound.

A standard visual representation of sound is a two-dimensional graph, plotted as amplitude over time. A mathematical sine wave produces a single-frequency tone and gives us a chance to examine the basic characteristics of an audio wave.

In Figure 2.1, a simple sine wave is plotted as a sound. The vertical axis, labeled as *"Amplitude,"* represents the strength of the pulses. Note that amplitude is measured in both directions from a center axis because sound generally has both positive and negative pressures. The horizontal axis measures variation of the amplitude over time. Since the wave is periodic, we can precisely measure the frequency at which the wave pattern repeats. This is usually simply referred to as the sound's *frequency*. Frequency is measured in *hertz* (Hz), which defines the number of times a sound repeats in a second. Human hearing ranges from approximately 20 Hz to 20,000 Hz.

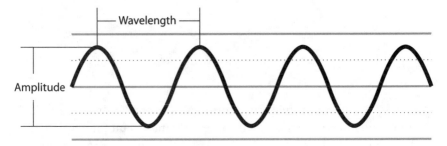

FIGURE 2.1   Visual representation of a basic sine wave.

FREQUENCY, PITCH, AND TUNING

Although related to each other, frequency and pitch are not synonymous. Frequency is an absolute measurement, but *pitch* may be described as the perceived frequency of a sound. For example, a perfect, mathematically tuned piano will tend to sound slightly off-tune because people tend to perceive high notes as a slightly lower frequency and low notes as a slightly higher frequency. It is important to remember that pitch and frequency are not the same thing.

Knowing the correct tuning frequencies is important if you plan to implement your own low-level musical synthesizer. Otherwise, it has little significance to the average game audio programmer. Most modern Western music uses a tuning called *equal tempering*, which has the advantage of flexibility over tuning that is geared to favor specific keys. That is, all the

TABLE 2.1   Frequencies for Equal-Tempering Tuning

	0	1	2	3	4	5	6	7	8
C	16.352	32.703	65.406	130.81	261.63	523.25	1046.5	2093.0	4186.0
C#	17.324	34.648	69.296	138.59	277.18	554.37	1108.7	2217.5	4434.9
D	18.354	36.708	73.416	146.83	293.66	587.33	1174.7	2349.3	4698.6
D#	19.445	38.891	77.782	155.56	311.13	622.25	1244.5	2489.0	4978.0
E	20.602	41.203	82.407	164.81	329.63	659.26	1318.5	2637.0	5274.0
F	21.827	43.654	87.307	174.61	349.23	698.46	1396.9	2793.8	5587.7
F#	23.125	46.249	92.499	185.00	369.99	739.99	1480.0	2960.0	5919.9
G	24.500	48.999	97.999	196.00	392.00	783.99	1568.0	3136.0	6271.9
G#	25.957	51.913	103.83	207.65	415.30	830.61	1661.2	3322.4	6644.9
A	27.500	55.000	110.00	220.00	440.00	880.00	1760.0	3520.0	7040.0
A#	29.135	58.270	116.54	233.08	466.16	932.33	1864.7	3729.3	7458.6
B	30.868	61.735	123.47	246.94	493.88	987.77	1975.5	3951.1	7902.1

keys can be used more or less equally well when using this tuning. Table 2.1 shows the tuning frequencies in hertz for a range of nine octaves.

We won't be discussing the finer points of tuning or the long history and mathematical theory that accompany it. Suffice it to say that entire books have been written on the subject, and that we really couldn't do the topic justice here.

AMPLITUDE, LOUDNESS, AND THE DECIBEL SCALE

A sound's amplitude is a measure of its power, which directly corresponds to its perceived loudness. As a visual representation, this can be thought of as the wave's height. Again, refer to Figure 2.1 to see this measurement graphed. The measurement of sound amplitude is commonly measured in *decibels*. A decibel is one tenth of a *bel*, which is a less-commonly used unit of measurement. Technically, the decibel (dB) scale does not measure absolute loudness. Instead, it measures the perceived difference in loudness between two sounds. Since perceived loudness increases linearly as power increases on a logarithmic curve, this is reflected in the scale. If a sound is twice as loud as another sound, it is $10 \log_{10}(2)$, or approximately 3.01-dB louder.

To help in measuring absolute volume, a standard has been defined as the approximate, quietest average sound a human can hear. All other sound volumes are then measured against this value, resulting in an absolute scale. When sound volumes are reported in decibels as an absolute volume, it is likely that this is the scale against which it is being measured.

For the case of digital audio, we are mostly interested in perceived relative volume rather than absolute volume. After all, we likely do not have any control over what the master volume is set to on the speaker hardware (or even if we did, it would be presumptuous of a program to adjust it).

DIGITAL STORAGE OF AUDIO

When dealing with audio in our games, we are obviously not dealing with an analog signal. Instead, we work with a digitally sampled representation of the original recorded sound. Although there are a few different methods of storing basic audio data, we will mostly be working with *Pulse Code Modulation* (PCM) audio files. This is the most common storage method for wave files (*.WAV) on the Windows platform.

PCM data storage is a fairly simple concept. Analog samples are turned into digital signals by a process called *sampling*. The measurement of the signal's height is sampled at regular intervals, and stored as a discrete value, usually ranging from 4–24 bits per sample. Typically, audio is sampled at rates ranging from 4,000 to 96,000 samples per second, or hertz. Note that in the context of analog audio, hertz refers to cycles per second; but in digital audio, it refers to samples per second.

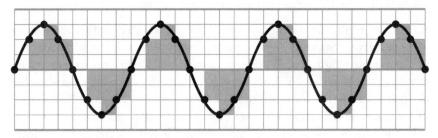

FIGURE 2.2   Sampled representation of a basic sine wave.

At each sampling time, the amplitude of the waveform is recorded as an integer value. The precision of this value directly corresponds to both the signal-to-noise ratio and/or the distortion of the digital representation of the waveform. We can see that the accuracy of the digital representation directly corresponds to two factors, the rate of sampling and the resolution of the sample value. These values affect the resolution of the sampling 'grid' that is used to convert the signal from analog to digital. As you can see in Figure 2.2, there will obviously always be some inaccuracy in the sampling process; but with a high-resolution grid (meaning a high sample rate and a large number of bits per sample), the human ear will eventually be unable to distinguish between the analog and digital representations. This perceptibly perfect 'target resolution' is generally acknowledged as 16 bits per sample and 44,100 samples per second. This, incidentally, happens to be the sampling rate and bit depth of the audio data stored on a standard music CD, also known as Redbook audio format.

In the past, it was common to conserve disk space and memory by reducing either the bit depth or the sampling rate of all the game samples—and this is still often done on console systems with their memory-constrained environments. Because powerful PCs with abundant disk space and physical memory are now available to consumers, most games are now able to ship with CD-quality samples. The advent of high-quality compression algorithms has also helped in this regard. However, it is still important to understand the ramifications of reducing either bit depth or sampling rate.

THE EFFECTS OF SAMPLING BIT DEPTH

The bit depth directly corresponds to the resolution of the sample on the y-axis (amplitude). In Figure 2.3, you can clearly see a problem with a low-resolution bit depth; the resolution does not adequately represent the sample accurately without introducing a significant amount of quantiza-

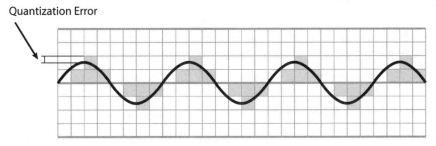

FIGURE 2.3   Waveform showing maximum quantization error.

tion error—the rounding error that occurs when converting sample points to a value with a fixed resolution. In a regular signal, such as the sine wave shown, the error will be a consistent value and will therefore create regular distortion in the signal. In a more complex signal, the quantization will be somewhat unpredictable, in essence causing random amounts of noise to be added to the signal. The lower the resolution of the bit depth value, the more distortion and noise will be inherent in the signal.

Engineers often refer to this as the signal-to-noise ratio (SNR), which is the comparison of the loudest possible signal to the average quantization error that occurs during the analog-to-digital conversion process. In this case, the higher the ratio, the better the quality of sound. To determine the value, simply compare the loudest possible sound with the average quantization error. In the case of an 8-bit sample value, your largest absolute sample is 128 (the values are positive and negative), and the quantization error is one half of a sample in the worst case. Thus, the SNR is 256:1, which translates into 48 dB. A 16-bit sample value, on the other hand, gives a much more impressive SNR of 65,536:1, or 96 dB. Note that the effective range of human hearing is approximately 100 dB, so a 16-bit digital recording will contain very little, if any, discernable noise if done with optimum efficiency. Figure 2.4 shows how the quantization error will be much less noticeable with this particular wave, due to the increased resolution of the stored sample values.

Reduced Quantization Error

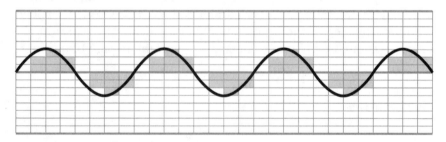

FIGURE 2.4   Increased bit-depth resolution decreases quantization errors.

THE EFFECTS OF SAMPLE RATE

The other direct effect on audio sampling quality is the rate at which samples are recorded. This is usually simply referred to as the *sample rate*, and is measured either in hertz or kilohertz (kHz), defined as 1 kHz = 1,000 Hz.

Just as the sample bit depth directly affects the resolution in the vertical axis, the sampling frequency can be considered the determining factor for resolution in the horizontal axis of the waveform. Let's see how sampling frequency can affect how high-frequency waveforms are represented.

Orginal Analog Sample

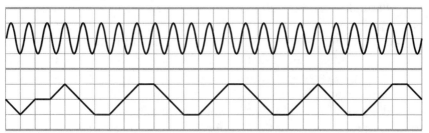

Digital Reproduction

FIGURE 2.5   Digital sampling cannot accurately represent the original analog signal.

In Figure 2.5, we've increased the resolution of the sine wave frequency to represent a frequency just below that of the sample rate. It quickly becomes obvious that the sampled waveform looks absolutely nothing like the original analog waveform. Because we've created the 'digital' representation using a very unsophisticated algorithm—locating the nearest grid point and then connecting the dots—the resulting digital representation has missed all of the higher frequencies that were inherent in the original

Original Analog Sample

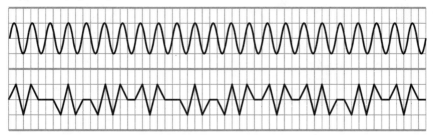

Digital Reproduction

FIGURE 2.6   Doubling the sample rate creates a closer, more accurate digital representation of the analog signal.

waveform. While analog-to-digital converters might not be quite this naive, the truth is that there is simply no way to represent the waveform accurately by using the sampling resolution in Figure 2.5, even if we were to attempt to intelligently recreate the digital waveform by hand. This is a result of the *Nyquist limit*, which essentially states that only frequencies up to half of the sampling rate can be properly recorded. We can visually verify this by doubling the resolution on our graph and again plotting the sampled waveform.

You can see that the waveform looks much closer to its original form. In addition, you might notice that there is also a bit of distortion in the waveform, preventing a perfect reproduction. While it was tempting to create a sample that would have perfectly matched the new frequency to the increased resolution of the grid, this would have missed a chance to demonstrate another property of the Nyquist limit: the closer a waveform gets to this limit, the less accurate the high-frequency representation will be. Although the amount of distortion in our figure is amplified because of the extremely low resolution of the graph's bit depth, it is still important to remember that this will happen to some degree in any high-frequency waveform that approaches the Nyquist limit. As a further demonstration, consider Figure 2.7, which again doubles the resolution used in Figure 2.6. This time, the digital signal closely resembles the original signal, even with the poor bit-depth resolution we are still working with.

Original Analog Sample

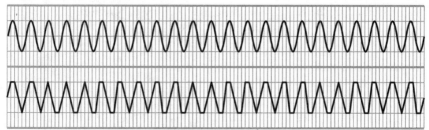

Digital Reproduction

FIGURE 2.7 Another doubling of the sample rate finally provides a reasonably accurate representation of the original waveform.

From this example, it becomes apparent that when working with sounds, the frequency of the original sounds will determine what hertz rate should be used to store the sampled data. Obviously, if you are using extremely high-frequency sounds, it may be best to use 44.1 kHz sounds, as these will reproduce nearly any humanly audible frequency. On the other hand, for low-frequency sounds, there is little harm in storing them at lower frequencies, except for run-time conversion overhead, which we will talk about in Chapter 30.

OVERSAMPLING AUDIO

It is partially because of the Nyquist limit that many professional digital recorders boast resolutions far beyond what normal human hearing could possibly distinguish, such as 24-bit audio and 96 kHz sampling rates. This helps ensure that there are very few quantization errors apparent in first-pass digital representation of the original sound. In addition, by *oversampling* the original recordings (extracting a higher digital resolution than is needed for the final output), applying digital manipulation or effects such as reverb or echo will be less likely to introduce additional quantization errors, since each pass of an effect is basically subject to the same quantization error rules as the original digital recording, and the error is accumulative.

Oversampling reduces these quantization errors to a negligible level. After all processing is applied to the oversampled sounds, they are converted back to lower-frequency sounds that are appropriate for the target medium, such as an audio CD. In the case of game production, the target sampling resolution should typically be a single target frequency and bit depth. (The reasons for this will be discussed in Chapter 30. Some 22.05 kHz sounds might initially sound adequate (except extremely high-frequency sounds, such as cymbal crashes or chirping crickets). However, the combination of mixing effects and digital processing, which is likely to occur on today's cards and audio systems, may make the increased resolution and decreased signal-to-noise ratio of 16-bit, 44.1 kHz sounds worth the extra storage space.

MONO AND STEREO SAMPLES

We haven't yet discussed the last major sample format modifier: stereo versus monaural (mono) sounds. A stereo sample is simply a dual-channel recording and can be considered two completely independent waveforms playing side by side. The digital samples are typically interleaved in the audio data stream. Most digital samples used in computer games, with the exception of ambient sound effects and music, are mono sounds for a couple of reasons. First, having two channels obviously doubles the required storage of PCM data. Second, stereo samples cannot be panned, nor can they be placed in a true 3D environment. This is because the two channels are inherently mapped to the left and right speakers, and so additional mapping via panning or 3D algorithms makes no sense.

DOLBY SURROUND DECODERS

One exception to the stereo mapping rule is when a Dolby algorithm is applied to a specially encoded stereo audio stream. Dolby Surround decoders have the ability to steer a 3D sound signal encoded into a two-channel audio output. (We will discuss various Dolby decoding techniques in more detail in Chapter 28.)

CONCLUSION

It is not crucial for today's audio programmers to be experts in acoustical physics, but a certain degree of basic knowledge is indeed a prerequisite for many tasks, especially when going beyond the basics of simply loading and playing a simple audio file. Later, we will delve deeper into the physics of audio propagation when theorizing how to properly calculate EAX (*Environmental Audio Extension*) settings for a given acoustical environment. But for now, in Chapter 3, we will discuss the capabilities of modern PC audio hardware, and what you need to understand in order to take advantage of them.

MODERN AUDIO HARDWARE CAPABILITIES

Today's modern PC-based audio hardware has taken a staggering leap forward from just a few years ago. It's now common to find audio cards with anywhere from 32 to 128 distinct voice channels, 3D hardware-implemented HRTF algorithms, and on-board mixing with hardware-based reverb and effects processors. This advance in hardware-accelerated functionality matches the trend of video cards, off-loading more and more work to a dedicated processor, which leaves more CPU time available for high-level game production code instead of the more mundane audio processing tasks.

Unfortunately, because the benefits of a high-end sound card are a bit less obvious than those of a high-end video card, we are still in the position (for the present, at least) where we must support nonaccelerated systems while maintaining a minimum level of quality. This usually means some sort of software emulation or, at the least, graceful degradation of features where possible. The good news is that falling back to some sort of basic effect emulation, or even dropping advanced effects altogether, is not as difficult or traumatic as with video, although a loss in aural quality will certainly be noticeable.

THE PC AUDIO LEGACY

The earliest audio cards were fairly crude by today's standards and provided a bare minimum of audio functionality. These cards utilized the

Industry Standard Architecture (ISA) bus, a standard developed for early PCs. The ISA bus standard was originally 8 bits, and later expanded to 16 bits in 1984, with a maximum speed of 8.3 MHz. This provided a maximum theoretical bandwidth of 15.9 MB per second. The ISA bus provided much less bandwidth than the modern Peripheral Component Interconnect (PCI) bus. The PCI bus is a 64-bit standard (although it is often implemented in 32 bits), and can be run at clock speeds of 33 or 66 *megahertz* (MHz; 1 MHz = 1,000 Hz). At 32 bits and 33 MHz, a PCI bus can transfer a maximum of 127.2 MB of data per second.

Because of the low bandwidth of these early ISA-based cards, it was not practical to stream a large amount of digital audio data to the audio card's hardware mixer in real-time. Thus, most cards utilized on-board sample memory so that multiple samples could be mixed and played back in real-time without overloading the ISA bus bandwidth. As new samples were needed, they were downloaded to the card's audio memory. Obviously, this was not an instantaneous process—it was also done over the already overburdened ISA bus.

However, for audio files too large to fit into available audio memory, the data was usually premixed by the CPU (for multiple streaming files) into a single data stream and then transferred in real-time to the hardware across the limited bandwidth for final mixing. Thus, it was important to differentiate between static (on-board memory) and streaming buffers for older hardware.

All modern audio cards now make use of the PCI bus, which is fast enough to allow audio hardware to utilize system memory for storing and mixing samples directly, eliminating the need for expensive on-board memory. Because no on-board storage is required with PCI cards, the differences between static and streaming buffers are essentially eliminated; and, as such, references to these must be understood as legacy systems. This will be important to understand when working with DirectSound Caps (capabilities) structures when determining what sort of buffers are available for use. Modern sound cards often make no distinction between streaming and static, and so the best answer for how many streaming and how many static buffers are available might be the exact same number— making these statistics somewhat useless for real-world use.

Additionally, storing samples in main system memory eliminates any firm, maximum size restrictions on buffers; a buffer can take up any amount of available system memory, ranging from 4 bytes to over 4 billion bytes in size.

■ **AMPLIFICATION VS. ATTENUATION**

Modern audio hardware does not actually amplify sounds, but rather attenuates them to achieve volume control. In other words, it reduces the power of sounds from a maximum, unchanged value. This is important for audio designers to understand when creating sounds. Additionally, this is why most audio APIs represent a volume control with a range of values from a negative number to zero. For instance, DirectSound volume control ranges from −10,000 to 0. These numbers represent hundreths of a decibel that the volume attenuated. In the *GAP* API, however, we have found that converting the volume range to a linear scale ranging from zero to one has certain advantages, such as ease-of-use, as well as simplicity in combining audio levels—just multiply them together.

3D AUDIO

As hardware-accelerated PC games began to proliferate in the market, it was soon realized that audio was a missing component of the experience. Simulating sounds in 3D space using simple pan and volume approximations worked fairly well, but new audio capabilities revealed that even more could be done to enhance the overall 3D experience.

HRTF

ON THE CD   Since most computers had (and still have) only two speakers, audio engineers have worked for years to figure out a method of simulating true three-dimensional sound utilizing *only* these two speakers. After all, humans only have two ears, and if the algorithms used to signal the brain about sound location can be reverse-engineered, then two speakers should be able to reproduce those algorithms and essentially fool the brain into thinking that a sound is originating from somewhere other than the speakers. These algorithms are generally known as HRTF (Head Relative Transfer Functions). There are some whitepapers written by Sensaura provided on the CD-ROM that explain the details of HRTF functions and its history of development in their company. It is excellent reading if you wish to learn more about these algorithms.

Although HRTF can produce excellent results in many cases, inadequacies in the final effect of some implementations often arise due to factors ranging from nonoptimal speaker placement to physical differences in the listeners' ear shapes. Other problems result from *crosstalk*, a phenomenon in which sounds meant for one ear are invariably heard by the other as well. Although impressive work has been done in canceling crosstalk, listening on headphones will often still provide much more convincing results. While aural positioning in the forward hemisphere is modeled quite realistically (often startlingly so), there are a few areas where HRTF still needs work. These include simulating the positioning of sounds directly behind the listener or sounds positioned above and below the horizontal plane occupied by the speakers.

However, despite the less-than-perfect results of these functions, there is no doubt that the result of HRTF output is substantially better than simple pan and volume simulation of 3D sound, and provides a significant degree of realism in many cases. And because these algorithms are typically implemented in hardware (although software algorithms are available in DirectSound), it provides a greatly enhanced user experience with minimal CPU overhead.

NATIVE MULTISPEAKER SURROUND SUPPORT

There is another approach to producing 3D audio that is a bit more direct than HRTF algorithms: setting up speakers all around the user. Higher-end audio cards now all have built-in multispeaker capability. These configurations might have either four or five mid- and high-range speakers, and typically utilize a subwoofer for low-frequency audio. Four-speaker systems utilize front-left, front-right, rear-left, and rear-right speakers surrounding the user. Five-speaker systems add a center channel, much like a theater-sound system. Because low frequencies are nondirectional (i.e., you can't tell what direction they're coming from), only one subwoofer is needed, and it can be placed anywhere. Figure 3.1 shows these layouts.

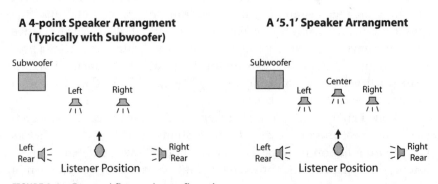

FIGURE 3.1   Four- and five-speaker configurations.

Because of the inherent simplicity of these systems, it is fairly easy to achieve very convincing three-dimensional sound effects, at least in the horizontal plane. Unfortunately, although the number of multispeaker configurations is growing, most users do not have such a system set up, mostly because of the inconvenience of placing speakers behind the listener.

Technically speaking, some hardware does actually still apply HRTF and noise-cancellation functions to sound, even in a multispeaker environment, in order to more effectively move the sound in all three dimensions, as well as increase the size of the listening 'sweet spot'—the area in which a user will hear optimal results from the speaker system.

DOLBY DIGITAL 5.1 HARDWARE SUPPORT

Some newer audio cards are now sporting support for Dolby Digital 5.1 encoding in hardware. Hardware-based Digital 5.1 encoding is a great benefit if you have a Dolby Digital receiver system connected to your PC. While there are currently only a handful of hardware devices capable of doing this, it is likely you will see an increasing number of such devices in the near future. Currently, Dolby decoders and receivers are considered high-end products, but the power of consumer electronic devices continues to skyrocket, even while prices drop, and soon it will not be unusual for every gaming-equipped PC to come with a Dolby Digital 5.1 surround encoder/decoder, which will sit either on the desktop or inside the audio card itself. For those interested in learning more about Dolby and its various encoding/decoding technologies, we discuss this in more detail in Chapter 28.

ENVIRONMENTAL REVERBERATION AND EFFECTS

A large portion of what modern 3D-capable cards do today is to dynamically add environmental reverberation and other effects to sounds through the use of hardware-based algorithms. This is an important method of providing audio cues that help to reinforce visual images on the screen. For instance, the same footstep samples that sound muted or muffled when walking in an office will become more pronounced and echoed when walking in a parking garage. By applying effects to the sound as it is played, the gamer is more readily immersed into the environment shown on the screen. These types of reverberation algorithms are generally too expensive to be done in software, and so audio cards have taken up the job.

Many cards have a single effects processor through which sounds can be processed, but newer cards allow for even more effects, which will in turn demand environmental reverberation models that can support this added functionality. (You might wish to visit *http://developer.creative.com/* to find out about the latest developments in EAX technologies.)

Currently utilizing interfaces such as I3DL2 or EAX 2.0, effects are applied to the concept of a 'listener' object, which represents a virtual microphone or ear in the 3D world. Because of the physical nature of the audio modeling, it usually does not make sense to apply different effects to different sounds, although individual parameters are often changed to help simulate the differences in the ways sounds reach the listener from different sources. However, newer audio cards are indeed starting to ship with multiple effects processors. It will be interesting to see how these new capabilities might be used in the future.

There are currently several challenges in using environmental effects in games. Not only is there a fairly steep learning curve to EAX and other related technologies, the question often remains: how to optimize audio data sets that take advantage of EAX while still supporting a sensible fallback. (We'll be discussing environmental reverberation in much greater detail in Chapter 24.)

OTHER HARDWARE PROPERTIES

In addition to EAX, which was pioneered by Creative Labs, Inc. and released to the industry as a general standard, there are other manufacturers who have developed special hardware-only capabilities either exposed through proprietary APIs or as DirectSound property sets. One chipset manufacturer with a large percentage of the market is Sensaura, a brand name that is not widely known among consumers, but is utilized by manufacturers of many audio cards—excluding the SoundBlaster® line—on the market, including clients such as Turtle-Beach and Hercules. Sensaura has also recently made inroads with consoles. NVIDIA is a recent client, so Xbox natively supports Sensaura algorithms and effects, helping to make it widely acknowledged as far and away the most advanced audio system ever developed for a gaming console, rivaling or even out-performing most modern PC sound cards. As such, it makes sense to natively support Sensaura-specific property sets as well.

MUSIC

Hardware-based music on the PC got off to a rather shaky start. The earliest attempts were usually based on MIDI (Music Instrument Digital Interface) combined with very poor-quality two-operator FM synthesis chips to produce the standard MIDI voices. The greatest failing of this system was the unpredictable quality of the end-user experience. Thus, many people whose only experience with MIDI was with early PC titles tend to regard all MIDI music as low quality, which is unfortunate. In reality, the only problem with MIDI was the delivery system.

DIGITAL AUDIO STREAMS

Once digital compact discs (CDs) became standard issue on PCs, a new avenue of music became available and is still in use today, although not nearly as widely used as before due to a number of factors (see the section on Redbook audio in Chapter 29). However, there were definite benefits to this delivery method: the musical quality was superb and consistent, and it required very little processing because the CD player did all of the work.

One variant of simply playing Redbook audio was to stream the data (either off the CD or off the hard drive) as a pure digital data stream instead of an analog stream. There are a few advantages to this method: no additional capabilities other than a streaming buffer are required, and the quality of the music stream can be reduced slightly to save space. This requires slightly more CPU time, but the overhead proves to be negligible for powerful modern PCs. As more CPU power became available, increasingly better lossy compression algorithms were used. Currently, several excellent algorithms are available for use, which we'll discuss in Chapter 20 through Chapter 22. The use of high-compression lossy formats remain an extremely popular method for playing music and other types of audio due to the high quality and consistency of output, along with the relative simplicity of preparing both code and content.

MIDI PLUS DLS

Surprisingly, MIDI has recently been making a comeback, thanks in large part to both the DLS (DownLoadable Sound) standard and Microsoft DirectMusic. Despite the early failings of MIDI, it nonetheless has some very attractive properties. First, since only note and velocity (volume) information is typically stored, very little data is required to store enormous amounts of music. This makes it the most efficient music-storage system possible—an attractive notion for developers of downloadable games. Second, because musical playback is done algorithmically, using MIDI makes it easy to manipulate the music in real-time. This has given new life to the concept of dynamic (interactive) music. Although interactive music can be achieved using digital streams, it is much more flexible with MIDI segments; it is a more-algorithmic format that can be manipulated even at the note-by-note level.

Many audio cards are making support for DirectMusic more feasible by directly supporting DLS (and more recently DLS2) in hardware. Regardless of this, and as welcome as any accelerated features may be, though, the primary reason for the success of DirectMusic in revitalizing MIDI is that Microsoft provides a software synthesizer—consistent playback is guaranteed on *all* systems, regardless of acceleration features.

CONCLUSION

PC audio hardware has definitely come a long way, but unlike PC graphics, where acceleration is now mandated by the requirements of most high-profile games, there is a frustrating disparity between the high and low ends of audio hardware. Many computers are still shipped with high-end video cards right alongside unaccelerated, bare-bones audio cards that only synthesize a single stereo waveform, meaning that everything else must be done in software. Therefore, for the present, the audio programmer must struggle to support high-end features while continuing to support legacy and low-end systems—all the while maintaining a decent level of performance and audio quality. In the next chapter, we will begin looking at what is required in order to design a robust and long-lasting, low-level audio API.

CHAPTER 4

DESIGNING A ROBUST AUDIO API

Perhaps, the most important part of your job as an audio programmer is to design an easy-to-use, yet highly functional application programming interface (API). Even if you are planning to write all of the sound functionality yourself (both the sound code and the game code that calls it), it still is worthwhile to create a clean separation in the system through a well-defined set of objects and functions. Doing so will ensure that the code remains better compartmentalized, which in turn provides simpler debugging, cleaner implementations, and better reusability.

AUDIO SYSTEM DESIGN GOALS—THE *GAP* LIBRARY

Before any code is written, it helps to have a very clear understanding of what the final goal is when we create an audio library. In creating a new audio library for this book (we've dubbed it the *GAP* library, for *Game Audio Programming* library), an effort was made to avoid creating cool features for their own sakes. Instead, our focus was on what was likely to be necessary or interesting to game developers. The *GAP* library is not intended to be an all-purpose audio API. After all, that is pretty much what DirectSound is. Nor does it attempt to be a commercial library, written in a generic-enough way to appeal to a wide audience in nearly all circumstances.

Instead, what we have created is a mid-level demonstration audio system ready for integration into a game engine, as well as a platform on which we could later build more high-level audio abstractions, similar to the soundscapes and dynamic music scripts we've already built. Our system is defined as 'mid-level,' meaning that many tasks are automatically performed for you instead of you having to manage them yourself (e.g., wave loading, disk-based streaming, etc.); but enough generality is left to make it useful for most games or entertainment applications. Let's examine the most important features of our *GAP* library and categorize them as low-, mid-, or high-level functionality.

LOW-LEVEL FUNCTIONALITY

- Perform basic manipulation (e.g., play, pause, stop, pan, volume, pitch) on 2D sounds.
- Perform basic manipulation and control properties (e.g., position, velocity, etc.) of 3D sounds.
- Expose all basic functionalities of 3D listener objects.
- Perform basic manipulation (e.g., play, pause, stop) on 2D musical segments.
- Expose hardware property sets on individual sound objects.

MID-LEVEL FUNCTIONALITY

- Load PCM wave files from disk.
- Stream large audio files from disk.
- Allow basic queuing of sequential music segments.
- Intercept segment notifications for user-defined processing tasks.
- Automatically manage hardware resources, loading and unloading sounds dynamically to ensure optimum usage, based on a prioritization scheme that includes user-set priority values.
- Maintain persistent information so audio properties can be set while a sound is unloaded or retained between an unload/reload of the data.
- Allow one-function loading and playback on demand.

- Asynchronously load audio data from disk while maintaining the simplicity and ease-of-use of a synchronous API.
- Handle multiple compressed audio formats, including Ogg Vorbis, MP3, WMA, and Windows ACM compressed wave files.
- Use helper objects and dedicated interfaces to assist in calculating environmental reverberation or other known hardware extensions.
- Allow use of custom file loaders through optional interfaces (e.g., WAD-like file-packing systems).

HIGH-LEVEL FUNCTIONALITY

- Provide the script parsing and loading system used for scripting advanced audio property and behavior objects.
- Create a high-level soundscape system based on the generic audio API, utilizing a script or programmatic interface.
- Create an advanced dynamic musical cueing and transition system based on the audio scripting system.

You can see that the low-level functionality we are after is barely more than what is provided by DirectSound. It's for this reason that we've claimed in earlier chapters that many of the lessons learned in this book can be applied even if you plan to use a third-party library. While most of the libraries offer some of the functionality found in our mid-level goals, it's a sure bet that most of them do *not* offer anything found in the high-level design goals list. The fact of the matter is that almost no library is going to work exactly in the manner you want it to. In this case, it's going to be up to you to dig into a system and make it work the way you want it to—adding features that are not available, or perhaps removing those that you do not need (if you have the source, that is).

The basic strategy we will employ is to create a two-tiered system. (We delve into multitiered systems later on in this chapter, and Figure 4.1 shows a visual representation of this concept.) All our low-level requirements are essentially provided by DirectX Audio (or can be provided by your audio library API of choice), with minimal programming effort on your part. The functionality we will be providing on top of this is in the mid-level section. Finally, the advanced functionality, which will eventually be placed into a separate library, is designated as the high-level goals.

GENERAL API DESIGN PRINCIPLES

Creating a robust, easy-to-use, powerful, and flexible API for a library or system can sometimes be an art in itself. How much do you abstract, how much do you hide, and what implementation details do you try to manage behind the user's back? Do you enable low-level, raw power at the expense of simplicity; or is ease-of-use your primary concern? These are a few of the questions you should be asking yourself at the beginning of your design phase.

The most important aspect of all is, though, that there actually *is* a design phase. Despite the complexity of today's engineering and programming challenges, there still is an alarming number of programmers who prefer to simply jump in and begin coding, letting the design sort itself out logically as they progress and experiment. While this is not a bad way to tinker with a new technology for the sake of learning, it must be understood that an API designed in such a manner is not going to be nearly as useful in the long term as one that is well planned before coding even begins.

INTERNAL VS. EXTERNAL APIS

All this talk of APIs may sound a bit strange if you're like most small-team game developers: you're writing a sound library for internal use, possibly even your own. You are most likely not releasing a documented sound library that others will be using. Creating abstract interfaces and hiding implementation details almost seems silly if the programmer using the library happens to be the same one who wrote it—again, mostly likely you. In this case (in which you will not be releasing your API to a third party), you can consider your library to have an *internal API* instead of an *external API*. By 'internal' and 'external,' we are referring to the library's accessibility to the outside world. Internal libraries and APIs are only available to programmers within your own company, and are considered proprietary information. An external library, however, is documented and can be used outside your company.

External libraries have some unique challenges of their own. The most important aspect of an external API is the simple fact that it must be documented and supported with greater longevity than an internal API. You are likely to lose customers rather quickly if you break your own API every week with changes, even in the interest of improving it. Stability is consid-

■ **LIBRARY DOCUMENTATION**

"Document an internal library? Are you nuts? Who has time for that?" Unfortunately, this attitude tends to be the rule among game developers rather than the exception. With today's high-pressure, high-profile, fast-paced projects, it seems as though no one is considering the importance of good library design, let alone even (gasp) documenting it. While there is an obvious limit to what should actually be formally documented (e.g., game specific code), the whole purpose of documentation seems to have been forgotten: documentation actually saves the developers time over the long run. Granted, you should not be writing volumes about interfaces that are likely to change next week, but there are some tools available to assist in the documentation process without causing too much pain.

Documentation extracted from the source code itself is perhaps one of the best methods to ensure that programmers both do the actual documentation work and keep it up to date. Moreover, the automated tools help to ensure that the actual program structures are never out of synch with the code, since they are extracted right from the source files. Specially formatted comments typically provide the actual documentation text, and these comments can serve as good documentation both inside the source and when extracted and formated by external tools.

One great source documentation tool that also happens to be completely *ON THE CD* free is Doxygen (Web site: *http://www.doxygen.org/*). You can see how Doxygen was used in documenting the *GAP* library by examining both the interface source code and the resulting documentation in the /audio_sdk/docs folder located on the CD-ROM.

ered essential, which is why it is critically important to design your API properly right from the beginning. Naturally, it is impossible to foresee every advance or change needed down the road, but you can minimize the time between *refactoring*. Refactoring can be described as the complete restructuring of a software system and is usually done when incremental improvement is no longer a feasible option. In fact, with a well-designed API using an abstract interface, some degree of refactoring can take place without having to revise the interface in a significant manner, or even at all.

Internal libraries, on the other hand, tend to be a bit more dynamic and flexible, since the company is its own customer; it can choose when to break compatibility for the sake of improving the library. Granted, revising an internal API has consequences, just as it does for an external API. And so the same consideration should be given when designing it.

In other words, your goal in either case is to design an API that can remain externally consistent for the longest period of time, along with the obvious goals of functionality, intuitiveness, and ease of use. In this light, the same design lessons for both types of libraries can be applied because they both have the same benefit—namely, improved productivity.

■ **API REFINEMENT DURING DEVELOPMENT**

Don't simply assume that because designing your API is the first step, your interfaces cannot subsequently be changed during the implementation phase of the library. On the contrary, you will undoubtedly think of new and better ways to represent your interface, and you should not be afraid to alter your API accordingly. Often, you will discover that an idea you had earlier about the way the system should work was just not practical, or was redundant, or was just too clumsy to use. Alternatively, you may discover yourself implementing similar functionality on a number of different objects, and so decide to unify them under a common, abstract base interface. During the initial implementation is when you should take these lessons to heart and be willing to throw out ideas and bring in new ones.

The *GAP* API was revised a number of times over the course of writing this book. Minor modifications were made right up until the text and code was sent off to the publisher. However, each successive change tended to be more of a refinement and less of a rewrite of the system. It is difficult to demonstrate this iterative process; you are only presented with the final product. In the end, the final API actually resembled the very first draft to a remarkable degree, despite numerous alterations, which helps to underscore the lessons of solid initial design considerations.

THE API PAYOFF

In fact, this lesson underscores the entire reason for designing an API in the first place, instead of just creating a random set of audio functions or classes as you need them. The biggest payoff that comes with a robustly designed API is improved productivity. This productivity is a simple matter of programmers learning and effectively using a stable API. The longer someone uses a system, the more proficient he or she becomes with it, and a programming interface is no exception. Productivity gains are also made when the system itself takes into account the expected users.

There are other less-immediately tangible benefits in creating a solid API layer, as well. An interface is essentially an implied contract with the programmer calling the function. The function or object is expected to behave in a certain manner, given a known set of circumstances and supplied parameters. For instance, the member function:

```
bool Sound::Play()
```

is expected to play a loaded sound, with the function returning true on success and false on failure. Expected behavior might be defined as follows: the function will return true on successfully playing the sound. The function will return false if the sound is unable to play for any other reason, including if the entire sound system was not initialized, or if the sound object itself had not been initialized properly.

By creating a fixed set of well-known entry points in the library's functionality in the form of classes and functions, you are defining the expected behavior of the library. It becomes a simple matter to determine when the library deviates from expected behavior, assisting in the tracking down of any bugs or other issues.

THE ABSTRACT INTERFACE

One of the most powerful conceptual models in modern-day object-oriented programming is the *abstract interface*. Simply put, an abstract interface allows you to create a generic interface to a particular subsystem without worrying about implementation details. This allows you to focus on the usability of your interface instead of trying to create an interface that matches internal functionality. This is an important concept for designing APIs. Although it is impossible to design an API without some notion of how things are working internally, it is best to keep usability at the forefront, as long as it does not interfere with the optimal functioning of the code. (Graphics programming often has to make usability sacrifices in order to gain efficiency. However, audio code rarely has this problem.)

A true abstract interface has some other advantages, as well, especially regarding cross-platform or cross-library coding. Instead of coding in a native API directly from game code, using a more-generic interface means a library's implementation can be changed; for instance, instead of using DirectSound, you may switch to using a commercial sound library. As long as calling conventions at the interface level do not change, the change can be made entirely at the library level, avoiding the need to rewrite a large amount of game code.

Don't be misled by the academic-sounding term, "abstract interface." Although we will be looking at more-sophisticated object-oriented methods of creating abstract interfaces, simple C-style functions can work just as well. In fact, it is sometimes better to avoid over-designing a system if you know you are never going to do anything too fancy with it. More features simply mean more to go wrong—and more to maintain. If you're designing a simple puzzle game, some simple PlaySound() function variants will probably suffice quite nicely.

However, throughout this book, we'll be assuming that you are interested in designing a cutting-edge sound system, and we will orient the code and designs based on that assumption. Too often, game programming books provide extremely simplistic audio samples, which tend to be easy to understand (and to write). Unfortunately, once you are beyond the basic concepts, you find you don't have the instructions to help with the more-advanced issues. In *Game Audio Programming*, we are instead covering all relevant audio topics in as much detail as is practical; and we are assuming that you can extract relevant information for your own project. Remember, it is feasible to cut out the sections of code that you are not interested in using, to simply use the concepts presented here to create a simpler version for your own project, or even to use them as a starting point for more-advanced systems. The audio libraries provided and described in this book are certainly usable by a large number of different project types, but our goal is to explain all relevant portions in as much detail as possible. In this way, you have the option of reworking the sound system to specifically match your project's needs.

THE MULTITIERED AUDIO SYSTEM

In designing audio systems, you will quickly discover that there are essentially two basic usage types when playing a sound. The first and most simplistic case can be summed up by a single sentence: the program is required to play a sample of digital audio at a specified time and with specified parameters. Essentially, this is the PlaySound() case, or the most basic requirement of an audio system—simply load and play a digital audio sample.

The second case is a bit more convoluted and can vary greatly from game to game. Usually, this involves more-complicated logic, as well. Here's an example: play a low background loop of ambient audio while the listener is in a specified area, moving the volume and pitch randomly within certain constraints over time. Periodically, fire a specified set of 3D audio samples of various other types of periodic background sounds, randomly selecting relative direction and distance from the listener, while maintaining relative position to the listener.

Are you surprised that both of these can be considered part of the same audio system? Even more surprising is that with proper coding, both of these tasks should be as easy as calling a single object's member function. The trick in being able to do both of these without too much entangling code is to use a *multilayered audio library*. Essentially, this is a fancy way of saying that we will have multiple layers of libraries, each representing different levels of functionality. The first, referred to as either our "base" or "core" library, is a low-level wrapper for an audio SDK. It handles the basics of simple audio playback, managing all low-level audio playback for us. On top of this, we will build higher-level libraries with greater amounts of very specific functionality. We can see this organization in Figure 4.1. These libraries will make use of the core library to perform more-advanced audio-related tasks, such as creating an entire dynamic ambiance track from a small script file that can be loaded and played with relative simplicity.

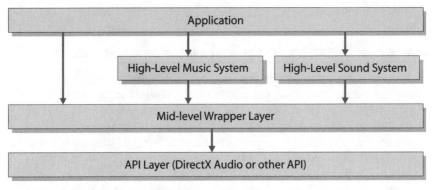

FIGURE 4.1   Multilayered audio system configuration and interface.

It is sometimes tempting for game programmers to put too much game-specific information into their core systems. It is easy to simply keep adding functionality once a basic system is in place. However, this can create potential problems down the road. Though adding more and more advanced functionality to a core system might seem harmless enough, too often what ends up happening is that unless the programmer is *extremely* conscientious, he or she will begin to over-utilize internal classes, functions, and structures that were originally designed for the lower-level audio system.

Later, when it is decided that the audio system needs to be revamped, rewritten, or just cleaned up, the unlucky maintenance programmer finds a nightmarish web of interdependencies, making it almost impossible to replace any low-level functionality without destroying the high-level functionality that is supposed to remain in place.

By creating specific higher-level libraries that *only interface with the low-level systems through the abstract interface layer,* we avoid this problem by creating a dedicated place for game-specific or high-level audio code, which is easier to maintain in a separate library module. In this manner, if the lower-level audio system is ever replaced, only code that is specifically relevant to playing audio need be changed, while higher-level functionality need not be touched if you have ensured that the new library conforms to the abstract interface you designed for your original low-level system. Moreover, because the systems are physically in separate libraries, it is relatively simple to ensure there is no 'cheating' or peeking behind an abstract interface to tinker with a concrete class's members. If you cannot do what you need to with the abstract interface, then you should address this by fixing your general-purpose API instead of by creating a quick hack to bypass the established interfaces.

■ **ALL-VIRTUAL FUNCTIONS? BUT WHAT ABOUT PERFORMANCE ISSUES?**

If you have been programming since the days of DOS gaming, you will likely remember when C++ was considered by some to be too bloated and inefficient for serious game development. Nevertheless, the days of counting cycles for each function are long behind us. While performance in games is, and always will be, a top priority, it is important to decide where your CPU time is actually going to be spent. Audio calls are not made in tight loops, unless you happen to be writing a low-level audio decoder or filter. At the API level, you need to worry about stability, usability, and functionality, not counting cycles. Leave the cycle counting to those that truly need to do it. *Don't fear the abstract interface....*

SOME BASIC PRINCIPLES

Before we actually begin designing the audio API, we are going to establish a few core principles. We will attempt to adhere to these principles during the design phase.

OBJECT-ORIENTED DESIGN

Our design is strictly object oriented, which means we are using C++. Theoretically, we could create an equivalent interface in C, using handles to represent audio objects and functions that operate on those handles; but in all honesty, this is simply a less-robust and more-tedious method of doing what a well-designed object can easily do for you. Both our audio system manager and the sounds themselves will be represented by objects, with member functions providing any required functionality.

OBJECT DESIGN AND NAMING CONSISTENCY

All of our sound and music objects will be designed with a base interface class containing a core degree of required functionality. This will help to ensure that function names are easy to remember—no matter what type of object or whatever parameters have been set, playing an audio object is as simply as calling its Play() member function.

NO-ARGUMENT PLAY FUNCTIONS

Any parameters required to properly play a sound should be defined as a property of the sound itself. This might seem odd to those of you who would naturally follow the DirectSound example of including an argument in the Play() function that indicates whether or not the sound should be looped. However, there is an excellent reason for *not* doing so. By storing these variables internally in the object, we are essentially defining them as part of the sound itself. Most sounds do not switch between looping and nonlooping; they are created this way by your sound designer and should be played as specified, with no intervention from the programmer. Because every aspect of the way a sound is played is defined either as an initialization parameter or a property, this gives total control over playback to the sound designer, since the load-time properties can easily be represented in a text-based script file. (We'll examine this technique in further detail in Chapters 16 and 17.) Naturally, most properties have corresponding Get and Set member functions so that, if needed, parameters can be easily changed at run-time.

WRITING FROM THE API DOWN

Quite simply, writing our audio library from the API down means that we will be designing an abstract interface according to the following concept:

usability should shape the design and layout, rather than implementation details. This may seem like an odd way to design a library; but as you will see, it helps to keep a larger plan in mind as you start filling in low-level pieces. It also helps to ensure that your library doesn't end up looking like a simple, lightweight wrapper over the DirectSound COM (Component Object Model) objects, with just a bit of added functionality thrown in here and there, and a myriad of confusing and seemingly unrelated or redundant functions to choose from.

However, there are still choices to be made regarding the use of Direct-Sound- or DirectMusic-specific features. For example, we will expose the concept of DirectMusic-specific objects such as segments, DLS collections, and scripts. At our API level, though, we have avoided exposing any interface that, in theory, could not be practically coded or at least simulated on other platforms. Thus, an ISegment object, while obviously influenced by DirectMusic design, could also represent a generic piece of MIDI music or a streaming digital audio track on platforms on which DirectMusic is not available.

Moreover, many of these interfaces represent important portions of DirectMusic technology, and so they are worth examining. After all, while showing how to create a clean and portable API is one of the design goals of this book, learning about all the important DirectX Audio interfaces is equally critical.

API design is always a balancing act between functionality and portability, and between simplicity and direct control. Your particular design goals will always represent a unique reflection of your project's needs, which is why designing a custom wrapper layer around an existing API is so beneficial; it not only to improves clarity and functionality, but it allows you as a programmer to shape the API to match your specific project's needs, ensuring the audio system will be easy to use and integrate into your game.

CONCLUSION

Taking the time to design your sound system's interface with some serious thought instead of simply throwing together a few sound-playback functions will reap rewards in the future. Audio design, although it will never be as high a priority as graphics, is still becoming a more important and sophisticated component in any game. This is especially true in tomorrow's sophisticated, seamless-world games, where a dynamic management system must underlie the foundation of the library because of the large volume of data it must handle. By critically considering the long-term flexible design, you will also enable your audio engineers and composers to do more in less time, instead of fighting the inherent technological limitations of the target platform.

In the next chapter, we will move from theory to practical application as we design our new audio API from the ground up.

CHAPTER 5

AUDIO API
IMPLEMENTATION

We're ready now to begin designing the *GAP* audio library's API. Keep in mind that we're building a rather advanced 2D/3D audio and music system that deals with large numbers of audio-related resources, managing them in real-time. The benefit of designing a system with more-advanced resource-management capabilities is that it's fairly easy to use the library for smaller or simpler projects, if needed. Some features, such as the more-advanced dynamic buffer-management system or the asynchronous loading mechanism, might go unused, but these advanced features have been designed to be as unobtrusive as possible. If you don't want to use them, you can simply ignore them.

ON THE CD
The code listed in this chapter can be found in \Game_Audio\ audio_sdk\include\audiolib\IAudio.h.

INTERFACE CLASSES

Our audio API is object-oriented, meaning that sounds and other resources are managed through the use of interface pointers. We're taking a pseudo COM-like approach in that the user will never directly allocate or deallocate a sound object. Allocation/creation is done through the audio manager, which is somewhat of a controlling authority for the entire audio system. Deallocation of the object is handled by a Destroy() function, which each object derives from a base class. Initialization of the object is performed as separate step from creation, and each class interface has a unique set of parameters needed for proper initialization. This step provides the audio object with everything it needs to know in order to load and unload itself on demand, and this information is preserved for the lifetime of the object—that is, until Destroy() is called, or until the audio manager is shut down. Figure 5.1 shows all the primary class interfaces in the *GAP* library and their relationships to each other.

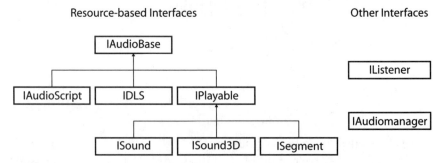

FIGURE 5.1   Interface class hierarchy.

IAUDIOBASE

IAudioBase defines a set of functionality and interface common to all managed audio object in our API. As you can see, all managed audio objects—defined as objects in which multiple instances can be created and used simultaneously—are derived from this common interface. The two exceptions are IAudioManager and IListener, since only one of these objects can logically exist at any time. Let's examine the common interface for all of our audio objects in Listing 5.1.

LISTING 5.1

```
class IAudioBase
{
public:
    virtual void Destroy() = 0;
    virtual bool IsInitialized() const = 0;

    virtual bool Load() = 0;
```

```
    virtual bool Unload() = 0;
    virtual bool IsLoaded() const = 0;

protected:
    virtual ~IAudioBase() {};

};
```

Here we've defined a core set of functionality that all our resource-type interfaces should support. Each managed object (or resource object) has a Destroy() function that will unload and destroy the object. The interface should be considered invalid after this function has been called, in the same way as if the memory to which the object has been pointing has been deallocated. Technically speaking, our objects will go into an object cache for later reuse. (You can see how this works in Chapter 30.) So the program would not really crash if it were accessed; but this is simply an implementation detail/optimization and should not be relied on.

The IsInitialized() function can be safely called after the object has been created but before it has been initialized. It is often used internally inside function calls to prevent accidental dereferencing of things like null pointers. Likewise, the IsLoaded() function works in a similar manner, determining if an object is currently loaded or not.

When an object is initialized, it does not actually immediately load the data from a file or resource. Rather, it stores the information required to load and prepare the object for use at any time with a call to its overloaded Load() function. This is a very important property of the *GAP* library to understand—any object, once initialized, can be loaded or unloaded via a simple, no-argument function call. For IPlayable-derived classes (ISound, ISound3D, and ISegment), all settings and properties of the sound will also be preserved, even when unloaded. This gives us the freedom to implement a very dynamic buffer allocation and prioritization system without the fear of losing critical information when discarding a low-priority buffer.

IPLAYABLE

The IPlayable interface is designed to enforce basic audio-control mechanisms for individual sound and music objects. Listing 5.2 shows the functions required to control and check the status of a playable object.

LISTING 5.2

```
class IPlayable : public IAudioBase
{
public:
    virtual bool Play() = 0;
    virtual bool Pause() = 0;
    virtual bool Stop() = 0;

    virtual bool IsPlaying() const = 0;
    virtual bool IsPaused() const = 0;
    virtual bool IsLooping() const = 0;
};
```

Here's a basic rundown of the functions and how they are expected to behave. Play() is fairly straightforward—it simply plays the resource file from the current play location. Calling Pause() will pause the sound at the current playing position, and calling Play() again will resume playing the sound from where it left off. The controls are analogous to what you would expect to find on a standard CD control panel. Calling Stop() will stop the sound and reset the position to the beginning of the audio file.

ISOUND

We've reached our first actual interface class: ISound. This interface represents a single 2D sound created by the audio manager. Let's examine it in Listing 5.3.

LISTING 5.3

```
struct SoundProp              property  structi
{
    SoundProp()
    {
        Clear();
    }
    void Clear()
    {
        m_fVolume = VOLUME_MAX;
        m_fPan = PAN_CENTER;
```

```
        m_fPitch = PITCH_ORIGINAL;
        m_nReadCursor = 0;
    }
    float m_fVolume;
    float m_fPan;
    float m_fPitch;
    uint32 m_nReadCursor;
};

struct SoundInit          ← INIT STRUCT
{
    SoundInit()
    {
        Clear();
    }
    void Clear()
    {
        m_sFileName.erase();
        m_bStreaming = false;
        m_bLooping = false;
        m_bMusic = false;
        m_nPriority = 0;
        m_Prop.Clear();
    }
    std::string m_sFileName;
    bool m_bStreaming;
    bool m_bLooping;
    bool m_bMusic;
    uint32 m_nPriority;
    SoundProp m_Prop;
};


class ISound : public IPlayable    ← INTERFACE
{
public:
    virtual bool Init(const SoundInit& init) = 0;

    virtual bool SetProperties(
        const SoundProp& prop) = 0;
    virtual bool GetProperties(
        SoundProp& prop) const = 0;
```

```
      virtual bool SetVolume(float fVolume) = 0;
      virtual bool GetVolume(float& fVolume) const = 0;

      virtual bool SetPan(float fPan) = 0;
      virtual bool GetPan(float& fPan) const = 0;

      virtual bool SetPitch(float fPitch) = 0;
      virtual bool GetPitch(float& fPitch) const = 0;

      virtual bool SetReadCursor(uint32 nBytes) = 0;
      virtual bool GetReadCursor(
          uint32& nBytes) const = 0;

      virtual bool GetSourceSize(
          uint32& nBytes) const = 0;
};
```

The sound interface is actually separated into three components: the initialization structure, the properties structure, and the interface class. Using a single initialization structure allows us to easily add parameters to the structure with less chance of breaking existing code, since the structure is designed to always properly initialize itself with correct default values. The SoundInit structure contains the required information for loading a sound and creating a corresponding sound buffer for it. The information in SoundInit is stored in the sound object until the Destroy() method is called. The members of this struct should be considered properties of the sound, required for internally loading the sound data and creating a suitable sound buffer for it. So altering them would be problematic, given the dynamic nature of this audio system. The various members include the name of the audio file to play, whether this file should be played as a full buffer or streamed, whether the sound loops, a sound fx/music file flag, and a user-set priority value. This structure is passed to the ISound::Init() function, which returns a simple bool indicating success or failure. The initialization structure also contains a SoundProp structure as a member, which allows us to tweak the initial settings of the buffer before it is actually initialized or loaded.

One quick note about the SoundInit::m_bMusic flag. This is a simple mechanism used in all IPlayable-derived interfaces in the *GAP* library to categorize audio files. Every audio object is designated as either "sound effects" or "music" for control purposes. For instance, there is one global volume control for sound effects and another one for music. Selecting this flag allows you to choose which volume control works on which particular sounds. You'll notice this flag in the ISound3D and ISegment initialization structures, as well.

Because ISound is derived from IPlayable, which is similarly derived from IAudioBase, all of their functions are naturally implemented for ISound and work as described earlier. In addition, the ISound interface provides some additional functionality. SetPan() and GetPan() can set or retrieve the current pan settings. The pan parameters are floats in the range of −1.0 to 1.0, making them slightly easier to use and visualize than larger integer ranges.

SetCursor() and GetCursor() provide low-level control over the play cursor, and GetSourceSize() gets the total size of the audio source in bytes.

ISOUND3D AND ILISTENER

Next, we'll move into the realm of 3D positional audio. Creating a sound in 3D space is a two-step process. A sound source must be defined and created, and a listener must be placed so that it can hear the sound source. Three-dimensional audio, instead of modeling the typical two-speaker system on a computer or stereo, attempts to emulate real-life positional audio and spatial orientation. Thus, like in real life, we need both an object that produces sound and someone to listen to it—both located and oriented in 3D virtual space for the sound path to be complete. Let's examine the 3D sound source's first interface. In Listing 5.4, note that the type AUDIOVEC-TOR is a typedef of D3DVECTOR in this implementation.

LISTING 5.4

```
struct Sound3DProp
{
    Sound3DProp()
    {
        Clear();
    }
    void Clear()
    {
```

```
        m_vPosition.x = 0;
        m_vPosition.y = 0;
        m_vPosition.z = 0;
        m_vVelocity.x = 0;
        m_vVelocity.y = 0;
        m_vVelocity.z = 0;
        m_vConeOrientation.x = 0;
        m_vConeOrientation.y = 0;
        m_vConeOrientation.z = 1.0f;
        m_nInsideConeAngle = 360;
        m_nOutsideConeAngle = 360;
        m_fConeOutsideVolume = VOLUME_MAX;
        m_fMinDistance = 1.0f;
        m_fMaxDistance = 100.0f;
        m_nMode = MODE_NORMAL;
        m_fVolume = VOLUME_MAX;
        m_fPitch = PITCH_ORIGINAL;
        m_nReadCursor = 0;
    }
    AUDIOVECTOR m_vPosition;
    AUDIOVECTOR m_vVelocity;
    AUDIOVECTOR m_vConeOrientation;
    uint32 m_nInsideConeAngle;
    uint32 m_nOutsideConeAngle;
    float m_fConeOutsideVolume;
    float m_fMinDistance;
    float m_fMaxDistance;
    uint32 m_nMode;
    float m_fVolume;
    float m_fPitch;
    uint32 m_nReadCursor;
};

struct Sound3DInit
{
    Sound3DInit()
    {
        Clear();
    }
    void Clear()
    {
        m_sFileName.erase();
```

```
            m_bStreaming = false;
            m_bLooping = false;
            m_bMusic = false;
            m_nPriority = 0;
            m_Prop.Clear();
        }
        std::string m_sFileName;
        bool m_bStreaming;
        bool m_bLooping;
        bool m_bMusic;
        uint32 m_nPriority;
        Sound3DProp m_Prop;
};

class ISound3D : public IPlayable
{
public:
        virtual bool Init(const Sound3DInit& init) = 0;

        virtual bool SetProperties(
            const Sound3DProp& prop) = 0;
        virtual bool GetProperties(
            Sound3DProp& prop) const = 0;

        virtual bool SetPosition(
            const AUDIOVECTOR& vPosition) = 0;
        virtual bool GetPosition(
            AUDIOVECTOR& vPosition) const = 0;

        virtual bool SetVelocity(
            const AUDIOVECTOR& vVelocity) = 0;
        virtual bool GetVelocity(
         AUDIOVECTOR& vVelocity) const = 0;

        virtual bool SetMaxDistance(float fMaxDist) = 0;
        virtual bool GetMaxDistance(
            float& fMaxDist) const = 0;

        virtual bool SetMinDistance(float fMinDist) = 0;
        virtual bool GetMinDistance(
            float& fMinDist) const = 0;
```

```
virtual bool SetConeAngles(uint32 nInside,
    uint32 nOutside) = 0;
virtual bool GetConeAngles(uint32& nInside,
    uint32& nOutside) const = 0;

virtual bool SetConeOrientation(
    const AUDIOVECTOR& vOrientation) = 0;
virtual bool GetConeOrientation(
    AUDIOVECTOR& vOrientation) const = 0;

virtual bool SetConeOutsideVolume(
 float fVolume) = 0;
virtual bool GetConeOutsideVolume(
 float& fVolume) const = 0;

virtual bool SetMode(uint32 nMode) = 0;
virtual bool GetMode(uint32& nMode) const = 0;

virtual bool SetVolume(float fVolume) = 0;
virtual bool GetVolume(float& fVolume) const = 0;

virtual bool SetPitch(float fPitch) = 0;
virtual bool GetPitch(float& fPitch) const = 0;

virtual bool SetReadCursor(uint32 nBytes) = 0;
virtual bool GetReadCursor(
 uint32& nBytes) const = 0;

virtual bool GetSourceSize(
 uint32& nBytes) const = 0;

virtual IEAXBuffer* EAX() = 0;
virtual IZoomFX* ZoomFX() = 0;

virtual bool QuerySupport(const GUID& guid,
    uint32 nID, uint32* pTypeSupport) = 0;
virtual bool Get(const GUID& guidProperty,
    uint32 nID, void* pInstanceData,
    uint32 nInstanceLength, void* pPropData,
    uint32 nPropLength, uint32* pBytesReturned) = 0;
virtual bool Set(const GUID& guidProperty,
    uint32 nID, void* pInstanceData,
```

```
        uint32 nInstanceLength, void* pPropData,
        uint32 nPropLength, bool bStoreProperty) = 0;
};
```

The 3D sound object interface looks very similar to the 2D sound object, with the obvious exception of the addition of numerous 3D audio parameters. Like the previous object, `ISound3D`'s `Init()` function takes a initialization structure (`Sound3DInit`) that must be filled out with information, such as the source file to load. And like the 2D sound, there is a second structure that contains all of the run-time 3D parameters, which in this case are considerably more numerous than for 2D sound.

Also note `QuerySupport()`, `Get()`, and `Set()`. These functions mirror the DirectSound `IKsPropertySet` interfaces, essentially giving the user low-level access to EAX or other property sets. This is one case where we do slightly bend our rule of top-down API design. However, these functions are rather fundamental to DirectSound programming, and any audio API should easily adapt to the interface if it has any sort of concept of generic properties. (Later on, we'll look at creating EAX and other property-set-specific interfaces, as demonstrated by the `EAX()` and `ZoomFX()` functions, which return these additional interfaces.)

The second half of creating a 3D sound object involves creating a global listener object: `IListener`. Unlike 3D sounds, there can obviously only be a single listener object, and this is enforced by the audio manager. Again, because we've hidden these objects behind an abstract interface, there is no way for a programmer to accidentally or intentionally create objects that are not allowed. In addition to creating a clean interface, abstract interface classes are a great way of enforcing required behavior, helping to keep the client's code safer. Here's the `IListener` class in Listing 5.5:

LISTING 5.5

```
struct ListenerProp
{
    ListenerProp()
    {
        Clear();
    }
    void Clear()
```

```
    {
        m_vPosition.x = 0.0f;
        m_vPosition.y = 0.0f;
        m_vPosition.z = 0.0f;
        m_vVelocity.x = 0.0f;
        m_vVelocity.y = 0.0f;
        m_vVelocity.z = 0.0f;
        m_vOrientFront.x = 0.0f;
        m_vOrientFront.y = 0.0f;
        m_vOrientFront.z = 1.0f;
        m_vOrientTop.x = 0.0f;
        m_vOrientTop.y = 1.0f;
        m_vOrientTop.z = 0.0f;
        m_fDistanceFactor = 1.0f;
        m_fRolloffFactor = 1.0f;
        m_fDopplerFactor = 1.0f;
    }
    AUDIOVECTOR m_vPosition;
    AUDIOVECTOR m_vVelocity;
    AUDIOVECTOR m_vOrientFront;
    AUDIOVECTOR m_vOrientTop;
    float m_fDistanceFactor;
    float m_fRolloffFactor;
    float m_fDopplerFactor;
};

struct ListenerInit
{
    ListenerInit()
    {
        Clear();
    }
    void Clear()
    {
        m_Prop.Clear();
    }
    ListenerProp m_Prop;
};

class IListener
{
public:
```

```
virtual bool Init(const ListenerInit& init) = 0;
virtual void Term() = 0;

virtual bool SetProperties(
    const ListenerProp& prop) = 0;
virtual void GetProperties(
    ListenerProp& prop) const = 0;

virtual bool SetPosition(
    const AUDIOVECTOR& vPos) = 0;
virtual void GetPosition(
    AUDIOVECTOR& vPos) const = 0;

virtual bool SetVelocity(
    const AUDIOVECTOR& vVel) = 0;
virtual void GetVelocity(
    AUDIOVECTOR& vVel) const = 0;

virtual bool SetOrientation(
    const AUDIOVECTOR& vFront,
    const AUDIOVECTOR& vTop) = 0;
virtual void GetOrientation(
    AUDIOVECTOR& vFront,
    AUDIOVECTOR& vTop) const = 0;

virtual bool SetDistanceFactor(
    float fDistanceFactor) = 0;
virtual void GetDistanceFactor(
    float& fDistanceFactor) const = 0;

virtual bool SetDopplerFactor(
    float fDopplerFactor) = 0;
virtual void GetDopplerFactor(
    float& fDopplerFactor) const = 0;

virtual bool SetRolloffFactor(
    float fRolloffFactor) = 0;
virtual void GetRolloffFactor(
    float& fRolloffFactor) const = 0;

virtual IEAXListener* EAX() = 0;
```

```
virtual bool QuerySupport(const GUID& guid,
    uint32 nID, uint32* pTypeSupport) = 0;
virtual bool Get(const GUID& guidProperty,
    uint32 nID, void* pInstanceData,
    uint32 nInstanceLength, void* pPropData,
    uint32 nPropLength, uint32* pBytesReturned) = 0;
virtual bool Set(const GUID& guidProperty,
    uint32 nID, void* pInstanceData,
    uint32 nInstanceLength, void* pPropData,
    uint32 nPropLength) = 0;
};
```

The IListener object must be initialized like any other object, although there are currently no members in the initialization struct other than a set of initial properties. Again, like the 3D sound object, we've created a struct that holds all of the listener's 3D properties. Using this structure, users have a choice of setting parameters either individually or all at once.

You should note the default parameters used in setting the listener's orientation, which are currently set to the DirectSound default values. Depending on how your coordinate system works, you might wish to adjust these default values to achieve a more appropriate default direction.

ISEGMENT AND IDLS

In addition to simple wave files, our sound system can also handle more-abstract concepts of sound or music. Because DirectSound and DirectMusic are more closely related than in previous versions of DirectX, it's possible to use segments as sound effects, for example. Thus, it is beneficial to integrate sound effects and musical playback functionality at a fairly low level. Eventually, we'll separate higher-level music and sound functionality into separate manager classes, which both utilize the combined low-level audio engine.

Our audio engine is primarily designed to utilize DirectMusic segments as musical components. We have a fairly full-featured DirectSound-based engine already designed for sound effects, so there is less incentive to use DirectMusic in this capacity. In Chapters 6 and 12, we'll discuss the pros and cons of this decision in regards to DirectMusic as a sound effects engine. For now, let's examine our DirectMusic-specific structures, starting with DLS and segment-based interfaces.

LISTING 5.6

```
struct DLSInit
{
    DLSInit()
    {
        Clear();
    }
    void Clear()
    {
        m_sFileName.erase();
    }
    std::string m_sFileName;
};

class IDLS : public IAudioBase
{
public:
    virtual bool Init(const DLSInit& init) = 0;
    virtual bool Lock() = 0;
    virtual bool Unlock() = 0;
};

struct SegmentInit
{
    SegmentInit()
    {
        Clear();
    }
    void Clear()
    {
        m_sFileName.erase();
        m_bMusic = true;
        m_bLooping = false;
        m_pDLS = 0;
    }
    std::string m_sFileName;
    bool m_bLooping;
    bool m_bMusic;
    IDLS* m_pDLS;
};
```

```
class ISegment : public IPlayable
{
public:
    virtual bool Init(const SegmentInit& init) = 0;
};
```

In Listing 5.6, we see interfaces for both a DLS file and a segment. There are no real surprises here. Both work exactly like previous interfaces we've examined, although they are even simpler than the sound effects classes. Each has an initialization structure and requires a filename containing a path to the persistent object that is stored on disk. One thing to note, the bool m_bMusic in SegmentInit is of particular importance if you wish to create a segment to be used as a sound effect. If you set this to false, the segment will be created as a secondary segment and will play on a separate performance than the standard musical segments.

There are several reasons for this. First, an optional global reverb is applied to the default audiopath of the musical performance (you'll learn more about this in Chapter 12), which likely not desired for the sound effect. Second, musical notifications are required to ensure any musical playback system knows when segments are playing and when they are finished. Since it is not practical to turn these on and off on a per-segment basis, the best thing we can do is to play them on different performances. For now, you must simply remember to designate all files as either music or non-music (sound effects) in order to make sure they play properly. The SegmentInit structure initializes this to true by default, meaning a segment will play as music unless specifically designated as a sound effect.

IAUDIOSCRIPT

Our only other resource-based class is IAudioScript. This class is a thinly disguised wrapper for the DirectMusic scripting interface. Again, for the sake of demonstrating code, we stretch out API-neutral design's credibility, but we'll still examine the implementation here, as shown in Listing 5.7.

LISTING 5.7

```
struct AudioScriptInit
{
    AudioScriptInit()
```

```
    {
        Clear();
    }
    void Clear()
    {
        m_sFileName.erase();
        m_bMusic = true;
    }
    std::string m_sFileName;
    bool m_bMusic;
};

class IAudioScript : public IAudioBase
{
public:
    virtual bool Init(const AudioScriptInit& init) = 0;

    virtual bool SetVariable(std::string sVarName,
        int32 iVal) = 0;
    virtual bool GetVariable(std::string sVarName,
        int32& iVal) = 0;
    virtual bool CallRoutine(
        std::string sRoutineName) = 0;
};
```

IAudioScript objects are initialized using a string identifier (m_sFile-Name), similar to any other object. Unlike our sound objects, we cannot afford to load scripts asynchronously, since a user will expect to be able to execute routines and set variables immediately after loading is complete. Moreover, there should be no significant strain in loading a small script file unless a large number of resources are embedded inside the script. In this case, you must take responsibility for loading the script manually at an appropriate time in your game's execution.

DirectMusic scripts allow arbitrary routines and variables to be defined within an authored script object, and the IAudioScript interface provides mechanisms to set and retrieve variable values or to call script functions through its members SetVariable(), GetVariable(), and CallRoutine().

IAUDIOMANAGER

We'll now examine the heart of the audio system: the manager. As noted
earlier, the audio manager is a low-level system designed to give direct control over sound and musical playback, while at the same time providing a
level of automatic resource management with regard to both total memory
usage and the number of allocated channels used on a sound card. This
gives programmers the freedom to simply initialize and play sounds in a
logical fashion, without having to worry about low-level implementation
or resource management.

LISTING 5.8

```
struct AudioMgrInit
{
    AudioMgrInit()
    {
        Clear();
    }
    void Clear()
    {
        m_hWnd = (HWND) 0;
        m_bLoadAsyncronously = true;
        m_bForceSoftware = false;
        m_bUseMusicReverb = true;
        m_bUseEAX = true;
        m_bUseZoomFX = true;
        m_n2DHardwareBufferMin = 8;
        m_n3DHardwareBufferMin = 8;
        m_n2DHardwareBufferMax = 256;
        m_n3DHardwareBufferMax = 256;
        m_n2DSoftwareBufferMax = 256;
        m_n3DSoftwareBufferMax = 256;
        m_nSegmentMax = 256;
        m_nOptimalSampleBits = 16;
        m_nOptimalSampleRate = 44100;
        m_sWorkingPath.erase();
        m_pAudioStreamFactory = 0;
        m_pMusicCallback = 0;
    }
    HWND m_hWnd;
```

```cpp
    bool m_bLoadAsyncronously;
    bool m_bForceSoftware;
    bool m_bUseMusicReverb;
    bool m_bUseEAX;
    bool m_bUseZoomFX;
    uint32 m_n2DHardwareBufferMin;
    uint32 m_n3DHardwareBufferMin;
    uint32 m_n2DHardwareBufferMax;
    uint32 m_n3DHardwareBufferMax;
    uint32 m_n2DSoftwareBufferMax;
    uint32 m_n3DSoftwareBufferMax;
    uint32 m_nSegmentMax;
    uint32 m_nOptimalSampleBits;
    uint32 m_nOptimalSampleRate;
    std::string m_sWorkingPath;
    IAudioStreamFactory* m_pAudioStreamFactory;
    IMusicCallback* m_pMusicCallback;
};

struct AudioMgrStats
{
    AudioMgrStats()
    {
        Clear();
    }
    void Clear()
    {
        m_bForce2DSoftware = false;
        m_bForce3DSoftware = false;
        m_n2DSoundsLoaded = 0;
        m_n3DSoundsLoaded = 0;
        m_nSegmentsLoaded = 0;
    }
    bool m_bForce2DSoftware;
    bool m_bForce3DSoftware;
    uint32 m_n2DSoundsLoaded;
    uint32 m_n3DSoundsLoaded;
    uint32 m_nSegmentsLoaded;
};


class IAudioManager
{
```

```
public:

    virtual bool Init(const AudioMgrInit& init) = 0;
    virtual void Term() = 0;

    virtual bool IsInitialized() const = 0;

    virtual bool GetStats(
        AudioMgrStats& stats) const = 0;

    virtual bool CreateSound(ISound*& pSound) = 0;
    virtual bool CreateSound3D(ISound3D*& pSound3D) = 0;
    virtual bool CreateSegment(ISegment*& pSegment) = 0;
    virtual bool CreateDLS(IDLS*& pDLS) = 0;
    virtual bool CreateAudioScript(
        IAudioScript*& pScript) = 0;

    virtual bool GetListener(IListener*& pListener) = 0;

    virtual bool SetSoundVolume(float fVolume) = 0;
    virtual bool GetSoundVolume(
        float& fVolume) const = 0;

    virtual bool SetMusicVolume(float fVolume) = 0;
    virtual bool GetMusicVolume(
        float& fVolume) const = 0;

    virtual bool StopAll() = 0;
    virtual bool PauseAll() = 0;
    virtual bool ResumeAll() = 0;

    virtual bool GetCurrentSegment(
        ISegment*& pSegment) const = 0;
    virtual bool GetNextSegment(
        ISegment*& pSegment) const = 0;

    virtual bool CreateAudioStream(
        IAudioStream*& pStream) = 0;
};

inline IAudioManager* AudioMgr()
{ return AudioLibFactory::GetAudioMgr(); }
```

5 creation functions [handwritten annotation in left margin]

In Listing 5.8, we can see that, like in the other classes we've examined so far, the audio manager requires us to fill out a structure containing all the parameters required to initialize the audio system. For details on what all these parameters do, you can read the SDK help documentation found on the CD-ROM. Most of the parameters and functions' behaviors can be intuitively deduced based on their names. We'll discuss some of the more important functions and parameters in particular, though.

There are five object-creation functions, each corresponding to an IAudioBase-derived interface (e.g., CreateSound(), CreateSound3D(), etc.). These five object-creation functions do the actual work of allocating an audio object and return the proper interface to the user. By deferring allocation to the manager, it gives us the opportunity to perform a couple of tasks. First, object creation can be made more efficient through the use of cached object pools, allowing us to reuse previously 'destroyed' objects as new ones. This helps to prevent memory fragmentation, especially if the user creates and destroys sound objects rather frequently. Second, it gives us an opportunity to store all created objects for later cleanup, meaning that the client need not even be responsible for cleaning up all the individually created audio resources—thus, drastically reducing the chances of memory leaks.

To retrieve the IListener interface, we use a function called GetListener(). This is a minor but important distinction, because unlike other object types, only one listener is created, and this listener can only be accessed via GetListener(). The "Get" implies that the same listener object will be retrieved on every call to the function. Again, like all other objects retrieved, this one is also managed and requires no cleanup by the programmer, although a Term() function is supplied if the listener must be cleaned up manually for some reason. In the case of both the listener and audio manager interfaces, you'll notice that Term() is used as a cleanup function rather than Destroy(). In the *GAP* library, Term() is used to designate simply cleaning up an object's initialized components, not destroying and deallocating the object like Destroy().

In addition, basic volume controls are provided. SetSoundVolume() adjusts the volume of any IPlayable object with the m_bMusic initialization flag set to false, and SetMusicVolume() likewise adjusts the volume of any object with the m_bMusic flag set to true.

Some basic global playback controls are provided with StopAll(), PauseAll(), and ResumeAll(). These functions operate on all playing sounds, regardless of their music/sound effect designation, as you would expect them to.

There is also one additional detail to note regarding how clients may access this class. We've utilized a singleton methodology to create and then access a single global instance of this class through the inline function, AudioMgr(). This gives a convenient, single-entry point into the object. The function returns the address of the object, which is always guaranteed to be valid. The code to initialize the audio manager then might look something like this: *should uses: " mgrInit Struct "*

```
// Initialize the audio system
AudioMgrInit init;
init.m_hWnd = MainWindow()->GetHWnd();
if(!AudioMgr()->Init(init))
    return Error::Handle("Could not initialize audio system")
```

Unlike some of our managed objects, the programmer is also responsible for calling Term() when finished with the audio system. This gives the class a chance to clean itself up properly.

ARCHITECTURAL CONSIDERATIONS

When creating a large system such as a sound and music library, it is important to understand both the theoretical goals of the system and the practical matter of how to implement those goals. We have already addressed a large portion of the theoretical goals when we designed our abstract interface, which defines the relationship between the library's objects and the client. At this point, we now must begin to address the practical matter of implementing this interface with concrete classes from an architectural standpoint.

ON THE CD The obvious (and required) way to start is by mirroring the abstract classes with concrete classes and logically filling out any required functionality, such as the Init() and Term() functions. However, beyond the public interface of the abstract interface lies a different interface that is only available internally to the audio libraries' concrete classes. Because of the arrangement of the code in separate folders on the CD-ROM (see Figure 5.2), the abstract interfaces are available in the /include folder, while the concrete class header files and implementation files are contained in the /src folder.

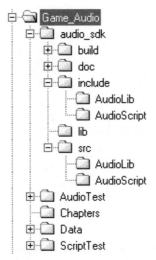

FIGURE 5.2 Arrangement of library code on the companion CD-ROM.

■ **INCLUDING THE GASspk HEADER FILES**

In any project, the application should ideally only add the /include folder to the source path. You can look in the project settings of the AudioTest project to see how this was done. Select Project | Settings in the menu, and make sure the AudioTest project is selected. Go to the C++ tab, then select Preprocessor from the Category: drop-down menu. You will note in the "Additional Include Directories" field that the relative path "..\audio_sdk\include" points to the audio sdk header.

If you simply wish to place the sdk in a fixed location and link to the libraries instead of compiling the project, you can simply point the general include path to this folder, and point the library include path to the /lib folder.

This means that we have two layers of interface to work with: an external interface defined by the abstract classes and an internal interface defined by the concrete classes. Although it may not seem like an important thing to point out, these distinct interface layers help to keep the code both encapsulated and clean. How does this work though?

■ NO CHEATING!

Because the source is distributed in our sample audio, it would naturally be simple to set an include path to point straight to concrete classes and to use those classes in unintended ways. This is something that cannot be practically prevented; but at the same time, it is such an obvious violation of the design intentions that it's not even worth trying to prevent. The power of C++ always demands a certain level of intelligent and responsible usage. While having to add members to both an abstract interface and a concrete implementation isn't quite as convenient as simply going directly to the source, it does encourage a bit more planning and foresight, which is not necessarily a bad thing.

You might recall that we used a singleton pattern to provide one, and only one audio manager object to any portion of the code via the function AudioMgr(), which returns a pointer to IAudioManager. Internally, we add the following function to provide the same object, except cast to the concrete AudioManager class.

```
static AudioManager* DXAudioMgr()
{ return static_cast<AudioManager*>(AudioMgr()); }
```

Now, when we need access to public members of AudioManager that are not derived from the public IAudioManager interface, we can simply use this access function instead of the public one.

This may not seem like a big deal; and in truth, it is a very simple concept. But it is a powerful mechanism for organizing your code's functionality, helping to guarantee that any internal functionality can be cleanly exposed in public members at the concrete implementation level. Without the abstract interfaces and the corresponding concrete-level access function, you would be forced to utilize protected or private functions to expose functionality that other classes needed to use, but which shouldn't be accessible to the user. This often results in supporting classes being declared as friends, leading to a dangerous temptation to access private data directly. Ultimately, your code is far less encapsulated and object-oriented because of this interdependency. A simple combination of abstract interfaces and multilevel access functions prevents this from being a problem.

CONCLUSION

This gives you a general overview of how the *GAP* library's basic API both looks and works to some degree. As we delve into the various components, you'll learn how to create these systems yourself, so that whether you need a fully featured sound system or just need to play a few simple sounds, you'll have the information and the reference material to do the job easily and quickly.

We've reached the end of Part I—Introduction and Theory of *Game Audio Programming*. It's time now to get down to the metal and start actually coding. The next section will cover DirectX Audio programming. We'll begin with a brief introduction that gives us an overview of DirectX, and then we'll jump right into DirectSound programming.

PART II

DIRECTX AUDIO

CHAPTER 6

DIRECTX AUDIO OVERVIEW

In this chapter, we will give a basic overview of the Microsoft DirectX Audio API. The goal of this and other chapters on DirectX is to bring a different perspective to the practical usage and application of DirectX components by examining how they are implemented in a full-featured audio engine that is designed from the ground up for high-performance games. Moreover, we will be taking a critical and honest look at the API, examining where design flaws exist, and what can be done to circumvent these flaws to produce a high-quality, flexible audio system.

DIRECTX AUDIO

In case you missed it, the combined *DirectX Audio* API was introduced in DirectX 8.0. Unlike DirectX Graphics, which combined DirectDraw and Direct3D into a completely revamped and seamless new API, the result of combining DirectSound and DirectMusic, while an admirable goal, mostly amounted to packaging the two APIs side by side while encouraging developers to use the much higher-level DirectMusic API for managing not only music, but all system-wide sound effects as well. The unfortunate effect of this merger was a slightly confusing set of documents and APIs that jumped between the low-level DirectSound and the rather high-level DirectMusic, often leaving audio programmers unsure about exactly where they should begin or which system they should really be using. Officially, developers are encouraged to use the DirectMusic interfaces because the tutorials in the help file demonstrate basic wave playback in this fashion. But, as we'll see, there are some drawbacks—some serious and some minor—to this approach that require consideration when deciding how the audio system should be set up. Fortunately, the slightly confusing 'combined' documentation has been improved with separate audio sections in DirectX 9.0, but much of the fundamental confusion about the level of integration between the two systems remains.

However, despite some minor nitpicking over issues, the DirectX Audio API contains a wealth of functionality for your use, as long as you clearly recognize the important roles of the two combined APIs, and how they can effectively work side by side, drawing on the strengths of each other.

■ INTRODUCTORY MATERIAL

The primary goal of *Game Audio Programming* is to provide audio developers real, working, detailed examples of advanced audio concepts and production code, not just simplistic examples that could be found in the DirectX documentation. To this end, we have attempted to avoid repeating what is contained in the DirectX SDK documentation and substituting different wording or different examples.

As an example, while we *do* present introductory material in the DirectMusic chapters, you might notice that we dispense with the typical "here is how you load and play a wave file" example. Unlike DirectSound wave file loading, which has no explanation in the documentation (other than sample code) showing that basic concept, the DirectMusic documentation covers this introductory material quite nicely. Thus, while we will spend a considerable amount of time covering DirectSound wave loading and playback, we will not cover this in the DirectMusic chapters.

Instead, we will be exploring the relevance of specific functions of each component as they relate to creating an entire DirectX-based audio system. Hopefully, the SDK documentation you read later (or perhaps have read already) will fill in the details and make much more sense when understood in the context of what is being presented here. Don't assume this book is a substitute for the DirectX documentation. Such duplication of effort would make little sense; and in the end, it would be far less useful when you are ready to move on to more advanced topics.

DIRECTSOUND

DirectSound is the low-level audio component of DirectX Audio. It essentially has two basic jobs to perform. First, it manages chunks of sampled audio data in container objects called *sound buffers,* or just "buffers." Second, it instructs the hardware to mix all audio data in a master buffer, called the *primary buffer,* and send the resulting waveform to the audio output device. We'll learn in Chapter 7 how the primary buffer has actually been depreciated; but the concept is still important, since DirectSound acts as though the primary buffer is still there. These buffers might be located in hardware, but DirectSound provides software audio mixing if hardware is not available.

Beginning with DirectX 3, DirectSound provided 3D aural capabilities in addition to traditional 2D stereo mixing. By using the concept of sound sources located in true 3D space and a 'listener' object that simulated the position of a person's head in the 3D world, a greater sense of realism could be achieved than by using simple panning stereo buffers. This form of audio manipulation was increasingly popular as 3D video and audio hardware became commonplace, enabling a large number of games to make the jump to true 3D.

Because DirectSound is the lowest level in the audio chain, audio card device drivers are written to be 'DirectSound compatible,' meaning that they conform to the interface needed to accelerate audio functions. As an audio programmer, you support a greater range of hardware functionality than 3D graphics programmers do. Most modern games no longer need concern themselves with software-only versions of rendering engines; but the same is certainly not true for sound and music. While reasonably priced hardware-accelerated audio cards are readily available, a surprising number of modern computers still ship with very limited-function audio hardware that does little more than offer a single basic mixing buffer, requiring all other functions to be performed entirely by the CPU.

In addition, you must be prepared to deal with a much wider variety of quality in sound drivers. Because the quality of these drivers is (if you'll pardon the expression) not as easily visible as those of video drivers, too often consumers are either stuck with, or don't know enough to upgrade, their old, buggy drivers. This leaves you, as an audio programmer, in a bit of a sticky situation. Consumers are far less likely to blame faulty audio drivers; instead, they assume the game or audio library is at fault. Thus, it is in your own best interest to ensure your audio system is as robustly designed as possible, even to the extent of accounting for situations where you might have to completely fall back on software audio rendering.

While the new, combined DirectX Audio API and instructions on how best to use it can be a bit obtuse at times, there are few real restrictions with regard to how you choose to implement your audio system. Using Direct-Sound and these property-set extensions is an easy way to ensure that an audio card's hardware is being utilized to the best degree possible, since hardware acceleration is automatically used unless specifically prohibited. DirectSound was also designed from the ground up as a low-latency audio solution. With good hardware support, *audio latency* (the time from the point at which a sound is triggered in software to final audio output) can be as low as 10 ms, a nearly imperceptible delay for gaming purposes. In addition, DirectSound utilizes a property-set mechanism that allows third-party hardware extensions (such as Creative Labs EAX or Sensaura MacroFX) to be used with relative ease.

Although playing a standard 2D sound is an inexpensive proposition in terms of CPU usage, hardware-accelerated audio really pays for itself when playing 3D positional audio. The algorithms that position a sound in 3D space using only a pair of speakers can certainly be done in software, but it is definitely more efficient (and more effective) to use dedicated hardware for this. An even greater benefit comes when applying environmental re-verberation to 3D audio. While this, too, can conceivably be done in soft-ware, it is enormously expensive and generally not worth the CPU cycles.

DIRECTMUSIC

DirectMusic is the latest addition to the DirectX Audio system, providing musical capabilities to the existing audio capabilities of DirectSound. Es-sentially, you can think of DirectMusic as sitting on top of DirectSound as a higher-level API. After DirectMusic synthesizes its music (or sound ef-fects), the resulting audio is sent to one or more DirectSound buffers for mixing.

Although DirectMusic started out as a MIDI (Musical Instrument Dig-ital Interface) plus DLS (DownLoadable Sound) system, it has since evolved to play any form of digital audio, as well. This considerably en-hances the attractiveness of the DirectMusic system for those interested in creating an interactive music system. Even those not interested in using MIDI can still make use of DirectMusic to sequence segments composed of digital audio, instead of MIDI notes.

When browsing through the DirectX Audio documentation, notice that DirectMusic-related content takes up the majority of the space. This is par-tially because DirectMusic is a more complex system than DirectSound. However, Microsoft is also actively encouraging developers to utilize

DirectMusic as both a music playback system *and* a sound-effects playback system. While some programmers might want to consider this approach, it is important to understand both the benefits and problems that can be encountered by doing so. These issues will be discussed in more detail in Chapters 12 and 13.

However, if these issues are not a concern to you, it is well worth your time to look at the benefits of DirectMusic in playing all of your sound effects. Numerous advantages quickly become apparent when comparing DirectMusic to DirectSound. The number of lines of code required to simply get a wave file loaded and playing are *drastically* reduced, saving a huge amount of initial coding time. Likewise, since DirectMusic is, by nature, a streaming architecture, playing a streaming audio file is no more difficult than playing any other sound. DirectMusic also automatically takes advantage of the Windows Audio Compression Manager, meaning that any audio which has a corresponding codec installed on the machine can be automatically loaded and played by DirectMusic. While all of these features are technically possible with DirectSound (and we'll be examining how to do them all), the onus falls to the programmer to implement them, requiring a fair amount of effort, even to load a simple wave file from disk or from memory.

Overall, DirectMusic is a fantastic system for music playback; it is quickly becoming a viable alternative for handling all audio-management tasks. As audio development continues on DirectX Audio, and DirectMusic in particular, there is a good chance that someday, most application developers' need for DirectSound might disappear entirely (or at least be minimal). So it is worth keeping an eye on the overall development of DirectMusic API and its capabilities. However, DirectSound is still very much a required component for today's audio systems, and so it is important to cover both systems in detail.

DIRECTX AND COM

Like all DirectX components, both DirectSound and DirectMusic are based on COM (Component Object Model). Understanding and utilizing COM in its entirety is a daunting task, worthy of numerous books dedicated to the subject. Fortunately, *using* COM-based components is a simple matter. However, in order to utilize these libraries most effectively, and to avoid common COM-related pitfalls, a bit of information about COM and how it works will be helpful.

WHAT IS COM?

COM is a complex beast that can be a bit difficult to precisely define, but for our needs, a simple definition will suffice. Put simply, COM enforces a standardized object model at the binary level, enabling library compatibility across different languages. In addition, COM rules require that once an interface is published, all subsequent releases must use a different interface version if compatibility is broken in any way. In this manner, installed DirectX 9 system components continue to function properly with games released with any previous version of DirectX because the internal binary interfaces that these games use remains unchanged in DirectX 9.

USING COM

To the C++ programmer, COM objects look very much like standard C++ objects, but they operate with a few specific rules of their own. To first ensure that COM is initialized properly, your application must call the function `CoInitialize()`. When your program is finished, it must call `CoUninitialize()`, even if the initial call to `CoInitialize()` has failed.

Most COM methods, including `CoInitialize()`, return an HRESULT error value, which is nothing more than a typedef'd 32-bit integer. The sign bit determines success or failure, with the remaining bits used to determine the particular success/error code. In fact, the HRESULT error code is a bit more complex than a simple error number—but this is something we are not too concerned about when simply *using* the error codes. For this reason, it is very important to avoid explicitly checking for a particular value to determine the success or failure of COM functions, unless there is a documented reason to do so. For instance, the following code incorrectly checks for a common success code:

```
// Bad HRESULT checking
HRESULT hr = CoInitialize(NULL);
if (hr == S_OK)
    // Success!
```

Because COM might return a success or error code that is different than what you might expect, the only sure way to check for success or failure is to use the SUCCEEDED() or FAILED() macros. For instance, some functions might return a value of S_FALSE if the function did not necessarily fail, but there was no need to perform the requested action. Here is how to properly check for successful completion of a COM function:

```
HRESULT hr = CoInitialize(NULL);
if(SUCCEEDED(hr))
    // Success!
```

Likewise, failure can be checked as follows:

```
HRESULT hr = CoInitialize(NULL);
if(FAILED(hr))
    // Failure!
```

Most COM interface documentation will tell you the specific error codes for which you can check. Although numerical error codes are certainly efficient, they are someone difficult to decipher.

■ **HRESULT TO STRING HELPERS**

DirectX 9 provides the convenient functions DXGetErrorString9() and DXGetErrorDescription9(), which return character-based string descriptions of an error code and its corresponding description for easier debugging. You must also explicitly link to the DxErr9.lib, as well as include the header file dxerr9.h. DirectX 8 also provides this functionality using its own functions and libraries—simply replace the "9" with "8" in the function, header, and library names.

COM OBJECT CREATION

Unlike standard C++ objects, you do not directly allocate a COM object yourself. Instead, COM utilizes a factory methodology to allocate and give you a requested object. The process looks like the following:

```
IFoo *pFoo = NULL;
HRESULT hr = CoCreateInstance(
    CLSID_Foo,
    NULL,
    CLSCTX_ALL,
    IID_IFoo,
    (void**)&pFoo);
```

This code retrieves an IFoo interface. You really don't need to understand all the details of the call, but the basic idea is that you request a class type and a specific interface of that class. These identifiers are CLSID_Foo and IID_IFoo. The function allocates and retrieves a pointer to a COM object, which it assigns to pFoo and hands back to you. At this point, you can think of this as a pointer to a standard, dynamically allocated object. For instance, let's pretend IFoo (sometimes referred to as just Foo) has a function called DoSomething(), which takes no arguments and returns an HRESULT. The code would look like this:

```
HRESULT hr = pFoo->DoSomething();
```

Essentially, the binary interface of COM objects map perfectly to standard C++ function calls, making it extremely easy to manipulate these objects—exactly as if they were simple C++ objects.

IUNKNOWN

All COM objects are reference-counted, meaning that they maintain an internal record of how many interface pointers are currently accessing the object. Additionally, COM objects may provide alternative interfaces, which can be requested at run-time. In order to standardize the COM reference counting and dynamic interface functionality, all COM objects are required to derive from an interface called IUnknown, which provides three methods: AddRef(), QueryInterface(), and Release().

```
ULONG IUnknown::AddRef();
```

AddRef() increments the internal reference count to an object and should be used when an interface pointer is copied and used elsewhere. The function returns the new reference count of the object. All COM objects are reference-counted through this interface and will not be destroyed until the reference count drops to zero. It is the programmer's responsibility to properly make use of the proper reference counting functions when copying the interface pointer. Alternatively, you could make use of _com_ptr_t, a *smart pointer* that will automatically handle the details of maintaining a proper reference count on COM objects by (among other things) automatically calling AddRef() when it is copied and Release() when it is destroyed.

```
HRESULT IUnknown::QueryInterface(
  REFIID riid,
  LPVOID* ppvObj
);
```

QueryInterface() allows you to obtain a different interface from an existing one, similar to upcasting or downcasting a class interface in C++. You will see this used when an interface has been upgraded to provide new functionality, and we must obtain the new interface from the old one. This mechanism allows code to retrieve and use a new interface without breaking compatibility with the older interfaces.

```
ULONG IUnknown::Release();
```

Release() is called when you are finished with an object. It returns the new reference count of an object, but this value should only be used for testing and debugging purposes. The object will be destroyed if the reference count drops to zero because of this call. For each CoCreateInstance(), AddRef(), or QueryInterface() call, there should exist a corresponding Release() call, much in the same way each call to new must have a matching delete call in C++. Often, other methods will add a reference count to an object as well. This will typically be documented, and the implication is that it is the programmer's responsibility to call Release() when finished with the object.

Once you have the basics down, you will find that using COM is a simple matter, and having to do so as part of using DirectX should not cause you too much trepidation.

■ SAFELY USING COM'S RELEASE FUNCTION

Do not simply call Release() on a COM object until the reference count drops to zero. If, at the end of your program, the reference count to a DirectSound or DirectMusic object does not return zero at release, it is likely that an extra reference is left over from somewhere in your code, and this needs to be fixed—not covered up by implementing a hack at the end of the program. As such, writing code like the following is not recommended:

```
while(m_pLoader->Release());
```

It is appropriate to monitor the value of Release() and use it for debugging purposes, but never alter your program's behavior based on this value.

INSTALLING AND USING THE DIRECTX 9 SDK

The DirectX 9 SDK is available from Microsoft at *http://msdn.microsoft* *.com*. This version supports Windows 98, Windows 98SE, Windows ME, Windows 2000, and Windows XP. Because only the beta version was available at the time this book went to print, we were obviously not able to distribute the SDK with the CD-ROM. In fact, the actual differences in the audio section between DirectX 8 and DirectX 9 are rather minor at the API level. If you are using DirectX 8, you should be able to compile the libraries with only a few small adjustments.

SETUP

Follow the download instructions found on the MSDN site (*http://msdn.microsoft.com*) to retrieve the DirectX installation program. DirectX comes as a complete package. There is no way to install just the audio component.

Once the installation process begins, you will be asked to choose a directory to install the SDK, which defaults to C:\DXSDK. You will also be asked if you wish to install the debug or retail run-time libraries. It is highly recommended that you install the debug run-times for doing any sort of DirectX developmental work, as these will assist you in finding bugs and errors in your code that the retail run-time might miss. As a simple example, the DirectSound run-times will initially fill buffers with random data, helping to find cases in which you might not have properly filled your buffers. (It will result in a burst of static-like noise.) Additionally, the debug run-times will spit out information to your debugger, providing you with another source of information.

USING THE SDK

In order to use the DirectX SDK in a Visual Studio project, you must first tell the program where to find the DX include files and libraries. In Visual Studio, click on Tools | Options, which will bring up the Options dialog box. Click on the Directories tab, and you will see a listing of directories for various types of files, similar to Figure 6.1. Typically, you should see a listing of include file directories when the dialog first is opened.

Type in or browse to the directory where you installed the DirectX SDK headers. By default, this should be found at C:\DXSDK\INCLUDE. Select it and click on the up-arrow to move this directory to the front of the list. This is important because there might be an older DirectX SDK installed

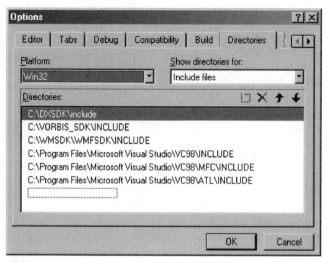

FIGURE 6.1   Visual Studio directories listing.

with your copy of Visual Studio. Because the directories are searched in the order listed, by placing this directory first, you ensure that the correct version of DirectX will always be found.

Next, select the dropdown item labeled "show directories for:" and select Library Files. This time, select the DirectX SDK library folder, which is found at C:\DXSDK\LIB if you installed DirectX in the default location. Again, move this directory to the front of the list to ensure linking with the latest versions of the DirectX libraries.

CREATING A DIRECTX AUDIO PROJECT

Now when you attempt to use DirectX Audio in a project, you only have to make sure you include the proper headers and libraries in your project settings or in your source code. In the sample audio library, this is done all in one step via a single header file called "AudioCommon.h."

LISTING 6.1

```
// DirectX Audio include files
#include <dmusicc.h>
```

```
#include <dmusici.h>
#include <dsound.h>
#include <dxerr9.h>

// Required Windows libs
#pragma comment(lib, "msacm32")
#pragma comment(lib, "winmm")

// Link DirectX 9 libs
#pragma comment(lib, "dxguid")
#pragma comment(lib, "dsound")
#pragma comment(lib, "dxerr9")

// Ogg Vorbis libs
#ifdef USE_VORBIS
#ifdef _DEBUG
#pragma comment(lib, "ogg_static_d")
#pragma comment(lib, "vorbis_static_d")
#pragma comment(lib, "vorbisfile_static_d")
#else
#pragma comment(lib, "ogg_static")
#pragma comment(lib, "vorbis_static")
#pragma comment(lib, "vorbisfile_static")
#endif
#endif // USE_VORBIS

#ifdef USE_WMA
#pragma comment(lib, "wmstub.lib")
#pragma comment(lib, "wmvcore.lib")
```

In Listing 6.1, we have included the required header files for DirectX: dmusicc.h, dmusici.h, dsound.h, and dxerr9.h. Obviously, the first two are for DirectMusic, and the third is for DirectSound. The last header file, as previously mentioned, is a handy utility library consisting of some functions that turn DirectX HRESULT error codes into human-readable strings, along with error descriptions.

Additionally, we use the #pragma comment feature to implicitly link the required library files to any project which includes this header file. This feature saves the client the bother of having to remember which library files must be linked with in order to use the audio system.

If you wish to link the files explicitly, simply add the files to the Link section in the Project Settings dialog box (click Project | Settings in the Visual Studio menu). Make sure you have the main project highlighted, then select the Link tab. Then, simply enter the names of the library files, as shown in Figure 6.2.

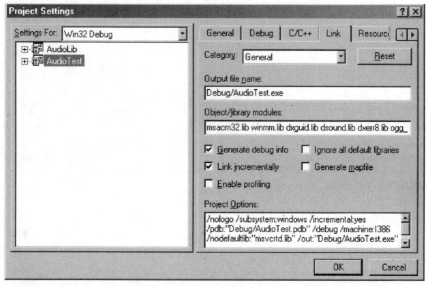

FIGURE 6.2   Explicitly linking with the DirectX library files.

One additional thing to keep in mind when linking libraries: it is imperative to ensure that the same C and C++ run-time libraries are used by all statically linked projects, or you'll encounter bizarre run-time errors. In general, Microsoft recommends dynamically linking to the multithreaded C run-time DLLs, as this is both more efficient and a safer practice for libraries such as audio systems, where it is almost guaranteed that calls to various C functions must be made in a thread-safe manner. You can find the selection of the C run-time libraries in the Project Settings dialog box. Click the C/C++ tab, and then select Code Generation in the Category drop-down selector. You should see a dialog box similar to those in Figure 6.3 and Figure 6.4. Note that both projects (the audio library and the application project) are selected, ensuring the same settings are used for both. The Win32 Debug version of the project use the debug builds of the C

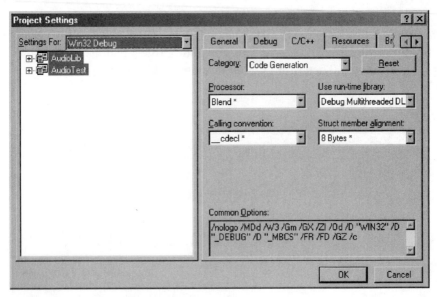

FIGURE 6.3   Run-time C library selection for debug.

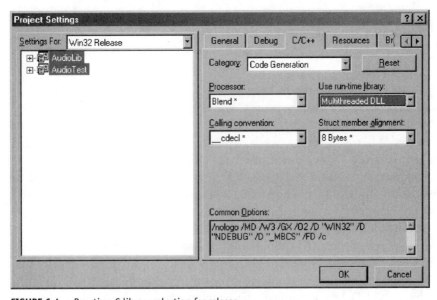

FIGURE 6.4   Run-time C library selection for release.

run-time library, and the Win32 Release version uses the optimized retail run-times.

CONCLUSION

You should now have a good idea of what the DirectX Audio system is all about and how to get started using the SDK with your own projects. In the next chapter, we will begin our DirectX Audio coverage by looking at DirectSound; and here we will lay the foundation for loading and playing a simple wave file.

CHAPTER 7

DIRECTSOUND IMPLEMENTATION

DirectSound programming at a rudimentary level is a rather straightforward proposition, but the real difficulty often involves issues somewhat outside of the realm of DirectSound itself. For instance, there is no built-in mechanism to load a wave file from disk or memory and then insert it into a buffer for playback. Instead, DirectSound makes a few assumptions about what and how you wish to implement these functions. As such, simply getting a sound to play can be a daunting proposition for the uninitiated.

DIRECTSOUND BASICS

At a very basic level, DirectSound is essentially a software interface to a hardware-based digital audio-mixing device. This interface is designed to play a number of simultaneous sounds, each with its own unique parameters, such as volume, pan, and frequency. In the case of 3D sounds, additional algorithms are applied by either the software emulation or the hardware before sending the sound to a final mixing buffer. This buffer then mixes the samples from individual sound buffers in real-time and converts the combined waveform to an analog signal, which is then amplified and transmitted to the user's speakers.

VxD and WDM Drivers

In the days of Windows 95 and Windows 98 (first edition), DirectSound utilized a driver model called VxD. Because DirectSound talked to this driver directly, no other audio devices were capable of producing sounds if DirectSound played in priority or exclusive mode, meaning that it was able to control the primary mixing buffer directly. You can see this illustrated in Figure 7.1, where only one application may utilize the hardware in exclusive mode. Taking control of the primary buffer was required in order to control the final output format of audio. For instance, the buffer might be set at 16-bit, 22 kHz, in order to most efficiently mix audio samples that match this format. Otherwise, the samples would be altered on the fly to match the destination buffer's format, a process known as *resampling*.

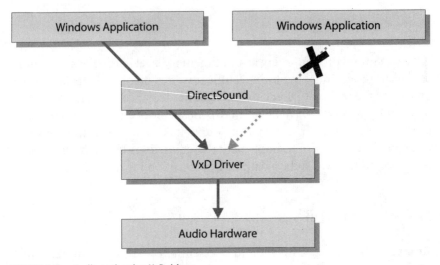

FIGURE 7.1 Audio path using VxD drivers.

In Windows 98 Second Edition, a new driver format, WDM (Windows Driver Model) was introduced. This new driver model no longer talks exclusively to DirectSound. Instead, DirectSound communicates with KMixer, the Windows system kernel-level mixer. You can see the communication path in Figure 7.2. KMixer receives input from both DirectSound and any waveout devices (and in fact any number of these applications simultaneously), meaning that the old restriction about only one application playing sound at a time is no longer true. This also means that Direct-Sound cannot control the primary buffer format of the audio hardware anymore. Instead, KMixer determines the optimal format based on the sample types mixed, which generally means it will choose the format based on the highest-quality mixed sample. Technically, the concept of a 'primary buffer' in DirectSound is still present, even when using WDM-based drivers, but this is more of an abstraction than an actual physical mixing buffer like it used to be.

While it is important to ensure that your sound code runs properly on an older VxD driver or on ISA sound hardware, it no longer makes sense to optimize your code to do this, as very few computers in the game market are still using this older hardware. Even low-end audio cards are generally PCI-based, not ISA; and ever since DirectX 8.1, Windows 95 is no longer supported, although you still might encounter VxD drivers in various versions of Windows 98 and beyond.

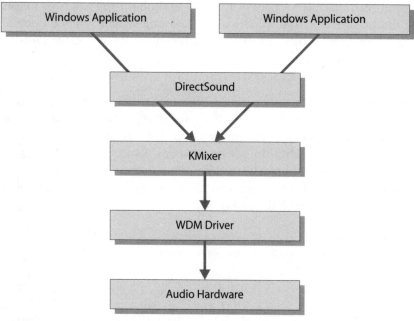

FIGURE 7.2   Audio path using WDM drivers.

SETTING UP A DIRECTSOUND PROJECT

In order to compile and link a DirectSound project, you will need to make sure your project is set up correctly. The code in this book was written using Microsoft Visual C++ version 6.0 with Service Pack 5 installed, was run on a Windows 2000 platform, and was tested on several other variants.

To set up a DirectSound-compatible project, first ensure that the DirectX 9 SDK is installed correctly on your system. (See Chapter 6 for detailed instructions on how to install the DirectX 9 SDK.) In addition, one or more library files must also be linked to your project. You must link to dxguid.lib, and if you use the `DirectSoundCreate8()` function, which is discussed in the next section, you must also link to dsound.lib. If you wish to use the handy `DXGetErrorString9()` or `DXGetErrorDescription9()` functions, which turn error codes into human-readable strings, then you must also link dxerr9.lib to your project.

IDIRECTSOUND8 INTERFACE INTRODUCED

The `IDirectSound8` interface is the first COM object you will need to use. From this interface, you will initialize the sound system, query the sound card and driver for their capabilities, and create audio buffer interfaces.

ENUMERATING DIRECTSOUND8 DEVICES

Most applications can simply use the Windows 'primary' sound output device when creating the DirectSound device (this is what users set as their default sound device in the Windows Control Panel). However, some applications might benefit from giving the user a choice of audio devices for their specific application. This can be done by enumerating the Direct-Sound devices using the `DirectSoundEnumerate()` function (which would also require linking with dsound.lib).

```
HRESULT WINAPI DirectSoundEnumerate(
    LPDSENUMCALLBACK lpDSEnumCallback,
    LPVOID lpContext
);
```

This function takes as parameters the address of an enumeration callback function and a void pointer, which is suitable for pointing back to an object, custom structure, or whatever you wish. For the callback function, simply create a function (or a static class member function) that matches the DirectSound enumeration callback function format.

```
BOOL CALLBACK DSEnumCallback(
    LPGUID lpGuid,
    LPCSTR lpcstrDescription,
    LPCSTR lpcstrModule,
    LPVOID lpContext
);
```

To properly select the appropriate output device, you should allow the user to choose a GUID (Globally Unique Identifier) value based on the lpcstrDescription field, which is a description of the sound card. Typically, you will see at least two descriptions from the enumeration: a 'primary sound driver' and a specific description of the sound card installed on the user's system. If only one sound card is installed, these both refer to the same output device. If a user does not choose a particular sound card, you should always default to the primary sound driver.

CREATING THE DIRECTSOUND8 OBJECT

To create a DirectSound8 object, you can use the DirectSoundCreate8() function to create the COM object and retrieve its interface.

```
// Create the DirectSound object
LPDIRECTSOUND8 pDirectSound;
HRESULT hr = DirectSoundCreate8(NULL, &pDirectSound, NULL);
if(FAILED(hr))
    // Handle failure here
```

The first parameter is the GUID of the enumerated sound cards within the user's·system. Since most users only have one card, and Windows has a concept of a primary card, most games can simply use NULL to indicate that the primary sound device should be used. The second parameter retrieves the IDirectSound8 interface pointer. The third parameter must be NULL. If the function fails, the user either has no suitable hardware or does not have the proper version of DirectX installed. Under older VxD drivers, this also might fail if another application is currently using the audio hardware.

DirectSound can also be initialized directly using standard COM methods, which would look similar to this:

```
LPDIRECTSOUND8 pDirectSound;
HRESULT hr = CoCreateInstance(
    &CLSID_DirectSound8,
    NULL,
    CLSCTX_INPROC_SERVER,
    &IID_IDirectSound8,
    &pDirectSound);
if(SUCCEEDED(hr))
    hr = pDirectSound ->Initialize(NULL);
```

After the object is created, you must call `Initialize()`, but only if you created the object through the COM interface. And, as mentioned earlier, if you create the DirectSound object this way, you do not need to link with dsound.lib.

SETTING THE COOPERATION LEVEL

Next, you must specify a cooperation level for DirectSound. Although this is a required step, the function is a bit archaic in that it was designed for VxD drivers; it enabled the application to determine how it would cooperate with other applications. By setting the cooperation to 'primary' or 'exclusive' mode, an application could ensure that the primary buffer was mixing at the optimum level. Setting this level (along with a primary buffer) for compatibility with older drivers will have no real effect on any modern WDM drivers, since an application can no longer set the hardware's mixing buffer directly. In fact, for WDM drivers, the 'exclusive' cooperative setting now means the same thing as 'priority.' For games, using the `DSSCL_PRIORITY` level is recommended. Here is how the cooperative level is set.

```
// hWnd is a valid window handle
hr = pDirectSound->SetCooperativeLevel(hWnd,
DSSCL_PRIORITY);
if(FAILED(hr))
    // handle failure
```

RETRIEVING DEVICE CAPABILITIES

At this point, it is not a bad idea to retrieve the device capabilities in order to determine how to best to utilize the hardware present. This is as easy as a single function call.

```
// Get the capabilities of this sound system
// m_DSCaps is a DSCAPS structure
hr = m_pDirectSound->GetCaps(&m_DSCaps);
```

There is a large amount of data collected from the audio driver in this single function call. You can read the detailed description of all the members and what they mean in the DirectX documentation, but here's a few tips on how to utilize and interpret this data.

One of the best things you can do for yourself is to ensure that the code you ship with has some method of dumping out the complete caps (capabilities) structure, even in release builds. This will help you considerably in the testing phase—you may discover a set of hardware that does not work the way you think it should with your audio system. By creating this capability in your system, you ensure that you will never have to guess at the capabilities of a sound card that might be experiencing problems with your code.

The most important data collected from this function is the number of hardware buffers available for use (dwMaxHwMixingAllBuffers). This number will range anywhere from zero to 256 on today's hardware, and the number of available buffers might grow even larger in the future. This effectively tells you how many simultaneous sounds can be played using hardware mixing. You will notice how the total number of sound buffers might not equal the sum of the 2D and 3D buffers. This is because a buffer can often be allocated as either, sharing the resources among buffer types. In addition, some cards have trouble accurately reporting the number of free buffers available; this number could depend on the buffer parameters, such as the total size of the buffer, for instance. In this case, any number of free buffers greater than zero signifies that at least one more buffer can be created. Generally speaking, this is the only truly safe metric (in terms of buffer counts) to rely on; and in fact, our library doesn't even rely on this. The *GAP* library (as you will see in Chapter 11) simply attempts to create hardware buffers until a failure occurs or until an arbitrary ceiling is reached.

Be aware that many sound cards today provide only rudimentary mixing, with no hardware channels at all available for use. Typically, these low-end cards are built onto motherboards or come by default with prepackaged systems. Because of the current number of these cards on the market, expect to have to support software-only solutions for a while.

In order to determine if a card is ISA or PCI, examine the memory statistics, such as `dwTotalHwMemBytes`, which is a member of the DSCAPS structure retrieved in the previous code listing. Because of the slower bandwidth available to ISA cards, many of these had on-board memory. If the memory is zero, it is likely a PCI card.

CREATING A PRIMARY BUFFER

Next, you will want to create a primary buffer and set it to an optimal format. Creating the buffer is required if you wish to obtain an `IDirect-SoundListener8` object or otherwise manipulate the buffer, but setting the optimal format is only helpful if a VxD driver is installed. At the same time, you can attempt to play the audio buffer for better performance. Again, this does nothing if a WDM driver is present, but it can help improve audio performance for older drivers. Note that for primary buffers, the `IDirect-SoundBuffer8` interface is not supported, so `IDirectSoundBuffer` must be used for the primary buffer interface.

```
// Create the primary sound buffer
DSBUFFERDESC desc;
ZeroMemory(&desc, sizeof(desc));
desc.dwSize = sizeof(desc);
desc.dwFlags = DSBCAPS_PRIMARYBUFFER | DSBCAPS_CTRL3D;
hr = m_pDirectSound->CreateSoundBuffer(
    &desc, &m_pPrimaryBuffer, NULL);
if(FAILED(hr))
    return false;

// Setting the format and playing the primary buffer does
// nothing with modern WDM drivers, but it's good to try in
// case older VxD model drivers are used.
WAVEFORMATEX wf;
memset(&wf, 0, sizeof(WAVEFORMATEX));
wf.wFormatTag = WAVE_FORMAT_PCM;
wf.nChannels = 2;
wf.nSamplesPerSec = 22050;
```

```
wf.nBlockAlign = 4;
wf.nAvgBytesPerSec =
    wf.nSamplesPerSec * wf.nBlockAlign;
wf.wBitsPerSample = 16;
m_pPrimaryBuffer->SetFormat(&wf);
if(FAILED(hr))
    return false;
m_pPrimaryBuffer->Play(0, 0, DSBPLAY_LOOPING);
if(FAILED(hr))
    return false;
```

RELEASING THE OBJECTS

When you are finished with the audio system, typically when the application is shutting down, you must release the objects you've created, or there will naturally be memory leaks.

```
// Release the primary buffer
m_pPrimaryBuffer->Release();
// Release the DirectSound interface
m_pDirectSound->Release();
```

CONCLUSION

In this chapter, we have examined the basic properties of DirectSound. We have also learned how to create the IDirectSound8 interface and use a number of its methods. This covers what you need to know for starting up and shutting down DirectSound. In the next chapter, we'll learn how to load a wave file, create a buffer, fill the buffer with audio data, and then play the sound.

CHAPTER 8

BASIC DIGITAL AUDIO SAMPLE PLAYBACK

Now that we know how to instantiate a DirectSound object, the next logical question is: how do we load and play a sound? We will be tackling the basics of 2D sound loading, playback, and manipulation in this chapter.

The code listed in this chapter can be found in \Game_Audio\ audio_sdk\src\audiolib\IAudioLoader.h, Wave.h, Wave.cpp, Sound.h, Sound.cpp, AudioMgr.h, AudioMgr.cpp.

LOADING A WAVE FILE

The DirectX sample code contains an excellent wave parser and loader called CWaveFile found in the DSUtil.h and DSUtil.cpp sample files. We've modified the code slightly for our own use by stripping out the file-writing code, as well as making some minor improvements in the reader. In addition, we added an abstract interface, which was modeled to some extent on this original class. We will see later how this can help us to easily write file readers for MP3, Ogg Vorbis, Windows Media, or any other format we want to load into a DirectSound buffer. But first, we need a bit of background information in order to understand the wave file format.

THE WAVE FILE FORMAT

Microsoft wave files (*.wav) are a type of RIFF (Resource Interchange Format File), which was originally based on the Electronic Arts IFF

(Interchange Format File)—but it is little-endian, instead of big-endian, designed to work more efficiently with Intel processors. RIFFs are designed as a portable, self-describing format, much in the same manner as XML files, except that IFFs and RIFFs are in binary format. The basic element in the RIFF is the *chunk*. You will see this referred to at times in the code. Essentially, a chunk consists of an ID, a value indicating how large the chunk is, and its corresponding data. By organizing a file into chunks that are defined in this manner, you can see how any RIFF can always be properly parsed, if not necessarily understood. Some types of chunks can also contain other chunks, such as catalogs and lists. All chunk types are identified with a four-byte set of characters. For instance, the wave chunk is logically identified with the uppercase characters "WAVE." This identifier is used to determine if the file is indeed a wave file. In Figure 8.1, you can see the minimum chunks required for a wave file—essentially a wave chunk containing a format chunk and a data chunk. Note that the identifier for the format chunk contains a space, since four characters are always required for identifiers.

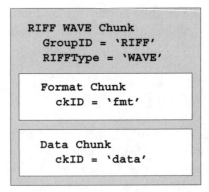

FIGURE 8.1   RIFF wave chunk file format.

Microsoft provides a special library for reading RIFFs, called Multimedia File I/O Services, which is a set of functions specifically designed to operate on RIFFs. These functions all begin with mmio, making them easier to spot in the code. Many of the functions should look familiar because they mimic traditional file functions such as mmioOpen() and mmioClose(). We won't be covering all the multimedia functions in great detail, but will instead show and explain the code specifically required to load a wave file properly.

THE WAVEFORMATEX STRUCTURE

The other notable structure you will be using quite often is the WAVEFORMATEX structure, so it's worthwhile to examine this in a bit of detail. This is the WAVEFORMATEX structure as defined in mmsystem.h.

```
typedef struct tWAVEFORMATEX
{
    WORD wFormatTag;        /* format type */
    WORD nChannels;         /* number of channels*/
    DWORD nSamplesPerSec;   /* sample rate */
    DWORD nAvgBytesPerSec;  /* for buffer estimation */
    WORD nBlockAlign;       /* block size of data */
    WORD wBitsPerSample;    /* bits per sample of mono data */
    WORD cbSize;            /* the count in bytes of */
                            /* extra information*/
} WAVEFORMATEX, *PWAVEFORMATEX, NEAR *NPWAVEFORMATEX,
    FAR *LPWAVEFORMATEX;
```

The first field in the structure, wFormatTag, designates the format type. Although vanilla PCM is the most popular format, there are many other types, usually involving some sort of compression scheme. For the purposes of DirectSound, we are initially interested in loading only PCM wave files, as this is by far the most common format that DirectSound natively supports. DirectSound on WDM also supports IEEE_FLOAT natively (in software). In addition, it can create hardware buffers in any format supported by the WDM driver, as long as the format satisfies certain basic WAVEFORMATEX validity rules. (Later, in Chapters 20 through 22, we will be learning how to convert other data formats to PCM data.) If a wave file is in PCM format, it will use this identifier:

```
/* flags for wFormatTag field of WAVEFORMAT */
#define WAVE_FORMAT_PCM     1
```

Next, nChannels designates the number of channels in the wave file. Although one or two channels are most common (mono or stereo), it is possible to use more than two channels for multispeaker playback; although this is not commonly used for games. When more than one channel is used, the samples in the data set are interleaved.

The nSamplesPerSec field describes the number of samples played per second for a single channel (hertz). Typical sample rates for wave files are 11025, 22050, and 44100, but other rates might be used.

The nAveBytesPerSec field indicates the bandwidth this wave file will require in bytes per second. This gives a simple method of creating a streaming buffer of a fixed audio length. For example, creating a two-second buffer is as simple as multiplying this value by two to determine the size of the buffer in bytes.

The variable nBlockAlign contains the size in bytes of a single sample group. For instance, a 16-bit stereo file should have an nBlockAlign value of 4 bytes. An 8-bit mono file will have an nBlockAlign value of one byte.

The number of bits in a sample is indicated by wBitsPerSample. A 16-bit wave file naturally has a value of 16 in this field. Although bit numbers other than 8 or 16 may be used, these are somewhat rare and really needn't be supported, especially for a game's wave reader. The following formulae might help you to understand the relationships between these fields:

nAvgBytesPerSec = nSamplesPerSec * nBlockAlign
nBlockAlign = nChannels * (wBitsPerSample / 8)

Finally, cbSize is a method of extending the wave format. You might have wondered what the "EX" stands for in "WAVEFORMATEX." The answer is: EXtensible. A method was needed to enable this standard structural head to extend with other data fields. The cbSize field indicates how many extra bytes need to be allocated to properly hold any wave file format extension header information. This essentially makes WAVEFORMATEX a variable-size structure. For now, we can just use the cbSize value to skip over any data we do not want to deal with at the moment, since we're mostly interested in PCM wave files. These typically have a cbSize set to zero. However, when using this structure, it is important to know how to use this field properly, as a fairly common coding mistake is to assume that wave headers are always a fixed size. Later on, you will see code that properly allocates a variable-size WAVEFORMATEX structure.

THE FILE-LOADING ABSTRACT INTERFACE

Let's first examine the abstract interface we've created, which was initially based on the basic CWaveFile class design. Note that unlike CWaveFile, there are no methods for saving audio files to disk. This is unnecessary in game code, and would simply complicate the task of writing other file format readers that must conform to this interface.

LISTING 8.1

```
class IAudioLoader
{
public:

    // This Open function is used by the current audio
    // system. It is expected that it will acquire
    // an IAudioStream interface using the filename,
    // which technically could simply be a string ID
    // for a custom file system, as well.
    virtual bool Open(std::string sFileName) = 0;

    // This decodes data directly to a memory buffer in
    // a single batch.
    virtual bool Open(BYTE* pbData,
        uint32 dwDataSize) = 0;

    // Close the input stream
    virtual bool Close() = 0;

    // Read from the input stream
    virtual bool Read(BYTE* pBuffer,
        uint32 dwSizeToRead,
        uint32* pdwSizeRead) = 0;

    // Get the total size of the input stream
    virtual uint32 GetSize() = 0;

    // Reset the input stream to the beginning
    virtual bool Reset() = 0;

    // Get the PCM format of the input stream
    virtual WAVEFORMATEX* GetFormat() = 0;

    // Return true if the end of the stream is reached
    virtual bool IsEOF() = 0;

    // Function used to destroy pool-managed objects
    virtual void Destroy() = 0;

protected:
```

```
virtual ~IAudioLoader()
{
}
};
```

Using this abstract interface as a template, we can create any file reader designed to pull data from either a file on disk or a buffer in memory. Readers based on this interface are required to be capable of loading/decoding data in small chunks for streaming code or all at once for typical sound-effects loading. A loader is simply opened using one of the two Open() functions. Data is read using one or multiple calls to the Read() function. Like a standard file, ILoaderInterface is required to track the current read pointer. You will note that we do not implement seeking functionality, as this would somewhat complicate our implementation of other readers at a later time, but it may be something you wish to add if, for some reason, your code must begin playback of audio streams at arbitrary points. Calling Reset() resets the read pointer back at the beginning of the file and prepares for reading again; and naturally, calling Close() shuts down the reader. Additionally, there are a couple of other functions, such as GetSize(), GetFormat(), and IsEOF() (end of file), which are used during the buffer creation and streaming processes. We'll see how these are both implemented and used a bit later.

CHOOSING A RUN-TIME LOADER

Because all of our loaders are based on a common interface, IAudioLoader, it becomes easy to create a run-time audio loader based on the extension of the filename passed into the Sound object's Init() function. We can extract a file type and create a specific loader using the following code:

LISTING 8.2

```
// Extract the extension - decide on a loader based on
// extension name.
string sExt =
m_Init.m_sFileName.substr(m_Init.m_sFileName.size() - 3);

// Use the Wave loader
if(stricmp(sExt.c_str(), "wav") == 0)
```

```
    m_pLoader = new Wave;
// Use the Windows Media loader
else if(stricmp(sExt.c_str(), "wma") == 0)
    m_pLoader = new WMA;
// Use the Windows Media loader
else if(stricmp(sExt.c_str(), "mp3") == 0)
    m_pLoader = new WMA;
// Use the Vorbis loader
else if(stricmp(sExt.c_str(), "ogg") == 0)
    m_pLoader = new Vorbis;
else
    return Error::Handle("Unsupported file type");
```

■ PLUG-INS

A more flexible approach to a general-purpose audio library would be to encapsulate each file loader into a separate dll and instruct the audio library to scan
through the directory, dynamically loading them as needed, based on a standardized method for associating specific file types with a given dll library. However,
such a system, while not too difficult to build, is beyond the scope of this book
and library. Unless you are actually selling a commercial library, there is little need
to provide run-time plug-in type functionality because there is no reason to use
more than one or two file types. Instead, it is far easier to simply link the specific
libraries you wish to support into your project. Most applications will only need to
support one or two types of basic audio files, not all of the four types we present
in this book.

CONCRETE CLASS WAVE LOADER

We're now going to examine the concrete class Wave, which can load or
stream a file either from disk or from a memory buffer.

LISTING 8.3

```
class Wave : public IAudioLoader
{
    DEFINE_POOL(Wave);
public:
    bool Open(std::string sFileName);
```

```
    bool Open(BYTE* pbData, uint32 dwDataSize);
    bool Close();

    bool Read(BYTE* pDestBuffer, uint32 dwSizeToRead,
        uint32* pdwSizeRead);

    bool Reset();
    WAVEFORMATEX* GetFormat()
    { return &m_DestFormat; }
    uint32 GetSize()
    { return m_dwSize; }
    bool IsEOF()
    { return m_bEOF; }
    void Destroy();
private:
    bool OpenMMIO();
    bool ReadMMIO();
    bool PrepareACMBuffers(uint32& nDataIn,
        uint32& nStreamRead, uint32 dwSizeToRead);
    bool DecompressData(uint32 nDataIn,
        BYTE* pDestBuffer, uint32 dwSizeToRead,
        DWORD* pdwSizeRead);

protected:
    virtual ~Wave();
private:
    Wave();

    WAVEFORMATEX m_DestFormat; WAVEFORMATEX structure
    HMMIO m_hmmio;      // MM I/O handle for the wave
    MMCKINFO m_ck;      // Multimedia RIFF chunk
    MMCKINFO m_ckRiff; // Use in opening a wave file
    uint32 m_dwSize;    // The size of the wave file
    bool m_bEOF;        // Has reached end of file?

    // ACM specific structures
    WAVEFORMATEX* m_pwfx;// Pointer to WAVEFORMATEX structure
    HACMSTREAM m_hACMStream;
    uint8* m_pCompressBuffer;
    uint32 m_nCompressBufferSize;
    uint8* m_pDecompressBuffer;
    uint32 m_nDecompressStart;
```

```
    uint32 m_nDecompressEnd;
    uint32 m_nDecompressBufferSize;

    static uint32 m_nWaveCount;
};
```

In Listing 8.3, we see the header file for the concrete wave-loading class. For the time being, we're going to ignore the bold code, as this is all specific to decoding compressed wave files. It will be simpler to first explain basic PCM reading. We'll worry about the additional complication of using the Windows Audio Compression Manager (ACM) later in Chapter 20. In our subsequent code listings, ACM-specific code will not be listed in order to help clarify the presentation; so you will notice a discrepancy when comparing the wave-reader code on the CD-ROM to that presented in the text.

After the file is opened, calling Read() pulls data out of the buffer. For a streaming buffer, calling Read() periodically in small amounts pulls the data off the disk, until the IsEOF() function returns true, signaling that the end of file (EOF) has been reached. At any time, the GetSize() function can be called to return the total file size, and the GetFormat() function is used when initially setting up the DirectSound buffer.

LISTING 8.4

```
Wave::Wave()
{
    memset(&m_ck, 0, sizeof(MMCKINFO));
    memset(&m_ckRiff, 0, sizeof(MMCKINFO));
    m_pwfx = NULL;
    m_hmmio = NULL;
    m_dwSize = 0;
    m_bEOF = false;
    memset(&m_DestFormat, 0, sizeof(WAVEFORMATEX));
}

Wave::~Wave()
{
    Close();
}
```

In Listing 8.4, we can see the constructor and destructor of the Wave class. In the constructor, all members are cleared; and in the destructor, the Close() function is called to help prevent memory or file resource leaks.

```
// Opens a wave file for reading from a file and offset
bool Wave::Open(string sFileName)
{
    // Open the wave file from disk
    m_hmmio = mmioOpen((char *) sFileName.c_str(),
                NULL,
                MMIO_ALLOCBUF | MMIO_READ);

    return OpenMMIO();
}

// Open a wave file format from a memory buffer
bool Wave::Open(BYTE* pbData, uint32 dwDataSize)
{
    // Indicate to read from a memory buffer
    MMIOINFO mmioInfo;
    ZeroMemory(&mmioInfo, sizeof(mmioInfo));
    mmioInfo.fccIOProc = FOURCC_MEM;
    mmioInfo.cchBuffer = dwDataSize;
    mmioInfo.pchBuffer = (CHAR *) pbData;

    // Open the memory buffer
    m_hmmio = mmioOpen(NULL, & mmioInfo, MMIO_READ);

    m_nWaveCount++;
    return OpenMMIO();
}

bool Wave::OpenMMIO()
{
    // Read the wave header file
    if (!ReadMMIO())
    {
        // ReadMMIO will fail if it is not a wave file
        mmioClose(m_hmmio, 0);
```

```
        return Error::Handle("Wave Error: ReadMMIO");
    }

    // Reset the file to prepare for reading
    if (!Reset())
    {
        mmioClose(m_hmmio, 0);
        return Error::Handle("Wave Error: Reset");
    }

    // Set the wave size
    m_dwSize = m_ck.cksize;

    return true;
}
```

We have two `Open()` functions for our `Wave` class in Listing 8.5, but the only real difference between them is the method of opening the multimedia file. The first function allows us to read directly from files. While the example listed simply opens a file, we'll learn in Chapter 20 how to install a handler that allows us to use our `IStream`-based file reader, meaning that we can even directly extract wave files from custom resource formats.

The second `Open()` function reads a file from a memory buffer, demonstrating an alternative method of retrieving wave files from custom resource systems. Typically, streaming would not usually be done from this type of buffer; the buffer would need to be allocated and read before the streaming began, which sort of eliminates the efficiency of it.

Both of the `Open` functions then call the internal function `OpenMMIO()`, which reads the file's header information, fills out the `WAVEFORMATEX` structure, and prepares the file for reading by calling `Reset()`.

LISTING 8.6

```
// Verifies that this is a wave file, and allocates and
// fills out the wave format header structure.
bool Wave::ReadMMIO()
{
    // chunk info for general use.
    MMCKINFO ckIn;
```

```
// Temp PCM structure to load in.
PCMWAVEFORMAT pcmWaveFormat;

// Make sure this structure has been deallocated
SAFE_DELETE_ARRAY(m_pwfx);

if (mmioSeek(m_hmmio, 0, SEEK_SET) == -1)
    return false;

if ((0 != mmioDescend(
    m_hmmio,
    &m_ckRiff,
    NULL,
    0)))
    return Error::Handle("Wave Error: mmioDescend");

// Check to make sure this is a valid wave file
if ((m_ckRiff.ckid != FOURCC_RIFF) ||
    (m_ckRiff.fccType != mmioFOURCC(
    'W','A','V','E')))
    return Error::Handle("Wave Error: mmioFOURCC");

// Search the input file for for the 'fmt ' chunk.
ckIn.ckid = mmioFOURCC('f', 'm', 't', ' ');
if (0 != mmioDescend(m_hmmio,
            & ckIn,
            & m_ckRiff,
            MMIO_FINDCHUNK))
    return Error::Handle("Wave Error: mmioDescend");

// Expect the 'fmt' chunk to be at least as
// large as <PCMWAVEFORMAT>; if there are extra
// parameters at the end, we'll ignore them
if (ckIn.cksize < (LONG) sizeof(PCMWAVEFORMAT))
    return Error::Handle(
    "Wave Error: sizeof(PCMWAVEFORMAT)");

// Read the 'fmt ' chunk into <pcmWaveFormat>.
if (mmioRead(m_hmmio,
        (HPSTR) & pcmWaveFormat,
        sizeof(pcmWaveFormat)) !=
    sizeof(pcmWaveFormat))
```

```
    return Error::Handle("Wave Error: mmioRead");

// Only handle PCM formats for now
if (pcmWaveFormat.wf.wFormatTag == WAVE_FORMAT_PCM)
{
    memcpy(&m_DestFormat,
        & pcmWaveFormat,
        sizeof(pcmWaveFormat));
    m_DestFormat.cbSize = 0;
}
else
{
    // We'd normally handle non-PCM formats here
    return false;
}

// Ascend the input file out of the 'fmt ' chunk.
if (0 != mmioAscend(m_hmmio, & ckIn, 0))
{
    SAFE_DELETE(m_pwfx);
    return Error::Handle("Wave Error: mmioAscend");
}

    return true;
}
```

Listing 8.6 shows the most complex function in the Wave class so far, ReadMMIO(). This function verifies that the file is indeed a valid wave file and reads the WAVEFORMATEX structure from the file. This may seem like a simple matter to do, but the matter is somewhat complicated by the variable-size nature of WAVEFORMATEX. However, since we're only concerned with PCM wave files for the moment, we can simplify the process somewhat.

The multimedia functions proceed to navigate to the format chunk, using the function mmioDecend(). Once the 'fmt' chunk has been found, the function then verifies that we are dealing with a PCM file; otherwise it returns an error. After the structure is properly stored in m_DestFormat, we then ascend out of the format chunk by using the function mmioAscend().

As you can see, the basic operations of RIFFs involve *seeking* a specified chunk type, *descending* down to perform operations within that chunk, then *ascending* back out of it. Later, the Read() function will operate in much the same way, although the operations will take place among several different functions to allow incremental reading of files, which is a requirement when streaming files from the disk.

LISTING 8.7

```
// Resets the internal m_ck pointer so reading starts from the
// beginning of the file again
bool Wave::Reset()
{
    m_bEOF = false;

    if (m_hmmio == NULL)
        return false;

    // Seek to the data
    if (-1 == mmioSeek(m_hmmio,
                m_ckRiff.dwDataOffset +
                sizeof(FOURCC),
                SEEK_SET))
        return Error::Handle("Wave Error: mmioSeek");

    // Search the input file for the 'data' chunk.
    m_ck.ckid = mmioFOURCC('d', 'a', 't', 'a');
    if (0 != mmioDescend(m_hmmio,
                & m_ck,
                & m_ckRiff,
                MMIO_FINDCHUNK))
        return Error::Handle("Wave Error: mmioDescend");

    return true;
}
```

The Reset() function now prepares to read the data chunk. It firsts seeks to the data and descends into the data chunk itself. Because the m_ck structure is filled out here, we were able to set the size after calling the first Reset() in OpenMMIO(). After the user is done reading the file, the Reset() function can be called to prepare the file for reading again.

LISTING 8.8

```
// Reads section of data from a wave file into pBuffer and
// returns how much is read in pdwSizeRead, reading not
// more than dwSizeToRead. This uses m_ck to determine where to
// start reading from. So, subsequent calls will
// continue where the last one left off,
// unless Reset() is called.
bool Wave::Read(BYTE* pDestBuffer, DWORD dwSizeToRead,
    DWORD* pdwSizeRead)
{
    MMIOINFO mmioinfoIn; // current status of m_hmmio

    if (m_hmmio == NULL)
        return false;
    if (pDestBuffer == NULL || pdwSizeRead == NULL)
        return false;

    if (pdwSizeRead != NULL)
        *pdwSizeRead = 0;

    if (0 != mmioGetInfo(m_hmmio, & mmioinfoIn, 0))
        return Error::Handle("Wave Error: mmioGetInfo");

    // Data member specifying how many bytes to actually
    // read out of the wave file.
    uint32 nDataIn = 0;
    BYTE* pWaveBuffer = 0;
    uint32 nStreamRead = 0;

    // If we're not decompressing data, we can directly
    // use the buffer passed in to this function.
    pWaveBuffer = pDestBuffer;
    nDataIn = dwSizeToRead;

    if (nDataIn > m_ck.cksize)
        nDataIn = m_ck.cksize;
    m_ck.cksize -= nDataIn;
    uint32 nRead = 0;
    uint32 nCopySize;
    while(nRead < nDataIn)
    {
```

```
    // Copy the bytes from the io to the buffer.
    if (0 != mmioAdvance(m_hmmio,
                & mmioinfoIn,
                MMIO_READ))
        return Error::Handle("Wave Error: mmioAdvance");

    if (mmioinfoIn.pchNext ==
        mmioinfoIn.pchEndRead)
        return Error::Handle(
            "Wave Error: mmioinfoIn.pchNext");

    // Actual copy.
    nCopySize = mmioinfoIn.pchEndRead - mmioinfoIn.pchNext;
    nCopySize = ClampMax<uint32>(nCopySize, nDataIn -
        nRead);
    memcpy(pWaveBuffer + nRead, mmioinfoIn.pchNext,
        nCopySize);
    nRead += nCopySize;
    mmioinfoIn.pchNext += nCopySize;
  }

  if (0 != mmioSetInfo(m_hmmio, & mmioinfoIn, 0))
    return Error::Handle("Wave Error: mmioSetInfo");

  // Report the number of bytes read
  if (pdwSizeRead != NULL)
    *pdwSizeRead = nDataIn;

  // Check to see if we hit the end of the file
  if (m_ck.cksize == 0)
    m_bEOF = true;

  return true;
}
```

In Listing 8.8, we see the Wave::Read() function, which has been slightly modified from the original CWaveFile source. The biggest difference is our inner reading loop, which has been modified to copy the wave data a block at a time, rather than the byte-by-byte copy that exists in the sample code; although the basic principles remain the same. Notice that we must be careful not to read too many bytes, and so we must check each actual copy against how much we are intending to read. This is presumably why a byte-by-byte copy was implemented. But, as you can see, there are other ways of accomplishing the same thing. Because the actual decent into the data chunk is performed in the Reset() function, which seeks to the proper location for the initial read, we can incrementally read data from the data chunk using this function.

LISTING 8.9

```
// Closes the wave file
bool Wave::Close()
{
    mmioClose( m_hmmio, 0 );
    m_hmmio = NULL;
    m_dwSize = 0;
    m_bEOF = false;
    return true;
}
```

Finally, as shown in Listing 8.9, we can close the reader with the Close() function, which appropriately calls mmioClose(), as well as clears out the appropriate data members. At about this point, if you are not familiar with this process, your jaw is likely dropping at the sheer volume of code needed to simply get a wave file loaded and its data extracted to a memory buffer. You're also probably beginning to understand exactly why DirectSound has a reputation for being slightly hard to use. This reputation is earned not so much for what DirectSound does, but more for what DirectSound *doesn't* do for you. The good news is, once you have your basic wave loader finished, 75 percent of the difficult work is done, at least in regard to playing a simple 2D sound. By cutting some corners and making some assumptions, we could have cut the code size down a bit, but it seems more useful to build a loader that will be worthwhile for the long haul, despite the initial amount of work involved.

THE IDIRECTSOUNDBUFFER8 INTERFACE

Now that we have a reliable and easy-to-use wave file loader, we can begin the much simpler business of creating a DirectSound buffer and playing it.

Before we start coding, though, we should take a moment to familiarize ourselves with the concept behind DirectSound buffers.

DIRECTSOUND BUFFERS

DirectSound's control of digital audio is at the buffer level, and this is essentially the heart of DirectSound. Each buffer contains a chunk of memory that defines the characteristic of the sound and that roughly corresponds to a single channel (or perhaps a pair of channels for a stereo buffer) in our 'digital mixer' paradigm.

One frequent complaint about DirectSound is that the current architecture does not separately represent the abstract concepts of the sound source (the actual digital data) and the sound channel (the hardware destination). Instead, DirectSound mixes them together into a single 'buffer' object. Part of the reason for this is historical. Since sound cards used to contain on-board memory, the concept of a package 'source + channel' buffer made much more sense than it does in the current context, where resources can easily be stored in system memory, independent of the number of hardware channels available on the sound card.

■ **DIRECTMUSIC'S ADVANTAGE**

One of the advantages of DirectMusic is that it actually does make a distinction between source data and buffer destinations (hardware channels). While it would be nice to have this functionality at a lower level in DirectSound, DirectMusic is not a bad alternative.

While this does complicate our task slightly, DirectSound *does* in fact have a voice-management mechanism that enables some degree hardware channel management that is separate from the buffers—albeit, somewhat of a tack-on solution. Also, because modern hardware utilizes buffers directly in system memory, it's not as CPU-intensive as it once was to create buffers on demand, allowing the user to more-effectively manage hardware resources themselves. Although the audio system in this book utilizes the latter method because it allows more control over how and when resources get removed, we'll also show you how to use the built-in voice management that comes with DirectSound, as well as how to roll your own management system (see Chapter 11).

As you can see in Figure 8.2, all DirectSound buffers begin life as 2D buffers. In order to create a 3D buffer, an addition interface is derived from the basic IDirectSoundBuffer8 interface. However, we will examine this in more detail when we begin discussing 3D sound. For now, let's focus on basic 2D sounds, as these are both the simplest interfaces as well as the prerequisite to creating 3D sounds.

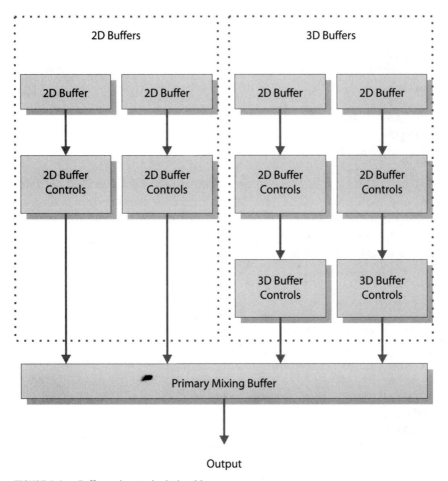

FIGURE 8.2   Buffer and control relationships.

The first thing we must do when playing a wave is to get the wave file and data into memory. This is a simple matter now that we have a convenient wave file loader. In addition, because we are using an abstract base class, it's much easier to utilize a factory system that creates a loader based on the type of file we're attempting to load. For these first examples though, we won't be doing anything quite so elaborate. Note that for the sake of brevity in our examples, we might not check for errors; but this is something you should always do in production code.

LOADING THE WAVE FILE

If you have an abstracted file system that extracts files and places them into memory buffers, you can use the memory-reading routines. Otherwise, it will likely be simpler to use the routines designed to read straight from a file.

```
Wave WaveFile;
if(!WaveFile.Open("somefile.wav"))
    // handle error
```

Now that the file has been opened successfully, we can extract both the size and the format of the data. We will need to use this information to construct a DirectSound buffer of the appropriate size and format. For now, we are going to simply construct a buffer that can hold the wave file in its entirety. In Chapter 9, we will see how to stream large files for more-efficient memory usage.

CREATING THE BUFFER

Let's first copy the WAVEFORMATEX data into our own structure. We will use a standard PCM structure (meaning the structure size is fixed), since DirectSound buffers cannot use any other format.

```
// copy the format and size information
uint32 nBufferSize;
WAVEFORMATEX WaveFormat;
memcpy(&WaveFormat, WaveFile.GetFormat(),
    sizeof(WAVEFORMATEX));
nBufferSize = WaveFile.GetSize();
```

Once we have the format and size, we can proceed to set up and create the DirectSound buffer.

```
// Create the actual sound buffer
HRESULT hr;
DSBUFFERDESC desc;
ZeroMemory(&desc, sizeof(desc));
desc.dwSize = sizeof(desc);
desc.dwFlags =
    DSBCAPS_CTRLPAN |
    DSBCAPS_GETCURRENTPOSITION2 |
    DSBCAPS_CTRLFREQUENCY |
    DSBCAPS_CTRLVOLUME;
desc.lpwfxFormat = &WaveFormat;
desc.dwBufferBytes = nBufferSize;
IDirectSoundBuffer* pDSB;
HRESULT hr = pDirectSound->CreateSoundBuffer(
    &desc,
    &pDSB,
    NULL);
if FAILED(hr)
    // handle error
```

In this code snippet, pDirectSound is a valid IDirectSound8 interface pointer. We use the CreateSoundBuffer() member that, if successful, returns a pointer to an IDirectSoundBuffer interface.

The DSBUFFERDESC structure is what defines all buffer characteristics. This has several important data fields that you should understand how to use. The first field, dwSize, is not the size of the buffer to create. Instead, it is the size of the structure itself. This convention of manually setting the size of a structure is used throughout DirectSound and DirectMusic as a form of structure verification. If this field is left unset, you'll typically see an INVALID_PARAMS (invalid parameters) error returned.

The dwFlags variable describes the type of buffer to create. In this example, we have created a standard 2D buffer with pan, frequency, and volume capabilities. You must be cautious when setting the DSBCAPS_CTRLPAN flag to avoid using this in conjunction with a wave file that has more than one channel. This combination is not allowed (i.e., panning a stereo source makes no sense) and will result in an invalid argument error.

Since we have not directed DirectSound to specifically use hardware or software resources, DirectSound will first attempt to find a hardware voice. If none is available, it will create a software buffer.

Next, the GETCURRENTPOSITION2 flag is used to choose an algorithm that returns the buffer's queried position more accurately than in previous versions of DirectSound. Unless you specifically need the older compatibility of the previous behavior, you should always use this flag.

Last, we set the buffer format and size using the lpwfxFormat and dw-BufferBytes fields, respectively. We then create the buffer with the Cre-ateSoundBuffer() function, passing in the description structure and the interface pointer. The last parameter must always be NULL.

However, before we proceed with playing and manipulating the sound, there is one more step to perform. You might have noticed that we have an IDirectSoundBuffer interface, not an IDirectSoundBuffer8 interface. In order to obtain the proper interface, we must call QueryInterface() to get the proper interface version. This is how it looks:

```
// Get the IDirectSoundBuffer8 interface
IDirectSoundBuffer8* pDSBuffer;
hr = pDSB->QueryInterface(
ID_IDirectSoundBuffer8,
(void**)&pDSBuffer);
if FAILED(hr)
    // Handle failure case

// Release the temporary DirectSoundBuffer interface
pDSB->Release();
```

Note that once we're done with the original interface, we must release it, or we'll end up with a memory leak. At this point, we have an IDirectSoundBuffer8 buffer that is ready for use. However, before we start using it, we must first fill the buffer with the wave data. This is done using the Lock() and Unlock() functions, which we'll see used next.

FILLING THE BUFFER

The Lock() and Unlock() functions are designed to allow direct access to a DirectSound buffer's memory. In the example shown in Listing 8.10, we are locking the entire buffer and copying data into it. Notice how the Wave class' Read() function is being used to copy data from the wave file to the DirectSound buffer's memory. After the data has been copied into the sound buffer's memory, we Unlock() the entire buffer once again to prepare the buffer for playback and manipulation.

LISTING 8.10

```
// Lock the buffer
void* pData;
uint32 dwBytes;
HRESULT hr;

hr = pDSBuffer->Lock(
    0,
    0,
    &pData,
    &dwBytes,
    NULL,
    NULL,
    DSBLOCK_ENTIREBUFFER);
if FAILED(hr)
    // Handle error

// Fill the entire buffer with audio data from source
uint32 dwBytesRead;
if(!WaveFile.Read((unsigned char*)pData, dwBytes, &dwBytesRead))
    // Handle error

// Unlock buffer
hr = pDSBuffer->Unlock(pData, dwBytes, NULL, 0);
if FAILED(hr)
    // Handle error
```

You might have noticed the specific mention of locking the *entire* buffer, leading you to wonder about locking *part* of a buffer, and why this might be done. In the next chapter, when we discuss streaming audio, we'll examine how a part of a buffer can be locked and unlocked while it is playing in order to continuously update it.

BUFFER PLAYBACK AND MANIPULATION

Congratulations! You now have a buffer and are ready to play it. From here, DirectSound is quite simple to use, but we will quickly go over a few of the basic control functions. Nearly all buffer functionality is encapsulated by the IDirectDirectSoundBuffer8 interface, so studying this interface in the SDK help documentation will give you a good idea of what manipulations are possible with a basic audio buffer. To play a sound, simply call the Play() member as follows:

```
HRESULT hr = pDSBuffer->Play(0, 0, 0);
```

If you wish to play the buffer so that it loops continuously (until you call Stop()), then play it in the following manner:

```
HRESULT hr = pDSBuffer->Play(0, 0, DSBPLAY_LOOPING);
```

The first parameter is reserved and should be zero, and the second parameter is a 32-bit, unsigned integer value designating the sound priority when using the voice manager. (We will discuss this in more detail in Chapter 11.) The last parameter is the options flag. DSBPLAY_LOOPING is currently the only play option.

In order to stop a sound, call the Stop() function:

```
HRESULT hr = pDSBuffer->Stop();
```

The GetStatus() call can be used to determine if a buffer is currently playing, stopped, or lost, among a few other states, as well. Here is a brief sample showing how to write a function to determine if a sound buffer is currently playing.

```
bool Sound::IsPlaying()
{
    DWORD dwStatus;
    m_pDSBuffer->GetStatus(&dwStatus);
    if(dwStatus & DSBSTATUS_PLAYING)
    return true;
    return false;
}
```

The complete set of status flags include: DSBSTATUS_BUFFERLOST, DSB-STATUS_LOOPING, DSBSTATUS_PLAYING, DSBSTATUS_LOCSOFTWARE, DSBSTA-TUS_LOCHARDWARE, and DSBSTATUS_TERMINATED. Most of these are somewhat obvious. If you have questions about them, you can find more information in the SDK help documentation.

VOLUME, PAN, AND FREQUENCY

In addition to creating a buffer to play, stop, and check the status of a sound, you might remember that when we created the buffer, we explicitly set flags that enable us to control volume, pan, and frequency. Like the play, stop, and check, these new flags are rather simple to implement.

In DirectSound, volume is controlled by attenuation, not by amplification. In simple terms, this means that volume can only be reduced. For this reason, it is important for sound designers to record audio at the maximum safe level, and this can easily be attenuated in the game itself. Volume is represented by an integer ranging from −10,000 to zero, representing hundredths of a decibel, or *millibels*. It is important to remember that this is not a linear representation of sound—it is logarithmic. If you set the audio volume of a buffer at −5,000, it will not be half the volume of what it was when it was at zero. As such, you'll need a method to convert a linear volume to a logarithmic one. Shown below is a function to turn a floating-point value ranging from zero to one into a integer value suitable for the DirectSound SetVolume() function.

```
static int LinearToLogVol(double fLevel)
{
    const int MIN_VAL = 0.0f;
    const int MAX_VAL = 1.0f;
    // Clamp the value
    if(fLevel <= MIN_VAL)
        return DSBVOLUME_MIN;
    else if(fLevel >= MAX_VAL)
        return 0;
    return (int) (-2000.0 * log10(1.0f / fLevel));
}
```

Using this function, we can easily set the volume linearly based on our earlier design of setting a volume using a floating-point value between zero and one.

```
HRESULT hr = pDSBuffer->SetVolume(LinearToLogVolume(fVolume));
```

If, for some reason, you wish to turn a DirectSound volume back into a linear range, we can apply the inverse of our previous function.

```
static float LogToLinearVol(int iLevel)
{
    // Clamp the value
    if(iLevel <= -9600)
        return 0.0f;
    else if(iLevel >= 0)
        return 1.0f;
    return pow(10, double(iLevel + 2000) / 2000.0f)
        / 10.0f;
}
```

Setting the pan value on the buffer is similarly easy. Technically, pan is a logarithmic value, and it works by attenuation as well by reducing the volume of the channel opposite to the direction of the pan. However, it tends to sound 'correct' enough when using the values linearly.

```
// Should give correct values assuming pan ranges from -1.0f
    to 1.0f
HRESULT hr = pDSBuffer->SetPan(static_cast<int32>(fPan *
    10000));
```

If you do wish to convert the value to a true linear range, you should be able to do this by modifying the algorithm found in the previous volume function.

Setting a new frequency is even easier. Simply choose a new hertz value, and call the function.

```
HRESULT hr = pDSBuffer->SetFrequency(nFrequency);
```

If you pass in a value of DSBFREQUENCY_ORIGINAL, the frequency is reset back to its original value.

All of the last three functions (SetVolume(), SetPan(), and SetFrequency()) also have corresponding Get functions that can retrieve the values as well. These work exactly as you might expect them to, and they can be found in the DirectSound SDK documentation along with more-detailed descriptions of all of the functions we've covered in this chapter.

CONCLUSION

Although getting a wave file loaded is the most difficult portion of writing a DirectSound file-playing system, we've seen that the rest of DirectSound buffer manipulation is rather trivial and can be controlled with just a few simple function calls. In the next chapter, we will examine the more complicated task of dynamically streaming a large wave file through a buffer.

CHAPTER 9

STREAMING DIGITAL AUDIO

One of the basic requirements of most audio systems is the ability to stream audio files from disk. Typically, games will stream digital soundtracks, long sections of spoken dialogue—any such large audio resource. The basic mechanism behind audio streaming is simple in concept. A small DirectSound buffer—enough to hold one second's worth of audio data—is created, and audio data is read and loaded into this buffer as it is playing. Like most simple concepts, however, the devil is in the details. We'll see exactly what you need to keep track of in order to properly stream your audio.

The code listed in this chapter can be found in \Game_Audio\ audio_sdk\src\audiolib\AudioMgr.h, AudioMgr.cpp, Sound.h, Sound.cpp.

CONCEPTS

When creating a streaming DirectSound buffer, instead of allocating space for all the sound data at once, we'll instead be creating a buffer large enough for one second of data. As data is needed, we'll pull it directly from the Wave class file reader and place it into the DirectSound buffer. Because it can read incrementally from a wave file, the Wave class is already capable of handling our streaming requirements. This will help to simplify our streaming code, which will be complicated enough without having to worry about the reader.

■ **STATIC BUFFERS DEFINED**

In this book, the opposite of streaming buffers will be refered to as *static buffers*. Do not confuse this with the notion of DirectSound 'static' buffers (indicated with the buffer description flag `DSBCAPS_STATIC`), which instructs DirectSound to place the audio data on board the audio card's memory, if available. 'Static,' in the more modern sense, simply refers to sounds that are created using a single, continuous buffer that holds the entire sample in system memory, even for hardware buffers.

As our streaming buffers are played, we'll be inserting them into a master streaming list, which will be periodically updated via a timing thread. As the list is traversed, a `ServiceBuffer()` member function will be called for each `Sound` object, which will read additional information from the disk via its corresponding `Wave` reader object. As playback of any particular buffer stops or is paused, it is removed from the list during the update cycle. So, there are two major components to streaming functions (see in Figure 9.1)—the sound buffer's update function, which performs the actual work of streaming, and the management and periodic updating of the master list of streaming files, which is responsible for invoking each buffer's update function.

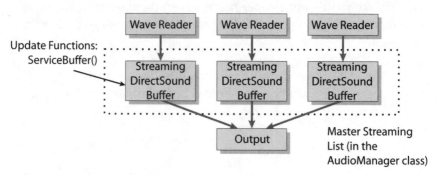

FIGURE 9.1   Streaming buffers and readers.

NOTIFICATIONS VS. TIMERS

You might see other code samples (such as the sample code that comes with the DirectX SDK) that use notifications instead of a periodic timer to update buffers. DirectSound notifications work fairly simply: a notification is set at a particular position in a buffer, and a corresponding Win32 event is created to signal the application when the specified position is reached. Typically, the application would create a dedicated thread that waits for the object's signal; it acts immediately when the signal is received.

We will not be covering DirectSound notifications for the simple reason that in real-world applications, notifications are not useful unless you only wish to create software buffers. According to the official DirectSound documentation, notifications can be set in hardware buffers; but often this is not the case. Whether this is an error of omission in the documentation or poor support at the driver level is irrelevant—the net result is the same. In many situations, every streaming buffer would have to be a software buffer, which is an especially bad proposition if we want to apply environmental effects to a streaming 3D buffer, for instance.

You are probably better off avoiding DirectSound notifications altogether, both in streaming buffers and elsewhere in your code, especially for such critical operations as streaming buffers. Thus, we will be demonstrating how to write notification-free streaming code in this chapter. A multimedia or thread-based timer works just as well as notifications, so it makes sense to use a more reliable method if it is available.

Managing the Streams

In our code, we'll create a one-second buffer and update it approximately five times per second. Since these updates are crucial to the progress of our streaming buffers, we'll begin by examining how to periodically update a set of streaming buffers.

Our basic strategy is to create a list of all currently playing streaming sounds and to iterate through these sounds periodically, calling each sound's ServiceBuffer() function, which will perform the actual work of reading the sound data into the buffer as well as keeping track of some other important information. We'll be working with two classes for this exercise—AudioManager and Sound—both of which are provided on the accompanying CD-ROM (audio_SDK/doc/GAPAudio system/Doc/HTML) for you to examine and study in further detail.

The AudioManager class, naturally enough, will be keeping track of all currently playing streaming sounds in a managed list. In addition, we must keep track of some other information as well: a list of sounds to be removed from the streaming list (we'll see why this is necessary in a bit) and a timing function, which actually calls the Sound object's ServiceBuffer() function. Listing 9.1 handles the data the AudioManager class must keep track of, as well as required stream-related functions. Naturally, we have removed a great deal of code from the actual AudioManager class listing in order to show you the relevant portions.

LISTING 9.1

```
class AudioManager : public IAudioManager
{
    // Interface functions
public:
    bool Init(const AudioMgrInit& init);
    void Term();

    // Stream insertion and removal
    void InsertStream(Sound* pStream);
    void RemoveStream(Sound* pStream);

private:

    // Separate thread for timed events
    static void TimeEvent(LPVOID lpv);
    // Service all currently playing streaming buffers
    void ServiceStreamingBuffers();

    // Streaming members
    SoundList m_SoundStreamProcess;
    SoundList m_SoundStreamRemoval;

    // Used to properly synchronize and shut down
    //the manager's multiple threads
    HANDLE m_hTerm[2];
};
```

When the AudioManager class is initialized, the following code should be executed:

```
// Set the callback for the timer function used for
// general periodic events.
```

```
if (_beginthread(&AudioManager::TimeEvent,
    4096,
    NULL) == -1)
    return false;
```

This launches a thread using the TimeEvent() function, which is shown in Listing 9.2. The function first checks to see if it must self-terminate, and proceeds to enter a critical section before calling the ServiceStreaming-Buffers() function. By incrementing and checking the static variable iServiceStreams, we ensure the function is only called once every four updates and performs a final approximate rate of five updates per second.

LISTING 9.2

```
void AudioManager::TimeEvent(LPVOID lpv)
{
    while (true)
    {
        // Wake up every 50ms to perform
        // some timed actions
        Sleep(50);

        // If the manager has been shut down
        // then terminate this thread
        if (!DXAudioMgr()->m_bInitialized)
        {
            SetEvent(DXAudioMgr()->m_hTerm[TIME_EVENT]);
            return;
        }

        // Enter the critical section to ensure that
        // functions that alter the contents of the
        // data through which we'll be looping cannot
        // continue until we are finished with
        // this function.
        EnterCriticalSection(
            &DXAudioMgr()->GetUpdateCS());

        // Use a static counter to make sure streams
        // only get updated five times a second. More
        // often is just wasteful.
```

```
static int iServiceStreams = 0;
if ((iServiceStreams++) % 4 == 1)
    DXAudioMgr()->ServiceStreamingBuffers();

// Update the listener object - calculate all
// deferred 3D settings
if (DXAudioMgr()->m_pListener)
    DXAudioMgr()->m_pListener->
        CommitDeferredSettings();

// We're done with the critical section now
LeaveCriticalSection(
    &DXAudioMgr()->GetUpdateCS());
    }
}
```

Because this is a static function, we must access the AudioManager object via DXAudioMgr(), which is based on a singleton pattern as previously discussed. Another option would be to pass the object pointer as user data, then cast the pointer to the appropriate object type inside the function. We now have our periodically updating function. Although we chose to use a thread and a sleep function, we could have also used the Windows multimedia timer to achieve approximately the same thing. This would have technically ensured a more constant update rate, but we are assuming the loads placed on this thread will not be so extreme as to cause problems of this nature.

Let's now examine the AudioManager functions that add, remove, and update the streams, as shown next in Listing 9.3.

LISTING 9.3

```
void AudioManager::ServiceStreamingBuffers()
{
    // Service all buffers
    SoundList::iterator itr;
    for (itr = m_SoundStreamProcess.begin();
        itr != m_SoundStreamProcess.end();
        ++itr)
        (*itr)->ServiceBuffer();
```

```
    // Remove requested buffers
    for (itr = m_SoundStreamRemoval.begin();
        itr != m_SoundStreamRemoval.end();
        ++itr)
    {
        SoundList::iterator itor = find(
            m_SoundStreamProcess.begin(),
            m_SoundStreamProcess.end(),
            *itr);
        if (itor != m_SoundStreamProcess.end())
            m_SoundStreamProcess.erase(itor);
    }
    // Clear the removal list
    m_SoundStreamRemoval.clear();
}

void AudioManager::InsertStream(Sound* pStream)
{
    m_SoundStreamProcess.push_back(pStream);
}

void AudioManager::RemoveStream(Sound* pStream)
{
    m_SoundStreamRemoval.push_back(pStream);
}
```

The first thing you might have noticed is the somewhat odd method of removing an object. Instead of simply removing an object from the list, it is instead placed into a removal list. Then, after the main update loop, the corresponding object is found and removed from the master list. In order to understand why this is done, a bit of explanation is in order.

The ServiceBuffer() function is on a separate thread than our other code. This creates two problems: first, we need to ensure that we never attempt to remove an element from the list as it is currently being updated. A bit of thought will reveal the obvious problems in an element trying to remove itself from a list from inside of an iteration loop. It simply can't be done safely without all kinds of messy convolutions. Second, we need to find a method to safely remove objects from the stream list via the Sound object's Stop() and Pause() functions, even though these functions may be called from inside the ServiceBuffer() function itself. As you can see, there are a lot of things that can go wrong here.

The solution is twofold. The first part you can see in the preceding code: a secondary 'removal' list is used to hold an element (or elements) that wishes to remove itself from the stream playback list. Only after the primary list is finished updating can the secondary list then iterate through and remove any designated elements. This 'deferred removal' technique is the safest and easiest method for removing objects from a list while inside an iteration loop.

The second part of the solution involves ensuring proper timing when removing a stream in order to avoid potential problems due to the multithreaded nature of the timing functions. The solution is to use a delayed removal, triggered by setting a bool value in the Sound object, m_bRemoveStream to true. Both the Pause() and Stop() functions set this value, and the next time the ServiceBuffer() is called, it checks for this value at the beginning of the function. If the value is true, the buffer is removed from the streaming list via the AudioManager::RemoveStream() function before exiting.

```
// If this flag has been set, it means that we should add this
// object to the list of those to be removed as soon as the
// service loop is completed.
if(m_bRemoveStream)
{
    DXAudioMgr()->RemoveStream(this);
    //...
}
```

You can quickly deduce that because the function is called only from ServiceBuffer(), there can never be any synchronization errors, even when calling Stop() from inside ServiceBuffer(). In this particular case, the buffer will simply remove itself on the next service cycle. Because the actual buffer is stopped immediately, it doesn't matter that the removal from the update list is slightly delayed.

Overall, it's a bit of effort to get around buffer notifications, but the robustness of the code is definitely worth the effort. Next, we'll examine what exactly happens inside the Sound::ServiceBuffer() function; but before we do, we must precisely understand how DirectSound buffers work.

UNDERSTANDING DIRECTSOUND CIRCULAR BUFFERS

We will take advantage of the DirectSound concept of a circular buffer to perform our streaming. The circular buffer has already been demonstrated when playing a looping sound. Internally, DirectSound maintains a pointer representing the current audio data being processed and sent to the primary buffer. This pointer is known as the *play cursor*. When the play cursor reaches the end of the buffer, and the buffer is designated as looping, it will jump to the front of the buffer and continue playing seamlessly. In front of the play cursor exists the *write cursor*. This marks the point at which it is safe to begin writing data. The space after the write cursor and before the play cursor is safe for an application to lock and modify the data. This concept is represented in Figure 9.2. The hatched area represents data currently in use by DirectSound, but all other areas may be safely locked and manipulated.

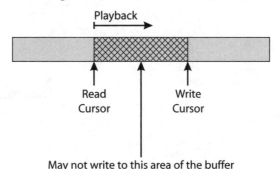

FIGURE 9.2   DirectSound read and write cursors.

DirectSound has a method for retrieving the play and write cursor positions in a DirectSound buffer: IDirectSoundBuffer8::GetCurrent-Position(). This function retrieves both pointers from a buffer and can be safely called while the buffer is either stopped or playing.

```
// Get the current play and write cursors for the buffer
DWORD dwPlayCursor;
DWORD dwWriteCursor;
```

```
HRESULT hr = m_pDSBuffer->GetCurrentPosition(
    &dwPlayCursor, &dwWriteCursor);
```

However, we'll soon see that we don't care at all about the write cursor. It may seem a bit odd at first, but with the nature of our streaming mechanism, the write cursor is not required at all. Instead, we must keep track of our own cursor based on how much data is actually written to the buffer, not based on where we are allowed to write. Let's call this custom cursor of ours the *data cursor*. We will use this simple integer value to keep track of how many bytes we have actually written into the buffer, thus telling us where we must write our next chunk of data on the next update. Figure 9.3 shows the two possible configurations in which the data might appear at any point.

Streaming Buffer

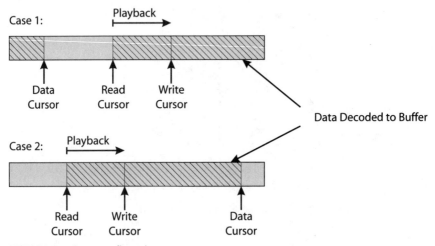

FIGURE 9.3   Cursor configurations.

The patterned areas represent data that has been written to the buffer, and the empty area indicates the area that we must lock and fill on the next update cycle. At the end of the update, we move the data cursor forward, indicating the amount of data newly written to the buffer, and the cycle will begin again on the next update. If we run out of data to fill the buffer with, we fill it with silence and stop the buffer when the play cursor reaches or exceeds the data cursor. If our streaming buffer is set to loop, however, we simply reset the source and continue filling the buffer.

You can see that there are two possible configurations of the space to which we must write our data. Figure 9.3's Case 1 represents the simplest case, with a single contiguous block of memory after the data cursor and before the read cursor to be filled. Case 2 represents a slightly more complex case, with the block of memory split by the end of the buffer. Fortunately, the DirectSound locking mechanism will automatically take care of this problem for us. We simply must indicate the position of the data to lock and the size of the data buffer. If the size exceeds the end of the buffer, DirectSound will return two locked data buffers. A bit later, we'll see exactly how the Lock() function can deal with this issue.

Preparing the Streaming Buffer

We'll now examine portions of the Sound class relevant to the mechanisms of streaming a sound. Our Sound object handles both static and streaming audio buffers in a single class and uses a switch to change the behavior of those functions. This is also handy because there are cases when a user's designation might be overridden because of practical considerations. Creating a streaming buffer with less than one second's worth of data doesn't work well, or you might decide to override a user's decision to load a huge buffer into memory all at once. In these cases, the class can simply flip the streaming flag and continue as normal.

Shown next are some of the required functions and data members of the Sound class for the streaming data buffer. We've simplified the code a bit to make it easier to follow, showing you only the portions relevant to streaming.

LISTING 9.4

```
public:
    bool Load();
    bool LoadSource(uint32& nBufferSize);
    bool FillBuffer();
    void ServiceBuffer();
    uint8 GetSilenceData();
private:
```

```
IDirectSoundBuffer8*  m_pDSBuffer;
WAVEFORMATEX          m_WaveFormat;
DSBCAPS               m_Caps;
ISoundSource*         m_pSource;
uint32                m_nDataCursor;
uint32                m_nBytesPlayed;
uint32                m_nLastPlayPos;
bool                  m_bRemoveStream;
```

Creating and loading a buffer occur exactly like when working with a standard, static buffer. Again, we've cut out some irrelevant portions, but you can see here the critical steps needed to set up the DirectSound buffers, exactly like we've seen in the previous chapter.

LISTING 9.5

```
bool Sound::DoLoad()
{

    // Make sure we don't reload the sound
    if(IsLoaded())
        return true;

    // First prepare and load the source
    uint32 nBufferSize = 0;
    if(!LoadSource(nBufferSize))
        return false;

    // Set the buffer creation flags depending on user
    // preferences
    uint32 nFlags =
        DSBCAPS_GETCURRENTPOSITION2 |
        DSBCAPS_CTRLFREQUENCY |
        DSBCAPS_CTRLVOLUME;

    // Check for pan flag
    if((m_WaveFormat.nChannels == 1) && !m_b3DSound)
        nFlags |= DSBCAPS_CTRLPAN;

    // Create the actual sound buffer
```

```
    HRESULT hr;
    IDirectSoundBuffer* pDSBuffer;
    DSBUFFERDESC desc;
    ZeroMemory(&desc, sizeof(desc));
    desc.dwSize = sizeof(desc);
    desc.dwFlags = nFlags;
    desc.lpwfxFormat = &m_WaveFormat;
    desc.dwBufferBytes = nBufferSize;
    hr = DXAudioMgr()->DirectSound()->CreateSoundBuffer(
        &desc, &pDSBuffer, NULL);
    if FAILED(hr)
        return false;

    // Get the IDirectSoundBuffer8 interface
    hr = pDSBuffer->QueryInterface(
        IID_IDirectSoundBuffer8, (void**)&m_pDSBuffer);
    if FAILED(hr)
        return false;

    // Release the temporary DirectSoundBuffer interface
    pDSBuffer->Release();

    // Get the caps to determine the actual
    // size of the buffer
    hr = m_pDSBuffer->GetCaps(&m_Caps);
    if FAILED(hr)
        return false;

    // Fill the entire buffer with source data
    if(!FillBuffer())
    {
        Unload();
        return false;
    }

    return true;
}
```

There are no flags to set in order to indicate to DirectSound that this should be a streaming buffer. One flag you would *not* want to use is DSBCAPS_STATIC, indicating that the buffer should be placed in on-board memory. Instead, a better choice is to make use of DSBCAPS_LOCHARDWARE or DSBCAPS_LOCSOFTWARE to control where the buffer is created. If a user has an older ISA card, you may want to give the user the option of forcing all buffers to exist in software, ensuring a more reliable, if less optimal experience. (We'll learn later in Chapter 11 how to dynamically manage buffer resources.)

LISTING 9.6

```
bool Sound::LoadSource(uint32& nBufferSize)
{
    if(!m_pLoader->Open(m_Init.m_sFileName))
        return false;

    memcpy(&m_WaveFormat,
        m_pLoader->GetFormat(),
        sizeof(WAVEFORMATEX));

    if(m_Init.m_bStreaming)
    {
        nBufferSize = m_WaveFormat.nAvgBytesPerSec;
        if(nBufferSize > m_pLoader->GetSize())
        {
            m_Init.m_bStreaming = false;
            m_pLoader->Close();
            return LoadSource(nBufferSize);
        }
    }
    else
    {
        // calculate the size of the DSound buffer
        nBufferSize = m_pLoader->GetSize();
    }
    return true;
}
```

When we load our source data, we also use this opportunity to calculate the size of our buffer, depending on whether it is streaming or not. For streaming buffers, we simply retrieve the value from m_WaveFormat. nAveBytesPerSec, which will always give us a one-second buffer, an appropriate size for streaming buffers. You may also notice an example of how we can determine if a buffer is too small to effectively stream and take corrective measures by turning it into a static buffer. Next, in Listing 9.7, we see how to fill the buffer.

LISTING 9.7

```cpp
bool Sound::FillBuffer()
{
    // Lock the buffer
    void* pData;
    uint32 nBytes;
    HRESULT hr;
    hr = m_pDSBuffer->Lock(0, 0, &pData, &nBytes,
        NULL, NULL, DSBLOCK_ENTIREBUFFER);
    if (FAILED(hr))
        return false;

    // Fill the entire buffer with audio data
    uint32 nBytesToRead;
    uint32 nBytesRead;

    nBytesToRead = nBytes;

    if (!m_pLoader->Read(
        (unsigned char*)pData,
        nBytesToRead,
        &nBytesRead))
        Error::Handle("Source read error");

    // make sure the cursor moves and wraps
    m_nDataCursor += nBytesRead;
    m_nDataCursor %= nBytes;

    // If we read less than the entire buffer
    // fill the rest with silence
    if (nBytesRead < nBytes)
        memset(((unsigned char *) pData) + nBytesRead,
            GetSilenceData(),
            nBytes - nBytesRead);

    // Unlock buffer
    hr = m_pDSBuffer->Unlock(pData, nBytes, NULL, 0);
    if (FAILED(hr))
```

```
      return false;

   return true;
}
```

Again, both `LoadSource()` and `FillBuffer()` should look just like the sample code you saw in the previous chapter. Notice how this line determines the size of the buffer:

```
// Calculate the size of the streaming buffer
nBufferSize = m_WaveFormat.nAvgBytesPerSec;
```

This creates a one-second buffer according to the information gathered from the source in the `WaveFormat` structure. Beyond this change, the only significant difference between the initial setups of static and streaming buffers is that for streaming buffers, you must not close the source reader object after you have initially filled the buffer. This object, obviously, will be needed to continue reading the file as the buffer plays. You'll see the `Wave` object represented as `m_pSource` in upcoming functions.

THE `ServiceBuffer()` FUNCTION

We now move to the most important function regarding streaming: `ServiceBuffer()`. Although the function can appear a bit daunting at first glance, it's not too difficult to comprehend when it's broken down into discrete steps. Here's the function shown in its entirety in Listing 9.8.

LISTING 9.8

```
// For streaming audio, ServiceBuffer() is invoked
// five times per second for each streaming buffer
// via a multimedia timer in order to fill and update
// the content of the circular buffer.
void Sound::ServiceBuffer()
{
    // If this flag has been set, it means that we
    // should add this object to the list of those
    // to be removed as soon as the service loop is
```

```
// completed, as well as resetting some variables.
if (m_bRemoveStream)
{
    m_bRemoveStream = false;
    DXAudioMgr()->RemoveStream(this);
    if (IsPaused())
        return;
    if (!m_pLoader)
        return;

    // Reset the source to play from the beginning of the
    // file
    m_pLoader->Reset();

    // Reset streaming variables
    m_nBytesPlayed = 0;
    m_nLastReadPos = 0;
    m_nDataCursor = 0;

    // Make sure the buffer plays from the beginning
    // when it starts up again
    if (!m_pDSBuffer)
        return;
    m_pDSBuffer->SetCurrentPosition(0);

    // The next time this buffer plays, we want it
    // set up properly with a full buffer of valid
    // source data.
    if (!FillBuffer())
        return;

    return;
}

// If we don't have a buffer or source, no use continuing
if(!m_pDSBuffer || !m_pLoader)
    return;

// Get the current play and write cursors for the buffer
DWORD dwReadCursor;
DWORD dwWriteCursor;
HRESULT hr = m_pDSBuffer->GetCurrentPosition(
```

```
        &dwReadCursor,
        &dwWriteCursor);

// Calculate how many bytes have played since
// the last update call
if (dwReadCursor > m_nLastReadPos)
    m_nBytesPlayed += dwReadCursor - m_nLastReadPos;
else
    m_nBytesPlayed += (m_Caps.dwBufferBytes -
        m_nLastReadPos) + dwReadCursor;

// Have we played the entire sound? If so, take
// appropriate action based on whether we're
// looping the file or not.
if (m_nBytesPlayed >= m_pLoader->GetSize())
{
    if (m_Init.m_bLooping)
    {
        // If we're looping, just start the count
        // back at the beginning
        m_nBytesPlayed -= m_pLoader->GetSize();
    }
    else
    {
        // Otherwise, stop playing and processing
        Stop();
        return;
    }
}

// Calculate how much data can be copied to the
// buffer this update
DWORD dwDataToCopy;
if (m_nDataCursor < dwReadCursor)
    dwDataToCopy = dwReadCursor - m_nDataCursor;
else
    dwDataToCopy = (m_Caps.dwBufferBytes -
        m_nDataCursor) +
        dwReadCursor;

// No need to allow more than 1/2 of the buffer to
// be read at a time. We're reading five times a
```

```
// second, so this should keep up without overtaxing
// the readers.
if (dwDataToCopy > (m_Caps.dwBufferBytes / 2))
    dwDataToCopy = m_Caps.dwBufferBytes / 2;

// Lock the buffer into one or two buffers
LPVOID pPtr1;
DWORD dwBytes1;
LPVOID pPtr2;
DWORD dwBytes2;
hr = m_pDSBuffer->Lock(m_nDataCursor, dwDataToCopy,
    &pPtr1, &dwBytes1, &pPtr2, &dwBytes2, 0);
if (FAILED(hr))
{
    Error::Handle("Error locking stream buffer!");
    return;
}

// If we're at the end of the wave data...
if(m_pLoader->IsEOF())
{
    // Fill the buffer with silence - we're at
    // the end of the file
    memset(pPtr1, GetSilenceData(), dwBytes1);
    if (pPtr2)
        memset(pPtr2, GetSilenceData(), dwBytes2);
    m_nDataCursor += (dwBytes1 + dwBytes2);
}
// Otherwise...
else
{
    // Fill the buffer with wave data as needed
    uint32 dwBytesRead = 0;
    if(!m_pLoader->Read((unsigned char*)pPtr1,
        dwBytes1,
                        & dwBytesRead))
    {
        Error::Handle("Error reading stream!");
        return;
    }
    m_nDataCursor += dwBytesRead;
    if(pPtr2 && (dwBytes1 == dwBytesRead))
```

```
    {
        if(!m_pLoader->Read((unsigned char *)
            pPtr2 dwBytes2, &dwBytesRead))
        {
            Error::Handle("Error reading stream!");
            return;
        }
        m_nDataCursor += dwBytesRead;
    }
}

// Unlock the buffer now that we're done with it
m_pDSBuffer->Unlock(pPtr1, dwBytes1, pPtr2, dwBytes2);

// If we want to loop the stream, reset the file
// to the beginning
if (m_Init.m_bLooping && m_pLoader->IsEOF())
    m_pLoader->Reset();

// Loop the write position around if it goes past
// the end of the buffer
m_nDataCursor %= m_Caps.dwBufferBytes;

// Set the last play cursor position for next
// update calculation
m_nLastReadPos = dwReadCursor;
}
```

Let's break this function apart and go through it step by step. You've already seen the code at the beginning of the function that checks for the removal flag, which is set in response to a Stop() or Pause() call. However, a bit more has to happen as well.

```
if (m_bRemoveStream)
{
    m_bRemoveStream = false;
    DXAudioMgr()->RemoveStream(this);
    if (IsPaused())
        return;
    if (!m_pLoader)
        return;
```

```
// Reset the source to play from the beginning of
// the file
m_pLoader->Reset();

// Reset streaming variables
m_nBytesPlayed = 0;
m_nLastReadPos = 0;
m_nDataCursor = 0;

// Make sure the buffer plays from the beginning
// when it starts up again
if (!m_pDSBuffer)
    return;
m_pDSBuffer->SetCurrentPosition(0);

// The next time this buffer plays, we want it
// set up properly with a full buffer of valid
// source data.
if (!FillBuffer())
    return;

return;
}
```

You can see how after the stream is marked for removal, we check to see if the Sound object is paused. If true, we can exit without resetting all the other streaming variables, which means that all we have to do to begin streaming again is to begin playing the buffer and reinsert the buffer back into the streaming list. Otherwise, we assume the buffer has been stopped and reset all the streaming-related variables. At this point, we also refill the buffer with data from the beginning of the file, which will allow the function to begin playing again without latency. The fill was done in the streaming thread (as opposed to being inside the Stop() function) to prevent a frame-rate drop from occurring in the main thread, since decoding a second's worth of data can be somewhat processor-intensive for some high-compression file formats (which are likely to be streamed the most).

Next, we do a simply sanity check to make sure we don't proceed without valid pointers to our buffers and source objects. Then, the first actual DirectSound function call comes into play. We retrieve the current DirectSound buffer's read pointer using the GetCurrentPosition() function.

```
// Get the current play and write cursors for the buffer
DWORD dwReadCursor;
DWORD dwWriteCursor;
HRESULT hr = m_pDSBuffer->GetCurrentPosition(
    &dwReadCursor,
    &dwWriteCursor);
```

Once these values are successfully retrieved, we use them to calculate how much data has been read since the last update. This is a key component of the streaming mechanism. By comparing the current read position against the last update's read position, we can tell how much data has been read per update. We add this to the variable m_nBytesPlayed, and this value is compared against m_pLoader->GetSize() (the size of the audio stream in bytes) to determine when we've actually reached the end of the file.

Because we're working with a circular buffer, we always have two cases to consider, because the cursors might be on either side of each other. The following algorithm interprets their relative position and returns the correct number of bytes read in the last frame:

```
// Calculate how many bytes have played since
// the last update call
if (dwReadCursor > m_nLastReadPos)
    m_nBytesPlayed += dwReadCursor - m_nLastReadPos;
else
    m_nBytesPlayed += (m_Caps.dwBufferBytes -
        m_nLastReadPos) + dwReadCursor;
```

Next, we use the m_nBytesPlayed value to determine if we have reached the end of our streaming. Depending on whether or not we want to loop the stream, different actions will be applied. We simply compare the total bytes read against the size of our data source, and if we've played enough, we perform the appropriate action.

```
if (m_nBytesPlayed >= m_pLoader->GetSize())
{
    if (m_Init.m_bLooping)
    {
        // If we're looping, just start the count
        // back at the beginning
        m_nBytesPlayed -= m_pLoader->GetSize();
```

```
    }
    else
    {
        // Otherwise, stop playing and processing
        Stop();
        return;
    }
}
```

Next in the function, we perform an algorithm that looks very similar to the one that calculates how many bytes have been read in the last update; except this time, we're calculating how much room we have to copy data into this update. As shown previously in Figure 9.3, we can update the buffer space between the data cursor and the read cursor. And, like the previous algorithm, we have to contend with both cases involving the cursors' relative positions.

```
// Calculate how much data can be copied to the
// buffer this update
DWORD dwDataToCopy;
if (m_nDataCursor < dwReadCursor)
    dwDataToCopy = dwReadCursor - m_nDataCursor;
else
    dwDataToCopy = (m_Caps.dwBufferBytes -
        m_nDataCursor) + dwReadCursor;
```

We now have the value `dwDataToCopy`, which we'll put to good use in the upcoming `Lock()` function. Let's look at how `IDirectSoundBuffer8::Lock()` works with a slightly more-complicated scenario than simply locking and filling the entire buffer front to back.

```
// Lock the buffer into one or two buffers
LPVOID pPtr1;
DWORD dwBytes1;
LPVOID pPtr2;
DWORD dwBytes2;
hr = m_pDSBuffer->Lock(m_nDataCursor, dwDataToCopy,
    &pPtr1, &dwBytes1, &pPtr2, &dwBytes2, 0);
if (FAILED(hr))
{
    Error::Handle("Error locking stream buffer!");
```

```
    return;
}
```

We simply pass in the data cursor and the size of the data to copy (we'll learn how to calculate this in a moment), and DirectSound returns two sets of pointers and size values. Unless an error is returned, the first pointer and size variable (pPtr1 and dwBytes1) should always be filled out. If pPtr2 is not NULL, then simply fill in this buffer next; otherwise, the data did not cross the buffer boundary on this update.

An additional wrinkle comes next. Because of the periodic nature of DirectSound buffer streaming, it is impossible for us to stop the streaming buffer exactly when the data runs out. Therefore, in order to provide the illusion of stopping exactly on cue, we must pad silence into any remaining data that might still be playing. So, at this point, we must check to see if the file has reached the end and take appropriate action.

```
// If we're at the end of the wave data...
if (m_pLoader->IsEOF())
{
    // Fill the buffer with silence - we're at
    // the end of the file
    memset(pPtr1, GetSilenceData(), dwBytes1);
    if(pPtr2)
        memset(pPtr2, GetSilenceData(), dwBytes2);
    m_nDataCursor += (dwBytes1 + dwBytes2);
}
// Otherwise...
else
{
    // Fill the buffer with wave data as needed
    uint32 dwBytesRead = 0;
    if(!m_pLoader->Read((unsigned char*) pPtr1,
        dwBytes1, &dwBytesRead))
    {
        Error::Handle("Error reading stream!");
        return;
    }
    m_nDataCursor += dwBytesRead;
    if(pPtr2 && (dwBytes1 == dwBytesRead))
    {
        if(!m_pLoader->Read((unsigned char*)
```

```
            pPtr2, dwBytes2, &dwBytesRead))
        {

            Error::Handle("Error reading stream!");
            return;
        }
        m_nDataCursor += dwBytesRead;
    }
}
```

In this code, we first check for an end of file (IsEOF) condition in the source object. If true, the buffer is filled with silence data via the Sound::GetSilenceData() function, which returns a single byte of either 8-bit or 16-bit silence. If we have not reached the end of the file, we fill the buffer as normal. Note how we update the data cursor with the number of bytes actually filled or read from the source, not the number of bytes we *intend* to read. This ensures an accurate count of where the next data must be written.

We now perform a series of steps to finish up the function:

```
// Unlock the buffer now that we're done with it
m_pDSBuffer->Unlock(pPtr1, dwBytes1, pPtr2, dwBytes2);

// If we want to loop the stream, reset the file to the
// beginning
if(m_Init.m_bLooping && m_pSource->IsEOF())
    m_pSource->Reset();

// Loop the write position around if it goes past the end of
// the buffer
m_nDataCursor %= m_Caps.dwBufferBytes;

// Set the last play cursor position for the next update
// calculation
m_nLastReadPos = dwReadCursor;
```

Since we're done with the sound buffers, we'll unlock them first. After this, if the file is intended to loop, and we're at the end of the file, we must reset the source object, which will prepare it for reading from the beginning of the file on the next update. Next, we mod the data cursor against the size of the buffer, which will ensure a proper wraparound of the cursor.

Finally, we set the last read position equal to the current read cursor, preparing it for the next update cycle.

This function is a bit much to absorb in one shot, but hopefully the step-by-step breakdown will make it a bit more palatable.

CONTROLLING A STREAMING BUFFER

For the most part, operations on a streaming buffer are no different than those on a static buffer, which is why we can get away with using the same class for both types of data. There are a few situations, however, where we need to branch out and perform special operations that are slightly different on streaming buffers than on static buffers.

Perhaps the first, most important, and most obvious difference in streaming buffers is the way we play them. No matter whether we want the *stream* to loop or not, the *buffer* must always be played with the looping flag set—for somewhat obvious reasons. In addition, we must also insert a streaming buffer into the streaming list every time it is played, which causes an additional branch. Thus, your Play() function is likely to look similar to the following:

LISTING 9.9

```
// If the sound is streaming, insert this buffer into a list
// managed by the audio manager, which periodically calls
// ServiceBuffer()
if(m_Init.m_bStreaming)
{
    m_bRemoveStream = false;
    DXAudioMgr()->InsertStream(this);
}


// Begin playing the buffer. If the looping flag is set or if
// the buffer is streaming, begin looping playback
HRESULT hr;
if(m_Init.m_bStreaming || m_Init.m_bLooping)
    hr = m_pDSBuffer->Play(0, 0, DSBPLAY_LOOPING);
else
    hr = m_pDSBuffer->Play(0, 0, 0);
if(FAILED(hr))
    return false;
```

When playing, we set the DSBPLAY_LOOPING flag if the buffer itself should loop *or* if it is a streaming buffer. As you might recall, the actual control mechanisms for looping streaming buffers is controlled in the Service-Buffer() function.

For our Stop() function, we only have to set a flag to indicate the object should be removed on the next ServiceBuffer() call.

LISTING 9.10

```
// Stop the DirectSound buffer
m_pDSBuffer->Stop();

if(!m_Init.m_bStreaming)
{
    // set cursor at buffer start
    SetReadCursor(0);
}
// remove stream on next update
m_bRemoveStream = true;
```

This function stops the DirectSound buffer, as might be expected. In the streaming branch, we simply mark the stream for removal on the next ServiceBuffer() call. This function will take on the work of cleaning up the stream for us and setting everything up to play again. For a non-streaming buffer, setting the m_bRemoveStream flag obviously has no effect, so we don't even need to bother putting this inside a branch.

The Pause() function has no branches, but you must be sure to remove the stream by setting the m_bRemoveStream value to true inside this function.

LISTING 9.11

```
m_bRemoveStream = true;

// Set the paused flag
m_bPaused = true;

// Stop the buffer if it's available
if (m_pDSBuffer)
    m_pDSBuffer->Stop();
```

Operations involving reading and setting the cursor must obviously differ between streaming and nonstreaming buffers. In the case of setting a cursor to an arbitrary point, because the IAudioLoader interface does not support seeking, we cannot jump to an arbitrary point using the Sound class. This was mainly done because of the difficulties inherent in seeking to arbitrary locations in some compressed formats.

One possible solution might be to add some sort of querying mechanism in the abstract interface to determine if seeking is supported or not, which at least gives us the option of seeking those file formats and SDKs that easily allow it.

LISTING 9.12

```
bool Sound::SetReadCursor(uint32 nBytes)
{
    if (m_Init.m_bStreaming)
        return false;
    m_Init.m_Prop.m_nReadCursor = nBytes;
    if (m_pDSBuffer)
    {
        HRESULT hr = m_pDSBuffer->SetCurrentPosition(
            m_Init.m_Prop.m_nReadCursor);
        if (FAILED(hr))
            return false;
    }
    return true;
}
```

Getting the read cursor is a simple matter, though. While the static buffer must query the DirectSound buffer to obtain the current read cursor, the streaming version can simply return m_nBytesPlayed.

LISTING 9.13

```
bool Sound::GetReadCursor(uint32& nBytes) const
{
    if (m_Init.m_bStreaming)
    {
        nBytes = m_nBytesPlayed;
```

```
    }
    else
    {
        nBytes = m_Init.m_Prop.m_nReadCursor;
        if (m_pDSBuffer)
        {
            HRESULT hr = m_pDSBuffer->GetCurrentPosition(
            &nBytes, NULL);
            if (FAILED(hr))
                return false;
        }
    }
    return true;
}
```

CONCLUSION

We've now covered both static and streaming buffers in as much detail as you need to implement your own basic loading and playback mechanism. By adding streaming buffers to your audio system's repertoire, you gain a degree of flexibility in the type of files you can play and the efficiency in how you play them. Again, you can see why DirectSound can be considered a bit unfriendly, given the amount of code required to simply get a buffer streaming. However, if you can get your streaming-buffer implementation finished and working solidly, you've conquered one of the more-difficult aspects of DirectSound programming.

In the next chapter, we'll look at the basics of 3D audio, such as how to create 3D buffers and listener objects. And we will discover what the most practical methods are for encapsulating these DirectSound interfaces.

CHAPTER 10

3D AUDIO BASICS

Visual imagery in computer game graphics has leapt into the third dimension, and so has sound. The viewer only has a constricted window into this game world—auditory clues are critical in helping to establish a real-world proximity to objects and the surrounding environment. Because of this, sound is arguably a much more important component in modern games than it was in those games of just a few years ago. The general public seems to agree, since many modern computers now come with high-quality desktop speakers, complete with subwoofers. Even better, many systems are even using theatre-like surround-sound with four-point and 5.1 speaker configurations capable of providing an astounding level of realism in both fidelity and spatial positioning, especially compared to the tinny-sounding $10 speakers that were standard until only a few years ago. Using Direct-Sound3D functionality, you can ensure that your game takes full advantage of any hardware/speaker configuration, from the most primitive desktop speakers to Dolby Digital 5.1-ready home theatre desktop systems.

ON THE CD
The code listed in this chapter can be found in \Game_Audio\ audio_sdk\src\audiolib\Sound3D.h, Sound3D.cpp.

3D AUDIO COORDINATES

Just as in 3D graphics, 3D audio works in a space designated by three orthogonal axes labeled *x, y,* and *z*. All 3D sound objects are stored with a number of properties, but the most important one is the three-component vector (or more properly speaking, a 3D point) designating the object's position in space.

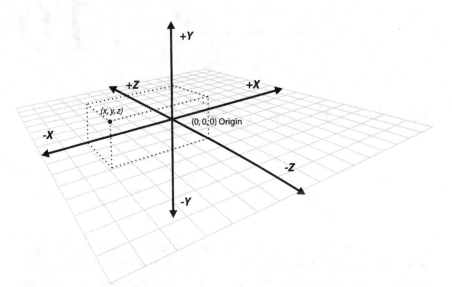

FIGURE 10.1 Cartesian coordinate system.

In Figure 10.1, you can see the location of a point in 3D space in a standard Cartesian coordinate system. The position is designated by the offsets of the *x, y,* and *z* component from the system's origin at (0, 0, 0).

So, what do these numbers actually represent? The measurements of these three offset values default to meters, but we'll see later how we can change the measurement system (scale) to anything we want. If your engine uses a different scale, you can designate a scaling factor so that a single unit of measurement can equal any distance. Likewise, it is important to remember that the positioning of your axes and what the labels represent is also entirely relative. As we'll demonstrate, it is the relative position between objects that is important.

Many 3D engines, including Direct3D samples and documentation, utilize a world coordinate system as follows: assume you are viewing the system and the avatar in a first-person perspective game (i.e., looking at the world's ground plane from the side). The ground plane is defined by the *x* and *y* axes. If your avatar stands on the origin and looks toward the positive *z* axis, the *x* axis will increase in value as it moves to the right side of the screen, and the *y* axis will increase in value as it moves upward. This is known as a *left-handed* coordinate system, which both Direct3D and DirectSound3D use by default.

■ DETERMINING COORDINATE HANDEDNESS

Coordinate handedness is defined in the following manner: from a first-person perspective, when looking at your coordinate system, point both of your hands, with your fingers straight, toward the positive end of the axis that runs horizontally across your monitor. (This is the x-axis in the standard Direct3D coodinate system and would require your palms to be facing up.) Curl your fingers up so that they now point toward the positive end of the axis that follows your screen vertically (y-axis by default). If the thumb on your left hand points toward the positive end of the third axis when this is done (z-axis by default), you are working with a left-handed coordinate system. If not, you are working with a right-handed coordinate system.

It is also possible to define the axis of your world in a different manner, yet still remain in a left-handed coordinate system. Some developers eschew the somewhat odd notion of defining the ground plane as *xz*, and instead define it as *xy*, using *z* to represent height. In this case, the coordinate system would look more like Figure 10.2.

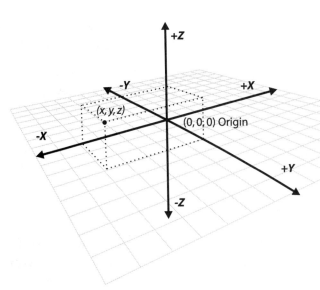

FIGURE 10.2   A coordinate system with an *xy* ground plane.

You can see that this is simply the coordinate system shown in Figure 10.1, only rotated 90° about the x-axis. Notice how that since the x-axis and z-axis are positive when right and up, respectively, and the y-axis increases as it moves *out* of the screen, this is considered a *right-handed* coordinate system. You should discuss the matter with your graphics programmer to determine which coordinate system your game engine is using, and what must be done to turn it into a standard left-handed coordinate system so that DirectSound3D can properly interpret the coordinates you give it.

■ **WHY Y EQUALS UP—DIFFERENT COORDINATE SYSTEMS**

You might be wondering why Direct3D (and consequently, DirectSound) uses a coordinate system defining a ground plane as using the x and z axes, instead of the x and y axes, as one might logically expect. From a mathematical and physics perspective (and indeed, in most modeling programs), the x and y axes are typically used as the ground plane; but 3D artists, mathematicians, and physics programmers were not involved in setting early standards and conventions.

It is likely that this practice started because of the similarity to the physical coordinates of the standard video monitor, where x and y represent the horizontal and vertical positions, respectively. Adding a third dimension means adding a z value that would perpendicularly travel in and out of the screen. Viewing these coordinates from a first-person perspective would result in world coordinates very similar to the screen coordinates, at least from one angle. Technically speaking though, there are no compelling reasons to use one coordinate system over another.

Whatever the reasons or history behind it, this somewhat nonintuitive coordinate system continues to appear even today, as evidenced by the DirectX documentation and many games that follow these guidelines, or those games built on legacy code that used this system.

THE SOURCE AND LISTENER CONCEPTUAL MODEL

3D audio, and more specifically DirectSound3D, creates the perception of three-dimensional audio through the concept of relative positioning of sound *sources*, which may be thought of as sound emitters, and a single *lis-*

tener, which is a sound receiver—both situated within the coordinate system described earlier.

There are three ways to interpret the coordinate system and the positional values of the source and listener objects in DirectSound, known as *sound processing modes*: *normal*, *head-relative*, and *disabled*.

In normal mode, both the sound sources and the listener are positioned in absolute world coordinates, and the spatial relationship between them defines the relative direction from which the sound sources appear to be originating. Generally speaking, this is the most commonly used mode (hence, it is called "normal"). You can see an example of a listener object and a single sound source positioned in world coordinates in Figure 10.3.

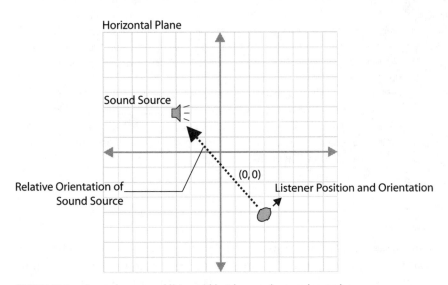

FIGURE 10.3   A sound source and listener object in normal processing mode.

In this model, a sound source is typically aligned with physical emitters of sound in the actual world, such as AI characters, cars, creaking doors, or a waterfall. The listener is usually located at the camera coordinates. By simply matching coordinates of sound and listener objects with those in the world coordinate system, we've instantly and simply created a 3D listening experience for the user.

■ **POINT SOURCES VS. AREA SOURCES**

Although many sound sources can be defined as point sources, such as a gunshot or a whistle blast, many sound sources, such as a waterfall, a tank, or a cheering crowd, are not as easily represented by a single point. Obviously, these larger objects emit sounds from a broader area than a single point. How can you as an audio programmer deal with this? You have several options available to you.

You may decide to represent a larger sound source as a 'composite' sound, placing individual sound sources at different points within the larger object's physical dimensions. In the case of a military tank, you could place an engine sound inside the chassis, some sqeaking and clanking sounds near the treads, and perhaps some crunching noises underneath it. This can produce amazingly realistic results, but obviously requires much more effort (both on your part and that of the audio designer) to produce well-balanced sounds. Generally speaking, it is not a practical approach if you are dealing with a potentially large number of objects on the screen, since it requires multiple 3D buffers per object, although it is conceivable that you might wish to implement your own level-of-detail system to compensate for this.

Another option is to use the ZoomFX hardware extension. This Sensaura technology helps to transform a single-point source into a wider-sounding result without requiring additional 3D resources. The obvious down side is that this is only available on Sensaura-based cards. You can learn more about ZoomFX and how to use this property set in Chapter 26.

In the head-relative processing mode, the source is always positioned in relative coordinates to the listener object. Or, another way of thinking about it is that the listener's position is simply set to the origin. This is demonstrated in Figure 10.4.

Head-relative mode can be used in a couple of different ways. One scenario might be that you wish to leave the listener positioned at the origin and instead perform your own translation on sound sources, moving them instead of the listener. In this way, your sound system remains centered on the listener, avoiding the problem of degrading floating-point accuracy as your listener moves far away from the world origin. Another use for head-relative modes is in nonstandard situations where you need relative instead of absolute positioning, such as a disembodied spirit voice whispering in

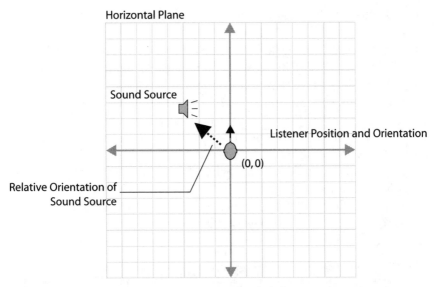

Horizontal Plane

Sound Source

Listener Position and Orientation

(0, 0)

Relative Orientation of
Sound Source

FIGURE 10.4   A sound source and listener object in head-relative processing mode.

the player's ear or a radio transmission coming from inside the player's vehicle.

The last mode—disabled—simply positions the sound directly on top of the listener, effectively removing any three-dimensional aspects to the sound. Why would you want to create a 3D sound buffer and then disable the 3D properties? This could be useful when you wish to play a sound that requires certain properties only available to 3D sound buffers, such as hardware-accelerated environmental reverberation; but you don't wish to associate the sound with a particular point in space. Any sound made by the player in a first-person perspective game is a good candidate for this type of sound processing. Another application might be the use of a global background sound, such as the constant rumbling inside a cargo ship. By playing the sound in disabled mode as a 3D buffer, you have the option of applying the current environmental effect experienced by the listener. In this manner, the rumbling would sound very different depending on whether the listener is in a large cargo bay or in a small corridor, simply due to the environmental effects being globally applied to the listener object.

SPEAKER CONFIGURATIONS AND HRTF FUNCTIONS

Because there are so many different possible configurations for speakers on a PC, Windows 98 (and its subsequent updates, including Windows 2000 and XP) provides a mechanism to configure the type of speaker setup that most closely matches the user's system. A speaker configuration dialog box can be found in the Windows Control Panel. (Note: Windows 2000 instructions follow. Different operating systems may vary slightly in the details.) Double-click the "Sounds and Multimedia" option, which will bring up the corresponding dialog box. Select the Audio tab, and then click on the Advanced button located in the "Sound Playback" section. This will bring up the Advanced Audio Properties dialog box. Click on the Speakers tab, and you should see an image similar to Figure 10.5.

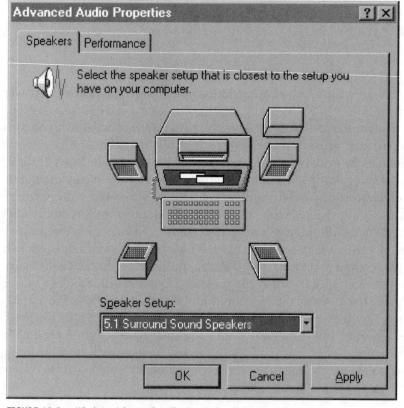

FIGURE 10.5   Windows Advanced Audio Properties dialog box.

However, you should be aware that some companies do not take advantage of the Windows settings and instead provide their own settings through a custom interface. An example of this is the Creative Labs Sound-Blaster Live! series. If a user were to install only the drivers without installing any of the management software, he or she would not be able to change the 3D settings or access other important functionality. In Figure 10.6, you can see the Creative Labs custom application for setting the speaker configuration.

FIGURE 10.6   The Creative Labs speaker configuration application.

The good news is that although enabling the correct settings might initially be awkward for some users, once the system is configured, it is automatically available for every application to use.

DirectSound does have methods for both setting and retrieving the speaker configuration settings via `IDirectSound8::SetSpeakerConfig()` and `IDirectSound8::GetSpeakerConfig()`, but this is a legacy interface from Windows 95, which did not have a mechanism for saving these settings system-wide. Since DirectX 8.1 no longer supports Windows 95, this interface has essentially become obsolete and should not be used by applications, except perhaps when retrieving the settings for informational purposes.

In addition to the obvious reason of needing to drive different numbers and types of speakers, one of the primary reasons Windows stores the configuration and placement of speaker systems is to allow drivers to configure their HRTF algorithms (which were described in detail in Chapter 3) to match the position of the speakers. For instance, a driver will likely use a modified algorithm for simulating a 3D sound depending on whether the user is wearing headphones or listening to a pair of standard desktop speakers, even though these are both technically two-speaker sound destinations. In the case of the desktop speakers, it is necessary to consider factors such as cross-talk cancellation, sound direction, and other factors that do not apply to headphones. As such, the driver might choose an algorithm better suited to individual configurations instead of a one-size-fits-all solution, resulting in a higher-quality listening experience.

BATCHING AND DEFERRED EXECUTION

When changing the 3D parameters of a listener object or an individual sound source, you will have a choice of when you want DirectSound to process this information. You can instruct DirectSound to either process the instructions immediately or batch the changes and apply them all at once. Because every changed parameter causes remixing to occur, and this requires CPU cycles, it is a good idea to enable batched (deferred) execution of all parameter changes. Most 3D parameter-setting functions have a DWORD parameter, dwApply, to which you may pass the flag DS3D_DEFERRED. This will postpone the processing of the new data until IDirectSound3D Listener8::CommitDeferredSettings() is called. Conversely, passing the DS3D_IMMEDIATE flag will instruct DirectSound to immediately process the new information.

PREPARING DIRECTSOUND FOR 3D

There are just a couple of things that must be done to prepare DirectSound for 3D playback. One task is to ensure the primary sound buffer is created with the DSBCAPS_CTRL3D flag, as shown in Listing 10.1.

LISTING 10.1

```
// Create the primary sound buffer
DSBUFFERDESC desc;
ZeroMemory(&desc, sizeof(desc));
```

```
desc.dwSize = sizeof(desc);
desc.dwFlags = DSBCAPS_PRIMARYBUFFER | DSBCAPS_CTRL3D;
hr = m_pDirectSound->CreateSoundBuffer(&desc,
&m_pPrimaryBuffer, NULL);
if(FAILED(hr))
    // report error
```

DIRECTSOUND BUFFER PREPARATIONS

As we will discover in more detail in the next section, all 3D sound buffers begin life as an IDirectSoundBuffer8 interface. This means that a 2D buffer must be created in the normal fashion, and from this, we will then retrieve an IDirectSound3DBuffer8 interface using QueryInterface().

There are few unique rules you must remember when creating a 2D buffer that will be used to create a 3D interface. The first and most basic rule is to remember to create the buffer with 3D capabilities, using the DSBCAPS_CTRL3D flag. The only other 3D-specific flag is DSBCAPS_ MUTE3DATMAXDISTANCE. Passing in this flag will tell DirectSound to stop processing a sound buffer if it gets beyond a maximum threshold, which will be covered in the next section, as well.

In addition, there are a few things you may *not* do when creating a 3D buffer. The DSBCAPS_CTRLPAN flag is mutually exclusive with the DSBCAPS_CTRL3D flag, as panning a sound makes no sense in the context of 3D audio. Likewise, you may not create stereo 3D buffers.

Creating either a hardware or software buffer also has obvious ramifications for 3D buffers, even more so than 2D buffers. Because 3D HRTF algorithms are more complex than performing basic 2D mixing operations, it is a good idea to ensure your 3D buffers are in hardware if possible. Not only that, because voices will sound differently when played on hardware or software, you should avoid mixing the two as well (see Chapter 11). Instead, you should adopt a buffer-management strategy that ensures only hardware voices are used. If a system does not have the minimum number of hardware voices to do this (or none at all), then you should use all software voices. In this way, you simply avoid the problem of inconsistent sounds between the different buffer types.

When creating a software buffer, you have a choice of three software algorithms to use for 3D voices: accurate but CPU-intensive HRTF, lightweight but less-accurate HRTF, and simple pan-and-volume approximation. Additionally, you have a choice of using what is known as the "default" algorithm, which in most cases simply means using the pan-and-volume method. These selections are made in the guid3Dalgorithm member of the DSBUFFERDESC structure, which is filled out before creating the sound buffer. One of four GUIDs may be assigned: DS3DALG_DEFAULT, DS3DALG_NO_VIRTUALIZATION (pan-and-volume mapping), DS3DALG_HRTF_ LIGHT, or DS3DALG_HRTF_FULL. Note that the HRTF algorithms are only available on Windows 98 Second Edition or later with WDM drivers. You might want to consult the DirectX SDK documentation for a more-detailed description of these algorithms.

THE IDirectSound3DBuffer8 INTERFACE

At this point you are ready to create and start using the IDirect Sound3DBuffer8 interface. It is a fairly simply process, once you understand the basic relationship between IDirectSoundBuffer8 and IDirect-Sound3DBuffer8, and how to use them.

RELATIONSHIP TO THE IDirectSoundBuffer8 INTERFACE

Although the 3D controls on a buffer might be thought of as a superset of a 2D sound buffer, DirectSound has implemented a separate interface exclusively for control of the 3D properties of the buffer. This means that playing, stopping, and positioning the 3D buffer is done with the old IDirectSoundBuffer8 interface just as with a 2D sound buffer. However, to control the three-dimensional positioning and properties of the sound, you will be using the IDirectSound3DBuffer8 interface. In essence, control of a single sound is maintained through two different interfaces. This is one of the reasons wrapper classes are almost an absolute requirement with DirectSound; keeping track of dual interfaces for each 3D sound, along with other required data, is tedious at best.

After the IDirectSoundBuffer8 interface is created, use QueryInter-face() to obtain the 3D interface:

LISTING 10.2

```
// Get the 3D sound buffer interface
// m_pSound is a valid IDirectSoundBuffer8 interface ptr
HRESULT hr = m_pSound->m_pDSBuffer->QueryInterface(
    IID_IDirectSound3DBuffer8, (void**)&m_p3DBuffer);
if FAILED(hr)
    return false;
```

Note that unlike previously when we released the old interface after getting the new one (such as with `IDirectSoundBuffer` and `IDirectSoundBuffer8`), we will not do so in this case, because we must continue to use both of them for the lifetime of the buffer.

PROPERTIES AND METHODS FOR 3D BUFFERS

Setting and retrieving properties using the `IDirectSound3DBuffer8` interface is quite straightforward. For each basic property, there is a corresponding `Get()` and `Set()` call. We won't be showing the definition and example of every function, but these all have the characteristic `HRESULT Set<`*property name*`>(<`*data*`>, DWORD dwApply)`, where `dwApply` requires either the `DS3D_DEFERRED` or the `DS3D_IMMEDIATE` flag, or `HRESULT Get<`*property name*`>(<`*data*`>)`. (For more details on the actual functions and their usage, see the DirectX SDK documentation.) For instance, when setting or retrieving the distance property, there are two functions: `IDirectSound3DBuffer::GetPosition()` and `IDirectSound3DBuffer::SetPosition()`. They look like this:

LISTING 10.3

```
D3DVECTOR vPosition;
vPosition.x = 5.0f;
vPosition.y = 10.0f;
vPosition.z = 0.0f;

HRESULT hr = m_p3DBuffer->SetPosition(
    vPosition.x,
    vPosition.y,
    vPosition.z,
    DS3D_DEFERRED);
```

```
if FAILED(hr)
    return false;

hr = m_p3DBuffer->GetPosition(&vPosition);
if FAILED(hr)
    return false;
```

Note that the position, velocity, and orientation property functions are a bit mismatched. The Set() call uses three float values, while the Get() call uses a D3DVECTOR struct. In this example, we are also making sure to use the DS3D_DEFERRED setting, which is recommended as normal practice because it is more efficient. The D3DVECTOR structure is defined as follows:

```
typedef struct _D3DVECTOR {
    float x;
    float y;
    float z;
} D3DVECTOR;
```

When representing a distance, these floating-point values represent meters by default, but the global scale can be changed through the IDirectSound3DListener interface, if required.

Additionally, there are methods for setting or retrieving all the properties at once. Let's examine all the properties of a 3D sound buffer.

Position
This property describes the sound's *position* in world space or relative space. The actual interpretation of the values depends on the *mode* property. The position is represented by three floats when setting the value and a D3DVECTOR when retrieving it.

Velocity
Velocity describes the number of units per second a sound is currently traveling. This value is also represented by a D3DVECTOR structure. Any change to the distance scale will similarly affect velocity, as well as any other unit that uses distance values. DirectSound tracks velocity in order to provide Doppler effects to sounds when they are rapidly changing relative distances to the listener.

Doppler shift is a phenomenon that will cause a sound's pitch to rise or drop, depending on whether a sound is moving toward or away from the listener, respectively. This is caused by compression or expansion of the sound waves as perceived by the listener (see Figure 10.7).

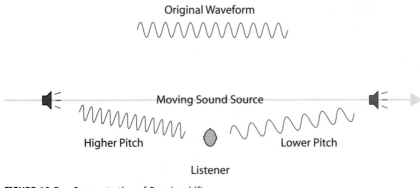

FIGURE 10.7   Demonstration of Doppler shift.

The actual effect of the Doppler shift can be modified through the listener interface.

Inside and Outside Cone Angles, Cone Orientation, and Outside Cone Volume

DirectSound additionally has a concept of sound directivity. This is manifested in four different properties: *inside cone angle, outside cone angle, cone orientation,* and *outside cone volume*. Because these are all related to sound direction, we'll discuss them as a group.

The cone orientation property is perhaps the most pivotal (no pun intended) of the group, so we'll begin here. The orientation is simply a D3DVECTOR, usually a unit vector (a vector with a total length of one), which defines how the sound is oriented. There is no need to supply an 'up' vector, as with the listener's orientation. A directional sound has no concept of up or down, being perfectly symmetrical around the directional axis.

Centered on this orientation vector are two cones, the angles of which are defined by the inside cone angle and outside cone angle properties. The values of the angles are set and retrieved in degrees. These cones mark volume borders for the sound. Within the inside cone (i.e., the one closest to the orientation ray), the volume of the sound is defined by the normal buffer volume property, which is set using the IDirectSoundBuffer8 interface. Outside the outermost angle, the volume is defined by outside cone volume. Between these two angles, the volume of the sound gradually ramps down as the angle moves from inside to outside, providing a smooth transition as the sound changes orientation relative to the listener. You can see a diagram of this in Figure 10.8.

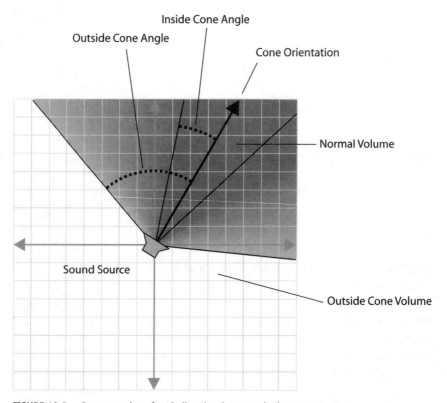

FIGURE 10.8   Demonstration of a 3D directional cone and relevant parameters.

Directional sounds are handy if you want to simulate a highly directional physical source, such as a bullhorn or trumpet. Even a person's vocalizations are somewhat directional. However, DirectSound models the sound cone uniformly across the frequency spectrum, which is atypical of the real world. High frequencies are highly directional, while low frequencies are omni-directional. Depending on the level of realism you want to attain, you might or might not care about this discrepancy. If you are interested in greater realism, you can use environmental property sets such as EAX to properly attenuate the high frequencies outside the directional cone.

Minimum and Maximum Distance

Because of the nature of digital audio, it is considered optimal to record all sounds as loud as possible within specified volume tolerances, no matter what the real-world volume. This results in a set of recorded samples that are all approximately the same volume when played back, regardless of the actual source. Thus, a nuclear explosion and a quiet conversation will play back at the same approximate volume. It is not technically incorrect that a whisper can be perceived at the same 'loudness' as a large explosion, but this is only true if the whisper is directly in the listener's ear, and the explosion is far away. The problem then becomes how to specify desired volume relative to distance.

The *minimum distance* and *maximum distance* properties work in conjunction to provide a level of control over the volume of a sound with respect to distance from the listener. Together, they define a sound curve that attenuates over distance.

The minimum distance marks the point at which the sound first begins to attenuate. This value also defines the steepness of the attenuation curve. For each doubling of the distance, starting with twice the minimum distance, the relative volume is halved. For instance, the default minimum distance is one 'distance unit' (which defaults to one per meter). At two units, the sound will be half of the original volume. At four units, the sound will be one quarter of the original volume, and so on. The global steepness of this attenuation curve can be set through the listener property rolloff factor, which is described a bit later.

The maximum distance indicates the point at which a sound will no longer get any quieter. This can be used in two different ways. If you set the maximum distance to the approximate point at which a sound will drop to an imperceptible volume, and if you have set the DSBCAPS_MUTE3DAT-MAXDISTANCE flag when creating the buffer, all processing on the sound will stop when the sound is farther away from the listener than the maximum distance. Needless to say, this is a significant optimization and should be taken advantage of.

The other way maximum distance can be used is to ensure a sound never drops below a certain level. When the sound moves beyond the maximum distance, instead of muting, the level will remain constant. This may be handy for creating a directional background sound on a small level, such as a wailing siren that can be heard throughout the entire level.

You should note that the default DirectSound maximum distance is 1 billion, meaning that for most cases, no optimizations will take place unless you specifically set these values. The *GAP* library, instead, defaults to 1,000 units, which is a somewhat more typical maximum range for loud sounds. It is important for the sound designer to understand how to properly set these values for the best effect.

Mode

The last parameter for 3D sound buffers is the processing *mode*, which we've already covered in some detail earlier in this chapter (see The Source and Listener Conceptual Model). There are three possible choices. "Normal" means that both the source and the listener are defined in terms of world coordinates. "Head-relative" means that the coordinates of the sound are defined relative to the listener's position. "Disabled" means that we simply remove any positional aspects to the sound and treat it like a standard 2D sound.

SETTING AND RETRIEVING ALL PROPERTIES

If you wish, you have the option of setting and retrieving all the parameters of a 3D buffer at once by using the DS3DBUFFER structure, which holds all the parameters of a buffer, along with the functions SetAllParameters() and GetAllParameters(). The DS3DBUFFER is defined as follows:

```
typedef struct {
    DWORD       dwSize;
    D3DVECTOR   vPosition;
    D3DVECTOR   vVelocity;
    DWORD       dwInsideConeAngle;
    DWORD       dwOutsideConeAngle;
    D3DVECTOR   vConeOrientation;
    LONG        lConeOutsideVolume;
    D3DVALUE    flMinDistance;
    D3DVALUE    flMaxDistance;
    DWORD       dwMode;
} DS3DBUFFER, *LPDS3DBUFFER;
typedef const DS3DBUFFER *LPCDS3DBUFFER;
```

The SetAllParameters() function, like the other Set() functions, also requires either the DS3D_DEFERRED or DS3D_IMMEDIATE flag as the second parameter. Here's what these functions look like in code:

LISTING 10.4

```
DS3DBUFFER dsprop;
memset(&dsprop, 0, sizeof(DS3DBUFFER));
dsprop.dwSize = sizeof(DS3DBUFFER);
// Assign properties here...

// Set all the parameters
HRESULT hr = m_p3DBuffer->SetAllParameters(
    &dsprop, DS3D_DEFERRED);
if FAILED(hr)
    return false;

// Now retrieve all the parameters
hr = m_p3DBuffer->GetAllParameters(&dsprop);
if FAILED(hr)
    return false;
```

THE IDirectSound3DListener8 INTERFACE

The second half of the 3D audio solution is the listener. As previously explained, the listener represents the receiver for the sound objects and can be positioned or oriented freely, just like the sound objects. You will notice that these two interfaces in fact share many properties, along with correspondingly similar functions to operate on them.

CREATING THE LISTENER OBJECT

Just like the 3D sound buffers, the IDirectSound3DListener8 interface must be obtained from a 2D sound buffer interface. However, instead of obtaining the interface from a secondary buffer, you must instead retrieve the interface from the primary buffer. The code to do so will look something like this:

LISTING 10.5

```
// The listener interface
IDirectSound3DListener8* pListener;

// Get the listener interface from the primary buffer
// interface. pPrimaryBuffer is a valid primary buffer.

HRESULT hr = pPrimaryBuffer ->QueryInterface(
    IID_IDirectSound3DListener8, (void**)&pListener);
if FAILED(hr)
    return false;
```

Once you have the listener interface, you are ready to begin setting and retrieving properties.

PROPERTIES AND METHODS FOR THE LISTENER

The `IDirectSound3DListener8` interface shares basic 3D properties with `IDirectSound3DBuffer8`, such as position, velocity, and orientation. In addition to these, however, the listener has some unique properties of its own, which are listed in the following sections. The discussion of some of the properties is slightly abbreviated because they are identical to the 3D sound buffer properties, such as when setting 3D buffer properties, you must always pass an additional parameter, `DS3D_DEFERRED` or `DS3D_IMMEDIATE`, to determine how these changes are processed.

Position
The *position* property represents the listener's position in the world, similar to the way the 3D sound buffer works. The relative position of each sound in the world is determined by a combination of the listener's position and orientation, and the sound's position.

Velocity
The *velocity* property is used to determine the relative movement between a listener and source object. From this information, the Doppler effect for each sound is calculated. The effect of Doppler on all sounds can be adjusted with the *Doppler factor* property, which is part of the listener interface.

Orientation

Unlike 3D sounds, the *orientation* of a listener object must store more than just a direction represented by a single vector. With the listener, there is a concept of 'up' and 'down.' To provide this direction, DirectSound uses a pair of vectors at right angles to describe both the front and top of the listener object, as shown in Figure 10.9.

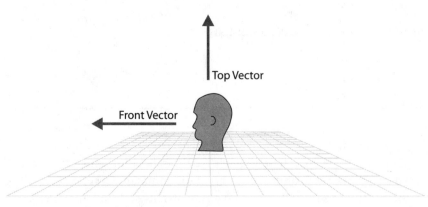

FIGURE 10.9   A listener's front and top vectors.

These angles should always be set 90° apart. If they are not, DirectSound will adjust the forward vector so that it is perpendicular with the top angle. The following code demonstrates how to set and retrieve the listener's orientation.

LISTING 10.6

```
D3DVECTOR vFront;
D3DVECTOR vTop;
vFront.x = 0.0f;
vFront.y = 0.0f;
vFront.z = 1.0f;
vTop.x = 0.0f;
vTop.y = 1.0f;
vTop.z = 0.0f;

HRESULT hr = m_pListener->SetOrientation(
    vFront.x,
```

```
        vFront.y,
        vFront.z,
        vTop.x,
        vTop.y,
        vTop.z,
        DS3D_DEFERRED);
if FAILED(hr)
    return false;

hr = m_pListener->GetOrientation(
        &vFront,
        &vTop);
if FAILED(hr)
    return false;
```

Distance Factor

By default, all distance-based values, such as position and velocity, are based on the standard unit of a meter. Some games, however, utilize a different measuring scale. DirectSound automatically scales all distance-based values by this *distance factor*. Naturally, the default value for this property is one. The effective range of the distance factor is any valid floating-point value.

It is important to remember that setting the distance factor will not actually directly affect the rolloff rate of a sound because the minimum distance, which is defined in generic units and not as an absolute distance, determines this. Instead, there is a special rolloff factor property that can be used to accomplish this.

The distance factor itself will mainly adjust the Doppler shift, since this is based on real distances rather than a generic distance unit like the rolloff rate. And, of course, it will have an effect on any other properties that make use of positional information, such as EAX, ZoomFX, or MacroFX.

Rolloff Factor

The standard attenuation over distance in DirectSound is based on somewhat simplified real-world acoustics. For every increase in distance based on the minimum distance setting, DirectSound will decrease the volume by half. The *rolloff factor* will globally adjust the rate at which sounds decrease in volume over distance by a specified factor. The default setting is 1.0 (DS3D_DEFAULTROLLOFFFACTOR), and it ranges from no rolloff factor

(DS3D_MINROLLOFFFACTOR) to 10 times the real-world rolloff factor (DS3D_MAXROLLOFFFACTOR).

Doppler Factor

The *Doppler factor* property directly controls the intensity of the pitch change (the Doppler effect). By default, this is also set to 1.0 (DS3D_DEFAULTDOPPLERFACTOR) and ranges from no Doppler effect (DS3D_MINDOPPLERFACTOR) to 10 times the real-world Doppler effect (DS3D_MAXDOPPLERFACTOR).

CONCLUSION

You should now have a basic understanding of the essential mechanics of creating 3D sounds and listener objects using DirectSound. While there is still much more work to be done in creating a full audio engine, this chapter provides the core components for a large amount of functionality in DirectSound.

In the next chapter, we'll discuss buffer management and its problems—how to play a nearly infinite supply of sound sources on a decidedly finite number of hardware channels.

CHAPTER 11

DIRECTSOUND BUFFER MANAGEMENT

An audio system by its very nature deals with a large amount of raw data, and so resource management is a primary concern when dealing with more data in a single session than can fit into memory at any one time. For simple games and applications, it may be acceptable to simply load up all sounds at the beginning of the game or level, keep them resident in memory, and play them on demand. For many games, however, there are potentially far more sounds to play than there are hardware buffers to play them, and more audio data than is practical to fit into memory at a single time.

The code listed in this chapter can be found in \Game_Audio\ audio_sdk\src\audiolib\AudioMgr.h, AudioMgr.cpp, Sound.h, Sound.cpp.

THE BASICS

There are two aspects to audio system resource management. The first area of concern is the number of hardware buffers available for playing audio. Although software buffers are available for use, it is highly recommended to use hardware buffers to minimize impact on the CPU, especially when playing 3D sounds.

In addition to the limited amount of hardware buffers available, there is also a matter of memory usage. DirectSound requires audio data to be stored as PCM data, which requires a large amount of memory. The good news is that, unlike earlier ISA cards and some console systems, modern

PCI sound cards make use of general-purpose system memory. However, this does impose a burden of responsible memory usage. Even though Win32 platforms have a flat memory model with a nearly unlimited virtual pool of memory on any system, the result of using this virtual memory when it's not really available is massive disk thrashing, obviously something to be avoided. Disk access might occur from time to time, but it's much more desirable for your program to control it, rather than the operating system, for performance and tuning reasons.

RESOURCE MANAGEMENT VS. MEMORY MANAGEMENT

Technically, what we've opted to do in the *GAP* audio library is not true memory management. We are not overriding the `new` and `delete` operators, and managing our own pool of memory. Instead, we are managing resources at the object level, delegating the responsibility of memory allocation to each class type. We do this because each class has different memory needs. DirectSound allocates memory for its own buffers; but with DirectMusic, we have a choice of using our own buffers or letting DirectMusic allocate and use internal memory.

In a sense, managing objects is simply a higher-level approach to memory management. By enforcing a hard limit on the number of buffers that may be allocated and loaded at any one time, we are also enforcing a limitation on memory usage, although the variable size of the buffers creates a somewhat flexible ceiling. This suitably balances the reasonable implementation complexity and decent functionality in real-world situations.

It should, however, be possible for you to override the `new` and `delete` operators for specific classes in order to optimize your game engine if need be (or perhaps provide a generic allocation method, similar to the file system). The *GAP* audio engine attempts to avoid any unnecessary run-time allocations and deletions. Where dynamic allocation is necessary, we often try to reuse the allocated pool instead of immediately discarding it. Some game companies strictly forbid any dynamic allocation at run-time, and while this might lead to some performance benefits in certain situations, someone must write custom allocation routines that can handle the game's demands. Implementing this sort of system is a bit beyond the scope of this book.

DIRECTSOUND BUFFER MANAGEMENT

An integral part of the *GAP* audio library is the automatic management of DirectSound buffers. This is an important requirement of a sound system, since hardware buffers are a finite resource on all platforms. DirectSound, unlike some other audio APIs, has no concept of a sound voice (sometimes called a "channel") that is separate from a sound buffer. Allocating a DirectSound buffer reserves a corresponding hardware buffer, if available, and will not release it until the buffer has been destroyed—meaning that you can never load more sounds than you have hardware buffers for, even if the memory is available to do so. You can see in Figure 11.1 how even though hardware channels are discrete elements from system memory, they are still coupled into a single DirectSound buffer object.

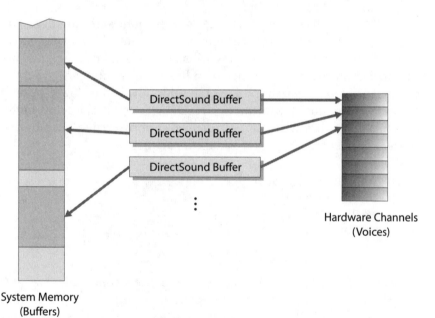

System Memory
(Buffers)

Hardware Channels
(Voices)

FIGURE 11.1   Representation of hardware channels (voices) and memory in relation to DirectSound buffers.

There are essentially two ways to get around this problem—you can either use the built-in DirectSound voice management, or you can carefully manage your own set of buffers to ensure that you never exceed the hardware limit. Although the sample audio library utilizes the latter approach, we'll first examine how we might have used dynamic voice management with our library as an alternative method.

In order to overcome the problem of limited numbers of hardware channels assigned to buffers, DirectSound introduced the concept of *deferred voice assignment*. Normally, DirectSound will attempt to assign buffers to hardware voices as they are created. When hardware buffers run out, DirectSound then begins creating software buffers (assuming we hadn't forced hardware-only buffers). The obvious problem here is that in order to ensure that the most-important voices are contained in hardware, you must always allocate the important voices before the less-important ones, which may not always be easy or practical to do. Or, we might simply wish to allocate more buffers than we actually have channels for, which will again cause a certain number of our sounds to be allocated as software buffers instead of hardware buffers.

By adding the flag DSBCAPS_LOCDEFER to the buffer-creation flags, you tell DirectSound not to assign the buffer to a voice until it is actually played. This is a simple and efficient way to ensure that hardware voices are allocated more effectively. When a buffer using voice management is played, DirectSound has the option of shutting down other, lower-priority voices to make room for the new voice. DirectSound decides on a buffer to shut down based on a user-defined priority value. Recall that IDirectSoundBuffer8::Play() had three parameters:

```
HRESULT IDirectSoundBuffer8::Play(
    DWORD dwReserved1,
    DWORD dwPriority,
    DWORD dwFlags
);
```

While the first parameter remains unused, the second parameter, dw-Priority, now specifies a DWORD value to use as a priority value. If this value is used along with the flag DSBPLAY_TERMINATEBY_PRIORITY passed via dwFlags, DirectSound will ensure that a hardware buffer is available by removing the lowest-priority sound currently loaded or playing. In addition to this flag, several other types of management options are available that use different flags. If DSBPLAY_TERMINATEBY_TIME is passed to the Play() function, the buffer that has the least amount of time left to play will be eliminated. If the DSBPLAY_TERMINATEBY_DISTANCE is specified, Direct-Sound will attempt to find a hardware buffer from among those that have the DSBCAPS_MUTE3DATMAXDISTANCE bit set and are out of playing range from the listener (this obviously only applies to 3D buffers). If one is not found, the Play() function will fail.

You can also force whether you wish the buffer to play in software or hardware with two flags, DSBPLAY_LOCHARDWARE and DSBPLAY_LOCSOFTWARE. The flag DSBPLAY_LOCSOFTWARE cannot be combined with any other voice-management flag, for obvious reasons.

Because DirectSound voice management has the ability to stop sounds from playing without the program's explicit instruction, it also provides a method to detect this status. Calling the IDirectSoundBuffer8::Get-Status() function will return a flag DSBSTATUS_TERMINATED if the buffer has been terminated by the voice manager.

There is one potential problem with DirectSound buffer management when using the Play() function. Because the buffer is not connected to the hardware until this function is called, you cannot set any hardware properties until the moment the buffer is played. Fortunately, there is an alternative method of connecting DirectSound buffers to hardware resources by using the IDirectSoundBuffer8::AcquireResources() method. In this way, you can connect the buffer to a hardware resource before the buffer is actually played. Between the time the AcquireResources() method is called and the Play() function is called, you must set any desired hardware properties on the buffer.

Although DirectSound voice management can be a bit awkward to use, it does provide an effective method of implementing hardware-level management to your audio system.

CUSTOM BUFFER MANAGEMENT

In addition to hardware-level management, you might wish to have higher-level resource management available to your system. In this way, you can let the sound system worry about which of 500 instantiated sounds might actually be loaded at any given time, freeing your game from having to micromanage the loading and unloading of individual sounds as the game progresses.

One reason for writing buffer-management routines at the game-library level is the same reason why many such optimizations work better at an application level than at a driver or system component level, even though these are closer to the hardware than the application or game libraries. No driver or system library can possibly understand the nature of your game better than you can. Thus, you can tune the management routines to work perfectly with your game engine, changing the algorithms and tolerances to suit your needs, something that would most likely be impossible if using driver-level or DirectSound-level management.

As such, we will demonstrate our own buffer and resource management in the *GAP* library. Again, because of our intrinsic knowledge of the game's properties and how sounds must be managed, this is not necessarily a bad thing. Keep in mind that you must be the final arbiter of whether the techniques presented here are correct for your game, or whether you should pursue a different route. This is one of the primary benefits of writing your own audio engine—*you* ultimately can create the best-suited audio engine for your game because you have a unique understanding of your game's requirements.

■ DO YOU REALLY HAVE TO CHOOSE?

One technique that may prove most effective for your engine could actually be a combination of DirectSound buffer management along with custom management routines to handle higher-level resources. In effect, there are two layers to be managed. While a sound card might only have enough hardware for 32 buffers, the system might have enough memory to hold 100 samples at a time. You could use a combination system to achieve both design objectives simultaneously.

Making the necessary modifications to the *GAP* audio library would not be terribly difficult. You would just alter creation flags; substitute DSBCAPS_LOCDEFER for DSBCAPS_LOCHARDWARE during buffer creation, and ensure the Acquire-Resources() function and restoration of property sets always occurs right before a buffer is played. (This is demonstrated later in Chapter 23.) While DirectSound buffer management takes care of managing hardware, the custom buffer management would then become an upper limit of how many resources are allowed in memory, regardless of how many hardware buffers you have. This could be a very effective two-tiered management scheme.

AUDIO DEVICE CAPABILITIES

Determining whether we should even be attempting to create hardware buffers is a bit of a challenge in itself. The decision must be based on both the capabilities of the hardware device and your determination, as the audio programmer, as to what the minimum requirement should be. Once this decision has been made, the library then knows what its limits are and attempts to continue adding voices (either hardware or software) until its limits (either hardware-based or artificially enforced) are reached. All sounds will be played exclusively in hardware or software, depending on these limits and the capabilities of the sound card itself.

■ **AVOID MIXING HARDWARE AND SOFTWARE VOICES**

It is highly recommended to either play all voices in hardware or all voices in software, rather than mixing the two. The reason is that there are perceptible differences in post-mixing volumes of voices, due to different algorithms being used in the mixing process. This causes a disparity in sounds that will make certain voices seem to play too loudly and others too softly. This problem is exacerbated by the fact that different drivers and hardware use different algorithms, and so results will be unpredictable, depending on the hardware and drivers used—not an ideal situation. This is why the *GAP* audio library enforces either an all-hardware or all-software solution, although mixing of hardware 2D voices and software 3D voices is allowed, and vice versa.

For some cards, the choice between using hardware or software is an easy one. Modern sound cards are designed for games, and many support anywhere from 32 to several hundred 2D hardware buffers, with anywhere from 16 to 64 3D hardware buffers. Other low-end cards support no hardware acceleration at all and provide only a single primary buffer for final mixing and output. In the former case, you might simply allow the audio hardware to reach its natural limit, or instead manually enforce a lower limit on the number of buffers. For the latter case, we could simply set a flag in our audio manager, dictating that all buffers must be created in software. In this way, we avoid the problem of hardware limitations altogether, though we might still want to enforce an arbitrary limit for performance reasons.

Unfortunately, you can't count on what DirectSound reports in its caps structure to be entirely accurate, for several reasons. The primary reason is because most modern audio cards share resources to a large extent. It might be possible to create 16 3D buffers *or* 32 2D buffers, but not both simultaneously. Or, buffers with certain attributes could require slightly more attributes than others. In truth, the DirectSound caps are good for determining general device capabilities and whether or not you should attempt to use all-hardware buffers or all-software buffers; but you should be aware that it might not return a *precise* number of each type of available buffer because these values might not be calculable.

LISTING 11.1

```
struct AudioMgrInit
{
    // HWND used for sound system initialization
    HWND     m_hWnd;
    // Force the system to use all-software buffers
    bool     m_bForceSoftware;
    // Threshold at which software buffers are
    // used instead of hardware
    uint32 m_n2dHardwareBufferMin;
    // Threshold at which software buffers are
    //used instead of hardware
    uint32 m_n3dHardwareBufferMin;
    // Maximum amount of 2d hardware buffers to allow
    uint32 m_n2dHardwareBufferMax;
    // Maximum amount of 3d hardware buffers to allow
    uint32 m_n3dHardwareBufferMax;
    // Maximum amount of 2d software buffers to allow
    uint32 m_n2dSoftwareBufferMax;
    // Maximum amount of 3d software buffers to allow
    uint32 m_n3dSoftwareBufferMax;
};

// <snip>

// Get the capabilities of this sound system
m_pDirectSound->GetCaps(&m_DSCaps);

// Determine how to configure the system based on stats and
// initalization requirements
if(init.m_bForceSoftware ||
        (init.m_n2dHardwareBufferMin >
        m_DSCaps.dwMaxHwMixingAllBuffers))
    m_bForce2dSoftware = true;

if(init.m_bForceSoftware ||
```

```
(init.m_n3dHardwareBufferMin >
  m_DSCaps.dwFreeHw3DAllBuffers))
 m_bForce3dSoftware = true;
```

In Listing 11.1, we see both relevant portions of the audio manager's initialization structure and the simple algorithm used to determine whether or not we should force 2D and 3D sounds into software buffers. Our strategy is as follows: in the initialization structure, we provide the capability to specify both the upper and lower limits for both 2D and 3D hardware sounds. If the hardware, according to the DirectSound caps, cannot apparently ever reach the lower limit or required numbers of buffers of a particular type (2D or 3D), we set a flag indicating that it is better to create all-software buffers for this specific type. The upper limit is by default set quite high, but you might wish to lower this in order to add constraints to the number of buffers loaded at one time. This will also tend to act as a cap for the amount of memory the audio system will use at any one time. Naturally, for a software buffer, there is no such thing as a lower-limit requirement, so we simply adhere to an upper limit set in the initialization structure. In addition, there is a flag that can be used to force all buffers to avoid using hardware altogether, which can be a useful way to alleviate some problematic or buggy sound drivers.

Because these values are exposed in the *GAP* API, the application can easily allow the user to indirectly customize the sound system for optimal performance. For example, many games employ a sound 'quality' slider. This may, in fact, simply adjust the upper boundaries of allowed 2D and 3D buffers. Or, you could add a check box that allows the user to select all-software buffers, or to 'autodetect' and use hardware when available.

Now that we have our buffer limits set up, let's look at exactly how to go about managing our buffers.

TRACKING THE DIRECTSOUND BUFFERS

In its most basic form, buffer management simply means keeping a list of currently loaded DirectSound buffers, sorting them by some criteria (priority), and discarding the lowest-priority item when it reaches a hardware or arbitrary limit. This is exactly the approach taken by the *GAP* audio library. Let's take a look at some of the code to see what we're dealing with.

LISTING 11.2

```
typedef std::vector<Sound*> SoundVector;
typedef std::vector<Sound3D*> Sound3DVector;
typedef std::vector<Segment*> SegmentVector;

class AudioManager
{
    // <snip>
private:
    // Ordered sets of all currently loaded objects by type
    SoundVector      m_LoadedSound;
    Sound3DVector    m_LoadedSound3D;
    SegmentVector    m_LoadedSegment;
};
```

In order to prioritize and manage our resources, we must first keep track of which resources are currently loaded. This is done with three STL vectors, shown in Listing 11.2. One of the benefits of using custom resource management is that we can apply it to any object, not just DirectSound buffers. In this case, we're also managing DirectMusic segments. Although we will be focusing on the DirectSound object because of its slightly more-complex management scheme, managing segments using the same basic mechanism works just as well.

As sounds are loaded and unloaded, they must be inserted and removed from these lists. This is a fairly straightforward operation when using standard STL techniques, which can be seen in Listing 11.3. We won't bother with showing all three object types, because they all work in the same way.

LISTING 11.3

```
void AudioManager::OnLoadSound(Sound* pSound)
{
    CRITICAL_FUNCTION(&m_csAudioUpdate);
    m_Stats.m_n2DSoundsLoaded++;
    m_LoadedSound.push_back(pSound);
}

void AudioManager::OnUnloadSound(Sound* pSound)
{
```

```
if (!IsInitialized())
    return;
CRITICAL_FUNCTION(&m_csAudioUpdate);
SoundVector::iterator itr;
for (itr = m_LoadedSound.begin();
    itr != m_LoadedSound.end();
    ++itr)
{
    if ((*itr) == pSound)
    {
        m_LoadedSound.erase(itr);
        m_Stats.m_n2DSoundsLoaded--;
        return;
    }
}
}
```

The OnLoadSound() and OnUnloadSound() functions are called from the Sound class when loading or unloading is successfully completed. Likewise, similar functions are called from the Sound3D and Segment classes.

Our list of loaded sounds is now ready for use. The next management stage comes at the point of actually creating the DirectSound buffer. This is where the real work of buffer management happens. Listing 11.4 shows the relevant portions of code inside the Sound class.

LISTING 11.4

```
// Ensure we're not over the buffer limit
if(!m_b3DSound)
{
    if(!DXAudioMgr()->CanAddSound())
        DXAudioMgr()->RemoveSound(this);
}

// Set the buffer creation flags depending on user preferences
uint32 nFlags =
    DSBCAPS_GETCURRENTPOSITION2 |
    DSBCAPS_CTRLFREQUENCY |
    DSBCAPS_CTRLVOLUME;
```

```
// Determine if we should be in hardware or software
if(DXAudioMgr()->ForceSoftware(m_b3DSound))
    nFlags |= DSBCAPS_LOCSOFTWARE;
else
    nFlags |= DSBCAPS_LOCHARDWARE;

// Create the actual sound buffer
HRESULT hr;
IDirectSoundBuffer* pDSBuffer;
DSBUFFERDESC desc;
ZeroMemory(&desc, sizeof(desc));
desc.dwSize = sizeof(desc);
desc.dwFlags = nFlags;
desc.lpwfxFormat = &m_WaveFormat;
desc.dwBufferBytes = nBufferSize;
hr = DXAudioMgr()->DirectSound()->CreateSoundBuffer(
    &desc, &pDSBuffer, NULL);
if(FAILED(hr))
{
    // First attempt failed. Remove a buffer and try again
    if(!DXAudioMgr()->RemoveBuffer(m_b3DSound))
    {
        Unload();
        return false;
    }
    hr = DXAudioMgr()->DirectSound()->CreateSoundBuffer(
        &desc,
        &pDSBuffer,
        NULL);
    if(FAILED(hr))
    {
        Unload();
        return false;
    }
}
```

There are several things that happen before and after a buffer is created, so let's go through them step by step. The first thing the buffer must check for is if the sound system is currently at its user-set maximum capacity for number of buffers. This is done with the call CanAddSound(). We only check the buffer limit if we are creating a 2D buffer. The Sound3D class checks 3D buffers. These functions examine the flags and initialization values we saw earlier and determine if we are allowed to create a new buffer of the type requested. If not, the RemoveSound() function, shown in Listing 11.5, will attempt to remove a buffer first, and then buffer creation will proceed.

LISTING 11.5

```
bool AudioManager::CanAddSound() const
{
    if(m_Stats.m_bForce2DSoftware)
    {
        if((m_Stats.m_n2DSoundsLoaded) >=
                m_Init.m_n2DSoftwareBufferMax)
            return false;
    }
    else
    {
        if((m_Stats.m_n2DSoundsLoaded) >=
                m_Init.m_n2DHardwareBufferMax)
            return false;
    }
    return true;
}
```

The function CanAddSound() compares the current number of buffers to the limits specified in the initialization structure in order to determine if another buffer can be added without exceeding the specified total. A value of true is returned if a buffer can be added, and false is returned if a buffer must first be removed.

LISTING 11.6

```
bool AudioManager::RemoveSound(Sound* pSound)
{
    CRITICAL_FUNCTION(&m_csAudioUpdate);
    // Check for the lowest-priority item in the segment set
    sort(m_LoadedSound.begin(), m_LoadedSound.end(),
        ptr_less<Sound*>() );
```

```
    if(m_LoadedSound.empty())
        return true;
    if(!pSound)
        return true;
    Sound* pFront = m_LoadedSound.front();
    if(*pSound < *pFront)
        return false;
    pFront->Unload();
    return true;
}
```

Note how the loaded object list is only sorted when a buffer must be removed. This helps to minimize the number of sorts to an absolute minimum. This was also why a vector was chosen instead of a continuously sorted structure, such as an STL set. You should also note that the argument passed to the RemoveSound() function does not indicate the sound to be removed. After all, we're attempting to load the current object's sound buffer. Instead, the pointer is used in the RemoveSound() function to determine if the sound is a higher priority than the lowest-priority sound currently loaded. If not, the sound will fail to load.

After we've determined if our audio system has reached its preset buffer limit and if appropriate action has been taken, we then set the flag to attempt creation of a buffer in hardware or software, depending on the current manager settings. The ForceSoftware() function simply returns one of the two flags we set earlier in the audio manager, based on the value of m_b3DSound.

```
// Determine if we should be in hardware or software
if(DXAudioMgr()->ForceSoftware(m_b3DSound))
    nFlags |= DSBCAPS_LOCSOFTWARE;
else
    nFlags |= DSBCAPS_LOCHARDWARE;
```

Next, we attempt the *first* DirectSound buffer creation. If we fail on the first attempt, we assume that we have likely run out of hardware buffers; and so we attempt to free a single buffer. This time, we pass a NULL pointer to the RemoveSound() or RemoveSound3D() function, forcing a load. Additionally, when a hard limit is reached, we call ResetSound3DLimit() or ResetSoundLimit(), depending on whether we're creating a 3D or 2D sound. This lowers the target number of buffers to the current number of buffers, helping to ensure that buffer management can proceed without having to rely on hitting the hard limit again.

LISTING 11.7

```
hr = DXAudioMgr()->DirectSound()->CreateSoundBuffer(
    &desc, &pDSBuffer, NULL);
if(FAILED(hr))
{
    if(m_b3DSound)
    {
        DXAudioMgr()->ResetSound3DLimit();
        if(!DXAudioMgr()->RemoveSound3D(0))
        {
            Unload();
            return false;
        }
    }
    else
    {
        DXAudioMgr()->ResetSoundLimit();
        if(!DXAudioMgr()->RemoveSound(0))
        {
            Unload();
            return false;
        }
    }
    hr = DXAudioMgr()->DirectSound()->CreateSoundBuffer(
        &desc, &pDSBuffer, NULL);
    if(FAILED(hr))
    {
        Unload();
        return false;
    }
}
```

This code is the remaining half of our management algorithm, allowing us to now limit buffer creation with either an artificial limit or a natural hardware limit. However, we're not yet done with our buffer management tasks. Although we can unload and load a buffer at will, a problem remains. Any changed buffer settings or properties will be lost along with the buffer. But this can be easily solved. In order to preserve buffer settings, the values must be kept separately and independent of the DirectSound buffer.

```
SetProperties(m_Init.m_Prop);
```

At the end of the Sound::Load() function, we call the SetProperties() function, passing the internally stored values, which are *not* cleared when the buffer is unloaded. Conveniently, everything needed to restore the buffer to its previous state is contained in the m_Init.m_Prop member. Thus, we ensure that the internal buffer settings will always be preserved between the time a buffer is unloaded and reloaded.

SOUND COMPARISONS AND RANKING

You've seen the sorting functions that operate on vectors of pointers to Sound objects (Sound3D and Segment objects work the same way), and you may be wondering exactly how this prioritization is working 'under the hood.' Quite simply, we define a less-than (<) operator for each object type, and the priority of two objects is determined inside this function. However, in order to properly get pointers to STL vector-sorted objects, we first must create a sorting function that will property dereference the pointer. Using the standard less-than algorithm in a sort function when working with pointers will only sort by the pointer's address in memory—not an extremely useful sorting criteria. Listing 11.8 shows the definition of the ptr_less class used in Listing 11.6 to sort the Sound objects.

LISTING 11.8

```
template<class _Ty>
struct ptr_less : std::binary_function<_Ty, _Ty, bool>
{
    bool operator()(const _Ty& _X, const _Ty& _Y) const
        {return (*_X < *_Y); }
};
```

Using this structure as the sorting mechanism will ensure that the objects are dereferenced before their less-than operators are invoked, which will allow the sorting to take place properly.

The only other consideration is how we want to define the objects' less-than operators, which will determine their overall priority. We have decided to use different approaches for each object type, and so we'll list all three less-than operator functions. We'll start with the simplest one, the Segment less-than operator shown in Listing 11.9.

LISTING 11.9

```
bool Segment::operator < (const Segment& seg) const
{
    if(GetLastPlayTime() < seg.GetLastPlayTime())
        return true;
    return false;
}
```

This is perhaps the simplest possible sorting function that is still effective. The segments are prioritized based on the last time they played. Simply put, the segments that have played most recently are least likely to be swapped out. This is known as a *least-recently used* algorithm, and can actually work fairly well if there are no better criteria to sort by.

Next, we'll look at the Sound sorting function. We have much more to choose from when sorting a Sound object because we have additional factors to consider, such as a user-defined priority value. Let's examine this in Listing 11.10.

LISTING 11.10

```
uint32 Sound::GetLastPlayTime() const
{
    if(IsPlaying())
        return 0xFFFFFFFF;
    return m_nLastTimePlayed;
}

bool Sound::operator < (const Sound& snd) const
{
    int iScore = 0;

    if(m_Init.m_nPriority < snd.m_Init.m_nPriority)
```

```
            iScore--;
      else if(m_Init.m_nPriority > snd.m_Init.m_nPriority)
            iScore++;

      if(IsPlaying())
            iScore++;
      if(snd.IsPlaying())
            iScore--;

      if(GetLastPlayTime() < snd.GetLastPlayTime())
            iScore--;
      else if(GetLastPlayTime() > snd.GetLastPlayTime())
            iScore++;

      return (iScore < 0) ? true : false;
}
```

We see a slightly different approach in this function. A general score is kept between the two objects, and each of a number of different criteria measured in the two objects will weight the object. This means that no single criterion has an absolute assurance of ranking one object higher than another. In this way, a high-priority sound that has not played in a very long time will still have a chance at being swapped out by a lower-priority sound that wants to play. However, a high-priority sound that is currently playing will definitely prevent a low-priority sound from loading and playing.

Notice the GetLastPlayTime() function. This function returns the last time played, except if the object is currently playing, in which case the maximum value is returned. This helps to ensure that currently playing objects always have a higher priority than objects that are not playing.

Our most complex comparison function belongs to the Sound3D class. We perform the same comparison operators as the 2D function, but we also perform several positional checks and comparisons. Let's examine this function in Listing 11.11.

LISTING 11.11

```
bool Sound3D::operator < (const Sound3D& snd) const
{
      int iScore = 0;
```

```
if(m_Init.m_nPriority < snd.m_Init.m_nPriority)
    iScore--;
else if(m_Init.m_nPriority > snd.m_Init.m_nPriority)
    iScore++;

if(IsPlaying())
    iScore++;
if(snd.IsPlaying())
    iScore--;

if(m_pSound->GetLastPlayTime() <
        snd.m_pSound->GetLastPlayTime())
    iScore--;
else if(m_pSound->GetLastPlayTime() >
        snd.m_pSound->GetLastPlayTime())
    iScore++;

AUDIOVECTOR vLP, vP1, vP2;
float fDist1, fDist2;
float fMaxDist;
IListener* pListener;
AudioMgr()->GetListener(pListener);
pListener->GetPosition(vLP);
GetPosition(vP1);
snd.GetPosition(vP2);
fDist1 = sqrt((vLP.x - vP1.x) * (vLP.x - vP1.x) +
    (vLP.y - vP1.y) * (vLP.y - vP1.y) +
    vLP.z - vP1.z) * (vLP.z - vP1.z));
fDist2 = sqrt((vLP.x - vP2.x) * (vLP.x - vP2.x) +
    (vLP.y - vP2.y) * (vLP.y - vP2.y) +
    (vLP.z - vP2.z) * (vLP.z - vP2.z));

GetMaxDistance(fMaxDist);
if(fDist1 >= fMaxDist)
    iScore -= 2;
snd.GetMaxDistance(fMaxDist);
if(fDist2 >= fMaxDist)
    iScore += 2;

if(fDist1 > fDist2)
    iScore--;
```

```
    else
        iScore++;

    return (iScore < 0) ? true : false;
}
```

After similar comparisons are made to those in the Sound class, the Sound3D comparison function compares the distances between each sound object and the listener, storing them in fDist1 and fDist2. These are then used for two more sorting criteria. First, the distance is checked against the sound's maximum distance, meaning that we check to see if the sound is even within hearing range. This is a very important sorting criterion, and so we add or subtract two instead of one to the score in this case. Next, we compare the distances to each sound against each other, and the closest sound is given a higher priority. Although not a perfect determination of sound priority, general distance to the listener is a fairly good method of determining what is most relevant to the current situation.

In this manner, we can completely customize each type of audio object's sorting criteria and management scheme. You may decide to utilize different sorting criteria for the objects, and doing so only requires changing a single function for each object, making it convenient to experiment with these functions and adjust them to suit your own needs.

CONCLUSION

Resource-management routines and systems are not exactly the most exciting part of an audio system, but they are a necessary and rewarding part of the project when you see the results of your efforts pay off. With proper buffer and resource management, even a modestly capable sound card can reproduce the full scope of your soundscape and musical themes.

Speaking of music, in the next chapter, we'll introduce the powerful, if somewhat intimidating, DirectMusic API; and you'll learn how you can use this library not only as an interactive music-playback system, but also to play any traditional 2D or even 3D sound effects.

CHAPTER 12

DIRECTMUSIC INTRODUCTION

DirectMusic is the high-level music and audio playback component of DirectX. Despite its name, Microsoft is encouraging programmers to use DirectMusic for both music and sound effects. However, the size and scope of DirectMusic is often intimidating to many programmers; and worse, DirectMusic capabilities are often not well understood, and so remain underused by a large percentage of game developers. By carefully evaluating its strengths and weaknesses, as well as learning a few Direct-Music-specific tricks, we can easily add a great deal of functionality to a game or audio engine with only a modest amount of effort.

 The code listed in this chapter can be found in \Game_Audio\ audio_sdk\src\audiolib\AudioMgr.h, AudioMgr.cpp, Segment.h, Segment.cpp.

DIRECTMUSIC OVERVIEW

DirectMusic was first introduced in DirectX 6.1 and was designed to provide additional MIDI-based musical capabilities to DirectX-enabled games. Previously, the only musical solution available to PCs was MCI MIDI playback, CD audio, or digital streaming audio written with custom DirectSound-based or software-accelerated code.

MIDI: A SPOTTY HISTORY ON THE PC

MIDI (Musical Instrument Digital Interface) has a horrible reputation among PC game developers—and frankly for good reasons. Back in the early days of PC gaming, the available musical options for many games were quite limited. CD-ROM drives had yet to become standard equipment, so many developers turned to MIDI as a solution.

In truth, MIDI was originally designed as a real-time communication protocol, and was intended to provide a standardized communication mechanism between different pieces of audio hardware. Typically, a musician would create a digital mapping of instruments based on a unique configuration of studio hardware voices, and so the typical MIDI-based setup was generally meaningless outside that specific environment. MIDI data is composed of individual messages broken into 16 discrete channels, representing different instruments in a musical environment. On each channel, individual notes with parameters such as velocity (volume), pitch, and duration are transmitted. In transmitted MIDI communication, these notes are sent in real-time to other instruments.

Eventually, a semistandardized file format containing a stream of this data was established in order to store the data on the PC, but in order to make any sense of a 'general' MIDI file, a standard set of voice mappings had to be established. Audio cards at the time began shipping with standardized sets of built-in instrument voices (pioneered by Roland), also referred to as General MIDI (GM).

Standardized voices sounded like a good idea, but the standard only consisted of names, such as "Piano" and "Flute." Each audio card manufacturer had a slightly different idea about what these voices should sound like and the required level of quality in reproducing them. Worse yet, most early audio cards had extremely low-quality, two-operator FM (Frequency Modulation) voices, as opposed to today's higher-quality digital samples. Although a composer would know, for instance, that assigning a track of music to voice one would produce a piano sound, there was no real guarantee what the final music might sound like on the user's system. This obviously was a source of frustration for composers and consumers alike. As such, MIDI has suffered from this confusion and has earned its terrible reputation in the PC world. To this day, it is often associated with a low-quality musical experience, even though professional studio musicians continue using MIDI in its proper studio role to this day.

DLS INTRODUCED

In order to alleviate the problem of poor-sounding MIDI audio, cards began shipping with digital audio samples built onto the cards. This later evolved into cards with general-purpose sample memory, allowing custom instrument banks to be used in conjunction with the MIDI data. The technology was eventually standardized and dubbed *DLS* (DownLoadable Sounds). The biggest problem with this technology, though, was its relatively rare hardware support, meaning that a standardized musical experience could still not be provided to users. This essentially relegated it to a compositional tool rather than a practical solution for game development.

ENTER DIRECTMUSIC

Microsoft DirectMusic has breathed new life into MIDI-based music because of a couple of key features. First, although DirectMusic takes advantage of DLS hardware when available, the key component is the Microsoft Software Synthesizer, which allows DLS-enabled MIDI music to be played on any computer with a DirectSound-compatible sound card. This had two very important ramifications:

- MIDI music could now be composed using custom sample sets, as it was originally intended, ensuring a much higher-quality playback than when using a standardized sample set.
- The music is guaranteed to sound the same on every computer platform, no matter what type of hardware is available. The only difference between systems will be the level of hardware acceleration.

MIDI's two biggest problems on the PC, quality and consistency, have now been solved with the introduction of DirectMusic. Because general computer performance has increased so drastically in recent years, it is now practical to devote a few percent of the total CPU time for a software synthesizer and even apply musical reverberation to the entire score for additional warmth and ambience.

In addition, DirectMusic gives composers and programmers a new slew of tools that are capable of creating truly *interactive music*. Interactive music, a buzzword in the game industry, simply means that in-game music can dynamically be altered to fit the on-screen game action. With the programmatic nature of MIDI music, it becomes quite easy to manipulate the data in real-time, allowing much more contextually relevant scores than are possible with linear audio tracks. While it's simple to create completely linear MIDI+DLS scores, DirectMusic really shines when using interactive composition elements to create subtle variations in a looping track pattern, or to use a dynamically created chord-map progression. In addition, MIDI takes so little disk space that literally hours of music can be stored in almost no space at all, other than the size of the sample set, which remains constant.

NOT JUST MIDI ANYMORE

Beginning with DirectX 8.0, DirectMusic provided the ability to load and play wave files in segments. This had a couple of major ramifications. First and foremost, for simple wave file playback, it was much simpler to use DirectMusic than DirectSound. This created somewhat of a blurring of capabilities and responsibilities between DirectSound and DirectMusic. Second and perhaps more subtle, DirectMusic became a powerful mechanism for streaming digital audio, even interactively, in the exact same manner as MIDI.

This means that DirectMusic can now be effectively used to create an interactive, streaming digital audio soundtrack just as easily as with MIDI. Many composers are more interested in digital audio streams for several reasons, whether for the simplicity of design and creation or for the ultimate control over the sound of the final product. Those composers and developers who aren't interested in DirectMusic because it means using MIDI in their projects should take another good look at it. DirectMusic automatically makes use of the Microsoft Audio Compression Manager (ACM), so any codec found on the user's system can be utilized for decoding digital audio streams, including MP3 codecs.

■ SO, WHY BOTHER WITH DIRECTSOUND?

We've covered a lot of ground with DirectSound and related technologies, and you may be wondering where all this DirectX Audio integration is supposedly taking place, and why we haven't been using any of it so far. In this book, we've presented DirectSound as a separate entity for several reasons.

Although DirectMusic is a wonderful high-level addition to DirectSound, it has a few drawbacks as a primary audio playback mechanism. While some tasks, such as loading a compressed wave file or streaming audio from disk, are greatly simplified, other tasks, such as managing and controlling your low-level buffers, become more difficult simply because you have less control over certain system aspects. In addition, using DirectMusic as both a music system and an audio playback system requires the successful pulling off of a few tricks. Previously, the biggest issue with DirectMusic was over the nature of its musical origin—high audio latency, which tended to be a problem for certain types of sound effects. However, with DirectX 9.0, Microsoft introduced a low-latency DirectSound sync buffer, making it feasible to use DirectMusic for even fast-action type sound effects. This has helped to mitigate the primary disadvantage when using DirectMusic over DirectSound.

Of course, there are currently many DirectSound-only solutions that exist in code, and some developers may simply feel more comfortable using DirectSound instead of DirectMusic; it is always a greater engineering risk to integrate a new audio system that requires a major paradigm shift. Or, in fact, a game simply might not need any of the features provided by DirectMusic, and so DirectSound might be a better choice there, as well. Ultimately, it will come down to a decision made either by the audio programmer or the game team as to whether it is better use DirectSound exclusively, DirectMusic exclusively, or use a combination of the two.

One thing to remember, as well: although DirectMusic might replace the mechanism for creating sound buffers or loading audio, you still need access to the low-level DirectSound buffer to control it the way you want. DirectSound, as an interface (and as a system), has simply not been completely superseded by Direct-Music yet, and so each API must still be thoroughly handled.

DIRECTMUSIC COMPONENTS

DirectMusic is indeed a powerhouse of functionality if properly understood and correctly utilized. The hundreds of lines of code that are required when using DirectSound can be replaced with only a handful of code when using DirectMusic, and the sheer volume of functionality provided is enough to make most audio engineers and composers happy. Despite this high-level functionality, DirectMusic remains surprisingly flexible in its usage and avoids any major constraints in how you design your musical system. Instead, it allows you to choose which components and capabilities are important for your sound engine. Unfortunately, at times, DirectMusic seems a bit too flexible; sometimes it seems difficult to even determine where to begin.

One of the requirements to utilize DirectMusic as an effective solution is to understand how the multitude of different classes and components work together. Because of the sheer number of interfaces and volumes of functionality, this can be a bit daunting at first. However, a game developer realistically needs only to understand four primary DirectMusic objects in order to take advantage of a good portion of its functionality: *Performances*, *Loaders*, *Segments*, and *Audiopaths*. Because each of these items is necessarily interconnected with other object types, we'll begin with a brief description of each object type and then proceed with investigating each object type in detail.

To help this make a bit more sense, look at Figure 12.1 to see the logical path of the audio data as it moves through or is controlled by the four different component types.

Data logically flows from a permanent storage medium, generally a hard drive or CD-ROM disc. There are two data paths into the loader. The simplest path is when you instruct the loader to get a file directly from a disk system. Alternatively, the client might load the file into a user-managed data buffer. In this case, the buffer must exist for the lifetime of the segment that uses it.

The loader then creates the individual segment objects and hands the data to them. These objects move the data to an audiopath, representative of the final mixing destination. Segments may share an audiopath with other segments (Figure 12.1, *left*), or they might have an audiopath of their own (Figure 12.1, *right*). The performance object is a little harder to define in terms of audio data flow. The best way to think of a performance object is as a controller of sorts, which is responsible for actual sequencing, timing, and playback. As such, in Figure 12.1, we have represented performances as dashed boxes that encompass the segment and audiopath elements. Note that two different performances are represented, indicating that multiple performance objects may be used simultaneously.

PERFORMANCES

A DirectMusic performance object (`IDirectMusicPerformance8`) is likely the first component you will create if you want to utilize DirectMusic. You can think of a DirectMusic performance in the literal sense of the musical

TABLE 12.1   DirectMusic Objects

Object Type	Description
Performance	Controls playback and coordination of multiple segments, as well as setting global parameters, such as volume and effects.
Loader	Responsible for loading wave files, segments, and other DirectMusic run-time elements.
Segment	The basic musical element of DirectMusic, encapsulating either a chunk of MIDI or digital audio data. Segments can be created statically or dynamically generated from other elements. Segments are designed to transition seamlessly from one to another, which is the basis for most interactive music.
Audiopath	Represents a destination buffer and effects chain on which a segment may be played. More than one segment can be played on a single audiopath, allowing for efficient use of DirectSound hardware resources.

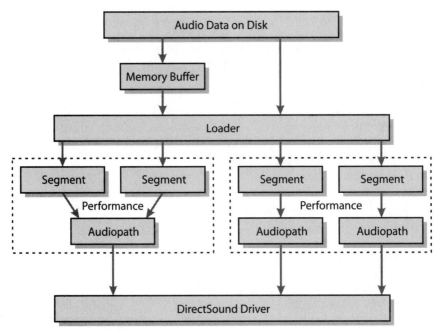

FIGURE 12.1   Data traveling through the four object types.

term—controlling the cueing, timing, and synchronization of playing segments. Although simple applications might only have a single performance object, we'll see a bit later how multiple performance objects can be used to effectively segregate DirectMusic-based sound effects from musical elements.

If you're anxious to get a sound loaded and playing, you can theoretically jump ahead to the more-exciting pieces of code to get up and running; but eventually, it will behoove you to understand what's going on in this function. For now, just copying the code in Listing 12.1 will work just fine to get you started.

The first thing to remember before calling any COM functions is to initialize COM by calling CoInitialize(NULL). After this, you create the DirectMusic performance object using the standard COM method CoCreateInstance(). Next, you must call InitAudio() to initialize the performance object. Let's take a moment to examine what this code looks like.

LISTING 12.1

```
HRESULT hr = CoInitialize(NULL);
if(FAILED(hr))
```

```
    return false;

hr = CoCreateInstance(CLSID_DirectMusicPerformance, NULL,
CLSCTX_INPROC, IID_IDirectMusicPerformance8,
(void**)&m_pPerformance );
if(FAILED(hr))
    return false;

// Initialize the music performance
hr = m_pPerformance->InitAudio(
NULL,
NULL,
m_hWnd,
DMUS_APATH_DYNAMIC_STEREO,
64,
DMUS_AUDIOF_ALL,
    NULL);
if(FAILED(hr))
    return false;
```

The InitAudio() function does some important work, so we'll take some time to explain it. The first two parameters are a double pointer to an IDirectMusic interface and a double pointer to an IDirectSound interface. Either of these parameters can contain NULL, a NULL pointer to the interface object, or a valid and initialized object of the specified type. More than likely, you will not actually need an IDirectMusic interface in your application. This interface is used to enumerate and query DirectMusic ports, but since DirectMusic utilizes ports a bit differently in DirectX 8.0 and its subsequent revisions, you have more control when choosing a default port; there is now less reason to do this manually.

However, there is more of an argument to create and use a Direct-Sound8 object and pass this in as the function's second argument. Unless you plan on utilizing DirectMusic exclusively for your audio playback needs, you will still want to create your DirectSound object exactly like always, and then pass the interface into this function. Additionally, this makes it easier to add DirectMusic to an existing DirectSound-based system, which is a likely scenario given the relative age of DirectSound compared to DirectMusic. Note that even though the function requests an IDirectSound interface, you can simply cast and use an existing IDirectSound8 interface.

Next, you pass in a standard window handle to the `InitAudio()` function. If you pass in `NULL`, it will use the current top-level window as the application window, but it is recommended to use your actual application window.

After this, you may direct this performance to use a default audiopath. We will discuss exactly what this means a bit later; but for now, suffice it to say that you may choose one of four basic types of audiopath. Our example will create a standard stereo audiopath. Think of it as creating a specific type of DirectSound buffer and effects combination (or lack thereof) for any segments that are played on this performance.

The next value indicates the number of performance channels available for use on this performance object. This corresponds roughly to simultaneous channels in a MIDI file, for example, or different wave file streams. Essentially, you can think of it as the number of simultaneous unique audio streams a performance may play at once. A value of 64 is a good number to use for now, as this is unlikely to be exceeded by a single performance.

The last two parameters contain information about what features DirectMusic should require when looking for an available port. While we can use the last parameter with a `DMUS_AUDIOPARMS` structure to request and obtain more detailed information about a chosen port, it is far simpler to pass the `DMUS_AUDIOF_ALL` flag to the second-to-last parameter, specifying that we wish to ensure that all features are available on the port that DirectMusic chooses for us.

As mentioned earlier, the DirectMusic performance object is responsible for coordinating all currently playing segments. In fact, the `IDirectMusic-Performance8` member functions `PlaySegment()` and `PlaySegmentEx()` are the mechanisms by which segments are played. The `IDirectMusicSegment8` interface (which contains the sound or song data) is passed as an argument to this function, along with parameters indicating how to interact with other possibly playing segments. One important function of a DirectMusic performance object is to queue segments so they will play sequentially. In this manner, you can easily switch between small musical sections, exactly on cue. In essence, only one segment may play at a time, as long as the segment is designated to play as a *primary segment*.

Obviously, this would be problematic for playing multiple sound effects, but there is a mechanism for triggering multiple segments to play simultaneously. By instructing the performance to play a *secondary segment*, we are able to play multiple segments on cue, even while a primary segment is playing or when no primary segment is playing. Unlike primary segments, there are no restrictions on overlapping secondary segments. In this manner, we can effectively play multiple, simultaneous sound effects on our performance object.

Here is a simple example of a segment-playback mechanism that can switch between sound effects and music based on the variable m_bMusic:

LISTING 12.2

```
// Set the flags based on the type of content (music or sound
// fx)
DWORD dwFlags = 0;
if(m_bMusic)
    dwFlags = DMUS_SEGF_QUEUE | DMUS_SEGF_DEFAULT;
else
    dwFlags = DMUS_SEGF_SECONDARY;

// Now play the segment
IDirectMusicSegmentState* pSegState = 0;
HRESULT hr;
hr = m_pPerformance->PlaySegmentEx(
    m_pSegment,
    NULL,
    NULL,
    dwFlags,
    0,
    NULL,
    NULL,
    NULL);
```

Listing 12.2 demonstrates how you might, in code, differentiate between a playing segment as part of a music track and a playing segment that must be fired off immediately, such as a sound effect. Likewise, other basic segment-control functions, such as stopping a segment or getting the current status of a segment, are also part of the IDirectMusicPerformance8 interface. (We'll be discussing the management of segments in much more detail in Chapter 13.)

Performances are also used to notify your program when performance-related events occur. For instance, a notification can be issued to your program on every measure or beat of a segment's playback, or it can notify your program that the current segment is about to finish playing, or that the last segment in the performance queue has stopped. It is these notifications that allow us to create a truly dynamic and interactive system.

Because we know when each segment is queued and played, our music-playback system has a chance to look at the current game state and decide what segment is most appropriate to play next, based on the current segment and current game state. The next segment is queued behind the current one, and DirectMusic will smoothly move from one segment playback to the next, regardless of whether the segment contains MIDI data or digital audio streams.

DirectMusic communicates with the program through the use of standard Windows events. Often called a "Win32 event," this mechanism is used to signal the occurrence of some event across different threads. What makes this both handy and powerful is the ability of a Win32 event to wake up a sleeping thread when the event is received, instead of requiring your application to waste cycles polling for information. For DirectMusic developers, this means creating a separate thread that just waits for events, and then responds immediately as they occur. This ensures immediate action no matter what else the program might be doing at the time—like loading a level, for instance. Unfortunately, writing thread-safe code is always a bit trickier than writing simple linear code, so we'll also look at a number of different ways to do so safely.

In Listing 12.3, we see a critical section initialized with the Windows function InitializeCriticalSection(). (Later, we'll discuss why this is occurring here.) Creating a Win32 event first requires the use of a standard Windows handle. Create an auto-resetting event with the Windows function CreateEvent() and give that handle to DirectMusic via the SetNotificationHandle() function. Next, we specify which notification types are to be handled by DirectMusic. In this example, we are telling the performance to signal us for measure and beat information, segment-related information, and performance-related information. (We'll look at source code a bit later that examines how to handle these events, and we'll see what these events can actually be used for.) Finally, we indicate that DirectMusic has been initialized with a Boolean value, and we start the notification-handling thread.

LISTING 12.3

```
InitializeCriticalSection(&m_csTerm);

// HANDLE m_hMusicNotify; declared in class header
// Create the Win32 event and set it in DMusic
m_hMusicNotify = CreateEvent(NULL, FALSE, FALSE, NULL);
```

```
m_pMusicPerformance->SetNotificationHandle(
    m_hMusicNotify, 0);

// Set notifications for the music performance
m_pMusicPerformance->AddNotificationType(
    GUID_NOTIFICATION_MEASUREANDBEAT);
hr = m_pMusicPerformance->AddNotificationType(
    GUID_NOTIFICATION_PERFORMANCE);
hr = m_pMusicPerformance->AddNotificationType(
    GUID_NOTIFICATION_SEGMENT);

// Audio system has been successfully initialized
m_bInitialized = true;

// Begin the DirectMusic event thread
_beginthread(AudioManager::MusicEventThread, 0, NULL);
```

You can see that AudioManager::MusicEventThread() is the function used as the entry point for the notification-handling thread. If you've never written multithreaded code, creating and using a thread in your application is most likely easier than you had imagined. The difficulty lies in making sure the different threads work properly together without accidentally causing errors or access violations. Because you may not pass a standard member function as a function pointer argument, the next best option is to use a static member function, since it still has the same rights to private data as any normal member function. Because our class uses a singleton to access the audio manager in which this code is found, our MusicEventThread() function can access any member data or function using the DXAudioMgr() access function. In Listing 12.4, you can see that the MusicEventThread() function simply calls the nonstatic member function UpdateMusic(). This is done to provide cleaner access to the class functions and data members, instead of having to use the singleton access function.

Let's look inside the UpdateMusic() function to see how to respond to DirectMusic message events.

LISTING 12.4

```
void AudioManager::MusicEventThread(LPVOID lpv)
{
    DXAudioMgr()->UpdateMusic();
}
```

```
void AudioManager::UpdateMusic()
{
    DMUS_NOTIFICATION_PMSG* pPmsg;
    while(true)
    {
        WaitForSingleObject(m_hMusicNotify, INFINITE);
        if(!m_bInitialized)
        {
            SetEvent(m_hTerm[MUSIC_EVENT]);
            return;
        }
        while (S_OK == m_pMusicPerformance->
            GetNotificationPMsg(
            &pPmsg))
        {
            // Intercept and handle messages here
            m_pMusicPerformance->FreePMsg((DMUS_PMSG*)pPmsg);
        }
    }
}
```

This function waits for and processes all DirectMusic messages until the m_bInitialized flag is set to false. The first thing you will notice in this semiperpetual loop is the function WaitForSingleObject(). This puts the thread to sleep until an event occurs (a DirectMusic message notification). If, for some reason, we wish the thread to continue after a specific amount of time regardless of the lack of notification messages, we can enter a time value in milliseconds instead of specifying INFINITE. This is known as the *timeout* value.

■ LET SLEEPING THREADS LIE

If you are not familiar with the term *sleep* in the context of multithreaded (or even single-threaded) applications, it simply means to halt a thread's execution for a specified amount of time, or until an event tells the thread to wake. However, it is much more efficient than simply putting an executing thread in a timing loop of some sort, or continuously polling to see if an event has arrived. Instead, it tells the operating system to suspend operation of the thread for the duration of the sleep period, therefore demanding few CPU resources while sleeping. Because the

WaitForSingleObject() message sleeps until the moment an event is signaled, it is an efficient way to wait for messages. And, equally handy, the message-handling operation of your interactive music system won't be interrupted by anything that is happening on the main thread, such as waiting for a loading screen to finish, so your music should always play uninterrupted, no matter what else is happening.

After we receive an event signal or timeout, we proceed with checking for and handling any waiting DirectMusic messages. Notice the thread that checks the m_bInitialized flag. If this is found to be true, it means the audio manager is shutting itself down and causes the thread to self-terminate. We'll examine this code in more detail in Chapter 15 when we discuss techniques for effectively and safely using multiple threads when shutting down DirectMusic. For now, simply understand that the thread exits when the m_bInitialize flag is set to false, which we will obviously do at some point when shutting down the audio manager.

Next, we check to see if the performance object's GetNotification-PMsg() function returns S_OK, and if so, proceeds inside the body of a conditional if block. You might recall how it is typically not a good idea to explicitly check for success by comparing against S_OK. Generally speaking, it is safer to check for success or failure using the SUCCEEDED() or FAILED() macros. However, we are not necessarily concerned with success or failure, but whether the function actually gives us a DirectMusic message to process. If no messages are available for us to process, the function will return S_FALSE, which by definition is still a success value. So, in this particular case, checking against S_OK is appropriate.

The GetNotificationPMsg() function takes the address to a DMUS_NOTIFICATION_PMSG pointer. If the function returns S_OK, a message has been allocated and filled out with a particular type of message, along with any corresponding information required. The DMUS_NOTIFICATION_PMSG structure looks like this:

```
typedef struct DMUS_NOTIFICATION_PMSG {
 DMUS_PMSG_PART
 GUID guidNotificationType;
 DWORD dwNotificationOption;
 DWORD dwField1;
 DWORD dwField2;
 } DMUS_NOTIFICATION_PMSG;
```

The DMUS_PMSG_PART is a macro that expands to a larger, common DirectMusic message structure. You can look up the DMUS_PMSG structure in the DirectMusic SDK documents, but it is not required reading for what we need to do. The guidNotificationType field indicates the class, or basic type of message received. This field corresponds to the GUID passed in to the AddNotificationType() function earlier. Each GUID we add then represents a class of message we are able to receive. There are six basic notification message types (Table 12.2):

TABLE 12.2 Notification Message Types

Value	Description
GUID_NOTIFICATION_CHORD	Chord change
GUID_NOTIFICATION_COMMAND	Command event
GUID_NOTIFICATION_MEASUREANDBEAT	Measure and beat event
GUID_NOTIFICATION_PERFORMANCE	Performance event, further defined in dwNotificationOption
GUID_NOTIFICATION_RECOMPOSE	A track has been recomposed
GUID_NOTIFICATION_SEGMENT	Segment event, further defined in dwNotificationOption

As you may recall, in our sample code, we chose to receive information about three of these message types: GUID_NOTIFICATION_PERFORMANCE, GUID_NOTIFICATION_SEGMENT, and GUID_NOTIFICATION_MEASUREANDBEAT.

The dwNotificationOption field in the DMUS_NOTIFICATION_PMSG further refines the message type, and is context-sensitive based on the GUID found in the guidNotificationType field before it. As an example, if the GUID is equal to GUID_NOTIFICATION_SEGMENT, the field might have the following values (Table 12.3):

TABLE 12.3 Segment Notification Subtypes

Value	Description
DMUS_NOTIFICATION_SEGABORT	The segment was stopped prematurely, or was removed from the primary segment queue.
DMUS_NOTIFICATION_SEGALMOSTEND	The segment has reached the end minus the prepare time.

(continues)

TABLE 12.3   Segment Notification Subtypes (*Continued*)

Value	Description
DMUS_NOTIFICATION_SEGEND	The segment has ended.
DMUS_NOTIFICATION_SEGLOOP	The segment has looped.
DMUS_NOTIFICATION_SEGSTART	The segment has started.

Further subtypes can be found listed in the SDK documents.

The fields dwField1 and dwField2 are both context-sensitive fields, depending on the message and submessage type. At the moment, only dwField1 is currently used for indicating the current beat number when the message type is GUID_NOTIFICATION_MEASUREANDBEAT. The field dwField2 is reserved for future message types.

The last major portion of code to examine is how to shut everything down safely. Because we are dealing with multiple threads, we must be cautious not to allow one thread to shut down an object while another thread is currently accessing that object. Without taking proper precautions, this is exactly what could happen with our message-handling thread. In general, this sort of problem is called a *thread-synchronization* issue. You can learn more about how we deal with shutting down multiple threads in Chapter 15 when we look at the audio manager in more detail.

There is one more lesson to be learned here regarding the use of the performance objects. One of the basic tenets of our audio system design so far has been to segregate, or at least differentiate in some manner, audio objects used for sound effects and audio objects used for music. This is desirable for a number of reasons, not the least of which is the ability to separately control the parameters (such as volume) of each without affecting the others. With DirectMusic, the easiest way to make this distinction is to *use separate performance objects for sound and music*. This provides a simple solution to a number of thorny problems, including:

- How do you choose a default audiopath that works for both sound and music? Typically, for music, you would want the standard shared+reverb audiopath, while for sound effects, you would likely want a standard stereo or mono dry buffer, or perhaps a standard 3D buffer.

- How do you differentiate between notifications received from sound effects and from music tracks? A 'segment is about to end' notification will fire for secondary segments, causing confusion in any code designed to handle the interactive music segment selection.

- How do you separately control the volume for all sound effects or all music?

With a separate performance object for each basic category of audio (we recognize two: sound fx and music), we mimic the same distinction made in other parts of the *GAP* audio library code. The following code demonstrates a simple mechanism for ensuring the correct performance is retrieved.

```
IDirectMusicPerformance8* Performance(bool bMusic)
{ return (bMusic) ? m_pMusicPerformance :
    m_pSoundPerformance; }
```

The Segment class has a member m_bMusic designating an object as either music or a sound effect (it's actually part of the initialization structure). Whenever a performance interface is needed, this variable is simply passed to the AudioManager::Performance() function, passing the music flag as a parameter, and the correct performance object is returned, depending on the value of the object's own flag.

The performance is also responsible for setting a number of 'global' parameters (i.e., global to the performance), such as volume, tempo, and *groove level*. Groove level is a user-defined property that can be used to alter the selection of variations in segments. A composer, for instance, might decide to use groove level instead of discrete segments to represent different levels of excitement or intensity within the same basic music structure of a single segment. This helps to provide a bit more control while cutting down the number of discrete variations needed in separate segments. You can use IDirectMusicPerformance8::SetGlobalParam() to set these global parameters and IDirectMusicPerformance8::GetGlobalParam() to retrieve them. The functions use a GUID identifier to indicate which parameter is being changed, and they use a void pointer to pass and retrieve generic data, which depends on the property being set or retrieved. Here is a simple example demonstrating how to set the volume of a performance object:

```
int32 nVol = -1000;
m_pPerformance->SetGlobalParam(
    GUID_PerfMasterVolume,
    &nVol,
    sizeof(int32));
```

Other parameters work in a similar matter. You can read about all of them in detail in the DirectX SDK documents under the topic "Setting and Retrieving Global Parameters."

LOADERS

The DirectMusic loader is a powerful and handy interface used to load audio data using a variety of methods, providing a simple means of retrieving DirectMusic objects from the disk. The loader is one of the first objects you'll likely create, and it should remain active throughout the life of your audio manager or application. You also should only need one loader for your application.

In addition to loading DirectMusic-related content and MIDI files, the DirectMusic loader now can load wave files. Like the wave file loader we so laboriously created in Chapter 8, The DirectMusic wave loader also uses the Windows Audio Compression Manager, so nearly any wave file recognized by installed Windows codecs will also be playable in DirectSound. For those wishing to use ACM-compressed wave files who are not willing to expend the energy to create their own general-purpose loader, this represents a considerable savings in effort.

Obviously, before anything else is done, the loader must be created. The most appropriate place to do that in our case is in our `AudioManager::Init()` function, where our performance objects were also created. This is accomplished exactly like any other COM object, as demonstated in Listing 12.5.

LISTING 12.5

```
HRESULT hr = CoCreateInstance(
    CLSID_DirectMusicLoader,
    NULL,
    CLSCTX_INPROC,
    IID_IDirectMusicLoader8,
    (void**)&m_pLoader);
```

There are two basic ways to load a wave file using DirectMusic. The first and simplest is to have the loader handle all the work of extracting the data from the disk. You simply supply the loader with the path and filename of an object, and it will load the object from memory and give you an `IDirectMusicSegment8` interface that points to a segment object that is loaded with the data from the disk. If you wish to load objects from disk using the DirectMusic loader, there are a few additional considerations that you may also wish consider, such as caching and enumerating objects in a directory, and setting a current search directory. We will deal with this after we first see how to load a simple wave or segment file.

LISTING 12.6

```
// IDirectMusicSegment8* m_pSegment; declared earlier

hr = m_pLoader->LoadObjectFromFile(
    CLSID_DirectMusicSegment,
    IID_IDirectMusicSegment8,
    L"SampleSound.wav",
    (void**) &m_pSegment);
```

You should note that DirectMusic uses only wide characters in its functions, meaning that you'll need to convert your ANSI, single-byte character strings into double-byte characters. Some handy utility functions can be found in the DXUtil.h and DXUtil.cpp files in the DirectX SDK. We've copied these functions for use in our library.

The `IDirectMusicLoader8::LoadObjectFromFile()` function does exactly what it says—loads a file from disk and gives the client a pointer to a segment object, since we requested a `CLSID_DirectMusicSegment` object in the first parameter, along with the proper interface ID in the second parameter. The third parameter requires a wide character string with the name of the file to load; and the fourth, like many other COM functions, uses `void**` to hand back an interface pointer to the user. On success, we have a segment that contains either wave or MIDI data.

With an unqualified filename (meaning no path is included), the DirectMusic loader will first look in the current directory, then in the Windows search path, and finally in the directory set by the last call to `IDirectMusicLoader8::SetCurrentDirectory()`. You can use this function to ensure that DirectMusic will always be able to find the files you are attempting to load, even if the current directory is set to some other location. There are other methods of loading files, even without necessarily knowing the filenames. You could, for instance, scan a directory using the `IDirectMusicLoader8::ScanDirectory()` function, which looks for all files or just a particular file type. These files can then be enumerated and loaded using the `IDirectMusicLoader8::EnumObject()` function. While these functions could come in handy for some types of applications, games and similar applications will usually know what particular files they are looking for and where they will be found, especially when using a script-based playback system, as we'll see later. Additionally, these functions will be useless for IStream-based interfaces that load data from custom file systems. In this case, you must be sure to explicitly load any files that might be referenced by other DirectMusic files.

The DirectMusic loader also has a slightly more general-purpose function for loading files and creating objects, called "GetObject()." This function uses a DMUS_OBJECTDESC to describe the object to be loaded. In addition to simply loading a file from a disk, you can choose to load primarily from the current search directory, using an absolute path, or you can load an object from a memory buffer that you manage yourself. The ability to load from a memory buffer is welcome news for many game programmers. Instead of having to implement a custom loader to load objects from packed file formats, applications can now simply use a memory buffer with the file image already loaded and pass this buffer to the Direct-Music loader. In addition, DirectMusic does not make an internal copy of the buffer and manage it. Instead, it relies on you to manage the buffer while the object exists. While this may seem unnecessarily burdensome, it is the most efficient way for DirectMusic to utilize memory that has already been allocated and loaded, and is well worth the slight extra effort of keeping track of this buffer manually. Let's see how to load a file from memory using the IDirectMusicLoader8::GetObject() function.

LISTING 12.7

```
// m_pBuffer contains a loaded file in a memory buffer
// m_nBufferSize is the size of m_pBuffer

DMUS_OBJECTDESC ObjDesc;
ObjDesc.dwSize = sizeof(DMUS_OBJECTDESC);
ObjDesc.guidClass = CLSID_DirectMusicSegment;
ObjDesc.dwValidData = DMUS_OBJ_CLASS | DMUS_OBJ_MEMORY;
ObjDesc.pbMemData = m_pBuffer;
ObjDesc.llMemLength = m_nBufferSize;

// Load the data and retrieve the segment interface
hr = DXAudioMgr()->Loader()->GetObject(
    &ObjDesc,
    IID_IDirectMusicSegment8,
    (void**) &m_pSegment );
```

```
if(FAILED(hr))
    return false;
```

Using the DMUS_OBJECTDESC structure flags, we describe the object as a segment and indicate that we're loading the data from a memory buffer. By changing the flags, we can also use this function to load files from disk, if desired. If you wish to stream large wave files from the disk, loading a file is the simplest solution, as DirectMusic will automatically stream from disk any sound file longer than 5,000 milliseconds. Obviously, this is not as beneficial if you have to load the entire file into a huge memory buffer. (In Chapter 19—Custom Resource Files, we'll deal with ways to get around this problem and show you how to use an IStream-compliant wrapper to allow streaming from any sort of custom file resource.)

Caching objects in memory is also another large part of the job of the DirectMusic loader. If automatic caching is enabled (which it is by default), every object loaded is cached in memory, ensuring that objects do not get loaded multiple times. This is particularly important with secondary loaded objects, like DLS files. When a DirectMusic run-time segment is loaded, this segment will likely reference a specific DLS file. The loader will automatically load this DLS file as needed and store it in the loader's object cache. When another segment uses this same DLS file, it will ask the loader to load it as well. Because it is already in the loader's cache, it does not need to reload the object from the disk. If caching were to be completely disabled, every segment would load its corresponding DLS file, which is obviously not a good thing.

All this functionality, however, requires some intervention by the client to ensure that objects are properly released from the cache when we are no longer using them. This will help to ensure the most efficient use of memory. Our basic audio objects always use Load() and Unload() methods to represent both the acquisition of the data and the creation of any internal objects. Therefore, we can safely release the cache of each object as its Unload() function is called, ensuring more-optimal memory usage in DirectMusic. Let's look at what happens in portions of the Segment::Unload() function.

LISTING 12.8

```
if(m_pSegment)
{
    m_pSegment->Unload(
```

```
                  DXAudioMgr()->Performance(m_Init.m_bMusic));

        // Since we're loading and unloading the segment
        // dynamically, it is important to release the loader's
        // internal reference to it.
        DXAudioMgr()->Loader()->ReleaseObjectByUnknown(m_pSegment);

        // Now release the actual segment
        SAFE_RELEASE(m_pSegment);

        // Instruct the loader to clear out unused memory.
        DXAudioMgr()->Loader()->CollectGarbage();
    }

    // Clear memory buffer
    SAFE_DELETE_ARRAY(m_pBuffer);
    m_nBufferSize = 0;
```

You can see in Listing 12.8 what the order of operations should be in order to properly clean up and release all memory associated with a segment loaded from memory or from disk. The segment should first unload its data via its Unload() member function. Next, the loader's Release-ObjectByUnknown() function is called, which tells the object to decrement the internal reference count of the object, which would keep it cached in memory even if Release() were called on it directly. We then release our own copy of the segment interface. This should drop the reference count of the object to zero, unless you have made copies of the object elsewhere in your code. After this, we call the loader's CollectGarbage() function. This checks internally cached objects, such as DLS collections, that are no longer be referenced and discards them from memory. Finally, we discard the memory buffer that was used to hold a copy of the file data, since our segment should be completely released and unreferenced at this point.

There are times, however, when DirectMusic data caching becomes a liability. This can occur when loading data through your own set of objects, such as through a custom IStream-based file loader. In this particular case, DirectMusic caching may inadvertently return an incorrect result if you reuse the same IStream object for more than one set of data. The caching may also return incorrect results if an allocated IStream object happens to have the same memory address and stream position as a previously cached IStream interface pointer. This is what exactly happens in the GAP audio library, since we reuse the allocated IStream objects as an optimization. In this case, it is best to simply remove the cached data from the loader immediately after the DirectMusic segment has been created. In this manner, we sidestep the problem of incorrect cache returns—and, because we are managing our own objects anyhow, there is no real performance penalty for doing so. You can see in Listing 12.9 how we immediately remove the cached object from the loader instead of waiting until the segment is unloaded as in Listing 12.8.

LISTING 12.9

```
DMUS_OBJECTDESC ObjDesc;
ZeroMemory(&ObjDesc, sizeof(DMUS_OBJECTDESC));
ObjDesc.dwSize = sizeof(DMUS_OBJECTDESC);
ObjDesc.guidClass = CLSID_DirectMusicSegment;
ObjDesc.dwValidData = DMUS_OBJ_CLASS | DMUS_OBJ_STREAM;
ObjDesc.pStream = pStream;

// Load the data and retrieve the segment interface
hr = DXAudioMgr()->Loader()->GetObject(
    &ObjDesc,
    IID_IDirectMusicSegment8,
    (void**) &m_pSegment );
if(FAILED(hr))
{
    Unload();
    return false;
}

// We must release the object from the cache since we
// are reusing the same IStream object to load
// different data.  This will otherwise confuse the
// cache system, resulting in errors.
hr = DXAudioMgr()->Loader()->ReleaseObjectByUnknown(
    m_pSegment);

// Instruct the loader to clear out unused memory.
DXAudioMgr()->Loader()->CollectGarbage();
```

You should note this issue is not confined to the use of IStream-based objects alone. Cache errors can also occur if you attempt to reuse memory buffers for reloading more data before removing the objects previously loaded using that buffer from the loader's cache. In this situation, the problem can easily be solved using the loader's member `SetObject()`. Immediately after creating the segment, passing the same `DMUS_OBJECTDESC` structure used to create the object, except with its `pbMemData` and `llMemLength` members set to zero, will force the cache to correctly reload data on the next object creation. For more detailed information on this procedure, refer to the DirectX SDK documentation under the sections *Cache Management* and *Loading an Object From a Resource or Memory Address.*

SEGMENTS

DirectMusic segments are perhaps the most important components. Yet oddly enough, the most important functions involving segments, including loading and playing them, are handled by the loader and performance objects. In truth, there are only a few critical functions for you to know about when dealing with segments, as they are primarily responsible for holding audio data, not necessarily manipulating it. (We'll learn in the next chapter about some of the more obscure or advanced functions available in both the `IDirectMusicSegment8` and the `IDirectMusicSegmentState8` interfaces.) A *segment state* object, as you'll discover later, provides methods to determine the current state of a playing segment, although many of its functions are duplicated in the performance object.

There are two very important member functions you should be aware of and know how to use, however: `IDirectMusicSegment8::Download()` and `IDirectMusicSegment8::Unload()`. These functions are responsible for transferring data from the segment to the audiopath that is responsible for playing it—or conversely, removing the data from the audiopath when it's no longer needed. The `Download()` function is generally called after the segment has been loaded, preparing it for playback. This is what's done in the sample audio library; `Download()` is called near the end of the `Segment::Load()` function.

The `Download()` function takes a single parameter, a pointer to the audiopath or performance object to which the file data is downloaded. Generally speaking, since the performance object is always going to exist, it seems simplest to use this object; and according to the DirectMusic documentation, it shouldn't matter which one you use, especially since we are just using the performance object's default audiopaths at this point.

In the sample audio library `Segment::Unload()` function, we reverse the procedure, making sure to call `m_pSegment->Unload()` before releasing the segment. Like the Download() function, it requires a pointer to the performance or audiopath object to which the data was originally downloaded.

AUDIOPATHS

DirectMusic also exposes a powerful audio paradigm called an *audiopath*, which is essentially the embodiment of the flow of data from the sound data source to the destination buffer, including effects and filters. While not entirely an accurate analogy, it helps to envision each audiopath simply as a DirectSound buffer, along with any associated effects. DirectMusic, in contrast to DirectSound, does not directly tie its audio data to a particular sound channel (DirectSound buffer). A segment is free to choose any audiopath, and therefore any buffer to play on. In addition, DirectMusic allows multiple sources to stream into the same destination buffer. This clever mechanism enables us to get around many of the voice-management problems imposed by DirectSound. However, since multiple sources must be mixed in software before being handed to the audio buffer, there is additional overhead associated with this technique. Likewise, the streaming nature of these buffers imposes some limitations on audio files in general—segments must be at least 250 milliseconds in length. Extremely short, one-shot sound effects are better left to DirectSound, as DirectMusic has no concept of static buffer playback.

So what exactly are the reasons you would want to create a unique audiopath for a segment or allow a group of segments to share a single unique audiopath? In the simplest terms, you should think of each audiopath as a unique DirectSound buffer that is a destination for any number of segment objects. If you require a set of unique properties for a particular sound that must be implemented at the buffer level, then a new audiopath is required. For instance, if you wish to play a segment with some unique effects, like EAX, you would be required to create a unique audiopath with a 3D buffer to manage these effects. If though, for instance, you were representing a monster that produced a number of individual sound effects, such as footsteps, breathing, roaring, and clinking armor, you could represent all of these with a single audiopath object, and each sound would use the same 3D buffer with appropriate effects applied.

The whole concept of audiopaths, while allowing a large amount of flexibility, also creates a bit of a conundrum when designing an audio system. When wrapping our DirectSound objects, we chose to present a 'sound' as a unified object, mostly for simplicity in management. Once the 'sound' object and its corresponding interface was presented to the client, all relevant functionality was incorporated into that interface, making the use of the object clean and simple to understand.

Audiopaths, however, create an additional layer of management that can be exposed in order to provide a great degree of flexibility in the management of buffer resources. In the end, though, the sample library ended up hiding the audiopath concept to a small degree for the sake of consistency and ease of use. Audiopaths, or an equivalent wrapper object, are not directly exposed to the user. However, Segment objects are allowed to create a unique audiopath, or even share audiopaths between objects by passing the ISegment interface pointer to another segment. Buffer-specific parameters will, by necessity, be shared in a single internal audiopath object; and to the external interface, it will simply appear as though setting a single parameter on a segment will also change parameters on any segment sharing that audiopath. In addition, by default, all segments are designed to utilize a default audiopath, unless explicitly set as otherwise in the initialization parameters.

It is important to recognize an important fact of API design: if a client deems a feature too much work to implement or too tricky to understand, the feature will likely not be used at all. In the end, it is your job to determine just how much functionality should be exposed to the user and how much responsibility that user must shoulder to manage the audio system.

With all of that out of the way, let's take a look at how audiopaths are actually created and used. Despite all the hand wringing about design and usage difficulties, audiopaths are fairly simple to create and use from a technical standpoint.

LISTING 12.10

```
// Create a standard 2D stereo audiopath
HRESULT hr = m_pPerformance->CreateStandardAudioPath(
    DMUS_APATH_DYNAMIC_STEREO,
    64,
    TRUE,
    &m_pAudioPath);
if(FAILED(hr))
    return false;
```

We see here a snippet of code that is executed *before* the segment is created. If the user wishes to create a unique audiopath for a segment, an audiopath is created by using the IDirectMusicPerformance8:: CreateStandardAudioPath() function. You may remember some of these parameters from the performance's `InitAudio()` function, which is not coincidental; they helped to create the default audiopath.

The first parameter describes the types of standard audiopaths to create. There are four basic types to choose from (Table 12.4):

TABLE 12.4   Audiopath Types

Value	Description
DMUS_APATH_DYNAMIC_3D	One bus to a 3D buffer. Does not send to environmental reverb.
DMUS_APATH_DYNAMIC_MONO	One bus to a mono buffer.
DMUS_APATH_DYNAMIC_STEREO	Two buses to a stereo buffer.
DMUS_APATH_SHARED_STEREOPLUSREVERB	Ordinary music setup with stereo outs and reverb.

The second parameter defines the number of performance channels to allow for this audiopath. It does not hurt to specify a large, safe number, so 64 seems to be a good value. The third parameter determines whether the audiopath is activated on creation. The fourth parameter retrieves the audiopath interface.

Since we've been referring to 'standard' audiopaths, you may be wondering what sort of 'nonstandard' audiopaths are available. In fact, audiopath configuration files, created in the DirectMusic producer tool, can also define custom audiopaths. This tool allows an author to define specific effects for different voices. For games, however, this is not quite as handy as it may seem. The effects currently directly supported by DirectMusic are software effects, which tend to chew up an inordinate amount of processing time. The function to load audiopath configuration files from disk is called `IDirectMusicPerformance8::CreateAudiopath()`. For game development, we'll likely be most interested in creating 3D audiopaths, as each unique 3D positional sound requires its own audiopath.

The standard audiopaths give us access to the DirectSound buffers used for rendering the audio; and using these, we can set any sort of hardware-based effect we want, as long as the hardware actually supports the effect we query for. We do this by using the `IDirectMusicAudiopath8::GetObject-InPath()` function.

LISTING 12.11

```
// Get the associated DirectSound buffer for more direct
```

```
// control
hr = m_pAudioPath->GetObjectInPath(
    DMUS_PCHANNEL_ALL,
    DMUS_PATH_BUFFER,
    0,
    GUID_NULL,
    0,
    IID_IDirectSoundBuffer8,
    (void**)&m_pDSBuffer);
if(FAILED(hr))
    return false;
```

The GetObjectInPath() function is designed to retrieve any number or type of objects from a given path, and so has some general-purpose parameters. However, to retrieve a specific buffer from a standard audiopath interface is fairly simple. You can read in the SDK what all the specific parameters do. Listing 12.11 demonstrates how to retrieve the DirectSound buffer object from the audiopath. Now that we have a DirectSound buffer from this audiopath, we can perform operations directly on the buffers, such as setting hardware properties like EAX.

This covers the basic functionality and usage of audiopaths. Like segments, audiopaths have few interface functions, but they are an important component in DirectMusic. Whether you utilize and actively create and manage audiopaths yourself, or simply use default audiopaths created in your performance object, understanding the audiopath model will go a long ways toward helping you to more effectively use DirectMusic.

CONCLUSION

In this chapter, we've examined the basic capabilities of DirectMusic to play digital audio and MIDI using four basic components: performances, loaders, segments, and audiopaths. By gaining a solid understanding of simple playback and operating mechanisms, we now have a firm foundation on which to build more-advanced concepts, such as interactive segment playback and dynamic soundtrack composition. In the next chapter, we'll look at some advanced, interactive composition and playback techniques.

CHAPTER 13

ADVANCED SEGMENT QUEUING AND CONTROL

In order to truly take advantage of the power of DirectMusic, you must have a solid understanding of how the DirectMusic *segment* fits into the scheme of your audio engine, and how exactly you plan to use this jack-of-all-trades object. The uses of segments in a DirectMusic system are amazingly diverse. The primary reason for this diversity is that DirectMusic segments are designed to have some musical intelligence embedded in the content, giving maximum control to the content creator. They are capable of holding MIDI or digital audio that is statically or dynamically created, representing music, 2D, or 3D sound effects. The most difficult aspect of DirectMusic programming is deciding which features you plan to take advantage of and how you plan to encapsulate this into a reasonably easy-to-use audio system.

ON THE CD
The code listed in this chapter can be found in \Game_Audio\ audio_sdk\src\audiolib\AudioMgr.h, AudioMgr.cpp, Segment.h, Segment.cpp.

INTRODUCTION TO SEGMENTS

As was emphasized in the previous, introductory chapter on DirectMusic, segments are perhaps the most critical component in the DirectMusic-based audio system, even though the `IDirectMusicSegment8` interface does not have a large number of member functions. While the definition and usefulness of segments has expanded dramatically in the past few versions of DirectX, the original purpose of segments was to hold musical content, whether generated statically or dynamically. Now, since segments can hold either digital data or MIDI-based content, interactive audio can even use digital audio streams, providing a boon to those developers who would like the flexibility of interactive audio but don't wish to be restricted to MIDI-based music. In this musical capacity, it is important to understand how to properly queue and sequence segments for a seamless musical experience. We'll demonstrate a number of tricks and techniques you can use when creating a dynamic music system using DirectMusic.

Segments have evolved into more-general-purpose audio containers. Because they can hold digital audio as well as MIDI data, segments can now be used for both 2D and 3D sound effects. And interestingly, since segments are logically separate from the sound buffer, the simultaneous sharing of sound buffers among multiple segments is actually encouraged. While a very powerful technique, this is something of a shift in emphasis from previous versions of DirectMusic and can present a bit of a design challenge when deciding how to implement your audio system.

THE MUSIC/SOUNDFX SWITCH

The first thing that must be done in any DirectMusic-based system is to make a clear distinction between segments played as music and segments played as sound effects. There are actually two mechanisms for handling this distinction. In the previous chapter, we discussed this when introducing DirectMusic performances, explaining how two performances should be used—one for music and one for sound effects. The first thing to do is to simply make sure we always play our musical segments using the performance created exclusively for music, rather than the alternative performance object created for sound effects.

Additionally, there is a difference in the way that music versus nonmusic segments are played. Music segments are typically meant to be played sequentially; one segment at a time is played, although there certainly are exceptions to this rule. These are known as *primary segments*, and the playback queuing mechanism is something we'll be examining in more detail. Sound effect segments, on the other hand, will always be played as *secondary segments*, meaning that they do not have to synchronize to other currently playing segments, although they can do so if need be.

In the sample audio library, a simple Boolean switch is used to indicate whether the segment is played as music or as a sound effect, much in the same way as it is done for Sound and Sound3D objects. This simplistic approach works well for our limited, music-emphasized design. But if you plan to implement a full-featured DirectMusic-based sound effects engine, you would likely want to subclass the two object types—one for music playback and one for sound effects.

SEGMENTS AS MUSICAL CONTAINERS

Before we discuss how to implement segments as sound effects, we'll be examining them in their original role—as musical containers. As stated earlier, segments can contain several types of data, but for the most part, it doesn't matter what the actual content of the segment is. DirectMusic handles a MIDI-based segment just like a wave audio-based segment, which makes the programmer's job a bit simpler.

INTERFACE CONSIDERATIONS

Because the role of segments for music playback is much less complex than when they're used as a sound effects container, our basic interface will tend to represent this inherent simplicity. Like the ISound and ISound3D interfaces, the ISegment interface is derived from IAudioBase and IPlayable, and shares basic functions, such as Play(), Stop(), Load(), and Unload(). Typically, these functions do not operate directly on members of the segment themselves, but they are representative of a single, global music track. We will see how the requirements are different with a DirectMusic system that assumes segments will be used as 3D sound effects later in this chapter.

SEGMENT QUEUING AND PLAYBACK

Using segments as musical components essentially means stacking segments end-to-end along a sequential playback track. Although there are conceivably many ways to implement a segment-queuing system, we'll be demonstrating a segment-queuing method that works well within the parameters of our audio system, such as dynamic background-threaded, on-demand object loading with interface simplicity. As such, we'll be creating a system based on a couple of simple principles. Our segment playback system has the concept of a *current segment* and a *next segment*. You might think of this as a queue that can only hold two segments.

Why only two segments? While DirectMusic can actually queue any number of segments, actually doing so might prove to be somewhat impractical and cumbersome to maintain and control. In reality, you never really need to know what's coming up more than a segment in advance. This gives the music system plenty of time to load and prepare the next segment for playback. Best of all, because of this, it is easy to redirect the music playback of the primary segment to a new segment at any time, allowing the creation of truly dynamic music sequences.

Here's how this works from the client's perspective: each call to ISegment::Play() actually performs several tasks, depending on the current state of the segment itself and of the music performance. Like other sound objects in our audio system, the Play() function first checks to see if the object is actually loaded. If not, it begins a background loading process and exits the function immediately. The segment is marked for playback, so as soon as the segment is finished loading, the Play() function will be called from the loading thread. (For more details on how this works, see Chapter 15—The Audio Manager, which demonstrates a general method used in all the playable audio objects for background loading.)

Once actually loaded, the segment's Play() function first checks to see if there is a current segment playing. If not, the segment plays immediately. If there is already a segment playing, it instead tells the audio manager that it will be the next segment to play. In essence, it places itself at the back of the two-segment queue.

When the current segment is finished playing, the audio manager smoothly transitions to the new segment. After this point, when a new segment's Play() function is called, it will then be placed in the queue for playback when the current segment is finished. In this manner, a segment can be played at any time and will always transition smoothly from the end of one segment to the beginning of another. Figure 13.1 shows the basic progression of events and important notifications during the queuing and playback process.

The segment-queuing process is quite simple for the client programmer and essentially allows a bulletproof system for basic transitions from segment to segment. The key to successfully implementing this transition system is in the combination of a dual-purpose Segment::Play() function and the use of performance-based notification messages to trigger the actual queuing/playback of sequential segments. Let's take a look at the Segment::Play() function to see how this works. Before we do, though, we'll introduce a couple of other functions that are important.

Inside the audio manager, we maintain a current pointer to both the current and next segments. These are set and retrieved with a set of four functions: AudioManager::SetCurrentSegment(), AudioManager::

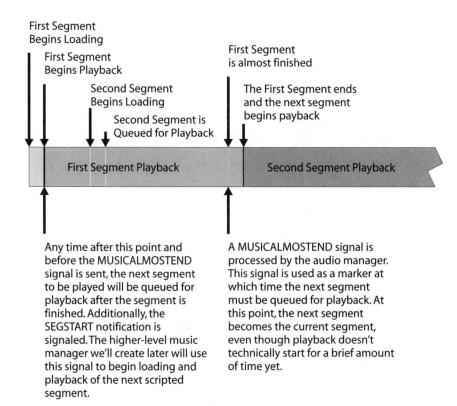

First Segment Begins Loading

First Segment Begins Playback

Second Segment Begins Loading

Second Segment is Queued for Playback

First Segment is almost finished

The First Segment ends and the next segment begins payback

First Segment Playback

Second Segment Playback

Any time after this point and before the MUSICALMOSTEND signal is sent, the next segment to be played will be queued for playback after the segment is finished. Additionally, the SEGSTART notification is signaled. The higher-level music manager we'll create later will use this signal to begin loading and playback of the next scripted segment.

A MUSICALMOSTEND signal is processed by the audio manager. This signal is used as a marker at which time the next segment must be queued for playback. At this point, the next segment becomes the current segment, even though playback doesn't technically start for a brief amount of time yet.

FIGURE 13.1   Timeline of segment queuing and events for musical playback.

GetCurrentSegment(), AudioManager::SetNextSegment(), and Audio Manager::GetNextSegment(), which work just as you would expect them to. Additionally, the real work of playing the segment actually happens in Segment::DoPlay(). The Segment::Play() function is actually used to determine whether the segment should be queued for playback next or should be played immediately, in which the DoPlay() function is called. You can see all this at work in Listing 13.1.

LISTING 13.1

```
bool Segment::Play()
{
    // Determine if we need to load this buffer before
```

```
// playing. After the buffer is finished loading,
// playback will begin automatically.
if(IsLoading())
    return true;
else if(!IsLoaded())
{
    m_bQueuePlayback = true;
    return Load();
}
// Clear queue play flag
m_bQueuePlayback = false;

// If this is a non-musical segment, play it
// immediately as a secondary segment
if(!m_Init.m_bMusic)
    return DoPlay();

if(DXAudioMgr()->GetCurrentSegment() &&
!DXAudioMgr()->GetCurrentSegment()->IsPlaying())
    DXAudioMgr()->SetCurrentSegment(0);

if(!DXAudioMgr()->GetCurrentSegment())
{
    DXAudioMgr()->SetCurrentSegment(this);
    DXAudioMgr()->SetNextSegment(0);
    return DoPlay();
}
else
{
    DXAudioMgr()->SetNextSegment(this);
}
return true;
}
```

The first part of the function, as explained earlier, checks the load status and loads the segment as necessary. Next, we check for the flag that indicates whether this is a music or sound effects segment. If it is a sound effect, the segment is played immediately by calling DoPlay(). Otherwise, we proceed to a series of conditional checks to determine what to do with the segment.

The first check we make is to see if there is a current segment that is *not* playing. In this case, we clear out the current segment variable in preparation for our next check. After this, we check to see if there is a current segment (which, if still there, is guaranteed to be playing because of our first test). If no segment is found, this segment becomes the current segment, the next segment variable is cleared, and the segment begins playing immediately. If, on the other hand, there is a currently playing segment, the segment becomes the next segment queued to play, which is accomplished by simply passing the this pointer to the SetNextSegment() function.

The DoPlay() function is in fact much less complicated than the Play() function. It's shown in Listing 13.2.

LISTING 13.2

```
bool Segment::DoPlay()
{
    if (!m_pSegment)
        return false;

    // Set the flags based on the type of content
    // (music or sound fx)
    DWORD dwFlags = 0;
    if (m_Init.m_bMusic)
        dwFlags = DMUS_SEGF_QUEUE | DMUS_SEGF_DEFAULT;
    else
        dwFlags = DMUS_SEGF_SECONDARY;

    if (m_bPaused)
        m_pSegment->SetStartPoint(m_iPauseTime);

    // Now play the segment
    IDirectMusicSegmentState* pSegState = 0;
    HRESULT hr;
    hr = DXAudioMgr()->Performance(
        m_Init.m_bMusic)->PlaySegmentEx(
            m_pSegment, NULL, NULL, dwFlags, 0,
            &pSegState, NULL, NULL);
    if (FAILED(hr))
        return false;

    // Reset the new start time to the beginning
```

```
// of the segment
if(m_bPaused)
{
    m_iPauseTime = 0;
    m_pSegment->SetStartPoint(m_iPauseTime);
}

// Not paused anymore...
m_bPaused = false;

// Get the segment state object
if (!pSegState)
    return false;
hr = pSegState->QueryInterface(
    IID_IDirectMusicSegmentState8,
    (void**) &m_pSegState);
if (FAILED(hr))
    return false;

// Get the time played for prioritization purposes
m_nLastTimePlayed = timeGetTime();

return true;
}
```

This play code looks pretty much like the example code you might find in the SDK, except for a few details. Pausing and restarting a segment is a little trickier in DirectMusic than it is in DirectSound, as there is no 'pause' type function. As such, we must determine the current read position when we call our Segment::Pause() function, just before we stop the segment and store it in our own variable. You can see we must manually set the start point of the segment (using the SetStartPoint() function) to begin at the time when we start it up again. After the segment is started, we must be sure to set the start point back to the beginning of the segment—position zero.

Note that for music performance segments, we apply the flags DMUS_SEGF_QUEUE and DMUS_SEGF_DEFAULT when calling the PlaySegmentEx() function. This tells the function to queue the segment for playback after the current segment is finished. Without these flags, the segment will interrupt the currently playing segment, which is not what we're after in this case. There may be cases in which you actually do wish to interrupt the currently

■ **PAUSING WAVE SEGMENTS IN DIRECTMUSIC**

Although wave files can be loaded directly and used as segments, there is at least one significant problem in doing so. A wave file that is loaded as a segment has an inherent DirectMusic length of one. Since you are not allowed to set the start position past the end of the length of the segment, pausing and restarting the segment at an arbitrary location will not work.

The only way to solve this problem is to use waves embedded in segment files instead of loaded at run-time, as the length can then be set inside the DirectMusic Producer authoring tool.

playing segment, and DirectMusic gives you control over how the interruption actually takes place. However, our music system does not take advantage of this functionality. See the DirectMusic documentation for details.

The Play() and related DoPlay() functions are only half of the interactive music queuing system. The other half of the system works by responding to DirectMusic performance events. In Chapter 12, we learned how to set up and handle various events. Now we'll see a practical application of a few of them. Listing 13.3 shows how to respond to two of these events in the music event thread described in Chapter 12.

LISTING 13.3

```
while (S_OK ==
    m_pMusicPerformance->GetNotificationPMsg(&pPmsg))
{
    if (pPmsg->guidNotificationType ==
        GUID_NOTIFICATION_PERFORMANCE)
    {
        if (pPmsg->dwNotificationOption ==
            DMUS_NOTIFICATION_MUSICALMOSTEND)
        {
            if (!m_pCurrentSegment)
                break;

            if (m_pCurrentSegment->IsLooping() &&
                !m_pNextSegment)
            {
```

```
                ISegment* pSeg = m_pCurrentSegment;
                m_pCurrentSegment = 0;
                m_pNextSegment = 0;
                pSeg->Play();
            }
            else if (m_pNextSegment)
            {
                ISegment* pSeg = m_pNextSegment;
                m_pCurrentSegment = 0;
                m_pNextSegment = 0;
                pSeg->Play();
            }
        }
    }
    else if (pPmsg->guidNotificationType ==
        GUID_NOTIFICATION_SEGMENT)
    {
        if (pPmsg->dwNotificationOption ==
            DMUS_NOTIFICATION_SEGSTART)
        {
            if (m_Init.m_pMusicCallback)
              m_Init.m_pMusicCallback->OnSegmentStart();
        }
    }
    m_pMusicPerformance->FreePMsg((DMUS_PMSG*)pPmsg);
}
```

The mechanism is fairly simple. When a performance is about to finish playing, it sends a DMUS_NOTIFICATION_MUSICALMOSTEND message. We respond to this event in a couple of different ways. If the currently playing segment is designated as a looping segment, and there is no segment queued to play behind it, we simply play the current segment again. This may seem like an odd way of looping segments instead of using the normal DirectMusic looping mechanism, but it is really the simplest way to transition from a looping segment to another segment. The disadvantage of this method is that we are giving up the feature of loop points set inside segments (but only for musical segments, remember). Generally speaking, though, anything that can be done with loop points can also be done by splitting up the segment into multiple parts and queuing them independently, so it's not too much of a deterrent.

If there is a new segment queued behind the current playing segment, the segment pointers are set to `null` and the new segment's `Play()` function is called. This will then appropriately set the next segment as the current segment, and the cycle will begin again.

This is the heart of the DirectMusic-based interactive music system—the ability to queue segments for playback and ensure a smooth transition from music section to music section. In Chapter 18—An Interactive Music Playback System, we'll see how we can build on this basic functionality to create a dynamic and flexible interactive music system that can be driven entirely from data scripts and simple state commands.

One other thing you may notice is that we are also making use of a callback function that is called every time the `DMUS_NOTIFICATION_SEGSTART` notification message is handled. This is the only event that our high-level music system needs in order to properly load and queue segments. However, for various reasons, it may be beneficial for you to add notification-related callback functions of your own. For instance, you might be interested in receiving a notification on every beat if you have a character that is supposed to dance to the music in your game. These should be simple to add to the existing notification structure in the audio engine, or you may decide to create your own.

■ INTERACTIVE MUSIC SYSTEM DESIGN CHOICES

You may be wondering about other playback options, such as interrupting a segment at the closest beat or measure instead of at the end of the segment. We have specifically chosen to disallow partial-segment interruptions for the sake of simplicity, and also because this allows us to choose segment transitions immediately after the first segment begins playback in our high-level music manager. This happens to work best with our audio manager's ability to load segments in the background on a separate thread. However, there should be no problems if you wish to implement this sort of additional flexibility with your music system.

There are literally thousands of combinations of DirectMusic segment playback/queuing options and strategies that could be used, and it's simply not possible to utilize every single one of them, nor is it good design practice. After all, there is little point in creating an API wrapper layer that simply duplicates all the functionality of the lower-level API. Instead, it's best to offer a reasonable subset of functionality that you expect to be useful while offering enhanced functionality and greater ease of use with the features you do support. If features are not available in your original implementation that you later find could be useful, just add them as you go.

SEGMENTS AS DIGITAL AUDIO SAMPLES

Beginning with DirectX 8, and now even more so in DirectX 9, DirectMusic can be used not only for playback of MIDI-based and digital interactive music, but also for playing all the sound effects in an audio system. With the introduction of a low-latency audio sync, DirectX 9 can offer responsive performance similar to DirectSound, but with much greater functionality—and in some cases, greater efficiency.

SEGMENTS, AUDIOPATHS, AND API CONSIDERATIONS

One of the first steps in understanding how to effectively use segments for sound effects playback is to understand the conceptual differences between a DirectMusic segment and a DirectSound buffer. While on the surface these two objects might seem analogous, a segment is in fact very different from a simple buffer. The most obvious difference is, of course, the varied composition of a segment—it can contain MIDI data, digital audio data, or even a combination of the two. Not only that, it can also contain multiple tracks and variations of a piece of music or sound effect, as well as references to other DirectMusic composition elements, such as styles, bands, and DLS banks.

More fundamentally, though, a segment only represents the audio data; whereas a DirectSound buffer (or a DirectSound3D buffer) actually represents both the data and the hardware channel to play it. In DirectMusic, audiopaths most closely represent the concept of a destination channel in hardware.

As you can see in Figure 13.2, segments and audiopaths create a distinct separation between audio data and the destination where that data must play, unlike DirectSound buffers, which lump the data and destination into a single object. Additionally, segments are not restricted to playback on a single destination audiopath. A single segment can play on multiple audiopath destinations, even simultaneously. This is accomplished through the use of a separate segment-state object that is created when a segment begins playing. This segment-state object provides an interface for controlling the segment. Otherwise, a simple function call to the segment object itself, such as Stop(), would not know which instance was being referred to. It is clear that the segment+segment=state+audiopath paradigm represents a definite technical advantage in overall resource usage and flexibility. What is not clear, however, is how best to take advantage of this power.

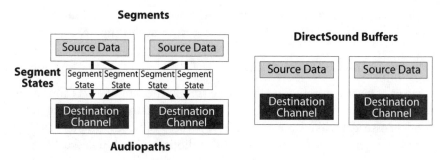

FIGURE 13.2   Relationship of data source and destination output for DirectMusic segments and audiopaths versus DirectSound buffers.

In fact, you may note that the sample audio library only uses segments in a fairly limited fashion, primarily for interactive musical playback, instead of providing a full implementation using the multiple audiopath techniques described previously. Why was this done? As must be obvious by looking at Figure 13.2, with the additional power of this paradigm comes a great deal of added complexity. In essence, if you wish to take full advantage of this sort of individual component-based system, you must be prepared to manage up to three interfaces for every sound you wish to play. Compare this to the simplicity of a DirectSound 'all-inclusive' sound buffer object, and you may begin to understand how it can be a design dilemma to create a streamlined and easy-to-use audio API using this approach.

There are other design considerations, as well, that must be taken into account. Generally speaking, there are very few audio APIs, even low-level ones, that provide this sort of power and flexibility in an audio system. If you know for certain that you will be developing only on platforms for which DirectMusic will be available (hint: there's only two of them), it may make sense for you to more-closely model your API on the DirectMusic objects, providing a very thin wrapper to the game system. If, however, you know that you will need to write multiple versions of the API interface (one for each platform), it is likely that you won't be able to easily duplicate this functionality on every platform.

In the end, how you decide to use the DirectMusic/DirectSound combination is a decision that can only be made by your knowing how and where your audio system will be used. Because the sample audio system provided with this book primarily utilizes the lower-level DirectSound API for sound effects, we'll spend some time examining how we might have designed a more-DirectMusic-focused API instead, and we'll look at some of the benefits that doing so can provide in your audio engine.

THE DIRECTMUSIC-CENTRIC API

Instead of basing our audio API on the simple concept of a '2D sound' or a '3D Sound,' where the entire object is self-contained, the DirectMusic model instead breaks up a sound into three basic components that are based on segments, segment states, and audiopaths. An API based on these three components would reflect the following functionality:

Segment Responsibilities
- Initialize and load segment and wave data.
- Begin playback on a specified audiopath, and return a segment state for control.

Segment State Responsibilities
- Allow interruption and continuation of a currently playing segment on a particular audiopath.

Audiopath Responsibilities
- Control buffer properties, such as volume, pan (2D only), and pitch.
- Control 3D buffer properties, such as position and velocity.
- Expose hardware property sets for buffers.

You can see how the API might be formed from these object responsibilities. To get an idea of what it might look like, simply examine the sample audio API's implementation of IAudioBase and ISound3D, reassigning the functions of each to three different objects based on the criteria listed previously. Listing 13.4 shows what some of the more-important functions might look like:

LISTING 13.4

```
class ISegment
{
public:
```

```
    virtual bool Init(const SegmentInit& init) = 0;
    virtual void Destroy() = 0;

    virtual bool Play(IAudioPath* pAudioPath) = 0;
    virtual bool Play(IAudioPath* pAudioPath,
        ISegmentState*& pSegState) = 0;
};


class ISegmentState
{
public:
    virtual bool Pause() = 0;
    virtual bool Stop() = 0;
    virtual bool Resume() = 0;

    virtual void Release() = 0;
};


class IAudioPath
{
public:
    virtual bool Init(const AudioPathInit& init) = 0;

    virtual bool Activate() = 0;
    virtual void Deactivate() = 0;

    virtual bool SetVolume(float fVolume) = 0;
    virtual bool GetVolume(float& fVolume) = 0;

    virtual bool SetProperties(
        const AudioPath3DProp& prop) = 0;
    virtual bool SetProperties(
        const AudioPath3DProp& prop) = 0;
};
```

The basic playback of sounds occurs by connecting segments to audiopaths with the Play() function. There are two overloaded versions available. If you are not interested in controlling the playback of the sound once it has begun, there is no need to obtain the `ISegmentState` interface, which helps to simplify things. Or, if you prefer, we might have included a `Play()` function in the `IAudioPath` definition and passed in an `ISegment` interface pointer instead. It works either way, depending on how you wish to view the connection being established between the two objects.

Note that the `IAudioPath` interface has the members and properties typically associated with a 3D DirectSound buffer, and in fact this is basically what it represents. The `Activate()` and `Deactivate()` methods determine whether the buffer is available for playback or not. This can be used as a way of maintaining a maximum number of DirectMusic-managed buffers.

An altogether different approach might be used, or might even be used alongside manual audiopath manipulation. You may decide that placing the responsibility of managing audiopaths with the client will be too cumbersome, and so you could have the audio system automatically create, assign, and use audiopaths as best it can. In order to conserve audiopath usage, you can create collections of segments designed to use a single audiopath, such as three or four sound effects that belong to a single 3D entity.

DIRECTMUSIC AUDIOPATHS AND DIRECTSOUND BUFFERS

So, if we wish to use DirectMusic as our primary sound effects playback mechanism, how exactly do we control, say, the position of a 3D sound or a listener object? DirectMusic does not actually have APIs for performing these tasks. Instead, it relies on the lower-level DirectSound APIs for performing these tasks. DirectSound buffers and listener interfaces can be retrieved from audiopaths, as long as the audiopaths were created with the proper settings; for instance, you can only retrieve a 3D buffer if the audiopath was created with 3D properties. In this way, the audiopath's interface is extended to include the lower-level DirectSound interfaces, in a manner of speaking. Listing 13.5 demonstrates what it looks like to retrieve 2D and 3D DirectSound buffer interfaces from an audiopath.

LISTING 13.5

```
// Get the DirectSound buffer
IDirectSoundBuffer8* pBuffer;
hr = m_pdmusAudioPath->GetObjectInPath(
    DMUS_PCHANNEL_ALL,
    DMUS_PATH_BUFFER,
```

```
    0,
    GUID_NULL,
    0,
    IID_IDirectSoundBuffer8,
    (void**)&m_pBuffer);
if(FAILED(hr))
    return false;

// perform some action with the buffer

// Release the buffer
pBuffer->Release();


// Get the DirectSound 3D buffer
IDirectSound3DBuffer8* pBuffer3D;
m_pdmusAudioPath->GetObjectInPath(
    DMUS_PCHANNEL_ALL,
    DMUS_PATH_BUFFER,
    0,
    GUID_NULL,
    0,
    IID_IDirectSound3DBuffer8,
    (void**)&m_pBuffer3D);
if(FAILED(hr))
    return false;

// perform some action with the 3D buffer

// Release the 3D buffer
pBuffer3D->Release();
```

If you plan to dynamically activate and deactivate audiopaths, it is probably a good idea to release the buffers immediately after you perform any required actions on them.

DIRECTMUSIC RESOURCE MANAGEMENT

Management of DirectMusic resources is a slightly different problem than with DirectSound, as well. While DirectSound imposes an artificial limit on the number of sounds loaded at once, based on the number of hardware resources, DirectMusic provides no such meaningful restriction. Instead, you will need to manage two sets of resources—segments and audiopaths. Audiopaths should be limited to a maximum number because audio systems are restricted as to the number of hardware 3D buffers that can be created, and the same general principles should apply to DirectMusic as to DirectSound: it's not a good idea to mix hardware and software buffers in the same audio environment.

In essence, we really only need to worry about the maximum number of *active* audiopaths at any one time. The function `IDirectMusic-AudioPath9::Activate()` takes a Boolean variable as an argument, setting the audiopath as active or not active. By using this feature of the audiopath interface, we can help to ensure that hardware resources are used most efficiently. An overview of buffer-management techniques was covered in Chapter 11—DirectSound Buffer Management. While it deals with DirectSound buffers, not audiopaths, the same principles would apply when dealing with DirectMusic audiopath management.

Segments, on the other hand, might well be managed simply by the amount of memory they occupy instead of their number, although either method could be effective in keeping a basic lid on the total resources used.

CONCLUSION

In this chapter, we've learned much more about the most important component in DirectMusic—the segment. These versatile objects can represent everything from a static chunk of digital audio to a dynamically composed piece of MIDI data, and can be used as the heart of both an interactive music system or a more-general-purpose audio effects playback and control system. While in some ways vastly simpler than basic DirectSound playback, DirectMusic has many complexities all its own. But DirectMusic can certainly pay big dividends in efficiency and functionality if you take the time to get to know how the system works.

In the next chapter, we'll demonstrate a few additional DirectMusic tricks and techniques that you may find useful.

CHAPTER 14

ADDITIONAL DIRECTMUSIC TECHNIQUES

DirectMusic is a vast API with an amazing amount of versatility. In addition to the basic mechanisms we've covered in the previous chapters, there are ways to squeeze even more functionality out of DirectMusic. We'll be briefly examining DirectMusic container files, scripts, and dynamically generated segments in this chapter. While most of these techniques are not utilized in the *GAP* audio library supplied on the CD-ROM (except for audio scripting), they are important components of DirectMusic that merit closer examination and discussion.

The code listed in this chapter can be found in
\Game_Audio\Voice Script\VoiceScript.pro
\Game_Audio\audio_sdk\src\audiolib\AudioScript.h,
AudioScript.cpp.

DIRECTMUSIC CONTAINER FILES

DirectMusic has the ability to load 'container' files that can hold any number of standard DirectMusic objects. These containers are created by the DirectMusic Producer application. So, what good is a container file, exactly, and why might you want to use it?

A DirectMusic container file is exactly what it sounds like—a digital version of a cardboard box. It's just used as a convenient way to pack things together for easier storage and/or loading. If your game, for instance, has a collection of scripts, segments, or DLS files, all of which are related in some manner (e.g., all of the objects for a particular musical theme), then it might be desirable for you to pack them all into a single container (see

Figure 14.1). One particularly useful occasion for containers is when they are used in conjunction with custom file-packing systems. Generally speaking, when using a custom file system, you will be loading the file into memory yourself via some custom routines and then passing the memory into the GetObject() function instead of having it load directly from a disk.

IDirectMusicContainer8

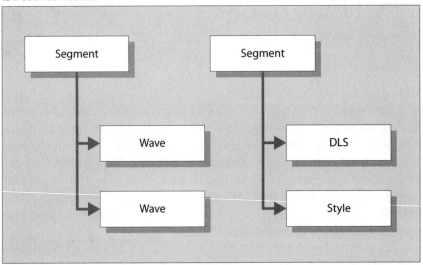

FIGURE 14.1   Container file with linked objects inside.

Many types of DirectMusic segments require implicit loading of the companion files to which they are linked. As an example, a segment might require a number of wave files to be loaded before it can be played. Using a traditional file system, you would use the loader to scan and enumerate the objects in the directory, ensuring that the loader can then find them when needed. Unfortunately, this is impossible to do with a custom file system.

However, an easy way of ensuring that all the necessary files are loaded and ready for use is to pack them all into a single container file that is explicitly loaded by the application. In this manner, when the container file is loaded, you ensure that all the necessary files are also loaded, such as a segment along with its linked wave files.

A DirectMusic container object is loaded just like any other DirectMusic object via the DirectMusic loader, using either GetObject() (as shown in the following code) or the somewhat more specialized LoadObjectFromFile().

LISTING 14.1

```
IDirectMusicContainer8* pContainer;

HRESULT hr;
DMUS_OBJECTDESC ObjDesc;
ObjDesc.dwSize = sizeof(DMUS_OBJECTDESC);
ObjDesc.guidClass = CLSID_DirectMusicContainer;
ObjDesc.dwValidData = DMUS_OBJ_CLASS | DMUS_OBJ_MEMORY;
ObjDesc.pbMemData = m_pBuffer;
ObjDesc.llMemLength = m_nBufferSize;

// Load the data and retrieve the container interface
hr = DXAudioMgr()->Loader()->GetObject(
    &ObjDesc,
    IID_IDirectMusicContainer8,
    (void**)&pContainer );
```

In Listing 14.1, we demonstrate loading a container from a memory buffer, which we would have previously filled by loading directly from the container file on disk or by loading it from a custom resource system. Once this container is loaded, we can now load other DirectMusic objects by name instead of loading them explicitly by filename. This means that instead of passing in the name of the file, you pass in the name of the object as it appears in DirectMusic Producer. When doing this, you must also let the loader know that you are attempting to retrieve an object by name, not by filename. Listing 14.2 demonstrates how to load a segment by name:

LISTING 14.2

```
IDirectMusicSegment8* pSegment;

HRESULT hr;
DMUS_OBJECTDESC ObjDesc;
ObjDesc.dwSize = sizeof(DMUS_OBJECTDESC);
ObjDesc.guidClass = CLSID_DirectMusicSegment;
ObjDesc.dwValidData = DMUS_OBJ_CLASS | DMUS_OBJ_NAME;
ObjDesc.wszName = wszObjectName;

// Load the data and retrieve the container interface
```

```
hr = DXAudioMgr()->Loader()->GetObject(
    &ObjDesc,
    IID_IDirectMusicSegment8,
    (void**)&pSegment);
```

Although we haven't added direct support for containers in the *GAP* audio library, it would be a fairly simple matter to use a Boolean flag in an object's initialization parameter to designate whether a file is loading by name or by filename. Additionally, a basic IContainer class would handle the actual loading and unloading of the container data itself. In this way, loading files from a custom resource becomes much simpler. Additionally, because the data is loading in a single large chunk, this method may end up being more efficient overall, as well.

If you wished to add this sort of functionality, you would be well advised to look at the DLS class as a potential model for a container class, as it is really nothing more than a specialized container class itself. The DLS class utilizes a COM-like reference-counting mechanism to ensure that it is loaded whenever any segment that is using the DLS collection is also loaded.

In addition to loading objects explicitly by name, it is also possible to enumerate objects already loaded via the container, using the function IDirectMusicContainer9::EnumObject(). However, this function seems less useful to games where the content is typically known in advance; but it would be useful for authoring applications.

DIRECTMUSIC SCRIPTS

DirectMusic scripting is a very powerful mechanism that can be used to provide a sound designer with an amazing amount of programming power. However, as with all things related to procedural scripting, you should definitely proceed with caution. As such, you must decide carefully if you wish to use this set of features.

SCRIPTING PROS AND CONS

DirectMusic scripting provides a set of functionality that actually goes beyond the original concept of an abstract audio system, mainly because this sort of scripting system is so specific to DirectMusic. Although we've exposed the concept of a 'generic' ISegment object that is roughly modeled on the DirectMusic segment, this limited abstraction could still apply to a MIDI file using sound banks on alternative platforms, for example. Creating an abstract interface for a script object is simple enough, and we've done this as a demonstration for you, but it would present a challenge to a programmer who wanted to duplicate this functionality on a non-DirectX platform. Even though our sample library only features a DirectSound/DirectMusic implementation, we've attempted to keep the feature set somewhat portable as a design exercise.

One way that an audio scripting system could be easily ported to other platforms is to cheat a bit with the script implementation. A game ported to a non-DirectX platform could simply create a hard-coded module (using standard C++) that would emulate the functionality of the script system. Each created script 'object' would simply be an entry point into a separate set of routines and variables, and these would individually perform identical behaviors, as the original DirectMusic scripts. Because we've enforced a simplified abstract interface on the DirectMusic script objects, this should be technically feasible, if not all that elegant.

■ LUA: A CROSS-PLATFORM SCRIPTING LANGUAGE

More realistically, if you need to perform audio scripting across different platforms on which DirectMusic is not supported, you should investigate the possible use of a true cross-platform scripting solution, such as Lua (*http://www.lua.org*).

As a final point, consider that in order to really be able to take advantage of DirectMusic scripts, your audio designer must be willing to actually take on a bit of simple programming, or at least have a need to do so. If you're finding that there's something that would just be too difficult using your engine, it could very well be that looking into scripts would be worthwhile.

SCRIPTING BASICS

There are two basic ways that DirectMusic scripts can be used. An application can either support scripts explicitly by loading them and calling routines using the object's interface, or a segment can call script routines from a script track embedded in a segment. The great thing about embedding segments is that it requires no additional work at all for the audio programmer—the sound designer simply creates the script to use, then makes appropriate calls using the script track. In practice, apart from some tricks such as automatically randomizing segment playback, there are not too many things that can actually be done without some sort of feedback from the program, mostly because the subset of Visual Basic that is actually used is fairly limited in scope.

This essentially leaves us with the first method—direct programming support in the audio engine—in order to make scripting really useful (or a combination of the two methods). Creating a scripting strategy is a lot like object-oriented programming class design. The internals of the scripts are less important than the defined interface and expected behavior. In the case of DirectMusic scripting, the interface consists of named variables with values that can be set and retrieved by the program, and routines that can be executed.

Sound designers and composers have a number of options at their disposal when creating scripts. Segments and other DirectMusic objects can be embedded inside scripts and referenced inside the script as objects, and simple variables and routines can be created using a subset of the Visual Basic language to perform basic tasks on these objects. The DirectMusic Producer help document has a comprehensive reference that includes a section on writing scripts. So if you're curious about what can actually be accomplished in these scripts, you should check it out.

As a C++ programmer working on either the engine or game side, however, your task is fairly straightforward. You are able to perform three tasks with DirectMusic scripts:

- Load and unload scripts.
- Set and retrieve variables or objects.
- Call script routines.

How and when each of these events happens is as specific to a game as when individual sounds are loaded and played. In fact, you will likely substitute a standard Sound::Play() call with a script routine call instead, with perhaps a preceding variable or two called as a primitive form of argument passing, and let the script decide what actually gets played and how.

Typically, you would sit down with your audio designer or composer and define a set of events and variables that you can agree will provide sufficient information to the scripts in order to do whatever is needed. For instance, the two of you may decide that every time the player encounters a new creature in your game, a preset number of variables would describe the player's health and level, the monster's name, and how many creatures are viewable. Then, the EncounterMonster routine would be called. The designer might then use this information to select a phrase that the game character can speak that is dependent on what the character is actually seeing. If the game character sees two snow bunnies hopping up to attack him, the "Bring it on!" sample is played (it would be a wave file embedded in a segment, most likely). If, on the other hand, 23 orcs are seen charging down the dungeon corridor, a sample playing "This is gonna hurt...." could be called instead. Additionally, the segments played could contain randomly chosen variations, which provides a bit more interest. In this manner, the sound designer has complete control over how sounds get played in very specific situations.

Let's examine a very simple script (VoiceScript.pro)that you can find in the examples on the CD-ROM Game_Audio/Voice Script. This script compares a player's strength to a monster's strength and plays one of three segments, each containing a number of variations of appropriate settings. Listing 14.3 shows this script it its entirety.

LISTING 14.3

```
dim PlayerStrength
dim MonsterStrength

sub EncounterMonster
    if PlayerStrength < MonsterStrength then
        negative.Play
    elseif PlayerStrength = MonsterStrength then
        even.Play
    else
        positive.Play
    end if
end sub
```

Even if you're not familiar with Visual Basic or VB script, it shouldn't be too hard to understand what is happening inside this script. We are using two variables, PlayerStrength and MonsterStrength, to determine what type of reaction a character in the game has when encountering a monster. The identifiers negative, even, and positive are all segments that are embedded in the script, and so are accessible as objects.

Each of these segments is designed to play one of a number of sample voice recordings at random, using track variations. You can open the DirectMusic project VoiceScript.pro again to see how this was done. Alternatively, we could have used the Rand function, which is a member of the Performance object, to randomly choose between individual segments.

In order to use this function, the script must first be loaded, of course. Then, whenever the game character encounters a monster, the relevant strengths of the player and the monster are sent to the script, and the EncounterMonster routine is called by passing the name of the function to DirectMusic (we'll see how this works later). The script will respond by playing a voice recording that is appropriate to the situation based on the variables you set inside the script.

Theoretically, much more information could be used in the routine (e.g., the number of monsters, what type of monster, etc.), and the response could be quite interesting and specific to the situation. The beauty of this system is that the programmer simply passes designated information, and the audio designer can use it however he wishes, without having to bother the programmer to continuously tweak and recompile a minor algorithm. And, this is done without having to write a complex and custom scripting language of your own.

You can read the DirectMusic Producer help files for specific information on creating audio scripts. Additionally, MSDN (*msdn.microsoft.com*) has some excellent online tutorials that describe some advanced audio-scripting techniques.

LOADING AND UNLOADING SCRIPTS

Loading and unloading a script should be no real mystery for you at this point. It works exactly like every other DirectMusic object—through the loader, using either LoadObjectFromFile() or GetObject(). Listing 14.4 shows a portion of the AudioScript::Load() function. Again, we're loading the file from a memory buffer using the IDirectMusicLoader8::GetObject() function.

LISTING 14.4

```
HRESULT hr;
DMUS_OBJECTDESC ObjDesc;
ObjDesc.dwSize = sizeof(DMUS_OBJECTDESC);
```

```
ObjDesc.guidClass = CLSID_DirectMusicScript;
ObjDesc.dwValidData = DMUS_OBJ_CLASS | DMUS_OBJ_MEMORY;
ObjDesc.pbMemData = m_pBuffer;
ObjDesc.llMemLength = m_nBufferSize;

// Load the data and retrieve the segment interface
hr = DXAudioMgr()->Loader()->GetObject(
    &ObjDesc,
    IID_IDirectMusicScript8,
    (void**) &m_pScript );
if(FAILED(hr))
{
    Unload();
    return false;
}

hr = m_pScript->Init(DXAudioMgr()-
>Performance(m_Init.m_bMusic), NULL);
if(FAILED(hr))
{
    Unload();
    return false;
}
```

Once the audio script is loaded, you must associate it with a particular performance. You can see how we choose either the sound effects performance or the music performance in our audio manager based on an initialization flag in the preceding code.

Unloading a script is similar to unloading a container. Unless specific objects that are embedded or referenced in the script are being used, they will be unloaded as well. Listing 14.5 shows how the script is unloaded. Note that we also ensure the loader's cache is flushed by calling `ReleaseObjectByUnknown()` and `CollectGarbage()`, helping to achieve more optimal use of memory in case multiple scripts are loaded and unloaded as the game progresses.

LISTING 14.5

```
bool AudioScript::Unload()
{
```

```
    if(m_pScript)
    {
        // Since we're loading and unloading segments
        // dynamically, it is important to release
        // the loader's internal reference to the segments.
        DXAudioMgr()->Loader()->ReleaseObjectByUnknown(
            m_pScript);

        // Instruct the loader to clear out unused memory.
        DXAudioMgr()->Loader()->CollectGarbage();

        // Now release the actual segment
        SAFE_RELEASE(m_pScript);
    }
    m_nBufferSize = 0;
    SAFE_DELETE_ARRAY(m_pBuffer);
    return true;
}
```

SETTING AND RETRIEVING VARIABLES OR OBJECTS

The only way to transfer data between the script and the program is to set and retrieve variables. This is no more difficult than calling the SetVariableVariant() or GetVariableVariant() routines. If you're just using integer variables, you have the option of using the functions SetVariableNumber() or GetVariableNumber(). Simply identify the name of the variable you wish to set or retrieve with a string identifier that matches the variable name in the script. Listing 14.6 shows the integer version of the AudioScript::SetVariable() function.

LISTING 14.6

```
bool AudioScript::SetVariable(string sVarName,
    int32 iVal)
{
    if(!m_pScript)
        return false;

    WCHAR wsBuffer[_MAX_PATH];
    ConvertAnsiStringToWide(wsBuffer, sVarName.c_str());
```

```
HRESULT hr = m_pScript->SetVariableNumber(
    wsBuffer, iVal, NULL);
if(FAILED(hr))
    return false;

return true;
}
```

If you are using 8-bit character strings, like in the *GAP* library, you will have to convert them to wide-character strings. We use a utility function, ConvertAnsiStringToWide(), which was copied from the DirectX SDK sample libraries.

CALLING SCRIPT ROUTINES

Calling a script routine is even simpler than changing a variable. Simply pass in the name of the routine to the IDirectMusicScript9::Call-Routine() function. Listing 14.7 demonstrates this.

LISTING 14.7

```
bool AudioScript::CallRoutine(string sRoutineName)
{
    if(!m_pScript)
        return false;

    WCHAR wsBuffer[_MAX_PATH];
    ConvertAnsiStringToWide(wsBuffer,
        sRoutineName.c_str());
    HRESULT hr = m_pScript->CallRoutine(wsBuffer, NULL);
    if(FAILED(hr))
        return false;

    return true;
}
```

That's really all there is on the programming side to using audio scripts. Generally speaking, the majority of work for you (the C++ programmer) is in defining the script names, variables, and routines that will act as an interface between the code and the audio scripts. This will involve working closely with the audio designer to determine what functionality should be exposed and utilized in the audio scripts. Once these interfaces are established, however, your work as a programmer is essentially finished, and the real work of creating the audio scripts and providing interesting content can then begin.

DYNAMIC SEGMENT CREATION

Up until this point, we've been considering DirectMusic segments as somewhat static entities. Any dynamic aspect of the musical score was created through the sequencing order of individual segments or by variations within the segment itself (although we, as programmers, don't really have to worry about that, since it is automatic). There are a few other ways to manipulate a musical score, which we'll be briefly examining here.

Although the capabilities for dynamic composition in DirectMusic are quite extensive, creating such a flexible and dynamic soundtrack might prove neither practical nor necessary for most titles. This is why most of the focus of this book regarding DirectMusic has been on utilizing simpler composition methods that do not require such huge conceptual leaps, making the audio system simpler to develop and compose for. For instance, the techniques used in segment-based interactive composition allow composers to choose their content delivery method of choice—either waveform audio tracks or MIDI+DLS-based segments. Interactive composition using this method simply involves creating small building blocks of segments that can be chained together to form larger patterns, with manually created transitional elements bridging the gaps between dissimilar pieces of music. This is not terribly unlike traditional linear composition, except that the soundtrack must be chopped into smaller segments and rearranged in pleasing patterns. This method of interactive music provides a good degree of dynamic responsiveness combined with the familiarity of more-traditional composition methods, making it an ideal combination for most developers. Indeed, from most anecdotal evidence as well as examination of current games on the market, this seems to be the level of interactivity generally preferred for modern games—that is, for those games that require any degree of interactivity at all.

However, there are some titles that demand a high degree of flexibility and dynamic expression in their musical scores, and these titles will push the boundaries of interactive musical expression, using some of the

DirectMusic objects described here. The DirectX documents discuss the use of these objects in detail, but we'll give a brief overview of the various elements and how they are used.

THE DIRECTMUSIC COMPOSITION ENGINE

The *composer* is the heart of the dynamic music-creation system. It coordinates and combines inputs from styles, templates, and chordmaps using parameters such as shape, activity, length, and others to create a segment at run-time. You can see an illustration of this process in Figure 14.2

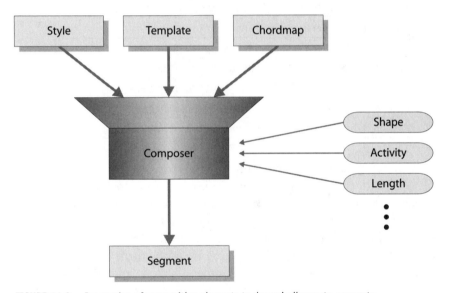

FIGURE 14.2   Interaction of composition elements to dynamically create segments.

Unlike the majority of the DirectMusic interfaces we've examined so far, the Composer object is not created using any other DirectMusic object. Instead, it is created using the standard COM method, CoCreateInstance(), as shown in Listing 14.8.

LISTING 14.8

```
IDirectMusicComposer8* pComposer;
hr = CoCreateInstance(CLSID_DirectMusicComposer, NULL,
    CLSCTX_INPROC, IID_IDirectMusicComposer8,
```

```
    (void**)&pComposer );
if(FAILED(hr))
    return Error::Handle("Composer object error = %s.",
        DXGetErrorString9(hr));
```

IDirectMusicComposer8 exposes eight methods for using composer segments dynamically or for altering music tracks in some manner. See Table 14.1.

TABLE 14.1   Eight Methods for Using Composer Segments Dynamically

IDirectMusicComposer8::AutoTransition()
IDirectMusicComposer8::ChangeChordMap()
IDirectMusicComposer8::ComposeSegmentFromShape()
IDirectMusicComposer8::ComposeSegmentFromTemplate()
IDirectMusicComposer8::ComposeTemplateFromShape()
IDirectMusicComposer8::ComposeTransition()

A complete explanation of all of these functions can be found in the DirectX SDK documentation. Without going into too much detail, most of these functions essentially construct more-concrete musical concepts from abstract expressions, and they use a number of additional parameters to determine the details of the final output. Except for ChangeChordMap(), the output of these functions generally appears in the form of a DirectMusic Segment object, which can represent either a concrete piece of music or a template (we'll look at this next). In fact, ChangeChordMap()'s output doesn't create a new segment, but modifies one that is playing based on changes made according to a chordmap. Once you have the segment, you queue, play, and control it like you would any statically composed Segment object.

TEMPLATES

A *template* is a segment that contains a signpost track and, optionally, a command track that is used to control playback aspects, such as groove level. Groove level, as you might recall, is a generic performance-wide property that can be used in any method chosen by the composer to affect selection of style patterns in segments. For instance, the groove level could control the intensity of a piece. A composer would designate certain pattern variations to play at specific groove levels inside DirectMusic Producer. Then, the higher the groove level in the final playback (again, which can be controlled by the command track in the template segment), the more intense the composed music will be. As a programmer, you do not need to do anything differently other than designate specified segments as "template segments" or just "templates." These templates are basic patterns that construct concrete segments for playback using the function `IDirectMusicComposer8::ComposeSegmentFromTemplate()`.

Templates can also be created programmatically from a *shape* using the function `IDirectMusicComposer8::ComposeTemplateFromShape()`. A shape can be defined as a change in time in musical structure and/or intensity. As an example, some predefined shape types are: rising, falling, level, loopable, song, loud, quiet, peaking, and random. In essence, the shape defines the basic structural and emotional characteristics of the section of music to be created. The composed template (defined using the specified shape and some other parameters, such as length or activity) can then be used in the `IDirectMusicComposer8::ComposeSegmentFromTemplate()` function as though it had been loaded from a file.

STYLE

A DirectMusic *style* is a component of music that typically contains one or more patterns of notes and built-in musical functionality. Most composer functions require the use of a style object. There are two ways that styles can be manipulated. First, you may notice the reference to a "pattern of notes," as opposed to "a short section of music." This is because changing the base chord, which is easily done with MIDI-based music, can substantially alter the 'pattern.' Second, the style may choose any number of complex patterns, which can be chosen at random or influenced by the performance's groove level. As a programmer, it is only important to understand that a style is a smaller building block used to compose segments. In this case, we're using a style to dynamically create a segment, instead of the more-typical method where an author inserts styles into a segment at authoring time.

From a programmatic point of view, you might need some method of choosing which style is appropriate at which point in the soundtrack. This means you will need to devise a method of choosing styles based on some game criteria. A likely candidate for this would be DirectMusic scripting, as this would give the composer the most direct control over music events and transitions. Nonetheless, you should expect a somewhat substantial challenge in coordinating this level of detail in your composition.

THE CHORDMAP

A *chordmap* is a particular track that, just like the name sounds, maps chord progressions in a logical fashion. After obtaining a DirectMusic chordmap interface, this ChordMap object can then be used in the functions that require this interface, such as ComposeSegmentFromTemplate() and ComposeSegmentFromShape(). In these functions, the wActivity parameter is used to determine how often the composer decides to change chords. Transitioning from one chordmap to another is done with the composer function IDirectMusicComposer8::ChangeChordMap().

As with styles, a decision must be made as to how chordmaps should be best used. There are several possible solutions, such as using a single chordmap through the course of an entire piece of music; or you can choose a more dynamic approach, such as using the chordmap associated with the currently used style. For even more control, you could expose an interface through DirectMusic scripting methods to allow the composer to choose when and how new chordmaps are chosen.

DYNAMIC COMPOSITION PAYOFF

The possibilities of how to implement a DirectMusic-based dynamic composition engine are nearly limitless. It can be exciting to imagine a piece of music that evolves and changes in subtle or dramatic ways, reacting to the mood and tempo of the game while maintaining continuity by transitioning on appropriate boundaries. Instead of a player growing bored with a continuously repeating loop of music, he or she instead takes pleasure in hearing familiar themes that, while based on statically composed patterns, always change and evolve in a way that prevents it from seeming lifeless or irrelevant to the game.

In most cases, it is simply a matter of balancing how much flexibility you wish to program into the system versus your expected gains in terms of music creativity and enjoyment for the player. For those who wish to truly push the boundaries of interactive music development, the advanced DirectMusic tools and interfaces are ready for you to use and experiment with.

CONCLUSION

The features presented in this chapter are powerful mechanisms, but they should be used with caution if there is a chance that your game could be ported to non-DirectX platforms, simply because most other platforms do not offer similar functionality at any sort of an API level. However, you may have different priorities with your own audio system and should judge for yourself whether or not to utilize these advanced DirectMusic features. If your game is a DirectX-only title, then this additional high-level functionality could, in fact, be a great boon to your game, giving your audio team even more power and control over the way the game sounds and behaves.

In the next chapter, we'll learn about the audio manager, a catch-all central repository for global sound- and music-management systems.

CHAPTER 15

THE AUDIO MANAGER

In covering DirectX Audio so far, we have seen a lot of discrete elements and various techniques covering everything from DirectSound buffers to advanced DirectMusic programming. One of the most important aspects of a solid audio system, though, is the creation and management of a centralized repository for all the audio data that must be managed and updated in real-time, such as background loading commands, streaming audio buffers, and resource management. This is what we call the *audio manager*.

Technically, in this chapter, some of techniques we will be demonstrating from the *GAP* audio system are not part of DirectX, but it is important to understand how to perform a number of basic management tasks. Some of these tasks include background-thread loading and management, global volume and playback controls, and factory-based object creation.

 The code listed in this chapter can be found in \Game_Audio\ audio_sdk\src\audiolib\AudioMgr.h, AudioMgr.cpp.

INTRODUCTION

In most programming systems or libraries, the concept of a single, central 'manager' object is not a new or particularly innovative one. In the classic book, *Design Patterns* (Gamma, et al.), a number of lower-level patterns are described that are often associated with manager classes. The singleton pattern, which enforces an interface so that only one object can be created and accessed, is often useful to ensure that all parts of the program are utilizing the same manager object. The facade pattern can also be used to describe a manager. Facades are described as a way of providing a unified interface to a number of interfaces in a subsystem. While not every interface is covered by the manager, this does accurately reflect the composite nature of the manager object, which often contains many discrete objects and provides a single, unified interface for the client programmer. Finally, the manager will sometimes take on the role of a factory pattern, a method in which creation of objects occurs by a third party in order to facilitate subclassing. The audio manager in the *GAP* library takes on characteristics of all three of these patterns.

Quite frankly, the audio manager is potentially the most confusing piece of code in the audio library, if for no other reason than it is responsible for so many different tasks, making the class large and at times somewhat difficult to follow. For this reason, we are taking an entire chapter to describe what the design goals of our manager class are and how these goals are implemented. We will start by listing the goals of our manager class:

- Allow simple, one-function initialization and shutdown of the entire audio system.
- Automatically handle all background tasks, such as updating streaming buffers, handling DirectMusic notification events, performing background loading, and enabling automatic volume ramping.
- Provide concise factory methods for creating audio objects.
- Provide an interface to global parameters, such as sound and music volume, and global pause, resume, and stop functions.
- Provide an interface to all callback mechanisms, such as music notification and internal file creation and usage.
- Provide an interface to a basic, interactive music playback system.
- Automatically handle all resource and buffer management according to user-defined preferences and priority values.

As you can see, the audio manager is responsible for a large amount of functionality that spans the entire audio system. All of this is accomplished in a single object, but many of the tasks are divided and handled completely independently on different threads, or within different functions called by a single timing thread, depending on the need.

A few of these tasks are described in detail in other sections of the book. For instance, we described in detail how to update and manage streaming sound buffers in Chapter 9—Streaming Digital Audio. However, any major functionality in the audio manager that is not specifically covered in another chapter will be covered here.

MULTITHREADED AUDIO PROGRAMMING

One of the things you will soon discover about this particular implementation of the audio manager, and in fact about audio programming in general, is that it relies heavily on multiple threads to perform many types of continuous processing or streaming operations. This is mostly due to the nature of processing large amounts audio data. It is often much more practical to create a background thread to handle the work of updating a streaming buffer or waiting for DirectMusic notification events than to require the client programmer to continuously poll for and handle these events manually. This also frees up the client programmer to perform tasks such as loading a new level while streaming audio or playing interactive music of some sort, even if they tie up the main thread with processor-intensive tasks.

Of course, there is a definite downside to creating and using multiple threads. It is very tricky to ensure that you never encounter conditions where one thread alters a variable in such a way that it might cause another thread to retrieve bad information, potentially even crashing the program. This can easily happen if one thread is accessing an object pointer, but another thread decides to manipulate or alter that pointer in some fashion at the same time (such as deleting the object). Even though you may check for a null pointer at the beginning of the function, a second thread could conceivably zero out the pointer after the check is performed, but before the pointer is accessed. In this case, the program will crash when the null pointer (or garbage pointer) is dereferenced. Fortunately, there are also a number of mechanisms provided to help ensure that scenarios like this do not occur.

CRITICAL SECTIONS

One of the handiest and most straightforward of these mechanisms is the *critical section*. Simply put, a critical section is a way of ensuring that two threads do not access specified sections of code at the same time. This is often done where two threads are both accessing a common resource, such as an object pointer. Listing 15.1 demonstrates a simple example that is similar to our previous scenario—the simultaneous access to a pointer by two or more threads.

LISTING 15.1

```
SomeClass* g_pPtr = 0;


void ThreadFunc1()
{
    if(!g_pPtr)
        return;
    g_pPtr->DoSomeFunction();
}


void ThreadFunc2()
{
    if(SomeConditionIsMet())
    {
        if(g_pPtr)
        {
            delete g_pPtr;
            g_pPtr = 0;
        }
    }
}
```

Assume that ThreadFunc1() and ThreadFunc2() are being executed on two concurrently running threads. It may seem at first as though this code should run safely, because ThreadFunc1(), g_pPtr is always checked to ensure that there is a value in the pointer before attempting to dereference it. Unfortunately, simple checks like this do not work, because threads do not operate on an entire function before moving to the next function, as happens in single-threaded code. The processor's execution can switch at any time between the two threads (or, in the case of multiprocessor machines, they might literally be executing simultaneously), meaning that the object might be deleted *after* the validity check in ThreadFunc1(), but *before* the pointer is dereferenced. Or, equally bad, the validity check might occur after the deletion of the object, but before the second thread has had a chance to set the pointer to null.

Using a critical section object and related functions, we can ensure that specific sections of code are blocked from executing simultaneously. This is done through the use of a shared CRITICAL_SECTION structure, along with the Windows API functions EnterCriticalSection() and Leave-CriticalSection(). Listing 15.2 demonstrates the same code, but this time safely blocking it from executing in a dangerous fashion.

LISTING 15.2

```
SomeClass* g_pPtr = 0;
CRITICAL_SECTION g_CS;

void ThreadFunc1()
{
    EnterCriticalSection(&g_CS);
    if(g_pPtr)
        g_pPtr->DoSomeFunction();
    LeaveCriticalSection(&g_CS);
}

void ThreadFunc2()
{
    if(SomeConditionIsMet())
    {
        if(g_pPtr)
        {
            EnterCriticalSection(&g_CS);
            delete g_pPtr;
            g_pPtr = 0;
            LeaveCriticalSection(&g_CS);
        }
    }
}
```

We must assume the critical section structure g_CS was first initialized with the function InitializeCriticalSection() and should be passed to DeleteCriticalSection()when the threads are finished executing.

We've wrapped the entire `ThreadFunc1()` inside calls to `Enter-CriticalSection()` and `LeaveCriticalSection()`. We have ensured that all exit paths call `LeaveCriticalSection()` by slightly altering the code logic. Likewise, we have also wrapped the code inside `ThreadFunc2()`, which actually deletes the object accessed by these two functions, as well. Because all of these critical section functions are using a common critical section structure, simultaneous execution of the code inside the two `Enter` and `Leave` blocks is impossible. If, for instance, code inside `ThreadFunc1()` is executing when `ThreadFunc2()` decides to delete the object, the `Enter-CriticalSection()` function in `ThreadFunc2()` simply waits for execution to finish (defined as when `LeaveCriticalSection()` is reached) in `Thread-Func1()` before continuing.

Essentially, any sections of code wrapped in these begin (`EnterCritical-Section()`) and end (`LeaveCriticalSection()`) functions while accessing a shared critical section structure becomes single-threaded code, even if that code actually resides in separately executing threads. This is an important point to make, because as you might surmise, it does absolutely no good at all if your design requires you to place so many critical sections inside your multithreaded code that it essentially becomes a single-threaded system. In fact, it actually can be harmful to your program's performance, since multithreaded code requires some additional overhead on single-processor machines. However, well-designed and carefully controlled multithreaded code can have a positive impact both on performance for multi-processor machines and ease-of-use for all systems by not requiring user polling, even if simultaneous execution is only simulated on single-processor machines.

Shutting Down Threads

Although shutting down a thread may not seem like one of the trickier aspects of multithreaded programming, it can be important to ensure the shutdown occurs cleanly and without destroying or accessing objects in the wrong order. In the audio manager, we use a synchronization technique using a combination of several elements. We will first examine the problem and then look at what needs to happen for a safe thread shutdown.

Typically, the threads we create are accessing some integral or common data, such as a list of pointers to sound objects. The problem is similar to our original problem—preventing an object from being accessed by multiple threads at the same time—but this time the problem is slightly more complicated because we must exit the thread, then shut down the critical section object used to synchronize the two thread's access to the common data. If these tasks are performed in the wrong order, it is almost guaranteed to crash the program due to an access violation. One solution involves using *notification messages* (communication signals between threads) to ensure proper synchronization before proceeding with a clean shutdown. Listing 15.3 shows a block of code from the audio manager's shutdown function, demonstrating the use of a combination of a notification message along with the use of a simple status flag to synchronize and shut down two periodically updating background threads.

LISTING 15.3

```
if(m_bInitialized)
{
    // Create event objects to be used by the threads
    // to signal a successful shutdown
    m_hTerm = CreateEvent(NULL, FALSE, FALSE, NULL);
    m_hTerm[MUSIC_EVENT] = CreateEvent(NULL, FALSE,
        FALSE, NULL);

    // Indicates the audio manager is now terminating
    m_bInitialized = false;

    // Wait for both threads to shut down
    // before continuing
    WaitForMultipleObjects(2, m_hTerm, TRUE, INFINITE);

    // Close the event objects now that
    // we're done with them
    CloseHandle(m_hTerm[TIME_EVENT]);
    CloseHandle(m_hTerm[MUSIC_EVENT]);

    // Delete the critical section now
    DeleteCriticalSection(&m_csAudioUpdate);
}
```

This code is used in combination with code in the background threads that check for the `m_bInitialized` flag to be set to `false` and then signal the main thread that it is now safe to proceed. Each background thread has code that looks similar to that shown in Listing 15.4.

LISTING 15.4

```
while(true)
{
    // Wake up every 50ms to perform some timed actions
    Sleep(50);

    // If the manager has been shut down then terminate
    // this thread
    if(!DXAudioMgr()->m_bInitialized)
    {
        SetEvent(DXAudioMgr()->m_hTerm[TIME_EVENT]);
        return;
    }

    // Enter the critical section to ensure that
    // functions that alter the contents of the data
    // through which we'll be looping through cannot
    // continue until we are finished with the function
    EnterCriticalSection(
        &DXAudioMgr()->GetUpdateCS());

    // do timing work next
```

This shows the beginning of the timing-thread loop and demonstrates how, on each iteration through the loop, the thread checks the audio manager's m_bInitialized flag, which indicates that it is attempting to shut down the audio system. When this flag is found to be false, the thread then signals, using the m_hTerm handle array before exiting. The audio manager's termination function will wait until both threads (the timer thread and music notification thread) have signaled that they are exiting before the function proceeds with the shutdown procedure, which also involves destroying the critical section object used to synchronize these two threads.

The asynchronous-loading thread must be shut down in a slightly different matter, since the thread is only activated when it receives a signal (using a Win32 event, again). Listing 15.5 shows the code used in the audio manager's termination function to signal the loading thread to shut down.

LISTING 15.5

```
// Set a load-notify event so the loading thread
// can exit
SetEvent(m_hLoadNotify);

// Enter and leave the loading critical section to
// ensure that the loading thread is finished
EnterCriticalSection(&m_csLoading);
LeaveCriticalSection(&m_csLoading);
DeleteCriticalSection(&m_csLoading);

// Close the load-notification handle now that
// we're done with it
CloseHandle(m_hLoadNotify);
```

Listing 15.6 shows the code used in the loading thread. Although very similar to the other threads, note that the thread does not notify the main thread when it is shutting down. This is because we can use the m_csLoading critical section object as a synchronization device in the shutdown process for this thread, eliminating the need for a separate signal handle. We could not do this in the previous example because a single critical section object was shared between three threads.

LISTING 15.6

```
while(true)
{
    WaitForSingleObject(m_hLoadNotify, INFINITE);

    if(!m_bInitialized)
        return;

    EnterCriticalSection(&m_csLoading);
```

The difference in the audio manager's shutdown code is twofold. First, we must signal the loading thread in order to make sure the thread is activated during the shutdown process. Next, we enter and leave the m_csLoading critical section. This is done in case the thread is currently loading some object. If so, the audio manager's termination function will simply wait until the thread is finished and only continue when the loading is completed. The loading thread will loop again and then exit because of the previously sent signal, regardless of what it was doing when the signal was sent.

In this manner, all three threads are safely shut down without any danger of inadvertently accessing lists of sound objects while the audio manager is busy destroying those objects—an obvious recipe for a crash.

ASYNCHRONOUS OBJECT LOADING

One of the neatest benefits of preserving the state information of audio objects, whether loaded or not, is that it facilitates background-thread, or *asynchronous* loading. In order to clarify our use of terms, we will discuss what is meant by "asynchronous loading."

Typically, loading a wave file or some other audio resource is done on the primary thread, meaning that all commands and instructions are executed sequentially. Thus, a call to pSound->Load() would not return until the entire sound had been loaded from disk. The biggest problem with an on-demand file-loading system is that if you happen to be loading a substantially large file, there can be a noticeable 'stutter' or drop in frame rate as the file is loaded.

An asynchronous loading mechanism, on the other hand, is less likely to cause a program to stutter quite so noticeably. While there is no such thing as a free lunch when it comes to disk/CPU usage, loading in the background has several distinct advantages. First, if the file is large and takes a considerable amount of time to load, the loading process can be spread over several frames, instead of having to completely finish before the main thread's execution continues. Second, this sort of system can benefit from a multiprocessor machine, since loading can occur on the idle processor, which should help to improve overall performance.

However, you may be wondering how a background loading system reacts to the following code:

```
m_pSound->Load();
m_pSound->SetVolume(0.5);
m_pSound->SetPitch(1.1);
```

```
m_pSound->SetPan(0.75);
m_pSound->Play();
```

After all, if loading takes place while the primary thread executes, won't all the setting changes made to the sound (e.g., setting the volume, pitch, pan, and, indeed, even the play call) be lost because the DirectSound buffer is not actually loaded and available when the functions are executed? If we simply routed all these calls to the DirectSound buffer without preserving the data, this would indeed be the case. Many asynchronous loading systems require complicated mechanisms, such as callback notifications, to tell you when it is safe to operate on the object.

However, one of the requirements of the sound system from the very beginning was that sound buffer settings must be preserved even while the sound buffer itself might not yet exist, or might have been unloaded at some point. Thus, every parameter call to a sound object is stored both in the object's data as well as in the DirectSound buffer, making it convenient to restore this information at any time.

Fortunately, this also happens to work equally well whether the sound buffer is unloaded or is still in the process of loading. There are just a couple of things we need to do at the end of the loading function to ensure that the all settings are properly applied, and we'll look at this in detail when we examine the sound objects' loading code. For this exercise, we'll be specifically examining the Sound class along with the AudioManager code, but keep in mind that all three Sound object classes, Sound, Sound3D, and Segment, work in exactly the same way.

The background loading process begins with the Sound::Load() function, as you might expect. This function is used both externally and internally, meaning that both client programmers and other functions inside the library may use this function. More specifically, the Play() function will always attempt to load a sound if it is not currently loaded. The Sound::Load() function is shown in its entirety in Listing 15.7.

LISTING 15.7

```
bool Sound::Load()
{
    // Make sure we don't reload the sound
    if(IsLoaded() || IsLoading())
        return true;
```

```
// If not loading asynchronously, load immediately and
// return
if(!DXAudioMgr()->LoadAsync())
    return DoLoad();

// Otherwise, schedule the audio manager to asynchronously
// load
m_bLoading = true;
DXAudioMgr()->ScheduleLoad(this);

return true;
}
```

The Load() function first does a simple check to see if the Sound object is currently either loaded or in the process of being loaded, and if so, returns success (true). Next, it checks to see if the user has disabled asynchronous loading, and if so, loads the sound buffer immediately before returning, using the function DoLoad().

The Load() function does not actually perform any loading itself. As you can see, it has delegated the responsibility of buffer creation and loading to the DoLoad() function. What we do instead is to schedule this function for loading on a background thread that is managed by the audio manager object. We also set the loading state of the object by setting the m_bLoading flag to true before we schedule the loading. This will prevent accidental and concurrent multiple loading of the same object, thanks to the check at the beginning of the Load() function.

The AudioManager::ScheduleLoad() function begins the process of loading in the audio manager. We can examine this in Listing 15.8.

LISTING 15.8

```
void AudioManager::ScheduleLoad(Sound* pSound)
{
    EnterCriticalSection(&m_csLoadScheduling);
    m_SoundLoadTemp.push(pSound);
    LeaveCriticalSection(&m_csLoadScheduling);
    SetEvent(m_hLoadNotify);
}
```

As you can see, this is a rather simple function. A critical section is used to prevent simultaneous access to a temporary loading queue. The temporary loading queue is used since we do not wish to block access to the main loading queue at any time. However, waiting for a temporary queue to copy a few pointers over to another queue is an event that can be synchronized without any performance penalties. It might be a bit difficult to understand what exactly is happening with the queues unless you examine the main loading thread; so we should look at that now. Listing 15.9 shows the entry function into the thread AudioManager::LoadingThread(), and shows the AudioManager::ServiceLoading() function, which does the real work.

LISTING 15.9

```
void AudioManager::LoadingThread(LPVOID lpv)
{
    CoInitialize(NULL);
    DXAudioMgr()->ServiceLoading();
    CoUninitialize();
}

void AudioManager::ServiceLoading()
{
    while(true)
    {
        // Wait until an loading notification event
        // is received
        WaitForSingleObject(m_hLoadNotify, INFINITE);

        // If the audio manager is terminating, then
        // exit the thread
        if(!m_bInitialized)
            return;

        // Copy the temporary queues to the main
        // loading queues
        EnterCriticalSection(&m_csLoadScheduling);
        while(!m_SoundLoadTemp.empty())
        {
            m_SoundLoadPending.push(
                m_SoundLoadTemp.front());
```

```
        m_SoundLoadTemp.pop();
}
while(!m_Sound3DLoadTemp.empty())
{
    m_Sound3DLoadPending.push(
        m_Sound3DLoadTemp.front());
    m_Sound3DLoadTemp.pop();
}
while(!m_SegmentLoadTemp.empty())
{
    m_SegmentLoadPending.push(
        m_SegmentLoadTemp.front());
    m_SegmentLoadTemp.pop();
}
LeaveCriticalSection(&m_csLoadScheduling);

// Do loading work
bool bFinishedLoading = false;
EnterCriticalSection(&m_csLoading);
while(!bFinishedLoading)
{
    if(!m_SoundLoadPending.empty())
    {
        m_SoundLoadPending.front()->DoLoad();
        m_SoundLoadPending.pop();
    }
    if(!m_Sound3DLoadPending.empty())
    {
        m_Sound3DLoadPending.front()->DoLoad();
        m_Sound3DLoadPending.pop();
    }
    if(!m_SegmentLoadPending.empty())
    {
        m_SegmentLoadPending.front()->DoLoad();
        m_SegmentLoadPending.pop();
    }

    if(m_SoundLoadPending.empty() &&
            m_Sound3DLoadPending.empty() &&
            m_SegmentLoadPending.empty())
        bFinishedLoading = true;
}
```

```
        LeaveCriticalSection(&m_csLoading);
    }
}
```

To begin, the LoadingThread() function wraps the thread's work function, ServiceLoading(), between calls to CoInitialize() and CoUninitialize(). DirectMusic will complain about COM not being initialized if this is not done. It is easy to forget that COM must be initialized on every thread that makes use of COM-related functions. Because Direct-Sound does not require COM to be explicitly initialized for most of its function calls, this is the first thread that has required this.

The ServiceLoading() function then goes into an infinite loading loop before waiting for a notification event, using the m_hLoadNotify handle. As previously noted, this notification is sent in the audio manager's Sched-uleLoad() function, which is in turned called by the Sound object's Load() function.

When a notification message is received, the function will move any object pointers originally placed into the m_SoundLoadTemp queue into the m_SoundLoadPending queue, as well as doing this with the other two object lists. You should take note of how the transfer is done entirely inside a critical section block defined by the m_csLoadScheduling critical section structure. This critical section object is also used by the AudioManager::ScheduleLoad() functions when adding an object to the temporary queue.

Why go through the work of using a temporary queue initially and then copying it to the 'real' loading queue before loading the objects? The reason we go through this somewhat convoluted procedure is because we have no guarantee that the STL queue container is thread-safe, and we could conceivably be adding an element to the queue at the same time the loading thread was removing another element, resulting in a potential problem. Typically, in dealing with this sort of access collision between threads, we would probably just block both functions with a single critical section object, forcing one function to stall until the other was finished, but this would defeat the entire point of the background loading thread if the main thread was forced to stall until an entire batch of objects was loaded. So instead, we place a block on an alternative section, where the only thing we potentially have to wait for is for one queue to transfer its contents to another queue—which seems like a reasonable and safe solution, if not entirely logical at first glance.

After the m_SoundLoadPending (and equivalents for the other audio object types) queue is filled with the contents of the temporary loading queues, the real work of loading up all the objects begins. The loop is fairly straightforward—all queues are emptied in turn while calling the Load() function on each object contained within. When all the queues are empty, the loading thread finishes its primary loop, which allows the thread to sleep again until it is signaled for another scheduled round of loading. The entire loading loop is also wrapped in a critical section m_csLoading, which is used when shutting down the audio manager to ensure the thread is not terminated while in the middle of a loading a set of objects, which would likely cause a crash.

You may also notice one potential drawback with this sort of asynchronous loading system. It is difficult to know what to do with loading errors. Because the main thread has finished with the loading function and has moved on to other tasks long before any potential errors are discovered, checking for errors at the actual point of loading is not feasible. The only practical solution is to log any errors for later retrieval—how those errors are handled at that point is a matter of individual preference.

GLOBAL SOUND AND MUSIC CONTROL

Controlling global audio levels is a task that naturally falls to the audio manager. As simple as controlling sound volume may seem, it is something that is quite easy to get wrong when programming your audio system. The very first thing you should know is what *not* to do, and then we will cover some other, more appropriate approaches that can be used.

As illogical as it seems, you should not adjust the master volume of the audio system by controlling the volume of the primary mixing buffer, as many programmers implementing a DirectX-based system mistakenly do. The reason for this is simple—on Windows systems with WDM drivers (i.e., those that use KMixer), the primary buffer is analogous to the master wave output control for the entire system, and so changing this affects the entire Windows system volume for all wave output. It is always bad form to adjust global Windows settings unless the user is well aware of what is happening, and a user hardly expects a volume control in a game to change the global Windows volume.

So then, how to you control volume globally using DirectSound? The short answer is: you cannot. At least, there is no built-in method in Direct-

Sound for attenuating all sound volumes. For this reason, as well the general practicality of having a list of all loaded sounds available for other management tasks (such as resource management), it is recommended to keep track of all currently playing sounds in your audio system. While the lack of global sound control might seem like a hindrance at first, you will soon understand why it is not such a bad thing after all, because in forcing you to implement low-level global volume control, DirectSound also provides you with an opportunity to design these controls in a way that best suits your game.

Many games have more than one master volume control. A typical scenario is a game that has separate volume settings for sound effects and music. This particular scenario is in fact so common that we have built these two separate volume controls directly into the audio system. All sound objects can be designated either as a sound effect or as music, giving the audio manager a simple method to differentiate between the two. Setting a master volume control is then nothing more than iterating through all currently playing sounds, checking for the sound fx/music switch, and then appropriately adjusting the volume, based on the type. Since our volume levels for this system always range from zero to one, combining the sound-specific level with the global sound volume is as simple as multiplying them together. Listing 15.10 shows the global sound controls for setting and retrieving both sound fx volume and music volume.

LISTING 15.10

```
bool AudioManager::SetSoundVolume(float fVolume)
{
    CHECK_INIT();

    // Ensure the volume stays within the allowed range
    m_fSoundVolume = Clamp<float>(fVolume, VOLUME_MIN,
        VOLUME_MAX);

    // Iterate through all the sounds designated as
    // sound fx, getting and setting the volume to
    // ensure each applies the new global sound setting.
    SoundVector::iterator itr;
    float fVol;
    for(itr = m_LoadedSound.begin();
        itr != m_LoadedSound.end(); ++itr)
```

```
    {
        if(!(*itr)->IsMusic())
        {
            (*itr)->GetVolume(fVol);
            (*itr)->SetVolume(fVol);
        }
    }
    Sound3DVector::iterator itr3d;
    for(itr3d = m_LoadedSound3D.begin();
        itr3d != m_LoadedSound3D.end(); ++itr3d)
    {
        if(!(*itr3d)->IsMusic())
        {
            (*itr3d)->GetVolume(fVol);
            (*itr3d)->SetVolume(fVol);
        }
    }
    return true;
}


bool AudioManager::GetSoundVolume(float& fVolume) const
{
    fVolume = 0.0f;
    CHECK_INIT();
    fVolume = m_fSoundVolume;
    return true;
}


bool AudioManager::SetMusicVolume(float fVolume)
{
    CHECK_INIT();

    // Ensure the volume stays within the allowed range
    m_fMusicVolume = Clamp<float>(fVolume, VOLUME_MIN,
        VOLUME_MAX);

    // Iterate through all the sounds designated as
    // music, getting and setting the volume to ensure
    // each applies the new global sound setting.
    SoundVector::iterator itr;
    float fVol;
```

```
    for(itr = m_LoadedSound.begin();
        itr != m_LoadedSound.end(); ++itr)
    {
        if((*itr)->IsMusic())
        {
            (*itr)->GetVolume(fVol);
            (*itr)->SetVolume(fVol);
        }
    }
    Sound3DVector::iterator itr3d;
    for(itr3d = m_LoadedSound3D.begin();
        itr3d != m_LoadedSound3D.end(); ++itr3d)
    {
        if((*itr3d)->IsMusic())
        {
            (*itr3d)->GetVolume(fVol);
            (*itr3d)->SetVolume(fVol);
        }
    }

    // Set the global volume on the performances
    int32 nVol = LinearToLogVol(m_fMusicVolume);
    Performance(true)->SetGlobalParam(
        GUID_PerfMasterVolume, &nVol, sizeof(int32));

    return true;
}


bool AudioManager::GetMusicVolume(float& fVolume) const
{
    fVolume = 0.0f;
    CHECK_INIT();
    fVolume = m_fMusicVolume;
    return true;
}
```

There are only a couple of differences between the sound fx controls and the music controls. First, we use the Sound and Sound3D class' IsMusic() function to determine if the sound should be designated as a sound fx or as music, and then filter the functions based on this result in the appropriate functions. It may seem odd to set the sounds' volumes via a pair of

GetVolume() and SetVolume() calls. The sound objects are internally scaling their own volume according to the master volume when applying it to the buffer (or segment), and this is why the technique works.

Additionally, you will notice that the two DirectMusic performance objects (one for sound fx and one for music) are differentiated by the Boolean parameter passed into the AudioManager::Performance() function, which returns different performances based on this value. DirectMusic works in a slightly different manner than DirectSound in that there *is* a mechanism to globally control volume via the performance objects, and so we naturally take advantage of it in these functions.

FACTORY FUNCTIONS

One of the tasks of the audio manager is to also provide a central point for all object creation. Why don't we simply allow objects to be created in the normal fashion via new and delete? The first and most obvious reason is that a client simply has no way of creating an object because all that is ever seen from the client's perspective are abstract interfaces. Additionally, by restricting object creation to an internal process, we are better able to optimize object creation and use. For our playable objects, such as the Sound, Sound3D, and Segment classes, this means that we can utilize an object-caching mechanism that maintains a global pool of objects, making destruction and subsequent recreation of objects a very inexpensive proposition as compared to typical, dynamic allocation via new and delete.

In other cases, using a central creation point allows us to use internal factories that can be supplied by the user, making the object-creation process much more flexible than if we hard-coded the class name in the library. We'll be examining both the object-caching system (Chapter 30—General Optimization Strategies) and a user-supplied file object factory (Chapter 19—Custom Resource Files) later on in this book. For now, we will touch on what they look like from the manager's point of view. The internal implementations are less important than the overall concept: why a factory mechanism can be useful.

AUDIO OBJECTS

There are three playable audio objects in the basic sound system: Sound, Sound3D, and Segment. Two other objects, AudioScript and DLS, can also be created. Additionally, there is one other object, the Listener class, which can be created by the audio manager, although it is slightly different in that only one object is ever created. These objects are all internally created by the audio manager, as shown in Listing 15.11.

LISTING 15.11

```
bool AudioManager::CreateSound(ISound*& pSound)
{
    CHECK_INIT();
    pSound = Sound::CreateObject();
    return true;
}


bool AudioManager::CreateSound3D(ISound3D*& pSound3D)
{
    CHECK_INIT();
    pSound3D = Sound3D::CreateObject();
    return true;
}


bool AudioManager::CreateSegment(ISegment*& pSegment)
{
    CHECK_INIT();
    pSegment = Segment::CreateObject();
    return true;
}

bool AudioManager::CreateDLS(IDLS*& pDLS)
{
    CHECK_INIT();
    pDLS = DLS::CreateObject();
    return true;
}


bool AudioManager::CreateAudioScript(IAudioScript*& pScript)
{
    CHECK_INIT();
```

```
    pScript = AudioScript::CreateObject();
    return true;
}

bool AudioManager::GetListener(IListener*& pListener)
{
    CHECK_INIT();
    if(!m_pListener)
        m_pListener = Listener::CreateObject();
    pListener = m_pListener;
    return true;
}
```

You can see that objects are not actually created by the audio manager itself. Instead, each of these objects has a CreateObject() function, a static member that returns either a previously discarded object if one is available or a newly allocated object if all other objects in a global pool are currently being used. You can see how the GetListener() function checks to see if a listener object has already been created, and if so, it creates a new listener object via the Listener::CreateObject() function.

You may be wondering why the listener bothers with object management like the rest of the functions. Technically speaking, it actually does not; but it hides the internal object creation and destruction in the same manner as the other objects.

This brings up an interesting point: how do you prevent a user from simply calling delete on an object pointer you hand over? The simple answer is to hide the object's destructor, making it private or protected. In the same way, we can prevent other classes from creating objects by making the constructor private or protected. Although the client is prevented from creating objects because of the abstract interface, hiding the creation and destruction of the objects inside static member functions simply provides us with an additional *internal* level of protection as well. Remember, part of good programming technique is to protect yourself from making silly errors, or to disallow (circumvent) innocent mistakes by programmers who may work on your code in the future.

ISTREAM FACTORY

One of the other tasks of the audio manager is to act as a mechanism for switching between a built-in, IStream-based file-reading mechanism or a user-supplied one. In the strictly technical sense of an abstract factory, the entire point of the mechanism is to be able to switch between different sets of objects without changing the interface. This is exactly what we have done here, even though we only have one object that we are creating.

Even though we discuss the custom file mechanism in more detail later, we can still look at the audio manager's part in the process. The AudioManager class definition contains a member that will track the custom factory:

LISTING 15.12

```
// Audio stream factory information
IAudioStreamFactory* m_pStreamFactory;
```

In the initialization function, we first determine if the user has supplied a custom stream factory via the initialization structure. We use a separate pointer in order to utilize the original AudioManagerInit struct member as a way of determining if a custom factory has been supplied. If the client has supplied the factory, then the client is also responsible for the destruction of the factory, because we cannot be certain in what manner it was created (on the heap or the stack).

Inside the AudioManager::Init() function, we see the following code:

LISTING 15.13

```
// See if the user has provided a custom stream factory
// object. If not, create our own disk-based system by
// default
if(m_Init.m_pAudioStreamFactory)
    m_pStreamFactory = m_Init.m_pAudioStreamFactory;
else
    m_pStreamFactory = new AudioStreamFactory;
```

The AudioStreamFactory class is a disk-based file loader that the audio manager uses by default. When it is time to destroy the factory, the same process is used in reverse. Here is what we see in the AudioManager::Term() function:

LISTING 15.14

```
// See if the user has provided a custom stream factory
// object. If not, destroy the one we've created
if(!m_Init.m_pAudioStreamFactory)
    SAFE_DELETE(m_pStreamFactory);
```

Now, we can use the AudioManager function interface that duplicates the IAudioStreamFactory interface used to create a file object. Listing 15.15 shows the single function used to create the stream objects. Because of the COM-compliant interface, destroying the stream only requires calling its Release() function.

LISTING 15.15

```
bool AudioManager::CreateAudioStream(IAudioStream*&
pAudioStream)
{
    CHECK_INIT();
    if(!m_pStreamFactory)
        return false;
    return m_pStreamFactory->CreateAudioStream(pAudioStream);
}
```

The reason we have created an external interface instead of simply using the internal factory object is because of our layered approach to building functionality. We will be using this interface in our higher-level sound and music managers. For instance, when we load script files, we do so using these stream interfaces. That way, any future extensions to the basic audio system can make use of a custom file system in exactly the same manner as the core library.

CONCLUSION

The audio manager contains a wealth of functionality; it is the logical place to store data and functionality for nearly everything of global consequence. By centralizing many common tasks, we allow ourselves the freedom to globally optimize our audio system without changing a large amount of code. It is important, however, to not attempt to centralize functionality that in fact belongs to the individual audio objects, and striking this balance between the convenience of centralized code and distributed object programming is sometimes a challenge. The audio manager is responsible for many important tasks, such as object creating (and caching), sound system initialization and shutdown, asynchronous file loading, and global control operations, as well as other tasks. Hopefully, you have learned enough about the design principles involved in each of these tasks to effectively modify the sample library for your own purposes or even write your own system from the ground up. Even if you use the example library as is (or nearly as is), it is still worthwhile to understand all that is happening 'under the hood,' so to speak.

This chapter concludes the DirectX Audio part of *Game Audio Programming*. In Part III—High-Level Audio Programming, we'll look at a specialized scripting system that can be used for simple construction of advanced data-driven programming concepts, and in doing so, demonstrate how to build a high-level sound system and interactive music system on top of an existing audio API.

PART III

HIGH-LEVEL AUDIO PROGRAMMING

CHAPTER 16

AN AUDIO-SCRIPTING FORMAT

Data-driven design is the key to flexibility and robustness in a modern game. Unlike other applications with rigid and often easily definable parameters, it is much harder to determine exactly what makes a game 'fun,' and so both code and content go through a process of evolution over the course of a product's development cycle. Audio is no different; therefore, it is worthwhile to examine techniques for exposing some of the basic controls of our audio system to the sound and game designers.

 The code listed in this chapter can be found in \Game_Audio\ *ON THE CD* audio_sdk\src\audioscript\Script.h, Script.cpp

AUDIO DATA FORMATS

Data-Driven Design sounds like a great buzzword, but what does it really mean? For a great answer to that question, read the first article in *Game Programming Gems* (Charles River Media, Inc., August 2000), written by Steve Rabin, entitled "The Magic of Data-Driven Design." In it, he explains a bit more about the data-driven design concept and how it can pay real dividends, even after the product has shipped:

> An example of this (data-driven) rule is the game *Total Annihilation.* The designer, Chris Taylor, pushed data-driven design to the limit. *Total Annihilation* was an RTS that featured two distinct races, the

Arm and the Core. Although the entire game was centered on these two factions, they were never hard-coded into the game. Theoretically, data could have been added to the game to support three races, even after the game shipped. Although this possibility was never exploited, *Total Annihilation* took full advantage of its flexibility. Since all units were completely defined by data, new units were released on a weekly basis over the game's Web site. In fact, many people created their own units with functionality that shocked even the game's developers.

Rabin also outlines a few requirements for getting this data-driven flexibility into your game, one of which is a text parser capable of extracting critical information from files at any point during the game. We'll see just such a system taken to a fairly advanced level. The parser used is built on the system first discussed in *Game Programming Gems 2* (Charles River Media Inc., August 2001), in the article, "A Flexible Text Parsing System." The code has been modified to tokenize vectors as a native type, and a hierarchical data system and accompanying navigation methods have been built on top of it, insulating the user from even having to examine individual tokens. Instead, we can now view data in a tree form, with nodes containing both names and optional data. This greatly simplifies the logic needed to read simple data formats.

CUSTOMIZED SCRIPT FORMAT—AN XML ALTERNATIVE

If you've worked with XML (eXtensible Markup Language), you understand the power inherent in a simple but robust self-describing text-based data format. However, straight XML has a few drawbacks as a native game format type. While it does have the properties we're interested in as a text file format, the format is a bit more verbose than it needs to be, causing additional parsing, which of course translates to additional load time. Moreover, there are a few tricks we'd like to employ with the script format to make it more compatible with a typical game engine. We've taken the best features of XML and streamlined them to meet our needs as game developers, while at the same time adding some features that are either prohibited or would be difficult in pure XML format. We're going to examine one such custom script language that you may wish to adopt or modify for your particular needs.

While this may seem like a bit of a stretch for audio programming, the data-driven concept is so important that it must be a part of every game system, including the audio engine. In this respect, topics such as solid OOP (Object Oriented Programming) design principles and data-driven programming are covered to a limited degree in this book; this doesn't seem inappropriate, as long as there is a direct correlation and application at some point for the creation of an audio system. And in fact, we'll be using this script system over the next two chapters to demonstrate how to easily create high-level sound and music systems that can operate on top of the existing audio API we've created, bringing together both solid design principles and data-driven techniques.

THE SCRIPT FORMAT

Our script language is a hierarchical, self-describing, text-based format just like XML. Here's an example of a sound as described by the script language.

LISTING 16.1

```
sound = "Menu Music"
{
    filename = "menumusic.wav";
    streaming = true;
    looping = true;
}
```

You'll notice the script has a striking resemblance to C code, which of course is no accident. Generally speaking, if conventions exist, it doesn't hurt to take advantage of them and lessen the learning curve of those new to the new system. We'll see in a moment why we're not actually using regular XML syntax. However, a brief glance at the equivalent text in XML will show how similar the definitions are.

LISTING 16.2

```
<sound id = "Menu Music">
    <filename>menumusic.wav</filename>
    <streaming>true</streaming>
```

```
<looping>true</looping>
</sound>
```

You can quickly determine that Listing 16.1 is much less verbose than the actual XML in Listing 16.2. To be precise (and including all of the spaces, carriage returns, and tabs), it's 90 characters versus 125 characters, respectively—Listing 16.1 is 72% the size of the XML data. While this may seem like splitting hairs, it's important to consider that since a file format could conceivably be used to hold a significant amount of data, a size reduction of this magnitude cannot be ignored. And while it may be tempting to argue that the savings really only represent the lack of duplicate tags, and this could be mitigated by using very short identifiers—part of the purpose of using text is to keep the data readable. If efficiency were the only concern, we would not be storing data in a text format to begin with.

XML is designed with many goals in mind, which do not always correspond to those of a typical game engine. A standardized format across different programs and platforms is usually far less important than a format that works well for the application at hand. Additionally, while XML readers like MSXML are robust and feature-packed, they are also quite memory-intensive—and memory is a precious commodity in games. For this reason, a custom format seems to make a lot of sense. However, keep in mind that almost anything our custom format does can also be done in XML, if you wish to use that instead. However, you lose the benefit of being able to customize your parser, reader, and even the basic data format to suit your needs. As a simple example, in our script language, types such as bools, floats, integers, strings, and even 3D vectors are already preconverted to native types during the tokenizing phase.

To define this data format a bit more robustly, every piece of data in the text file is represent by two components: a node and its corresponding data. The node names must follow the same rule the parser requires of variables: it must start with a non-numeric character and contain no whitespace, which is similar to C and C++ variable-naming rules. This also means that the parser treats identifiers as case-sensitive; so "var1" and "Var1" are two different variables. Each node may have optional data attached to it. Nodes may also contain children, each of which is also defined as a node with optional data and children of their own. If a node does not contain any children, it must terminate its definition with a semicolon.

Otherwise, C-style curly braces delimit the node's definition. We see all of the various permutations allowed in Listing 16.3. A graphical representation of this data is also shown in Figure 16.1.

LISTING 16.3

```
Node1
{
    Node2 = data1;
    Node3 = data2
    {
        Node4 = data3;
        Node5;
        Node6;
    }
}
```

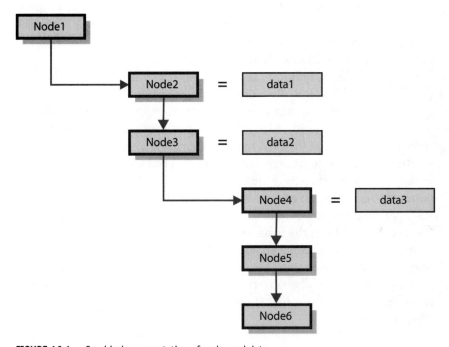

FIGURE 16.1   Graphical representation of nodes and data.

PARENTS, CHILDREN, AND SIBLINGS

You might have noticed the mention of "children." In our script format, like in most any hierarchical data format, there is a concept of parents, children, and siblings. Children are nodes directly under another node (their parent). Any children under one parent are also siblings to each other. For the purposes of our script, all top-level nodes are also considered siblings, even though they do not technically share a parent (or, you can imagine them sharing a 'null' parent). This notation will be used when using the ScriptNode object to navigate a tree.

SCRIPT DATA TYPES

There are a number of basic data types that the parser recognizes: variables, strings, reals (doubles), integers, and Booleans. These are all automatically determined by the content of the text. For instance, like C++, the parser recognizes *true* and *false* as keywords. For this reason, you may not use these words as other identifiers, such as the name of a node.

Strings are limited to 1024 bytes in length and may not span multiple lines. As in C, double quotes ("") delimit script strings. Escape sequences are not recognized, and because of this, certain characters, such as double quotes, are prohibited as such in text strings.

Our custom data-definition language also recognizes two other built-in data types: GUIDs (Globally Unique IDentifiers) and vectors. GUIDs are parsed as macros and must be in the form #DEFINE_GUID(guidName, 0x000000, 0x0000, 0x00, 0x00, 0x00, 0x00, 0x00, 0x00, 0x00, 0x00); (note the semicolon at the end) for the system to recognize it properly. This will be translated into a C-style definition that can then be used elsewhere in the script. For instance, if the GUID above was placed in a script at any point, the identifier guidName could be used as a variable elsewhere in the script, exactly as you would in C code.

Vectors must be in the form vector(0.0, 0.0, 0.0) to be recognized by the parser. It will return an AUDIOVECTOR, which in fact is currently defined as a D3DVECTOR in the *GAP* library. Note that in the case of vectors, the parser will automatically convert any integer values into real values, which is normally not done explicitly; most parsing is done without any knowledge of syntax.

SCRIPT COMMENTS

Our script code in this regard also allows both C- and C++-style comments, and follows the same general rules that pertain to well-formed C or C++ language.

CODING SCRIPT READERS

We'll now be reviewing the code you can use to parse a script file. *ON THE CD* The details of the inner workings of these classes will be discussed only insofar as may be useful for understanding how to use the objects. The code on the CD-ROM (game_audio/audio_sdk/src/audioscript) is available for you to examine at your leisure, but there is no need to describe the inner workings of the script-parsing mechanism in detail.

THE ScriptLoader CLASS

There are three classes you will use when loading and parsing script files. The first is the ScriptLoader class, which, as the name suggests, is responsible for loading script files. Before you begin using the class, you must call Init() to initialize an object. Internally, this creates and sets up a parser object to be used for tokenizing the script text. Although it does not hurt to have multiple copies, it is preferable to share a single loader among different script files, as this will save memory.

The Load() function loads a script file and tokenizes it, placing the contents into a node tree for later retrieval.

LISTING 16.4

```
if(!m_Loader.Init())
    return false;
Script script;
if(!m_Loader.Load(sFileName, script))
    return false;
```

We use a Script object as a container, controlling the lifetime of the data that is parsed by the script engine. When this object goes out of scope, all allocated memory for the parsed data will be freed.

The Script class is a very simple one. In fact, it has only one member function, GetNode(), and is primarily designed as a data holder.

LISTING 16.5

```
ScriptNode* pNode = script.GetRoot();
while(pNode)
{
    // Look for named "Sound" nodes in the script
    if(strcmp(pNode->GetName(), "Sound") == 0)
    {
        if(!LoadSound(pNode))
            return false;
    }
    // advance to the next sibling node if one exists
    pNode = pNode->GetSibling();
};
```

Once we have the Script object, our other only task with it is to extract the root node of the tree, using the GetNode() function. This function returns the first root-level node in the script, returning a ScriptNode pointer for us to use to iterate through the remaining nodes. To iterate through the remaining sibling nodes, use the ScriptNode's GetSibling() function to retrieve the next sibling. The function will return NULL after the last sibling is reached, and the loop will terminate.

Unlike XML, in our script language, there are no restrictions on how many root-level nodes you may have. This allows for multiple-tree hierarchies within a single script file. Our first example will demonstrate how to load a simple 2D sound, along with setting all of its initialization parameters. As a reference, the script code to load these files looks like this:

LISTING 16.6

```
Sound = "Menu Music"
{
    FileName = "menumusic.wav";
    Streaming = true;
    Looping = true;
    Music = false;
```

```
}

Sound = "Menu Thunder"
{
    FileName = "menuthunder.wav";
    Streaming = true;
    Looping = false;
    Music = false;
}
```

As you may recall, these initialization parameters match the SoundInit struct exactly. It is no surprise that our code will simply search for and match up data found in the script with initialization structures. Although we have listed every parameter for clarity, note that only parameters that are different from the defaults are actually required. So, for example, the last two parameters of "Menu Music" and the last three parameters of "Menu Thunder" are not required at all. In this way, the script file works exactly as though the structures were being initialized in C++ code.

You will also see that each parameter is given a unique string identifier. Even though nodes are generally not required to have data, we can define a particular format to parse that requires data, as we do here. Note also that we have chosen to use strings as the identifiers, but it is perfectly allowable to use more-efficient data, such as integers or guaranteed unique values, such as GUIDs.

Back in Listing 16.5, we saw the node iteration loops pass a node into the function LoadSound() if it finds a node named "Sound." Let's look at this function now to see how we navigate and extract data from the child nodes.

LISTING 16.7

```
bool SoundManager::LoadSound(ScriptNode* pNode)
{
    // We use string IDs in this scripting system
    if(pNode->GetDataType() != Script::STRING)
        return false;
    // Make sure the sound ID doesn't already exist
    if(IsSoundRegistered(pNode->GetString()))
        return false;
```

```
ISound* pSound;
if(!AudioMgr()->CreateSound(pSound))
    return false;
SoundInit init;
ScriptNode* pChildNode = pNode->GetChild();
while(pChildNode)
{
    if(strcmp(pChildNode->GetName(),
        "FileName") == 0)
        init.m_sFileName = pChildNode->GetString();
    else if(strcmp(pChildNode->GetName(),
        "Looping") == 0)
        init.m_bLooping = pChildNode->GetBool();
    else if(strcmp(pChildNode->GetName(),
        "Streaming") == 0)
        init.m_bStreaming = pChildNode->GetBool();
    else if(strcmp(pChildNode->GetName(),
        "Music") == 0)
        init.m_bMusic = pChildNode->GetBool();
    pChildNode = pChildNode->GetSibling();
}
if(!pSound->Init(init))
    return false;
m_SndMap.insert(make_pair(pNode->GetString(),
    pSound));
return true;
}
```

Inside our LoadSound() function, we will navigate and extract all required data to initialize a sound, then associate the sound with the unique string name given in the script. Our first task is to make sure the sound object actually does have string data associated with it. Otherwise, we'll have no way to retrieve the sound from code later.

We then use this string data to determine if a sound with this unique identifier has already been loaded. Once it has been determined that the identifier is unique, we retrieve a sound object pointer and create a sound initialization structure, which we will fill out next.

The next part of the code navigates by getting the first child node of the sound node. The code stores this as the ScriptNode pointer pChildNode. We then navigate through the code exactly as we did for the top-level nodes by iterating through sibling nodes. At each node, we check the node name and request the appropriate data type based on the name extracted.

When the iteration loop has finished, we are done filling out the initialization structure and can now fully initialize the sound object. Once this is done, we insert the object into a map, along with its name as the key value. We can now use the object name to retrieve a fully initialized sound object from the map. (This will be discussed in more detail in the next chapter.)

CONCLUSION

Now that we have a fully functional text-based data-definition script language and parser defined, we can easily add functionality that builds on top of the lower-level audio system we've previously created. By offering more control and power to the audio designers though simple scripts in text format, we ultimately reduce the coding time that you, as a programmer, must spend tweaking variables and adjusting sound parameters.

In the next chapter, we'll see exactly how to construct script readers and corresponding high-level sound code that will give your audio engine even more power and flexibility with minimal effort on the part of both the client programmer and the audio designer.

CHAPTER 17

HIGH-LEVEL SOUND SCRIPTING

Now that we have a functional script-based data-description language (see Chapter 16—An Audio-Scripting Format), it is much easier to create higher-level audio sound-management systems designed to provide a great deal of functionality with a minimal amount of effort. We will be demonstrating how to create a system that can read sound definitions from text data files, and then use these definitions to initialize sounds on demand. Additionally, the sound manager will provide a script-based soundscape system, providing complex layering of dynamic sound elements to create a rich sound environment with just a couple of lines of code on the client side.

ON THE CD

The code listed in this chapter can be found in \Game_Audio\ audio_sdk\include\audioscript\ISound.h\Game_Audio\audio_ sdk\src\audioscript\, SoundMgr.h, SoundMgr.cpp, SoundScape.h, SoundScape.cpp.

INTRODUCTION

One of the great things about effectively utilizing a well-designed abstract interface is that it makes creating higher-level systems much more straightforward. This interface ensures that the higher-level systems work with exactly the same interfaces as the game-side clients, making is much easier to rework any low-level components, if need be. If the interface remains the same (including functionality, of course), you are guaranteed that you could literally rewrite the entire back end of the audio system without ever affecting the high-level audio components.

One of the more interesting portions of the sound manager system is the concept of *high-level sound objects*. Basically, a high-level sound object is a sound component that contains one or more basic audio components, and it most likely uses some sort of algorithm to determine how these various components are played. The important point, though, is that if the sound object is derived from IPlayable, the client can then play and control the entire sound system as simply as if it were a single sound, no matter how complex the high-level sound object actually is.

For example, you could create a high-level sound object that is designed to play differently based on specific game information. An example of this might be a footstep sound object (or maybe a more generalized 'impact' object, even). This object produces any number of different sounds, depending on the material that a character is walking on, the size of the character, and how it currently moving (e.g., creeping, walking, running, jumping, etc.). By encapsulating this information into a single sound object, you avoid the need to build a lot of duplicate information into each character. Instead, you simply create a single sound object that is initialized with enough information to intelligently decide what the footsteps should sound like. The sound object can even provide built-in variations by either choosing one of multiple sounds to play or by altering the pitch slightly—or it can perform both of these variations. After that, it is simply a matter of manipulating and playing the sound just like any other sound.

We will be creating a SoundManager class that is designed to perform three tasks:

1. Load and maintain sound definitions (both 2D and 3D) from scripts, based on simple string identifiers. By "sound definition," we mean that an initialization structure can be retrieved using a simple string identifier.

2. Provide a create-on-demand object-caching system. This allows you to avoid having to create more sounds than are absolutely needed by easily reusing sound objects based on a sound-definition string identifier.

3. Load and play *soundscapes* from scripts. For our purposes, soundscapes are defined as layered groups of sounds with algorithmic properties that determine the random dynamics and placement of the sounds. These ISoundScape objects will be derived from IAudioBase, and will function like a single sound entity, able to Play(), Pause(), Stop(), and adjust the volume of the entire group with simple function

calls. (We will go deeper into the workings of soundscapes later on in this chapter.)

While there might be other tasks you want your higher-level sound manager to do, the point here is not to provide an all-inclusive list of features that could conceivably be needed for your game or engine. Instead, we are demonstrating several practical ways of expanding an existing sound system. Most games require many audio features, some fairly general and some quite specific to the game. By abstracting them to a limited degree where you can, and by placing them between the low-level audio interface and the game code via libraries, you can create a reusable set of highly functional audio components that can even be used in future games. Keep in mind that these features could just as easily be built on top of an existing system (say, a commercial sound library or a differently implemented DirectSound-based system).

INTERFACES

Let's first examine the basic interface used by the high-level sound system (from now on, just referred to as the "sound system." The low-level audio system will be called the "audio system".)

LISTING 17.1

```
class ISoundManager
{
public:

    virtual bool Init() = 0;
    virtual void Term() = 0;

    virtual bool IsInitialized() = 0;

    virtual bool LoadScript(std::string sFileName) = 0;
    virtual bool RemoveAll() = 0;

    virtual bool IsSoundRegistered(
        std::string sSoundName) = 0;
```

```
    virtual bool GetSoundInit(std::string sSoundName,
        SoundInit& init) = 0;
    virtual bool InitSound(std::string sSoundName,
        ISound*& pSound) = 0;
    virtual void ResetSoundItr() = 0;
    virtual bool GetNextSound(
        std::string& sSoundName) = 0;
    virtual bool RemoveSound(
        std::string& sSoundName) = 0;
    virtual bool RemoveAllSounds() = 0;

    virtual bool IsSound3DRegistered(
        std::string sSound3DName) = 0;
    virtual bool GetSound3DInit(
        std::string sSound3DName,
        Sound3DInit& init) = 0;
    virtual bool InitSound3D(std::string sSound3DName,
        ISound3D*& pSound3D) = 0;
    virtual void ResetSound3DItr() = 0;
    virtual bool GetNextSound3D(
        std::string& sSound3DName) = 0;
    virtual bool RemoveSound3D(
        std::string& sSound3DName) = 0;
    virtual bool RemoveAllSounds3D() = 0;

    virtual bool IsSoundScapeRegistered(
        std::string sSoundScapeName) = 0;
    virtual bool CreateSoundScape(
        ISoundScape*& pSoundScape) = 0;
    virtual bool InitSoundScape(
        std::string sSoundScapeName,
        ISoundScape*& pSoundScape) = 0;
    virtual void ResetSoundScapeItr() = 0;
    virtual bool GetNextSoundScape(
        std::string& sSoundScapeName) = 0;
    virtual bool RemoveSoundScape(
        std::string sSoundScapeName) = 0;
    virtual bool RemoveAllSoundScapes() = 0;
};

inline static ISoundManager* SoundMgr()
{ return AudioScriptFactory::GetSoundMgr(); }
```

`ISoundManager` OVERVIEW

The class interface `ISoundManager` defines the most important and fundamental class: the actual sound manager. Like the audio manager, this is a
facade-style class, and is based on a singleton model, meaning that only one
object may be created at any time. This is enforced through the use of a factory object that is hidden behind a convenient accessor function, `Sound-`
`Mgr()`. Thus, accessing the sound manager looks very much like accessing
the audio manager. For instance, to initialize the sound manager, you
would use the following code:

```
if(!SoundMgr()->Init())
    return false;
```

You may also note that the sound manager shares many design traits
with the audio manager, as well. For instance, objects specific to the sound
manager are created and managed through the manager itself. As an example, `ISoundScape` objects are created in the following manner:

```
ISoundScape* pSoundScape;
if(!SoundMgr()->CreateSoundScape(pSoundScape))
    return false;
```

However, one of the most important aspects of this manager is the ability to load sound and soundscape definitions from script files, and then access these definitions using a simple string identifier. Loading a script is as
simple as calling the `ISoundManager::LoadScript()` function. Any number of scripts can be loaded simultaneously, as long as they do not have
conflicting identifiers. They will be placed into a global pool for access until
the definitions are either explicitly destroyed or destroyed in a batch.

You may be wondering why we are talking about loading and storing
sound definitions rather than *sounds*. This is because we will be storing the
sound objects' initialization structures, not fully initialized sounds, which
makes much more sense when you consider how such a system is likely to
be used. In a script file, you might define "Goblin Grunt" as a 3D sound definition. Theoretically, you could store the actual position and other
specifics of one particular goblin grunt sound (e.g., `identifier` = `"Goblin`
`Grunt 974"`), but doing so would be an incredible waste of resources; you
would need a script entry for every single goblin in the game. Instead, by
storing the initialization structure, you need define the sound only once.

Your game can be made to understand that the "Goblin Grunt" sound should only be associated with goblins that come within a certain range from the player, so you can create this sound (or likely several instances of the sound), and associate each one with a goblin.

Storing one sound, or perhaps even several different sounds per goblin instance, may not be practical if you've got 20 goblins on the screen at one time. Technically, you only need to assign a sound to a goblin the moment that particular goblin actually must play a sound. In our example of a goblin grunt sound, this only happens when a goblin actually decides to grunt. One solution to this problem is to maintain a pool of sounds defined by the goblin grunt initialization parameters. In fact, we've built this capability into the sound manager via several functions, `ISoundManager::GetSound()` and `ISoundManager::ReleaseSound()` for 2D sounds, and `ISoundManager::GetSound3D()` and `ISoundManager::ReleaseSound3D()` for 3D sounds.

Whenever a goblin decides to grunt, it asks the sound manager for a goblin grunt sound. The manager determines if any free goblin grunt sounds have already been created and are not currently playing or in use, and returns one of these sounds. If no sounds are available, the sound manager creates a new sound object and returns it. In this manner, the total number of created goblin grunt sounds will never exceed the maximum number of these particular sounds played simultaneously.

There are two strategies for using these sounds in game-world objects, especially 3D sounds. Typically, a 3D object that needs to play a sound will use the `ISoundManager::GetSound3D()` function to retrieve the sound from the cache (or create a new one). The object then sets the appropriate parameters, such as the position or perhaps a small variance in the pitch. After this, the sound will likely be played. We then have two choices as to how the sounds are managed. In part, the correct choice depends on the particular task and on the environment for which you are programming.

In order for a sound to be released back to the sound manager's cache, the object and string identifier must again be passed to a `SoundManager` function—this time, `ISoundManager::ReleaseSound3D()`. This tells the sound manager that the sound is done and may be used by some other object. However, releasing a sound does not stop the sound. It will continue to play in full, making it convenient to quickly get, play, and release sounds in succession without a lot of extra management. The sound manager, in fact, will not reuse the sound until it has finished playing. For this reason, however, you should be careful when discarding a looping sound, as it will continue to play indefinitely until it is either stopped by a global command or discarded by buffer management.

This system allows a second management strategy wherein a 3D object gets a sound, plays it, and then releases it back to the sound manager only after the object has finished playing. This can be done by polling the `IsPlayed()` function in the object's update loop and calling `ISound-Manager::ReleaseSound3D()` when it's finished. This sound will then be stored until another request is made for a sound with the same definition. The advantage of this method is that the 3D object can move the sound around with it, only releasing it when it is completely finished. Additionally, you might even delay the release of the sound for a short time in order to avoid potentially cutting off any lingering reverberation or other effects that might still be audible. In this manner, you can ensure that your world object maintains control of the sound (and can position it appropriately) for as long as it needs to.

Technically speaking, you could rely on the audio manager's buffer-management systems to ensure that sounds are properly distributed. For instance, if there are not enough hardware 3D buffers to assign a sound to each goblin, sounds for goblins farthest away from the player will tend not to load or play, since the sorting algorithm takes distance from the listener into account. This is generally an acceptable proposition, as they would likely not be heard over the closer goblins' sounds, anyway. Unfortunately, for extremely brief and/or periodic sound effects, this means that the farther-away goblins would never grunt, even if the closer ones were currently silent. The advantage of using a higher-level management system is that buffers do not needlessly sit idle. It is simply a way to ensure more optimal use of buffers, at the cost of slightly more work for the client programmer in the way of management.

For all the object types that are tracked by the sound manager, you will also notice a number of enumeration and retrieval functions. For instance, for 2D sounds, two of these functions are:

```
virtual void ResetSoundItr() = 0;
virtual bool GetNextSound(std::string& sSoundName) = 0;
```

Using these two functions, an application can iterate through the entire internal set of sound definitions, getting the name of each in turn. Although a game could theoretically make use of this data in some way, most often a game will know in advance what string identifiers to search for.

These enumeration routines are primarily designed for use with editors and sample programs, such as the AudioTest application provided on the CD-ROM (game_audio\Audio_sdk\AudioScript\)that demonstrates many of the library features.

Additionally, routines are provided for removing sound definitions by name, by type, or all at once. Three examples of this are shown below:

```
virtual bool RemoveSound(std::string& sSoundName) = 0;
virtual bool RemoveAllSounds() = 0;
virtual bool RemoveAll() = 0;
```

Again, except perhaps for removal of all items (or maybe removal by type), these routines are less practical in games where the sound definitions will likely be left in memory over the course of the entire game, or at least until a new level or section is loaded.

SOUND MANAGER IMPLEMENTATION

In the rest of this chapter, we will examine the internal workings of the sound manager, including how to create and manage soundscapes. The SoundScape class implementation itself will be covered in an upcoming section, so don't worry if you don't understand all of the details yet. We will not only see how to create these operational classes, but how to integrate them with the script reader from Chapter 16. Using this system as a guide, you should be able to easily add your own customizations, create new objects, or even build your own sound manager system with your own objects instead of the ones presented here. The scripting system was kept independent of the main audio library. This way, you can more easily discard it and replace it with your own, if you already have a script system in your game engine.

Like the audio manager, our SoundManager class derives from an abstract interface class that defines which functions will be exposed to the client. Beyond this set of functions, though, there are no restrictions on how they are implemented. An advantage of this is that public member functions can be added to the concrete implementation class without fear of compromising or confusing the interface, since the client will never see these additional functions. This helps keep the implementation cleaner and easier to maintain in the long run.

CACHED OBJECT POOL IMPLEMENTATION

One of the more important, yet slightly complicated systems we have implemented is the cached object pool system. Essentially, the heart of the system is an associative STL map that pairs standard STL strings with a cached object structure that contains an initialization structure, along with a vector and a queue full of object pointers. Here are the structures involved in this system (Listing 17.2):

LISTING 17.2

```cpp
typedef std::vector<ISound*> ISoundVector;
typedef std::queue<ISound*> ISoundQueue;
typedef std::vector<ISound3D*> ISound3DVector;
typedef std::queue <ISound3D*> ISound3DQueue;

struct SoundPool
{
    ISoundVector    m_Used;
    ISoundQueue     m_Free;
    SoundInit       m_Init;
};

struct Sound3DPool
{
    ISound3DVector m_Used;
    ISound3DQueue  m_Free;
    Sound3DInit    m_Init;
};

typedef std::map<std::string, SoundPool> StrSndPoolMap;
typedef std::map<std::string, Sound3DPool> StrSnd3DPoolMap;
```

Because we are managing two different types of objects, we need two different structures, one for each object type. Each pool structure represents a single sound definition and is associated with a string identifier in a map. Figure 17.2 illustrates the relationships visually, showing two entries in the map, with three sounds in the in-use and free containers for both entries.

Inside each pool structure, an initialization structure is stored. This structure is used as a template for creating new sound objects on demand.

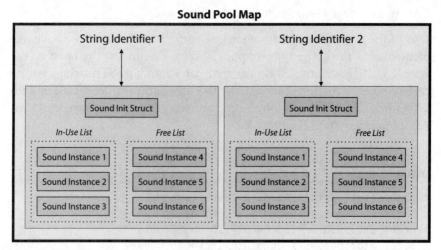

FIGURE 17.1   Internal representation of a sound pool map structure.

When an object is requested, the free queue is first checked to see if any objects are available. If so, the object is removed from the free queue and placed on the in-use vector. Using these two structures, the system keeps track of how many sound objects are free or in use at any time. When a sound changes status, it is simply moved from one container to the other. These two containers form the heart of the sound manager, so it is important to understand how they work.

THE SoundManager CLASS DECLARATION

In Listing 17.3, you can examine the concrete declaration of the Sound-Manager class. As should be expected, this concrete class is derived from ISoundManager for its enforced interface. The data members mainly include STL-based containers for tracking sound objects in various manners, including the pool container and iterators we've seen previously, and a couple of lists for tracking soundscape objects. We also maintain our own timer for use by the soundscape objects. Note also that, similar to the audio manager, we have an accessor function named CSoundMgr() that returns a concrete pointer, SoundManager*, instead of the abstract ISoundManager*. This allows easy access to the concrete class's public member functions via the SoundScape class. You should also note the private helper functions that begin with Load. Each of these functions are designed to load a specific object type from a script file. We will show how simple it is to add new supported object types and custom definitions by adding new functions. Or, if you prefer, you can extend the capabilities of existing definitions by adding new supported keywords in the loading functions.

LISTING 17.3

```
class SoundManager : public ISoundManager
{
// Interface functions
public:

    bool Init();
    void Term();
    bool IsInitialized() { return m_bInitialized; }


    // Load a sound script from a file
    bool LoadScript(std::string sFileName);

    // Removes all loaded sounds, 3d sounds,
    // and soundscape registrations from memory.
    bool RemoveAll();

    bool IsSoundRegistered(std::string sSoundName);
    bool GetSoundInit(std::string sSoundName,
        SoundInit& init);
    bool GetSound(std::string sSoundName,
        ISound*& pSound);
    bool ReleaseSound(std::string sSoundName,
        ISound* pSound);
    void ResetSoundItr();
    bool GetNextSound(std::string& sSoundName);
    bool RemoveSound(std::string& sSoundName);
    bool RemoveAllSounds();

    bool IsSound3DRegistered(std::string sSound3DName);
    bool GetSound3DInit(std::string sSound3DName,
        Sound3DInit& init);
    bool GetSound3D(std::string sSound3DName,
```

```
        ISound3D*& pSound3D);
    bool ReleaseSound3D(std::string sSound3DName,
        ISound3D* pSound3D);
    void ResetSound3DItr();
    bool GetNextSound3D(std::string& sSound3DName);
    bool RemoveSound3D(std::string& sSound3DName);
    bool RemoveAllSounds3D();

    bool IsSoundScapeRegistered(
        std::string sSoundScapeName);
    bool CreateSoundScape(ISoundScape*& pSoundScape);
    bool InitSoundScape(std::string sSoundScapeName,
        ISoundScape*& pSoundScape);
    void ResetSoundScapeItr();
    bool GetNextSoundScape(
        std::string& sSoundScapeName);
    bool RemoveSoundScape(std::string sSoundScapeName);
    bool RemoveAllSoundScapes();


// Concrete functions
public:
    SoundManager();
    virtual ~SoundManager();

    void Clear();

    void InsertSoundScape(ISoundScape* pSoundScape);
    void RemoveSoundScape(ISoundScape* pSoundScape);

    float GetCurrentTime() { return m_fCurrentTime; }
    float GetFrameTime() { return m_fFrameTime; }

    CRITICAL_SECTION& GetUpdateCS()
        { return m_csSoundScapeUpdate; }

// Internal functions and types
private:
    // Separate thread for timed events
    static void TimeEvent(LPVOID lpv);
    // Service all currently playing streaming buffers
    void ServiceSoundScapes();
```

```
bool LoadSound(ScriptNode* pNode);
bool LoadSound3D(ScriptNode* pNode);
bool LoadSoundScape(ScriptNode* pNode);
bool LoadBackground(ScriptNode* pNode,
    BackgroundElement& bge);
bool LoadPeriodic(ScriptNode* pNode,
    PeriodicElement& pe);

private:

    // Bool indicating initialization status
    bool                    m_bInitialized;
    // Script loader object
    ScriptLoader            m_Loader;

    // Map associating strings with sound pools
    StrSndPoolMap           m_SndMap;
    // Iterator for traversing through all sound
    // init structure names
    StrSndPoolMap::iterator    m_SndItr;

    // Map associating strings with Sound3D
    // initialization structures
    StrSnd3DPoolMap         m_Snd3DMap;
    // Iterator for traversing through all Sound3D
    // init structure names
    StrSnd3DPoolMap::iterator m_Snd3DItr;

    // SoundScape string-name to init structure map
    SSInitMap               m_SSMap;
    // Iterator for traversing through all
    // SoundScape init structure names
    SSInitMap::iterator     m_SSItr;

    // List of all updating soundscapes
    SoundScapeList          m_SoundScapeUpdateList;

    // Master list of all soundscapes
    SoundScapeVector        m_MasterSoundScape;

    // Shutdown synchronization handle
```

```
HANDLE                      m_hTerm;
// Critical section ensuring update thread is
// properly synchonized with other functions
CRITICAL_SECTION            m_csSoundScapeUpdate;

// Track the current time for all
// time-based calculations
float                       m_fCurrentTime;
float                       m_fFrameTime;
};


inline static SoundManager* CSoundMgr()
{ return static_cast<SoundManager*>(SoundMgr()); }
```

STARTUP, SHUTDOWN, AND UPDATING

One of the more important responsibilities of the sound manager is to dynamically alter the parameters of a soundscape over time in the background. As such, we will need another background thread for performing this operation without the direct intervention of the client. We will be taking a similar approach to that used with the audio manager. In fact, most of this code is copied almost verbatim, since we have already established how to safely create, maintain, and shut down threads in our managers. There is no need to reinvent a technique if we have already found one that works.

In the startup code, we also take care of a few other management issues, such as initializing our lexer object and storing the current time for future frame-rate calculations, which we will be using in the soundscape objects. Listing 17.4 shows the basic startup and shutdown code for the sound manager.

LISTING 17.4

```
bool SoundManager::Init()
{
    if(!m_Loader.Init())
        return false;
    m_bInitialized = true;
    m_fCurrentTime = float(timeGetTime()) / 1000.0f;
```

```
    SoundScape::InitPool(32);
    InitializeCriticalSection(&m_csSoundScapeUpdate);

    // Set the callback for the timer function used
    // for general events that need to happen 10
    // times per second.
    if(_beginthread(&SoundManager::TimeEvent, 4096, NULL) ==
        -1)
        return false;
    return true;
}

void SoundManager::Term()
{
    if(m_bInitialized)
    {
        // Create event objects to be used by the thread
        // to signal a successful shutdown.
        m_hTerm = CreateEvent(NULL, FALSE, FALSE, NULL);
        // Indicates the audio manager is terminating
        m_bInitialized = false;
        // Wait for the thread to shut down first
        WaitForSingleObject(m_hTerm, INFINITE);
        // Close the event object now
        CloseHandle(m_hTerm);

        // Delete all soundscape objects
        SoundScape::TermPool();

        // Enter and leave the critical section to ensure that
        // the soundscape update loop is done
        EnterCriticalSection(&m_csSoundScapeUpdate);
        LeaveCriticalSection(&m_csSoundScapeUpdate);

        // Remove the soundscape critical section
        DeleteCriticalSection(&m_csSoundScapeUpdate);

        // Clear all registration entries
        RemoveAll();
    }
```

```
    m_Loader.Term();
    Clear();
}
```

LOADING AND PARSING SCRIPTS

One of the sound manager's primary roles is to provide automatic script support. To give you an idea of how the script will both look and work, let's see what some sample sound definitions might look like in a script file.

LISTING 17.5

```
Sound = "Main Menu Music"
{
    FileName = "MainMenuMusic.mp3";
    Looping = true;
    Music = true;
    Streaming = true;
    Volume = 0.75;
}
Sound3D = "Goblin Grunt"
{
    FileName = "GoblinGrunt.wav";
    Volume = 0.8;
    MinDistance = 5.0;
    MaxDistance = 40.0;
}
```

The script definition looks suspiciously like an initialized C structure, which is no accident. In fact, if the script parsing is set up correctly, there should almost be no difference between creating sound definitions in code or from a script. Because of the known default values of the initialization structures, we can safely assume that certain parameters need not be filled out. For instance, you will notice how looping, music, and streaming are all set to true in the "Main Menu Music" sound, yet these are not defined in the "Goblin Grunt" 3D sound. This is acceptable because we know that both of these variables default to false in both the 2D and 3D sound initialization structures. Therefore, we know that any initialized sound based on the

"Goblin Grunt" definition will be nonlooping, nonstreaming, and defined as a sound effect (Music = false).

The LoadScript() function, shown in Listing 17.6, performs the actual task of parsing the script file and creating the appropriate objects based on the content.

LISTING 17.6

```
bool SoundManager::LoadScript(string sFileName)
{
    CHECK_INIT();
    Script script;
    if(!m_Loader.Load(sFileName, script))
        return false;

    ScriptNode* pNode = script.GetRoot();
    while(pNode)
    {
        // Look for named "Sound" nodes in the script
        if(SNDMGR_STRCMP(pNode->GetName(),
            "Sound") == 0)
        {
            if(!LoadSound(pNode))
                return false;
        }
        // Look for named "Sound3D" nodes in the script
        else if(SNDMGR_STRCMP(pNode->GetName(),
            "Sound3D") == 0)
        {
            if(!LoadSound3D(pNode))
                return false;
        }
        // Look for named "soundscape" nodes
        // in the script
        else if(SNDMGR_STRCMP(pNode->GetName(),
            "SoundScape") == 0)
        {
            if(!LoadSoundScape(pNode))
                return false;
        }
        // advance to the next sibling node
```

```
        // if one exists
        pNode = pNode->GetSibling();
    };
    return true;
}
```

The LoadScript() function is surprisingly simple, even with the bulk of the parsing work being done in other functions. As with all of our API-level functions, we are careful to first ensure that the manager has been properly initialized. We then create a Script object and pass it into the Script-Loader::Load() function, along with the name of the script file to parse.

Once the script has been successfully parsed, we begin iterating through the node tree built by the ScriptLoader and stored in the Script object. (For a more-detailed description of the parsing and traversal process, see Chapter 16—An Audio-Scripting Format.) In the node-traversal loop, we look for particular node names—in this case, "Sound," "Sound3D," and "SoundScape." When any of these names are found, the node pointer is passed to another function where it will be parsed, and an object will be created from the data contained under that node element. The SNDMGR_STRCMP identifier is a macro that can be switched between the case-sensitive and case-insensitive versions of the C-string comparison functions. The case-sensitive string comparison function is compiled by default, but this can be changed by commenting out the SNDMGR_CASE_SENSITIVE definition at the top of the file.

The LoadSound(), LoadSound3D(), and LoadSoundScape() functions are where the actual work of parsing the node tree takes place. You will notice that even these functions are relatively simple, thanks to the work we have invested in creating an easy-to-use parsing system. Let's look at each in turn, starting with the LoadSound() function shown in Listing 17.7.

LISTING 17.7

```
bool SoundManager::LoadSound(ScriptNode* pNode)
{
    // We use string IDs in this scripting system
    if(pNode->GetDataType() != Script::STRING)
        return false;

    // Just return true if the sound is already registered
```

```
if(IsSoundRegistered(pNode->GetString()))
    return true;

SoundPool pool;
ScriptNode* pChildNode = pNode->GetChild();
while(pChildNode)
{
    if(SNDMGR_STRCMP(pChildNode->GetName(),
        "FileName") == 0)
        pool.m_Init.m_sFileName =
            pChildNode->GetString();
    else if(SNDMGR_STRCMP(pChildNode->GetName(),
        "Looping") == 0)
        pool.m_Init.m_bLooping =
            pChildNode->GetBool();
    else if(SNDMGR_STRCMP(pChildNode->GetName(),
        "Streaming") == 0)
        pool.m_Init.m_bStreaming =
            pChildNode->GetBool();
    else if(SNDMGR_STRCMP(pChildNode->GetName(),
        "Music") == 0)
        pool.m_Init.m_bMusic =
            pChildNode->GetBool();
    else if(SNDMGR_STRCMP(pChildNode->GetName(),
        "Volume") == 0)
        pool.m_Init.m_Prop.m_fVolume =
            pChildNode->GetReal();
    else if(SNDMGR_STRCMP(pChildNode->GetName(),
        "Pan") == 0)
        pool.m_Init.m_Prop.m_fPan =
            pChildNode->GetReal();
    else if(SNDMGR_STRCMP(pChildNode->GetName(),
        "Pitch") == 0)
        pool.m_Init.m_Prop.m_fPitch =
            pChildNode->GetReal();
    else if(SNDMGR_STRCMP(pChildNode->GetName(),
        "ReadCursor") == 0)
        pool.m_Init.m_Prop.m_nReadCursor =
            pChildNode->GetInteger();
    else
        return false;
    pChildNode = pChildNode->GetSibling();
```

```
    }

    // Insert the sound definition into the map
    m_SndMap.insert(make_pair(pNode->GetString(),
        pool));
    return true;
}
```

The first thing this function does is to ensure that the top-level `"Sound"` node is assigned a string variable. At an example, in the script text:

```
Sound = "Some Sound"
```

The string "Some Sound" is the data contained in the node named "Sound". Because we need a way to differentiate between the different sounds we create, we require each Sound definition to have a string identifier. We have chosen strings as our method of uniquely identifying objects in our scripts, but there is no reason that integers or some other variable type cannot be used. The only requirements are that the data type must be supported by the lexer and script loader code, and the data type must be compatible with an STL map—that is, it must support the less-than ($<$) and equals ($=$) operators.

Once the sound data has been established, we check to see if a sound of that name (or rather, one with that associated ID value) has already been parsed. You may notice that we simply abort parsing and return success if a duplicate name is found. Duplicate names are not considered fatal errors because of the difficulties in determining which registered sound definitions to remove if a soundscape definition is removed. In fact, we don't even attempt it, because multiple soundscapes could be using a single sound definition. Instead, sound definitions may be enumerated and removed individually or in batches, if desired. When a soundscape is removed, there is no way to reload the soundscape if we do not allow the parser to skip over sounds that are already registered. Quite frankly, there is little reason to remove individual sound/soundscape definitions once they are in memory, but the ability to do so is available for completeness's sake, along with the more-practical ability to remove them all at once. Remember, only the initialization structures are kept in memory, not actual instantiated objects. The objects are only created once the appropriate function is called, such as CreateSound() or CreateSoundScape().

A SoundPool structure is created next, which contains a single initialization structure that will be used when creating new objects. As previously discussed, the SoundPool struct will also be responsible for holding multiple instantiated objects, and it will track which ones have been used and which have not. For now, however, we are only interested in the initialization structure, which will be used as a 'template' for creating any number of sounds based on this common data.

The function extracts the child node from the sound node next, and iterates through all the subsequent siblings of that first child node, looking for any nodes that match the parameters of the initialization structure. When a match is found, the data from that node is copied to the appropriate field in the initialization structure. In this manner, there is a one-to-one match-up between initialization members in both the C++ code and those available in the script. It should also be noted that there is no run-time error-checking performed on the variable types. It is assumed that the correct variable types will be used. An assertion will catch any mismatched types in debug mode, but will silently return an incorrect data type in release mode. In this scripting system, run-time safety/checking is usually neglected in favor of efficiency, since most game environments will be using static scripts that can be well tested in advance. There is typically no need for a large amount of run-time script-checking in production code. However, you may wish to add more-extensive error checking and reporting for use during development.

When there are no more child nodes to iterate through, the loop exits, and the SoundPool structure is inserted into an STL map along with the string ID of the parent node. We can now access this sound definition (based on the SoundInit structure) or the other sound pool data using a string identifier. (This will be described in more detail later on.) Soundscape objects and 3D sounds are parsed in a manner similar to the sound parameter. The only major difference for 3D sounds is in its different initialization parameters.

For soundscapes, we have to deal with a compound object, meaning that inside the script definition of every soundscape object we can expect to find multiple subobject definitions: namely, *background elements* and *periodic elements*. In script, each of these subobjects exactly mirrors the structures used in the programmatic interface (which can be seen in the upcoming Listing 17.13). In other words, you can simply look at the members of the two initialization structures Background and Periodic to determine what is supported in the script format. For reference, let's take a quick look at one of our sample soundscape scripts in Listing 17.8. Don't worry too much about what all these parameters mean. We will learn how soundscapes work in more detail later in the chapter.

LISTING 17.8

```
SoundScape = "Windy Forest"
{
    Background
    {
        Sound = "windloop01";
        MinVolume = 0.25;
        MaxVolume = 1.0;
        MinVolumeTime = 1.5;
        MaxVolumeTime = 3.0;
        MinPitch = 0.5;
        MaxPitch = 1.5;
        MinPitchTime = 1.0;
        MaxPitchTime = 4.0;
    }

    Background
    {
        Sound = "windloop02";
        MinVolume = 0.0;
        MaxVolume = 0.75;
    }

    Periodic = Default
    {
        Sound3D = "windfx01";
        MinDelay = 30.0;
        MaxDelay = 90.0;
        MinPitch = 1.25;
        MaxPitch = 0.75;
        XRange = 20.0;
        YRange = 20.0;
        ZRange = 20.0;
        MinDistance = 3.0;
    }
```

```
Periodic
{
    Sound3D = "windfx02";
}
Periodic
{
    Sound3D = "windfx03";
}
Periodic
{
    Sound3D = "windfx04";
}
Periodic
{
    Sound3D = "windfx05";
}
}
```

We can see that the soundscape Windy Forest is comprised of two background elements and five periodic elements. Our code takes the same approach as before when we dealt with child objects: we create a separate function for parsing each component. Listing 17.9 shows the code for reading soundscape definitions.

LISTING 17.9

```
bool SoundManager::LoadSoundScape(ScriptNode* pNode)
{
    // We use string IDs in this scripting system
    if(pNode->GetDataType() != Script::STRING)
        return false);

    // Just return true if the soundscape is
    // already registered
    if(IsSoundScapeRegistered(pNode->GetString()))
        return true;

    SoundScapeInternalInit init;
    BackgroundElement bge;
```

```
    PeriodicElement pe;

    ScriptNode* pChildNode = pNode->GetChild();
    while(pChildNode)
    {
        if(SNDMGR_STRCMP(pChildNode->GetName(),
            "Periodic") == 0)
        {
            if(!LoadPeriodic(pChildNode, pe))
                return false;
            init.m_aPeriodic.push_back(pe);
        }
        else if(SNDMGR_STRCMP(pChildNode->GetName(),
            "Background") == 0)
        {
            if(!LoadBackground(pChildNode, bge))
                return false;
            init.m_aBackground.push_back(bge);
        }
        pChildNode = pChildNode->GetSibling();
    }

    // Insert the sound definition into the map
    m_SSMap.insert(make_pair(pNode->GetString(), init));
    return true;
}
```

Again, this function looks very similar to previous parsing functions. We see that the two subelements "Background" and "Periodic" are searched for inside the "Soundscape" definition. In addition to passing the current node to these functions so they can parse the children, we also provide a BackgroundElement struct and a PeriodicElement struct for the functions to use. By using the same structures between function calls, we save the audio-script author typing time when creating a number of variables with similar types. Any changes made to the initialization structure are preserved for the next element unless the Default keyword is assigned to the top-level node, which clears all the values to their defaults. Let's look at the LoadPeriodic() function in Listing 17.10 to see how this works.

LISTING 17.10

```
bool SoundManager::LoadPeriodic(ScriptNode* pNode,
PeriodicElement& pe)
{
    // Check to see if the node has the "Default"
    // keyword, meaning it should clear all values
    // to their original defaults.
    if((pNode->GetDataType() == Script::VARIABLE) &&
        (strcmp(pNode->GetVariable(), "Default") == 0))
        pe.Clear();

    ScriptNode* pChildNode = pNode->GetChild();
    while(pChildNode)
    {
        if(SNDMGR_STRCMP(pChildNode->GetName(),
            "Sound3D") == 0)
            pe.m_sSound3DID =
                pChildNode->GetString();
        else if(SNDMGR_STRCMP(pChildNode->GetName(),
            "MinPitch") == 0)
            pe.m_Init.m_fMinPitch =
                pChildNode->GetReal();
        else if(SNDMGR_STRCMP(pChildNode->GetName(),
            "MaxPitch") == 0)
            pe.m_Init.m_fMaxPitch =
                pChildNode->GetReal();
        else if(SNDMGR_STRCMP(pChildNode->GetName(),
            "MinDelay") == 0)
            pe.m_Init.m_fMinDelay =
                pChildNode->GetReal();
        else if(SNDMGR_STRCMP(pChildNode->GetName(),
            "MaxDelay") == 0)
            pe.m_Init.m_fMaxDelay =
                pChildNode->GetReal();
        else if(SNDMGR_STRCMP(pChildNode->GetName(),
            "XRange") == 0)
            pe.m_Init.m_fXRange =
                pChildNode->GetReal();
        else if(SNDMGR_STRCMP(pChildNode->GetName(),
            "YRange") == 0)
            pe.m_Init.m_fYRange =
```

```
                pChildNode->GetReal();
        else if(SNDMGR_STRCMP(pChildNode->GetName(),
            "ZRange") == 0)
            pe.m_Init.m_fZRange =
                pChildNode->GetReal();
        else if(SNDMGR_STRCMP(pChildNode->GetName(),
            "MinDistance") == 0)
            pe.m_Init.m_fMinDistance =
                pChildNode->GetReal();
        else
            return false;
        pChildNode = pChildNode->GetSibling();
    }
    return true;
}
```

In the beginning of the function, we look for the keyword Default, and only clear the initialization structure if this keyword is found. In this way, the sound designer avoids having to needlessly duplicate settings from element to element, especially when it is likely that many of them will be identical, except for the name of the sound to play. This saves a lot of extra cut-and-paste work when making a small change that affects a large numbers of elements. In addition, any code changes that can bypass needless text-parsing is always welcome, especially if those changes don't come at the expense of the script format's usability. Remember, that is why we are storing data in a text format instead of a more-efficient binary format in the first place.

If performance becomes a concern at any point, there are two options for you to consider. You could add support to the script system to enable using precompiled script files, which is supported by the TokenFile class. Precompiled binary token streams are generally found to be about 5 to 10 times as efficient in regards to loading, since the stream does not have to be tokenized or heavily processed in any way. Alternatively, you may decide to add support for native binary formats. This could be accomplished by saving the initialization structures on disk, but referencing other items in a binary form does become a bit tricky, since it is obviously not feasible to save memory pointers on disk. Unless you actually demonstrate a noticeable performance problem when loading the text-based format, though, it seems like a good idea to stick with what works instead of creating more work for yourself.

SOUND CREATION AND POOL SYSTEMS

At this point, we have a system that can create a number of sound and soundscape definitions, and store them in an associative map with strings used to uniquely identify them. That's a great start, but what do we do with them next? Obviously, a definition does not do us a lot of good unless there is a way to turn it into an actual, instantiated object. Additionally, for our sound objects, we want to build a method into the system for creating and utilizing pools of reusable objects in order to ensure optimal use of resources. We have already laid the groundwork for this with the Sound-Pool and Sound3DPool structures. Each of these structures, in addition to being used to hold an initialization structure to be used when objects are created, also hold structures needed to maintain a pool of reusable objects, tracking which are used and which are unused. At the heart of this system are two complimentary functions, GetSound() and ReleaseSound(). In the case of 3D sounds, the functions are named GetSound3D() and ReleaseSound3D().

GetSound() takes a string name as an input parameter and has an ISound pointer as an output parameter. It is designed to create an ISound object, based on the initialization structure via the string ID passed to it. Before it creates an object, it first checks to see if there are any sound objects that have been discarded and are not currently playing. If one is found, this object is used instead of a new object being created.

Although an object-caching system is already used in the audio manager, the advantage of a higher-level object cache is that the caching takes place on a per-definition basis instead of on a global pool of objects. This means that the object, along with any internal buffers, might not have been destroyed before the occasion arises to use it a second time. This obviously adds a greater level of efficiency than simply reusing objects in a more simplistic manner. The downside of this more-advanced caching system is that in order to take advantage of the resource-saving benefits, more management is required on the part of the client programmer. However, there is certainly no need to worry about the object-caching system. All the details are handled internally, and there is no real penalty for not taking advantage of the object pool. Listing 17.11 shows how this function works.

LISTING 17.11

```cpp
bool SoundManager::GetSound(std::string sSoundName,
    ISound*& pSound)
{
    CHECK_INIT();
    StrSndPoolMap::iterator itr =
        m_SndMap.find(sSoundName);
    if(itr == m_SndMap.end())
        return false;
    // If there are existing free sounds,
    // use these first
    if(itr->second.m_Free.size() &&
        !itr->second.m_Free.front()->IsPlaying())
    {
        pSound = itr->second.m_Free.front();
        itr->second.m_Free.pop();
        itr->second.m_Used.push_back(pSound);
    }
    // Otherwise, create a new sound object
    else
    {
        if(!AudioMgr()->CreateSound(pSound))
            return false;
        itr->second.m_Used.push_back(pSound);
        if(!pSound->Init(itr->second.m_Init))
            return false;
    }
    return true;
}
```

The function begins by first finding the appropriate SoundPool structure based on the string ID passed into the function. If a structure is found, it then checks the free queue to see if there are any free sound items *that are currently not playing*. The second condition is an important design consideration for the system. The reason for this is that we want a client to have the ability to get a sound, play it, then release it again without worrying about stopping the sound. If a free sound is found, that sound is removed from the free list and placed in the used list, and the object interface is returned to the client. If no free sounds are found, a new sound is created using the initialization structure stored in the SoundPool structure. This sound is placed in the used list and the interface is returned to the user.

Here is one example in which this could be handy: say, for instance, a first-person shooter game uses a rapid-fire weapon of some sort (gee, you think?), and each firing of the weapon requires playback of a new sound to avoid cutting off the sound played before it. Because the sound length is longer than the required delay between successive firings, there will be a certain number of sounds needed to play this one weapon properly. Traditionally, the programmer would simply assign an array of several sounds to the weapon and play those sounds in sequential order. However, if the sound designer decides to shorten or lengthen the sound effect, or the game designer adjusts the firing time of the weapon, there will be either too many or too few sound buffers allocated, because the timing has changed. Instead, by using the object-caching system within the sound manager, the correct number of sounds will always be used because sounds will not be reused until they are finished playing.

The compliment to the GetSound() function is ReleaseSound(), shown in Listing 17.12

LISTING 17.12

```
bool SoundManager::ReleaseSound(std::string sSoundName, ISound*
pSound)
{
    CHECK_INIT();
    StrSndPoolMap::iterator itr = m_SndMap.find(sSoundName);
    if(itr == m_SndMap.end())
        return false;
    ISoundVector::iterator snditr;
    snditr = find(itr->second.m_Used.begin(),
        itr->second.m_Used.end(), pSound);
    if(snditr == itr->second.m_Used.end())
        return false;
    itr->second.m_Used.erase(snditr);
    itr->second.m_Free.push(pSound);
    return true;
}
```

The arguments are nearly identical, requiring a string ID and an ISound pointer. The only difference is that the ISound pointer is passed as a copy instead of by reference, since there is no need to modify the actual pointer for the client. The ReleaseSound() function moves the sound from the 'in-use' list (m_Used) to the 'is-available' list (m_Free). Note that the function must search through the list in order to locate the position of the ISound pointer passed to it. Because the algorithm works by pushing used pointers onto the back of the list, the search will be performed, roughly, from oldest to youngest items, meaning that the search should generally take less than the expected O(n) time (linear time). If you are expecting to use a very large number of sounds and cycle through them very rapidly, you may wish to consider changing the container to an STL set, which will ensure that both insertion and removal are O(log n) time (logarithmic time). However, for typical use this should not be necessary.

MANAGING SOUND DEFINITIONS

In addition to providing methods for retrieving objects created from sound definitions, we provide a way of managing the definitions themselves, including enumeration and removal functions. As previously mentioned, these functions are probably not as useful for a game as they are for an editor.

For each category of object definition, there are several navigation, administrative, and alternative-use type functions. Here is a brief listing of these functions and what they do:

TABLE 17.1 SoundManager Functions

bool IsSoundRegistered (std::string sSoundName);	Queries to see if a sound with a given string ID exists in the definition map.
bool GetSoundInit (std::string sSoundName, SoundInit& init);	Allows you to extract the SoundInit information from the definition map. This can be used if you want to manually create and initialize sounds instead of using the internal object pool.
void ResetSoundItr();	Points an internal iterator to the first definition ID in the map container.
bool GetNextSound (std::string& sSoundName);	Returns the current iterator's string ID, then increments the pointer. If no string can be returned, the function will return false.
bool RemoveSound (std::string sSoundName);	Removes a particular sound based on a string ID.
bool RemoveAllSounds();	Removes all the map elements.

You must be careful when using the remove functions. Because the sound definition is tied to the same structure as the sound pool, destroying the definition will also destroy any pool-managed objects, meaning any sounds created with the GetSound() function.

If you are interested in seeing how these functions work, you can ON THE CD examine the source code on the accompanying CD-ROM. Most of these functions are also available for 3D sounds and soundscapes, as well. Just substitute Sound3D or SoundScape for Sound in the function name.

SOUNDSCAPES

For the sound manager, we will demonstrate a high-level sound object based on the concept of an environmental 'soundscape.' Soundscapes are defined as a collection of two different types of objects, which we call *background elements* and *periodic elements*. You can see the initialization parameters defined in the struct's BackgroundInit and PeriodicInit. Each of these structures is used to define a single element that can be used in the function ISoundScape::AddElement().

Background elements are essentially 2D, looping sounds that can ON THE CD vary in pitch and volume over time. For instance, in the Game_ audio/data folder on the CD-ROM, you will find sample soundscapes, such as "Windy Forest," "Underwater," and "Spaceship Interior." The Windy Forest soundscape uses two overlapping wind loops that are interpolated between ranges of pitch and volume over a selected range of time. By appropriately layering several loops, along with the pitch and volume variations, we can create the illusion of a nonrepeating background sound with a great deal of variation and interest.

In addition to simple background loops, we also have periodic elements. These are randomly fired, single-shot sound effects positioned within 3D space. A number of parameters are used to constrain the sound effect, including maximum distances for each axis, as well as a minimal distance from the listener. Periodic elements are always positioned within absolute world coordinates, but are kept at a constant distance from the listener object. In this manner, the directional aspect of the sound effect is always properly preserved. Periodic elements can also be set to vary slightly in pitch on each play.

Figure 17.2 shows a series of graphs of a single background element and a single periodic element in use over time. The background element varies smoothly over time, while the periodic element plays discretely three times, with a different set of parameters on each play.

Although interfaces are provided to create soundscapes in code, the system truly shines when loading soundscapes directly from a script file. This

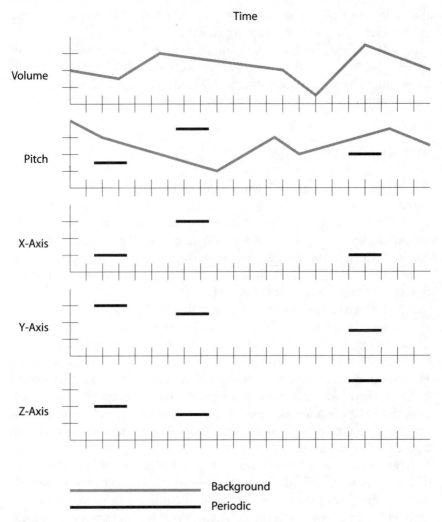

FIGURE 17.2   Soundscape parameters over time.

places the design and implementation of complex sound environments directly in the hands of the sound designer, since the only thing that must match is the name of the soundscape's string identifier. Every other aspect of the soundscape, including what sounds are played, what and how many of each element there are, and what each element's basic characteristics are, can be determined from the script. You can see how the initialization structures in Listing 17.13 correspond exactly with the sample script file previously shown in Listing 17.8.

LISTING 17.13

```
struct BackgroundInit
{
    BackgroundInit() { Clear(); }
    void Clear()
    {
        m_pSound = 0;
        m_fMinVolume = 1.0f;
        m_fMaxVolume = 1.0f;
        m_fMinVolumeTime = 0.0f;
        m_fMaxVolumeTime = 0.0f;
        m_fMinPitch = 1.0f;
        m_fMaxPitch = 1.0f;
        m_fMinPitchTime = 0.0f;
        m_fMaxPitchTime = 0.0f;
    };

    ISound*    m_pSound;
    float      m_fMinVolume;
    float      m_fMaxVolume;
    float      m_fMinVolumeTime;
    float      m_fMaxVolumeTime;
    float      m_fMinPitch;
    float      m_fMaxPitch;
    float      m_fMinPitchTime;
    float      m_fMaxPitchTime;
};

struct PeriodicInit
{
    PeriodicInit() { Clear(); }
    void Clear()
    {
        m_pSound3D = 0;
        m_fMinPitch = 1.0f;
        m_fMaxPitch = 1.0f;
        m_fMinDelay = 0.0f;
```

```
            m_fMaxDelay = 0.0f;
            m_fXRange = 25.0f;
            m_fYRange = 25.0f;
            m_fZRange = 25.0f;
            m_fMinDistance = 0.0f;
    };
    ISound3D*   m_pSound3D;
    float       m_fMinPitch;
    float       m_fMaxPitch;
    float       m_fMinDelay;
    float       m_fMaxDelay;
    float       m_fXRange;
    float       m_fYRange;
    float       m_fZRange;
    float       m_fMinDistance;
};


class ISoundScape : public IAudioBase
{
public:
    virtual bool Init() = 0;

    virtual bool AddElement(
        const BackgroundInit& init) = 0;
    virtual bool AddElement(
        const PeriodicInit& init) = 0;
};
```

ISoundScape AND ELEMENT INITIALIZATION STRUCTURES OVERVIEW

The base soundscape interface is ISoundScape, which is derived from IPlayable, which is derived from IAudioBase. You may recall that IPlayable defines a number of functions and operators common to all sound objects, such as a Play() and Stop() function. (IAudioBase and IPlayable can be examined in detail in Chapter 5, Listing 5.2.) One of the great benefits of using a common base class is the ability to extend its use, even beyond the basic audio component types. In this case, it makes sense to control an entire group of objects as a single entity, which is much more convenient than trying to control each element separately.

ISoundScape only has three functions (other than what it inherits from its parent class): Init() and two versions of AddElement(). Logically enough, Init() prepares the soundscape for use. Each of the AddElement() functions takes a different element initialization structure. AddElement() will create a new sound element in the soundscape, which is defined by the parameters of the structure passed into the function. Let's examine these two structures in more detail; and in doing so, we will understand what the intended behavior of the soundscape system is supposed to be.

The BackgroundElement struct has eight members, four volume- and four pitch-related. You can set minimum and maximum range values, as well as minimum and maximum interpolation times of these parameters. As an example, we may decide to set m_fMinVolume to 0.5 and m_fMaxVolume to 1.0. This will result in the element's random volume swing between 0.5 and 1.0 while the sound is playing. In order to determine what the rate of change will be, we must set the other two values, m_fMinVolumeTime and m_fMaxVolumeTime. If these two values are set at 2.5 and 5.0, respectively, the background element's volume will vary between 0.5 and 1.0, taking anywhere between 2.5 and 5.0 seconds to interpolate between the randomly selected volume changes.

The four pitch variables work in an identical manner to the volume controls. You can choose whether a background sound's pitch and volume should vary slowly and subtly, or fluctuate wildly and dramatically.

The PeriodicElement struct has different parameters to reflect the usage of periodically played sounds as opposed to continuous background loops. There are minimum and maximum values for setting a pitch range: m_fMinPitch, m_fMaxPitch. This controls the initial pitch setting as the element is played. Unlike background elements, periodic elements do not alter their pitch as they are played. Two other variables, m_fMinDelay and m_fMaxDelay, specify the time constraints between two successive play times of a single element. Note that this does not take into account the length of the sound being played. To control positional information, a combination of four additional variables are used: m_fXRange, m_fYRange, m_fZRange, and m_fMinDistance. The x-, y-, and z-range variables limit the random range (positive and negative) of the placement of a sound, relative to the listener object. Surround-speaker and multispeaker systems have poor spatialization of sounds in the vertical direction, so there is usually no need to limit the sounds in this direction, even if you are only trying to simulate random sounds in the horizontal plane, which is typical for most soundscapes. The `m_fMinDistance` variable is used to set a minimum allowed distance from the listener's position. In this way, you can prevent a sound event from occurring too close to the listener. This is important if you are trying to simulate sounds associated with real-world items that the user cannot actually see (i.e. they do not actually exist in the game). For instance, it makes little sense to simulate a bird call only a meter away from the listener if the bird is in fact nowhere to be seen.

One important point to make about positional elements: although the elements are positioned relative to the listener, we do not actually use the head-relative processing mode. Instead, we continuously update the position of the elements to remain a constant distance from the listener. This is done because the head-relative mode would cause the sound to appear from the same position in space as a listener changes orientation, which would tend to break the illusion of events happening in real-world space, especially if the sound effects are of a slightly longer duration where this effect would be most notable.

`SoundManager` SOUNDSCAPE SUPPORT CODE

The operation of soundscapes depends on two basic components: the soundscape implementation code and the support code in the sound manager. We will first examine the code needed to support the operation and updating of soundscapes in the sound manager.

The sound manager is responsible for maintaining a master list of currently playing soundscapes, very similar to the way the audio manager tracks all currently playing sounds and segments. In fact, you may notice some similarities in the code layout and tricks used to ensure thread synchronization. An update thread is created so the soundscapes can be updated without intervention required from the client, and the soundscapes are periodically updated using the master list.

We have already seen how soundscapes are loaded and created from scripts, so let's see what other functions are required for updating the soundscapes. Two important functions are used for inserting and removing the soundscape from the master list. While this may seem a bit trivial, manipulating lists is always slightly more complicated when working with multithreaded code. In order to ensure that a soundscape is not inserted or removed from this list while the update thread is in the middle of iterating through it, we need to make use of a critical section object that will be used to block simultaneous access to the list container from multiple threads. Listing 17.14 shows the functions used to insert and remove soundscapes from the sound manager's master list.

LISTING 17.14

```
void SoundManager::InsertSoundScape(
    ISoundScape* pSoundScape)
{
    CRITICAL_FUNCTION(&m_csSoundMgrUpdate);
    m_SoundScapeUpdateList.push_back(pSoundScape);
}

void SoundManager::RemoveSoundScape(
    ISoundScape* pSoundScape)
{
    CRITICAL_FUNCTION(&m_csSoundMgrUpdate);
    SoundScapeList::iterator itr = find(
        m_SoundScapeUpdateList.begin(),
        m_SoundScapeUpdateList.end(),
        pSoundScape);
    if(itr != m_SoundScapeUpdateList.end())
        m_SoundScapeUpdateList.erase(itr);
}
```

You can see the use of the critical section m_csSoundMgrUpdate in these functions. In Listing 17.15, which shows the update thread, note the use of that same critical section, which prevents these functions from executing at the same time and ensures safe operation.

LISTING 17.15

```
void SoundManager::TimeEvent(LPVOID lpv)
{
    while(true)
    {
        // Wake up every 50ms (20fps) to perform
        // some timed actions
```

```
        Sleep(50);

        // If the manager has been shut down then
        // terminate this thread
        if(!CSoundMgr()->m_bInitialized)
        {
            SetEvent(CSoundMgr()->m_hTerm);
            return;
        }

        CRITICAL_FUNCTION(
            &CSoundMgr()->m_csSoundMgrUpdate);

        // Calculate the current time and elapsed frame
        // time (in case we want to tweak timing).
        // Note that the frame value is always clamped
        // between .01 and .2 seconds.
        CSoundMgr()->m_fFrameTime = Clamp<float>(
            ((float(timeGetTime())) / 1000.0f) -
            CSoundMgr()->m_fCurrentTime),
            0.01f,
            0.2f);
        CSoundMgr()->m_fCurrentTime +=
            CSoundMgr()->m_fFrameTime;

        // Update all currently loaded soundscapes
        CSoundMgr()->ServiceSoundScapes();
    }
}

void SoundManager::ServiceSoundScapes()
{
    SoundScapeList::iterator itr;
    SoundScape* pSoundScape;
    for(itr = m_SoundScapeUpdateList.begin();
        itr != m_SoundScapeUpdateList.end(); ++itr)
    {
        pSoundScape = static_cast<SoundScape*>(*itr);
        pSoundScape->Update();
    }
}
```

These two functions are the heart of the sound manager's update loop. The `TimeEvent()` function is the beginning of the thread execution, so it must be a static function. It performs several operations, such as sleeping for 50 milliseconds between each update, checking for the sound manager shutdown, updating the manager's frame timers, and finally calling the `ServiceSoundScapes()` function. Inside this function, the sound manager iterates through the master list of soundscapes and calls `Update()` on each in turn. We'll look at the `SoundScape` class next, and, in particular, the `Update()` function, where the real work is done.

SoundScape IMPLEMENTATION

Because the `SoundScape` object derives from `ISoundScape`, which is in turn derived from `IPlayable`, we must implement all the basic sound control functions, such as `Play()`, `Pause()`, `Stop()`, `Load()`, and `Unload()`. Generally speaking, these functions are fairly simple to implement; and as such, we will not list them all here. You are encouraged, however, to examine the source code on the CD-ROM if you are interested in how these functions work. The `SoundScape` object has a vector of both background and periodic elements, and performing these operations generally means iterating through both of these containers and performing the equivalent operations on each element. There are a couple of functions that require some unique behavior; we'll briefly describe them so that you become aware of what happens inside these functions.

The `Play()` function does several things. First, it iterates through all the background elements, making sure to set both a random initial volume and a pitch setting that falls between the specified ranges. This is important, since it is possible to set either pitch or volume to an extreme range, and the sound would be slightly jarring if it always started from outside the expected normal range. Inside the iteration loop, the `SoundManager::Play()` function calls `Play()` on every background element. Periodic elements work a bit differently. Since these are not continuously played back, the only periodic elements that are played are those that are currently in a paused state. As you would expect, inside the `Pause()` function, all sounds that are currently playing are set to a paused state. The end result is a nice continuation of any sound that is interrupted by the `Pause()` function.

In contrast to other sounds, one thing that the `Play()` function does not do is to call the `Load()` function. Instead, the closest analogy to the principle of deferred loading is to avoid calling Load() at all in the Play() function. This has the result of allowing the audio manager to load sounds individually as they are played for the first time, which has a tendency to lessen the overall impact of loading a block of sounds from the hard drive. If the client wishes to force the entire block of sounds to load at once, it is simple enough to call the Load() function manually. The Load() function iterates through all the sounds, both background and periodic elements, loading them each in turn. And, of course, the Unload() function works in a similar manner, forcing an unload of all the sound elements.

Initializing a soundscape from a selection of data parsed from a script file could prove to be a bit tricky, especially considering that there can be an arbitrary number of two different types of elements, and these elements must be initialized using references to previously initialized objects. In order to help organize this somewhat intimidating collection of data, we've organized it all into a set of structures that will assist in both the initialization of the object as well as maintaining state information for each specific element. Let's take a look at a portion of the SoundScape header file shown in Listing 17.16.

LISTING 17.16

```
// Internally used to contain all data needed for playback
// of a background element
struct BackgroundElement
{
    BackgroundElement()     { Clear(); }
    void Clear()
    {
        m_Init.Clear();
        m_sSoundID.erase();
        m_fCurrentVolume = 1.0f;
        m_fTargetVolumeTime = 0.0f;
        m_fCurrentVolumeChangeRate = 0.0f;
        m_fCurrentPitch = 1.0f;
        m_fTargetPitchTime = 0.0f;
        m_fCurrentPitchChangeRate = 0.0f;
    }

    BackgroundInit  m_Init;
```

```
    std::string     m_sSoundID;
    float           m_fCurrentVolume;
    float           m_fTargetVolumeTime;
    float           m_fCurrentVolumeChangeRate;
    float           m_fCurrentPitch;
    float           m_fTargetPitchTime;
    float           m_fCurrentPitchChangeRate;
};


// Internally used to contain all data needed for playback
// of a periodic element
struct PeriodicElement
{
    PeriodicElement() { Clear(); }
    void Clear()
    {
        m_Init.Clear();
        m_sSound3DID.erase();
        m_fNextPlay = 0.0f;
        m_vPosition.x = 0.0f;
        m_vPosition.y = 0.0f;
        m_vPosition.z = 0.0f;
    }

    PeriodicInit    m_Init;
    std::string     m_sSound3DID;
    float           m_fNextPlay;
    AUDIOVECTOR     m_vPosition;
};


typedef std::vector<BackgroundElement> SSBEVector;
typedef std::vector<PeriodicElement> SSPEVector;

// Used to internally initialize a soundscape using scripts
struct SoundScapeInternalInit
{
    SSBEVector      m_aBackground;
    SSPEVector      m_aPeriodic;
};
```

As you can see, we have essentially created two new objects to wrap around the existing initialization structures, providing a means of storing the current information required by the elements that is not provided in the initialization structure. In addition, there are also some members specifically designed for use when loading from a script—in particular, a string member used for containing the ID of an element before it is converted into an object pointer. Each of these structures is then packed into a list, which is stored inside a single initialization structure. This is how the sound manager stores initialization information for a soundscape. When the soundscape is created, this structure is passed to a function called SoundScape::InternalInit(), where the information contained in the structure is used to fill out the internal-background and periodic-element vectors. Listing 17.17 shows how this function works.

LISTING 17.17

```
bool SoundScape::InternalInit(
    SoundScapeInternalInit& init)
{
    if(!Init())
        return false;

    ISound* pSound;
    ISound3D* pSound3D;
    SoundInit sndinit;
    Sound3DInit snd3Dinit;

    int i;
    for(i = 0; i < init.m_aBackground.size(); i++)
    {
        if(!AudioMgr()->CreateSound(pSound))
            return false;
        if(!SoundMgr()->GetSoundInit(
            init.m_aBackground[i].m_sSoundID, sndinit))
            return false;
        if(!pSound->Init(sndinit))
            return false;
        init.m_aBackground[i].m_Init.m_pSound = pSound;
        if(!AddElement(init.m_aBackground[i].m_Init))
            return false;
    }
```

```
    for(i = 0; i < init.m_aPeriodic.size(); i++)
    {
        if(!AudioMgr()->CreateSound3D(pSound3D))
            return false;
        if(!SoundMgr()->GetSound3DInit(
            init.m_aPeriodic[i].m_sSound3DID,
            snd3Dinit))
            return false;
        if(!pSound3D->Init(snd3Dinit))
            return false;
        init.m_aPeriodic[i].m_Init.m_pSound3D = pSound3D;
        if(!AddElement(init.m_aPeriodic[i].m_Init))
            return false;
    }
    return true;
}
```

This function iterates through the element initialization lists, creating the 2D and 3D sounds extracted from the string identifiers stored in the BackgroundElement and PeriodicElement structures. With the initialization structures updated, they are then passed into the AddElement() functions, where they are again wrapped in the element structures and stored in SoundScape's lists. Listing 17.18 shows these two functions.

LISTING 17.18

```
bool SoundScape::AddElement(const BackgroundInit& init)
{
    BackgroundElement element;
    element.m_Init = init;
    m_aBackground.push_back(element);
    return true;
}

bool SoundScape::AddElement(const PeriodicInit& init)
{
    PeriodicElement element;
    element.m_Init = init;
    m_aPeriodic.push_back(element);
    return true;
}
```

We now have a fully initialized object, ready to play. Now, the big question is: what happens in the Update() loop? As you might imagine, there is actually quite a lot happening in this single object, and there is quite a bit of code to cover here. The Update() function actually performs two updates, one for each element type; and these are represented by the functions UpdateBackground() and UpdatePeriodic(). With that in mind, let's look at the initial update call, shown in Listing 17.19, before moving on to the other functions.

LISTING 17.19

```
void SoundScape::Update()
{
    // Calculate the current volume, as it may be set to
    // dynamically change
    bool bVolumeChange = !m_VolumeAdjust.IsFinished();
    m_fVolume = m_VolumeAdjust.GetVar();

    // We track local time for each soundscape since
    // we don't want time to elapse when the object
    // is paused or stopped
    m_fCurrentTime += CSoundMgr()->GetFrameTime();

    // Update all background elements
    UpdateBackground(bVolumeChange);
    // Update all periodic elements
    UpdatePeriodic(bVolumeChange);

    m_bFirstUpdate = false;
}
```

Inside the Update() function, a couple of important steps happen. The first item of note is that the local volume for the soundscape is updated using a VarAdjust object, which assists in interpolating between volume settings over time. Next, we update the local time by adding the sound manager's current calculated frame time to the existing time. It is important for each SoundScape object to keep track of its own time. For instance, we do not want a paused soundscape to factor in the time during which it is paused when calculating when to play the next periodic element.

Next, the UpdateBackground() and UpdatePeriodic() functions are called, and finally the m_bFirstUpdate flag is turned off. Note also how the bVolumeChange flag is passed into the update functions to indicate whether the soundscape's volume needs change on a global level, in which case all currently playing elements must adjust their volume. UpdateBackground() can be seen in its entirety in Listing 17.20.

LISTING 17.20

```
void SoundScape::UpdateBackground(bool bVolumeChange)
{
 // Update all background sounds
 for(int i = 0; i < m_aBackground.size(); i++)
 {
    // Determine if this sound has modulating volume
    if(m_aBackground[i].m_Init.m_fMinVolume !=
        m_aBackground[i].m_Init.m_fMaxVolume)
    {
        // Adjust volume target if necessary
        if((m_fCurrentTime >=
            m_aBackground[i].m_fTargetVolumeTime) ||
            m_bFirstUpdate)
        {
            float fTime = GetRandom(
            m_aBackground[i].m_Init.m_fMinVolumeTime,
            m_aBackground[i].m_Init.m_fMaxVolumeTime);
            float fVolume = GetRandom(
            m_aBackground[i].m_Init.m_fMinVolume,
            m_aBackground[i].m_Init.m_fMaxVolume);
            float fRate = (fVolume -
            m_aBackground[i].m_fCurrentVolume) / fTime;
            m_aBackground[i].m_fTargetVolumeTime =
            fTime + m_fCurrentTime;
            m_aBackground[i].m_fCurrentVolumeChangeRate
            = fRate;
        }
    }

    // Adjust volume
    m_aBackground[i].m_fCurrentVolume +=
        (m_aBackground[i].m_fCurrentVolumeChangeRate *
        CSoundMgr()->GetFrameTime());
```

```
    m_aBackground[i].m_Init.m_pSound->SetVolume(
        m_aBackground[i].m_fCurrentVolume * m_fVolume);
    }
    else if(bVolumeChange)
    {
        m_aBackground[i].m_Init.m_pSound->SetVolume(
            m_aBackground[i].m_Init.m_fMaxVolume *
            m_fVolume);
    }
    // Determine if this sound has modulating pitch
    if(m_aBackground[i].m_Init.m_fMinPitch !=
        m_aBackground[i].m_Init.m_fMaxPitch)
    {
    // Adjust pitch target if necessary
    if(m_fCurrentTime >=
        m_aBackground[i].m_fTargetPitchTime)
    {
        float fTime = GetRandom(
            m_aBackground[i].m_Init.m_fMinPitchTime,
            m_aBackground[i].m_Init.m_fMaxPitchTime);
        float fPitch = GetRandom(
            m_aBackground[i].m_Init.m_fMinPitch,
            m_aBackground[i].m_Init.m_fMaxPitch);
        float fRate = (fPitch -
            m_aBackground[i].m_fCurrentPitch) / fTime;
        m_aBackground[i].m_fTargetPitchTime = fTime +
            m_fCurrentTime;
        m_aBackground[i].m_fCurrentPitchChangeRate =
            fRate;
    }
    // Adjust pitch
    m_aBackground[i].m_fCurrentPitch +=
        (m_aBackground[i].m_fCurrentPitchChangeRate *
        CSoundMgr()->GetFrameTime());
    m_aBackground[i].m_Init.m_pSound->SetPitch(
        m_aBackground[i].m_fCurrentPitch);
    }
    }
}
```

The basic function consists of a single loop, with two primary operations being performed inside the loop: updating the volume and updating the pitch. The basic adjustment works by storing the current volume or pitch target, along with a calculation of the change rate, which is applied to the current volume or pitch level on every update. New targets and rate changes are updated only if the current time exceeds the calculated time until the next update. Overall, the function may look somewhat intimidating at first glance, but the routine is actually pretty straightforward once you get past the lengthy notation required to access the necessary variables in the element's structures. For the volume-updating section, note how the volume is always multiplied by the soundscape's global volume. In this way, the client can easily adjust the soundscape's overall volume with a single function call, making it simple for a game to fade between soundscapes, ensuring a smooth, natural transition between virtual aural environments.

The `PeriodicUpdate()` function works in a manner similar to the `BackgroundUpdate()` function, although there are obviously some differences in the basic mechanics. For starters, none of the variables are dynamically updated, unless you count the periodic element's positional information or the sound volume, which has been adjusted. You can see for yourself how it works by examining the code in Listing 17.21.

LISTING 17.21

```
void SoundScape::UpdatePeriodic(bool bVolumeChange)
{
    IListener* pListener;
    if(!AudioMgr()->GetListener(pListener))
        return;
    AUDIOVECTOR vListenerPos;
    pListener->GetPosition(vListenerPos);
    AUDIOVECTOR vSoundPos;
    // Update all periodic sound effects
    for(int i = 0; i < m_aPeriodic.size(); i++)
    {
        // If enough time has elapsed, change all
        // the settings
        if(m_aPeriodic[i].m_fNextPlay <= m_fCurrentTime)
        {
            // Set a new position relative to the
            // listener
            m_aPeriodic[i].m_vPosition.x = GetRandom(
                -1 * (m_aPeriodic[i].m_Init.m_fXRange),
                m_aPeriodic[i].m_Init.m_fXRange);
```

```
        m_aPeriodic[i].m_vPosition.y = GetRandom(
            -1 * (m_aPeriodic[i].m_Init.m_fYRange),
            m_aPeriodic[i].m_Init.m_fYRange);
        m_aPeriodic[i].m_vPosition.z = GetRandom(
            -1 * (m_aPeriodic[i].m_Init.m_fZRange),
            m_aPeriodic[i].m_Init.m_fZRange);

    // Ensure the new position axis values are
    // outside the mininum range
    if(m_aPeriodic[i].m_vPosition.x < 0.0f)
        m_aPeriodic[i].m_vPosition.x =
          ClampMax<float>(
          m_aPeriodic[i].m_vPosition.x,
          -(m_aPeriodic[i].m_Init.m_fMinDistance));
    else
        m_aPeriodic[i].m_vPosition.x =
          ClampMin<float>(
          m_aPeriodic[i].m_vPosition.x,
          m_aPeriodic[i].m_Init.m_fMinDistance);
    if(m_aPeriodic[i].m_vPosition.y < 0.0f)
        m_aPeriodic[i].m_vPosition.y =
          ClampMax<float>(
          m_aPeriodic[i].m_vPosition.y,
          -(m_aPeriodic[i].m_Init.m_fMinDistance));
    else
        m_aPeriodic[i].m_vPosition.y =
          ClampMin<float>(
            m_aPeriodic[i].m_vPosition.y,
            m_aPeriodic[i].m_Init.m_fMinDistance);
    if(m_aPeriodic[i].m_vPosition.z < 0.0f)
        m_aPeriodic[i].m_vPosition.z =
            ClampMax<float>(
            m_aPeriodic[i].m_vPosition.z,
            -(m_aPeriodic[i].m_Init.m_fMinDistance));
    else
      m_aPeriodic[i].m_vPosition.z =
        ClampMin<float>(
            m_aPeriodic[i].m_vPosition.z,
            m_aPeriodic[i].m_Init.m_fMinDistance);

    // Hold the sound's position relative to the listener
    vSoundPos.x = vListenerPos.x +
```

```
        m_aPeriodic[i].m_vPosition.x;
vSoundPos.y = vListenerPos.y +
        m_aPeriodic[i].m_vPosition.y;
vSoundPos.z = vListenerPos.z +
        m_aPeriodic[i].m_vPosition.z;
m_aPeriodic[i].m_Init.m_pSound3D->SetPosition(
        vSoundPos);

        // Determine the pitch of the new sound
        float fPitch = GetRandom(
            m_aPeriodic[i].m_Init.m_fMinPitch,
            m_aPeriodic[i].m_Init.m_fMaxPitch);
        m_aPeriodic[i].m_Init.m_pSound3D->SetPitch(fPitch);

        // Calculate the next time for the sound to play
        float fRand = GetRandom(
            m_aPeriodic[i].m_Init.m_fMinDelay,
            m_aPeriodic[i].m_Init.m_fMaxDelay);

        m_aPeriodic[i].m_fNextPlay = m_fCurrentTime +
            fRand;

        // If this isn't the first update,
        // play the sound
        if(!m_bFirstUpdate)
            m_aPeriodic[i].m_Init.m_pSound3D->Play();
    }
    else
    {
        // Hold the sound's position relative
        // to the listener
        vSoundPos.x = vListenerPos.x +
            m_aPeriodic[i].m_vPosition.x;
        vSoundPos.y = vListenerPos.y +
            m_aPeriodic[i].m_vPosition.y;
        vSoundPos.z = vListenerPos.z +
            m_aPeriodic[i].m_vPosition.z;
        m_aPeriodic[i].m_Init.m_pSound3D->SetPosition(
            vSoundPos);
    }
    if(bVolumeChange)
    {
```

```
                m_aPeriodic[i].m_Init.m_pSound3D->SetVolume(
                m_fVolume);
            }
        }
    }
```

Like the previous function, UpdatePeriodic()'s most prominent feature is an iteration loop. However, there are a few unique features in this function. To start with, note how we obtain the position of the listener. At the end of the iteration loop, you can see how we use this information to ensure that the sounds we play maintain a constant distance from the listener, which in turn means that they will always appear to originate from a constant direction. The design was implemented in this manner to avoid the problem of a far-away sound appearing to move as the listener moves rapidly. Technically, this could be mitigated by moving the sound a long distance away, but this poses problems of its own. It is unlikely that anyone will ever be able to tell that the sound of wolf howling in the distance is in fact coming from only 20 meters away, as long as the distance remains constant and the sound is appropriately muted.

The function checks each sound to see if the required time has elapsed in order to play again. This time is randomly generated on each play and based on the two limiters chosen by the sound designer in the audio script or by the programmer in the initialization structures. The value is then clamped appropriately to ensure the minimum distance in any axis is never less than the minimum distance variable, another initialization parameter. Once this is done, the position is updated, a new random pitch is chosen (within the specified range), and the volume is updated, if needed.

This is the heart of the soundscape code. Obviously, there are a few functions that have not been examined in detail, but the most-critical functions, classes, and structures have. Naturally, it is always a good idea to open up a project and trace through the routines of a class you are interested in learning more about. Alternatively, if you are simply interested in using this class in your own project, you will find that the interfaces are all fully documented, just like the basic audio interfaces.

CONCLUSION

While there is certainly a large amount of code to digest in the sound manager and related classes, the basic concept is quite simple. By taking advantage of the clean audio object interface we've worked hard to create in Part II, we can now start seeing real dividends in functionality and ease of use. While it may seem like a lot of extra work to expose so much functionality in a text-based data format, it will tend to pay for itself over the long run. Sound designers will be free to implement sounds and effects the way they want to, without continually having to ask a programmer to tweak hard-coded variables or functions inside the game itself.

Next, we will look at how to create an interactive music system using our scripting system. In doing so, we will provide a convenient method for creating branching and interactive sequences of DirectMusic segments.

CHAPTER **18**

AN INTERACTIVE MUSIC-PLAYBACK SYSTEM

One of the most exciting and fundamental capabilities of DirectMusic is its ability to dynamically adjust soundtracks on the fly in response to game events. This is generally referred to as *interactive music*. Although there are many ways to create interactive music scores, one of the most basic and useful methods is to simply play small chunks of music sequentially, transitioning from chunk to chunk through the use of a predefined map, specific game events, or a combination of the two.

In the case of our music system, the atomic element is the DirectMusic segment, and we'll use a system of user-defined mappings and transition events to determine how the segments are arranged, and, ultimately, the way the final score sounds to the listener.

The code listed in this chapter can be found in \Game_Audio\ audio_sdk\include\audioscript\IMusic.h \Game_Audio\audio_sdk\src\audioscript\MusicMgr.h, MusicMgr.cpp, Theme.h, Theme.cpp

INTRODUCTION

The current audio manager has only the most rudimentary segment playback capabilities. It can play a single primary segment, and will allow one additional segment to be queued for playback after the first segment is finished. The manager will provide notifications when specific events occur, such as when a segment starts, stops, is just about to end, or hits a measure or beat. The music manager will be utilizing these basic capabilities to create a DirectMusic-based interactive music system. Our design goals are as follows:

1. Load segments and DLS files from a disk or other resource using a simple, text-based script format.

2. Create basic segment-to-segment transition maps in the form of 'themes.' Each theme defines a number of transition points, which in turn define the segments to play and how they should interact with each other. Additionally, themes will be able to contain theme-to-segment transition maps, as well, allowing easier use of transitional segments.

3. Allow users to choose a theme to invoke the proper segment transitions. Specific theme types, called "interludes," allow one theme to interrupt another, then automatically transfer back to the original when it has finished.

■ ONLY DIRECTMUSIC?

You may have decided that you don't wish to use DirectMusic, and instead plan to implement your music via a streaming DirectSound buffer using Ogg Vorbis-encoded files, for instance. As such, you might be wondering if this sort of interactive music playback system could still work for you. The answer is "Yes," but you'll need to do a bit of extra modification work, both in this system and in the core audio manager. The music system relies on a couple of features in the audio manager: the ability to queue a section of musical data behind a currently playing one, and a function callback when a new piece of music begins playing. While neither of these is directly supported in the audio system as it exists, it would not be terribly difficult to add basic queuing and callback capabilities to a streaming DirectSound buffer, allowing you to duplicate the essential abilities required for this music system by using only DirectSound. And, of course, you'll need to modify the internal mechanisms of the music manager to parse and load ISound objects instead of ISegment objects, but this should be a fairly simple conversion to make; references for your use of the sound manager class were discussed in the previous chapter.

MUSICAL SCRIPTING

The entire music system is based on the concept of a musical 'theme,' which is identified using a standard C++ string. Each theme contains a map that determines which segments may transition to which other segments. The client can switch between themes at any point, and this will affect how the transitions are made. A visual example may help to clarify how this process works. Figure 18.1 shows two simple themes with several segments in each. The arrows indicate the possible transitions that may be made between segments. Notice how while "Linear Theme" plays a fixed sequence of segments, "Random Theme" allows a great deal of variety in the sequencing of its segments. Additionally, you can see that "Linear Theme" plays a special transition segment when transitioning from "Random Theme."

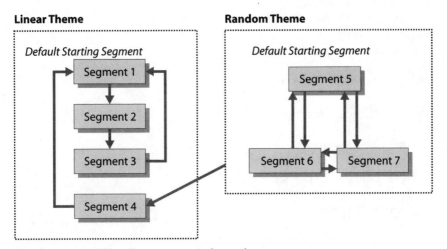

FIGURE 18.1   Transitions between segments in two themes.

So, how exactly do we define this set of segments, themes, and transitions? We use a custom-designed text-based data script. Using the text-parsing system discussed in Chapter 16, we can easily define all the required DLS files, segments, and themes required. For now, let's find out what the actual script for these two themes and their supporting objects look like in Listing 18.1.

LISTING 18.1

```
DLS = "SomeSounds"
{ FileName = "SomeSounds.dls"; }
```

```
Segment = "Segment1"
{ FileName = Segment1.sgt"; }
Segment = "Segment2"
{ FileName = Segment2.sgt"; }
Segment = "Segment3"
{ FileName = Segment3.sgt"; }
Segment = "Segment4"
{ FileName = Segment4.sgt"; }
Segment = "Segment5"
{ FileName = Segment5.sgt"; }
Segment = "Segment6"
{ FileName = Segment6.sgt"; }
Segment = "Segment7"
{ FileName = Segment7.sgt"; }

Theme = "Random Theme";

Theme = "Linear Theme"
{
    Src = "Segment1"
    {
        Dest = "Segment2";
    }
    Src = "Segment2"
    {
        Dest = "Segment3";
    }
    Src = "Segment3"
    {
        Dest = "Segment1";
    }
    Src = "Segment4"
    {
        Dest = "Segment1";
    }
    Src = "Random Theme"
    {
        Dest = "Segment4";
    }
}

Theme = "Random Theme"
```

```
{
    Src = "Segment5"
    {
        Dest = "Segment6";
        Dest = "Segment7";
    }
    Src = "Segment6"
    {
        Dest = "Segment5";
        Dest = "Segment7";
    }
    Src = "Segment7"
    {
        Dest = "Segment5";
        Dest = "Segment6";
    }
}
```

Music scripts are composed of three top-level object definitions: DLS, Segment, and Theme. Creating DLS and segment objects is as simple as defining each of the objects with a unique string ID, and ensuring the parameters, such as FileName, are properly filled out.

In the previous chapter on high-level sound scripting, we learned that when creating sound definitions in script, only the definitions are loaded when the script is loaded, not the actual instances of sounds. The instances are only created later, when requested based on the definition ID.

This new music system works somewhat differently. When the script is loaded, a corresponding segment is created and initialized for every definition listed in the script file. It makes more sense for the music system to simply keep a permanently associated and instantiated object with each ID instead of just a definition, since only one primary segment can ever be played at a time, anyhow. It is implied that segments will be using the most-recently defined DLS file in the script, so segments also do not explicitly need to be associated with the DLS file, but can be if needed.

After the DLS and segments are defined in Listing 18.1, we can then create our themes. You'll notice that the first theme is actually a forward declaration of "Random Theme". Forward declaration of themes has been implemented in the data definition format to allow themes to reference each other internally, which we'll see next.

The first defined theme is `"Linear Theme"`. As with the segments and DLS file, a unique string identifier is required as part of the definition. This string is what a client will use to play and transition between specific themes. Inside each theme definition are a number of nodes, labeled `src`. You can think of each `src` node as a method of identifying one half of a transition table. It identifies the currently playing segment or theme, and directs the music manager to play another segment, or allows it to randomly choose between a number of new segments. This particular transition only occurs, though, when the current theme is active. When a new theme is chosen, the new transition map directs the flow of segments.

What happens when there is no corresponding `src` node that matches up with the currently playing segment or theme? The very first `src` node definition that identifies a segment to transition from is used as the default starting segment. In our sample definition, this means that `"Segment1"` is the default starting node for `"Linear Theme"`, and `"Segment5"` is the default starting node for `"Random Theme"`.

Beginning with the definition of `"Random Theme"`, we see multiple paths for the transition. This allows, in fact, much more complex behavior than a basic map would, even though this is what we have been calling it. If fact, any source node may have as many random destinations as you wish. The destination is always chosen randomly. Particular choices are weighted by including more than one destination that points to the same segment.

There are a few additional options and nuances you should be aware of when creating themes. A theme may be designed to stop automatically by creating a source node that transitions to nothing. The music manager will interpret this by stopping the musical playback after that segment is finished. Alternatively, you have two choices if you wish to loop a single segment. You may either define the segment as looping inside the actual segment definition, or you may point the transition back to itself, inside the theme definition. You can also define a theme as an *interlude* by placing the following line inside the theme definition:

```
Interlude = true;
```

An interlude is a special type of theme. When a client switches to a new theme, the theme normally continues to play indefinitely, unless it is designed to stop by itself. An interlude, however, will always transition back to the previously playing theme when it self-terminates. For this reason, when you define an interlude, you should always be sure it has a way to stop, or the transition back to the previous segment will never happen. You should be aware that the interlude will not preserve the previous theme's currently playing segment. Instead, it will start playing at the default segment of the previous theme after it has finished, unless a specific transition is defined that would override this behavior.

THE `IMusicManager` INTERFACE

Now that we know what our music-script system looks like, we need to consider what the music manager interface will look like. The first step in creating a new system, as always, is to consider what functionality we want to provide to the client, and in doing so, we create an abstract interface. Here is what the manager will have to do:

- Start up and shut down
- Load themes from a file (or custom resource system)
- Play themes based on their string identifiers
- Manage themes based on their string identifiers

From this set of basic requirements, we'll construct our manager. Listing 18.2 shows what the `IMusicManager` interface looks like.

LISTING 18.2

```
class IMusicManager : public IMusicCallback
{
public:
    virtual bool Init() = 0;
    virtual void Term() = 0;

    virtual bool LoadScript(std::string sFileName) = 0;

    virtual bool PlayTheme(std::string sThemeName) = 0;
    virtual void ResetThemeItr() = 0;
    virtual bool GetNextTheme(
        std::string& sThemeName) = 0;
    virtual bool RemoveTheme(
        std::string& sThemeName) = 0;
    virtual bool RemoveAllThemes() = 0;
```

```
};
```

```
inline static IMusicManager* MusicMgr()
{ return AudioScriptFactory::GetMusicMgr(); }
```

As with our other manager interfaces, we have also provided a function as an access point, MusicMgr(). This function will retrieve a single static manager object from the AudioScriptFactory class, which actually creates the concrete object.

IMusicManager is publicly derived from IMusicCallback, which is an abstract interface that is used internally in the audio manager to receive specific DirectMusic notifications. IMusicCallback is shown in Listing 18.3.

LISTING 18.3

```
class IMusicCallback
{
public:
    virtual void OnSegmentStart() {};
};
```

At the moment, we are obviously only interested in one particular notification message, and so this is what we've defined. If more are needed at a future date for any reason, they can easily be added.

Since we're using a callback or notification object in the audio manager, this means that we must at some point pass in the music manager object to the audio manager. This is done in the audio manager's initialization function. The sequence of events required to initialize both the audio manager and the music manager is shown in Listing 18.4. The music manager requires the audio manager to be initialized before it will successfully initialize, so we must be sure to initialize them in the correct order. While technically we did not have to require this in the music manager, an initialized audio manager is eventually required anyhow, so it seemed simpler to just verify that the audio system is ready to go right from the beginning.

LISTING 18.4

```
AudioMgrInit init;
init.m_pMusicCallback = MusicMgr();
```

```
if(!AudioMgr()->Init(init))
    AfxMessageBox("Error initializing audio system");
if(!MusicMgr()->Init())
    AfxMessageBox("Error initializing music manager");
```

Using the IMusicManager should be fairly intuitive. After initialization, simply call the Load() function, passing in the name of the file. Once the music script is parsed and loaded, the client can play any theme by using the PlayTheme() function and passing in the name of the theme to play as a string. There are also a number of functions that can be used to enumerate and remove individual themes; these are less useful to most applications, but are handy for authoring or playback tools.

IMPLEMENTATION

Designing an interface is the easy part. Now, we have to actually implement our design. Let's begin by examining the concrete implementation of the IMusicManager interface, which is the MusicManager class.

THE MusicManager CLASS

The concrete MusicManager class, as you might guess, is the central repository and manager for the data loaded from the music scripts. Listing 18.5 shows the MusicManager class definition in full.

LISTING 18.5

```
class Theme;

typedef std::map<std::string, IDLS*> IDLSMap;
typedef std::map<std::string, ISegment*> ISegmentMap;
typedef std::map<std::string, Theme*> ThemeMap;

class MusicManager : public IMusicManager
{
// Interface functions
public:
    bool Init();
```

```
    void Term();
    bool LoadScript(std::string sFileName);
    // Theme functions
    bool PlayTheme(std::string sThemeName);
    void ResetThemeItr();
    bool GetNextTheme(std::string& sThemeName);
    bool RemoveTheme(std::string& sThemeName);
    bool RemoveAllThemes();
    void OnSegmentStart();
// Concrete functions
public:
    MusicManager();
    virtual ~MusicManager();
    void Clear();
// Internal functions and types
private:
    bool IsInitialized() { return m_bInitialized; }
    bool LoadDLS(ScriptNode* pNode);
    bool LoadSegment(ScriptNode* pNode);
    bool LoadTheme(ScriptNode* pNode);
    bool LoadThemeNode(ScriptNode* pNode,
        Theme* pTheme);
// Internal data
private:
    // Bool indicating initialization status
    bool                m_bInitialized;
    // Script loader object
    ScriptLoader        m_Loader;
    // DLS data
    IDLSMap             m_DLSMap;
    // Segment data
    ISegmentMap         m_SegmentMap;
    // Theme collection
    ThemeMap            m_ThemeMap;
    ThemeMap::iterator  m_ThemeItr;
    IDLS*               m_pCurrentDLS;
    // Currently playing theme
    Theme*              m_pPlayingTheme;
    Theme*              m_pPlayingInterlude;
    Theme*              m_pPreviousTheme;
    bool                m_bIsPlaying;
```

```
};
inline static MusicManager* CMusicMgr()
{ return static_cast<MusicManager*>(MusicMgr()); }
```

The public interface consists of the inherited interface from IMusic-Manager and a number of utility functions, such as IsInitialized(), LoadDLS(), and LoadSegment(). The Load() functions are each designed to load a specific type of data structure.

The private data consists of the ScriptLoader object m_Loader, which is used to load, tokenize, and format the script into a traversable tree structure. There are also three maps that store the three primary object types defined and created by the music manager: m_DLSMap, m_SegmentMap, and m_ThemeMap. Each of these maps associates objects with string identifiers, which are used both during the parsing process and at run-time.

There are a number of Theme* pointers designed to track current theme, current interlude, and previous theme, and a couple of status flags whose purposes should be fairly obvious. We'll see how all of these are used when we examine the member functions' implementations.

Initialization and shutdown are fairly straightforward. Listing 18.6 shows code for both the Init() and Term() functions. The Init() function ensures the loader is initialized, and the term function makes sure everything is cleaned up.

LISTING 18.6

```
bool MusicManager::Init()
{
    if(!AudioMgr()->IsInitialized())
        return false;
    if(!m_Loader.Init())
        return false;
    m_bInitialized = true;
    return true;
}

void MusicManager::Term()
{
    m_Loader.Term();
```

```
    RemoveAllThemes();
    Clear();
}
```

Next we examine the LoadScript() function in Listing 18.7.

LISTING 18.7

```
bool MusicManager::LoadScript(string sFileName)
{
    if(!IsInitialized())
        return false;

    Script script;
    if(!m_Loader.Load(sFileName, script))
        return false;

    ScriptNode* pNode = script.GetRoot();
    while(pNode)
    {
        // Look for named "DLS" nodes in the script
        if(MUSMGR_STRCMP(pNode->GetName(), "DLS") == 0)
        {
            if(!LoadDLS(pNode))
                return false;
        }
        // Look for named "Segment" nodes in the script
        else if(MUSMGR_STRCMP(pNode->GetName(), "Segment") == 0)
        {
            if(!LoadSegment(pNode))
                return false;
        }
        // Look for named "Theme" nodes in the script
        else if(MUSMGR_STRCMP(pNode->GetName(), "Theme") == 0)
        {
            if(!LoadTheme(pNode))
                return false;
        }
        else
        {
```

```
            return false;
        }
        // advance to the next sibling node if one exists
        pNode = pNode->GetSibling();
    };
    return true;
}
```

After checking to see that the music manager has been initialized, the m_Loader performs the work of loading and tokenizing the script via its own Load() function. The function fills out a single Script object, which is then used to obtain the root node of the data tree built by the loader. Again, you can learn more about the specifics of this process in Chapter 16—An Audio Scripting Format.

The function then iterates through the top-level nodes of the data tree, which correspond to the object definitions in the script file. When a recognized node is found, it is passed to one of the helper functions that is designed to load specific object definitions—LoadDLS()?, LoadSegment(), or LoadTheme().

The LoadDLS() and LoadSegment() functions are nearly identical, other than the different content and different parameters they are loading. As such, let's just look at one of them, LoadSegment(). This function is shown in its entirety in Listing 18.8.

LISTING 18.8

```
bool MusicManager::LoadSegment(ScriptNode* pNode)
{
    // We use string IDs in this scripting system
    if(pNode->GetDataType() != Script::STRING)
        return false;

    // Make sure the segment ID doesn't already exist
    ISegmentMap::iterator itr = m_SegmentMap.find(
        pNode->GetString());
    if(itr != m_SegmentMap.end())
        return true;

    SegmentInit init;
```

```
ScriptNode* pChildNode = pNode->GetChild();
init.m_pDLS = m_pCurrentDLS;
while(pChildNode)
{
    if(MUSMGR_STRCMP(pChildNode->GetName(), "FileName") == 0)
        init.m_sFileName = pChildNode->GetString();
    else if(MUSMGR_STRCMP(pChildNode->GetName(), "Looping")
      == 0)
        init.m_bLooping = pChildNode->GetBool();
    else if(MUSMGR_STRCMP(pChildNode->GetName(), "Music")
      == 0)
        init.m_bMusic = pChildNode->GetBool();
    else if(MUSMGR_STRCMP(pChildNode->GetName(), "DLS") == 0)
    {
        IDLSMap::iterator itr = m_DLSMap.find(
            pChildNode->GetString());
        if(itr != m_DLSMap.end())
            init.m_pDLS = itr->second;
    }
    pChildNode = pChildNode->GetSibling();
}
ISegment* pSegment;
if(!AudioMgr()->CreateSegment(pSegment))
    return false;
if(!pSegment->Init(init))
    return false;

// Insert the segment into the map
m_SegmentMap.insert(make_pair(pNode->GetString(),
    pSegment));

return true;
}
```

LoadSegment() is actually somewhat similar to the original Load() function, but it naturally has a few important differences. We first check to make sure the node has a valid string identifier assigned to it. Otherwise, we will have to figure a way to reference the node from other points in the script. Next, we double-check to make sure the node hasn't already been loaded. In the case of both segments and DLS collections, we allow duplicate loadings and simply exit the function prematurely, returning `true`. This is done for convenience in case more than one script attempts to load a segment or DLS. However, if you wish to prevent this, you can simply change the function to return `false`, which will signal a loading error and abort the creation process.

We'll see in the next function, `LoadTheme()`, how we use this initial check in a different manner to allow forward declarations of themes, which is necessary because themes have to be able to reference each other, much in the same way that C/C++ classes and structs reference each other.

Next, the function obtains a child node, which will allow us to iterate through the children that hold the object's properties in their nodes. The loop searches and sets the properties for `FileName`, `Looping`, `Music`, and `DLS`. These functions, because we use the standard C++ initialization struct, always have the same default values as in regular code and work exactly in the same manner.

After the properties are obtained, the segment object is obtained and placed in the segment map, associating it with the top-level node's string identifier for future access through the script-parsing process.

Now let's examine the `LoadTheme()` and `LoadThemeNode()` functions. You may notice a pattern in which we create a new helper function for every new subnode definition that must be loaded. This helps to keep the code cleaner and more concise. Listing 18.9 shows the first of these functions, `LoadTheme()`.

LISTING 18.9

```
bool MusicManager::LoadTheme(ScriptNode* pNode)
{
    // We use string IDs in this scripting system
    if(pNode->GetDataType() != Script::STRING)
        return false;
    Theme* pTheme = 0;
    // Make sure the theme ID doesn't already exist
    ThemeMap::iterator itr = m_ThemeMap.find(
        pNode->GetString());
    if(itr != m_ThemeMap.end())
        pTheme = itr->second;
    else
        pTheme = new Theme;
```

```
if(!pTheme)
    return false;

ScriptNode* pChildNode = pNode->GetChild();
while(pChildNode)
{
    if(MUSMGR_STRCMP(pChildNode->GetName(), "Src") == 0)
    {
        if(!LoadThemeNode(pChildNode, pTheme))
            return false;
    }
    else if(MUSMGR_STRCMP(pChildNode->GetName(),
        "Interlude") == 0)
    {
        pTheme->SetInterlude(pChildNode->GetBool());
    }
    else
        return false;
    pChildNode = pChildNode->GetSibling();
}

// Insert the theme into the map
m_ThemeMap.insert(make_pair(pNode->GetString(), pTheme));

return true;
}
```

This function is similar in most respects to the LoadSegment() function, except for a section that checks for an existing Theme using the same identifier. Instead of exiting when an existing node is found, this function simply returns the pointer to the Theme object if it has already been created, which allows the function to then fill out the object with appropriate data. In this case, we check for two nodes: "Src" and "Interlude". "Interlude" is a simple Boolean value; but for "Src", we pass the node and the theme pointer to a new function in order to process its child nodes for the theme object. Let's look at this function now, shown in Listing 18.10.

LISTING 18.10

```
bool MusicManager::LoadThemeNode(ScriptNode* pNode,
    Theme* pTheme)
```

```
{
    FN("MusicManager::LoadThemeNode()");

    if(pNode->GetDataType() != Script::STRING)
        return false;

    ISegment* pSegmentSource = 0;
    Theme* pThemeSource = 0;
    // First look for matching segments based on the
    // ID value
    ISegmentMap::iterator itr = m_SegmentMap.find(
        pNode->GetString());
    if(itr == m_SegmentMap.end())
    {
        // Next, look for matching themes
        ThemeMap::iterator itor = m_ThemeMap.find(
            pNode->GetString());
        if(itor == m_ThemeMap.end())
            return false;
        pThemeSource = itor->second;
        if(!pTheme->CreateNode(pThemeSource))
            return false;
    }
    else
    {
        pSegmentSource = itr->second;
        if(!pTheme->CreateNode(pSegmentSource))
            return false;
    }

    ScriptNode* pChildNode = pNode->GetChild();
    while(pChildNode)
    {
        if(MUSMGR_STRCMP(pChildNode->GetName(),
            "Dest") == 0)
        {
            itr = m_SegmentMap.find(pChildNode->GetString());
            if(itr == m_SegmentMap.end())
                return false;
            ISegment* pDest = itr->second;
            if(pThemeSource)
            {
                if(!pTheme->CreateTransition(
```

```
                    pThemeSource, pDest))
                    return false;
        }
        else
        {
            if(!pTheme->CreateTransition(
                pSegmentSource, pDest))
                return false;
        }
    }
    else
    {
        return false;
    }
    pChildNode = pChildNode->GetSibling();
}

return true;
}
```

For this function, we know the "Src" node should be assigned the name of either a segment or a theme, so we have to look for both, first the segment and then the theme. If neither are found, the function exits with an error. Depending on which object type is found, the appropriate pointer, pSegmentSource or pThemeSource is filled out with the object pointer, which is located with the node's string ID. This object is then used to create a transition node in the Theme object that was passed to the function via its pointer. Essentially, you can think of a theme's node as the source from where transitions occur. When we iterate through the loop, we'll find as many destination nodes as the script contains, and this will be associated with each node as a list of possible destination segments for each source node. It's a little hard to visualize this, so don't worry about it for now. We'll be covering this in more detail when we examine the Theme class next.

There are really only two more functions of any importance in the music manager: PlayTheme() and OnSegmentStart(). PlayTheme() is used to begin playback of our theme-based segment-mapping scheme, and OnSegmentStart() is the function called every time a musical segment starts. The music manager uses this to precache and queue all musical playback defined by the current theme. Let's first examine `PlayTheme()` in Listing 18.11.

LISTING 18.11

```cpp
bool MusicManager::PlayTheme(std::string sThemeName)
{
    if(!IsInitialized())
        return false;
    ThemeMap::iterator itr =
        m_ThemeMap.find(sThemeName);
    if(itr == m_ThemeMap.end())
        return false;

    if(m_pPlayingInterlude)
        m_pPreviousTheme = m_pPlayingInterlude;
    else if(m_pPlayingTheme)
        m_pPreviousTheme = m_pPlayingTheme;

    itr->second->StartTheme();

    if(itr->second->IsInterlude())
        m_pPlayingInterlude = itr->second;
    else
        m_pPlayingTheme = itr->second;

    OnSegmentStart();
    return true;
}
```

The function first checks to see if the manager is initialized properly, and then finds the theme based on the string identifier sThemeName, passed into the function. If the theme is successfully located, we then proceed with assigning the previously played interlude or theme to the m_pPrevious-Theme variable. This will be needed in case the new theme wishes to transition to a specific segment based on the previously played theme instead of the previously played segment. Next, the new theme's StartTheme() function is called, which resets internal variables inside the theme to let it know that it will become active. We'll look at why this is done a bit later.

The function then checks to see if the theme is defined as an interlude, which means it will play that theme, then transition back automatically to the last noninterlude theme after the interlude theme ends.

Finally, the `OnSegmentStart()` function is called, which actually does the work of loading, queuing, and playing segments located using the current theme object. Let's see how this function works in Listing 18.12.

LISTING 18.12

```
void MusicManager::OnSegmentStart()
{
    ISegment* pCurrent;
    ISegment* pNext;
    AudioMgr()->GetCurrentSegment(pCurrent);
    if(m_pPlayingInterlude)
    {
        if(!m_pPlayingInterlude->GetTransition(
            m_pPreviousTheme, pCurrent, pNext))
        {
            m_pPlayingInterlude = 0;
            if(!m_pPlayingTheme)
                return;
            m_pPlayingTheme->StartTheme();
            if(!m_pPlayingTheme->GetTransition(
                m_pPreviousTheme, pCurrent, pNext))
                return;
        }
    }
    else
    {
        if(!m_pPlayingTheme)
            return;
        if(!m_pPlayingTheme->GetTransition(
            m_pPreviousTheme, pCurrent, pNext))
            return;
    }
    pNext->Play();
}
```

The basic premise of this function is fairly straightforward: with both the previous theme and the currently playing segment as keys (m_pPrevious-

Theme and pCurrent), the current theme or interlude (m_pPlayingInter-
lude or m_pPlayingTheme) is used to determine the next segment (pNext),
which is then played.

We first check to see if we are working with an interlude or a normal
theme. If it is an interlude theme, we check for the end of the theme, which
is signaled by the Theme::GetTransition() function returning false. In
the case of the interlude, we then switch to the normal theme and continue.
If the normal theme is finished playing, then we simply exit, meaning that
playback will stop when the current segment finishes, unless it is designated
as a looping segment. When the next segment has finally been determined,
we simply call Play() to either prepare for playback after the currently
playing segment is finished or, if nothing is currently playing, the segment
will play immediately after it is loaded.

Because this is all happening on a signal from the music system that a
segment has started playing, the queuing process will always occur one
full segment ahead of the current segment. The advantage of this system
is its relative stability—this gives the segment plenty of time to load in
the background, even if an entirely new DLS set needs to be loaded, for
instance.

THE Theme CLASS

The only other class of significance used in the music manager is the Theme
class. Each theme may be thought of in the literal sense of the musical
term: it defines which segments should play and how these segments
should be connected to each other in something resembling a connection
map. However, the problem is slightly more complicated than a simple
map, because each segment is allowed to transition to one of any number
of randomly selected target segments.

This can be a bit hard to understand without being able to properly visualize it. Let's refer back to our sample shown in Figure 18.1 and listed in
script form in Listing 18.1. We have two themes, "Linear Theme" and
"Random Theme". Each of these themes is stored in a map in the music
manager and uses a string ID as the key or index. Inside each theme are two
more maps. Each of these contains a list of vectors to segments, and the
keys to these maps are a segment pointer and a theme pointer. These maps
are used to locate the final data—the destination segments. When more
than one destination segment is found, the destination is simply chosen
randomly from each list. Figure 18.2 shows all of this graphically to help
you make a bit more sense of how this is all arranged.

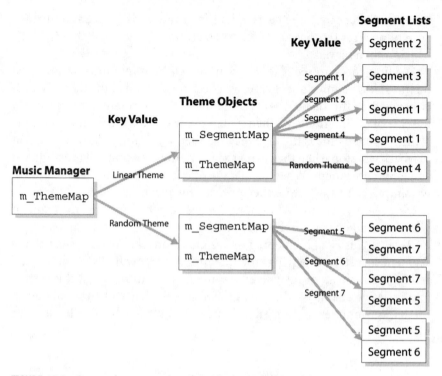

FIGURE 18.2   Structural representation of sample themes and transition maps.

By comparing Figure 18.2 to Figure 18.1 and Listing 18.1, you should be able to visualize how the data structures work and why they are arranged as they are. Essentially, the key values in the two next maps are used to locate the final segment destination, which is then chosen randomly from all the available choices.

As you can see in Listing 18.13, the Theme class declaration contains two maps: one associating segment pointers with a vector of segment pointers, and the other associating theme pointers with a vector of segment pointers.

LISTING 18.13

```
typedef std::vector<ISegment*> ISegmentVector;
typedef std::map<ISegment*, ISegmentVector*>
    SegmentTransitionMap;
```

```
typedef std::map<Theme*, ISegmentVector*>
    ThemeTransitionMap;

class Theme
{
public:
    Theme();
    ~Theme();
    bool IsInterlude()      { return m_bInterlude; }
    void SetInterlude(bool bVal)
    { m_bInterlude = bVal; }
    bool CreateNode(ISegment* pSegment);
    bool CreateNode(Theme* pTheme);
    bool CreateTransition(ISegment* pFrom,
        ISegment* pTo);
    bool CreateTransition(Theme* pFrom, ISegment* pTo);
    void StartTheme()
    { m_bFirstTransition = true; }
    bool GetTransition(Theme* pTheme, ISegment* pFrom,
        ISegment*& pTo);

private:
    void Clear();

    ISegment*              m_pDefaultSegment;
    SegmentTransitionMap   m_SegmentMap;
    ThemeTransitionMap     m_ThemeMap;
    bool                   m_bInterlude;
    bool                   m_bFirstTransition;
};
```

The basic operation for the Theme() class is to use CreateNode() to create the proper index entries (whether a theme or segment pointer) and to allocate a vector of segment pointers to insert into the map, as well. The very first segment pointer received in this function is set as the default segment to play during the first transition if no specific transition information exists. After this, the CreateTransition() function is used to fill out the map nodes, inserting destination segment pointers into the segment lists contained in the maps. These functions are shown in Listing 18.14.

LISTING 18.14

```
bool Theme::CreateNode(ISegment* pSegment)
{
    if(!pSegment)
        return false;
    if(!m_pDefaultSegment)
        m_pDefaultSegment = pSegment;
    ISegmentVector* pList = new ISegmentVector;
    if(!m_SegmentMap.insert(
        make_pair(pSegment, pList)).second)
        return false;
    return true;
}

bool Theme::CreateNode(Theme* pTheme)
{
    if(!pTheme)
        return false;
    ISegmentVector* pList = new ISegmentVector;
    if(!m_ThemeMap.insert(
        make_pair(pTheme, pList)).second)
        return false;
    return true;
}

bool Theme::CreateTransition(ISegment* pFrom,
    ISegment* pTo)
{
    SegmentTransitionMap::iterator itr =
        m_SegmentMap.find(pFrom);
    if(itr == m_SegmentMap.end() || (!itr->second))
        return false;
    itr->second->push_back(pTo);
    return true;
}

bool Theme::CreateTransition(Theme* pFrom,
    ISegment* pTo)
{
    ThemeTransitionMap::iterator itr = m_ThemeMap.find(pFrom);
    if(itr == m_ThemeMap.end() || (!itr->second))
```

```
      return false;
   itr->second->push_back(pTo);
   return true;
}
```

Once the maps have been constructed, we are ready to use them for segment transitions in our music system. The music system contains a concept of a current theme, and it calls the GetTransition() function using this theme to retrieve the next segment to play, which is based on the previously playing theme and what segment is playing now. These two pointers are used as key values in the transition maps, which simply return an element selected from whichever vector of segments is found. The segment map is always given precedence over the theme map, since this is the most detailed information and should produce the best-sounding results. If no specific segment or theme is found to transition to, a default selection is made. However, the default segment cannot be used more than once with looping segments, because otherwise, themes would never be able to self-terminate; they would always start over with the default theme. The m_bFirstTransition flag is used to track this. During the MusicManager::PlayTheme() function, the Theme::StartTheme() is always called for the current theme. As you can see in Listing 18.13, this function simply resets this flag to true, which allows the Theme::GetTransition() function to ensure that the default segment is only used once each time the PlayTheme() function is called. Listing 18.15 shows the GetTransition() function.

LISTING 18.15

```
bool Theme::GetTransition(Theme* pTheme,
    ISegment* pFrom, ISegment*& pTo)
{
    bool bFirstTransition = m_bFirstTransition;
    m_bFirstTransition = false;
    pTo = 0;

    // First check to see if we can find a specific
    // transition based on the pFrom segment
    SegmentTransitionMap::iterator itr =
        m_SegmentMap.find(pFrom);
```

```
    if(itr == m_SegmentMap.end() ||
        !itr->second->size())
    {
        // If we can't find a segment-based transition,
        // look for a theme-based transition instead
        ThemeTransitionMap::iterator itor =
            m_ThemeMap.find(pTheme);
        if(itor != m_ThemeMap.end() &&
            itor->second->size())
        {
            pTo = itor->second->at(rand() %
                itor->second->size());
            return true;
        }

        if(!m_pDefaultSegment || !bFirstTransition)
            return false;
        pTo = m_pDefaultSegment;
        return true;
    }
    pTo = itr->second->at(rand() % itr->second->size());
    return true;
}
```

One last, small note: because we are dynamically allocating the vectors in the maps, we must be sure to deallocate them cleanly when destroying the maps, or we'll see a lot of memory leaks. Listing 18.16 shows the Theme destructor.

LISTING 18.16

```
Theme::~Theme()
{
    SegmentTransitionMap::iterator itr;
    for(itr = m_SegmentMap.begin(); itr != m_SegmentMap.end();
        ++itr)
    {
        SAFE_DELETE(itr->second);
    }
    ThemeTransitionMap::iterator itor;
```

```
for(itor = m_ThemeMap.begin(); itor != m_ThemeMap.end();
    ++itor)
{
    SAFE_DELETE(itor->second);
}
}
```

CONCLUSION

That's all there is to the music manager. You've seen how the manager works both from a scripting and a conceptual side, as well as the actual code needed to implement such as system. The amount of actual coding saved by an intelligent data-loading system, such as the one we've built, can't be overstated. Previous versions of this system, written before the audio-scripting format and loader were completed, required nearly twice the amount of parsing code in order to yield the same approximate results.

Because the hierarchical structure of the data format makes it so simple to define any sort of object or structure in data, you should have no problems extending this system or even creating new systems for your own use. Simply create a code interface that performs the task you need, then write script support to allow the audio designer or composer to 'script' any audio system they want.

This finishes up Part III—High-Level Audio Programming. In Part IV, we'll be looking at both custom file systems and alternative data formats. We will also demonstrate how to extend DirectSound and DirectMusic to handle just about any audio format you'd care to use.

PART IV

CUSTOM AUDIO FORMATS AND LOADERS

CHAPTER 19

CUSTOM RESOURCE FILES

While a resource packing and extraction system does not necessarily belong in an audio library, it certainly must deal with any custom resource system that a game might be using, and do so in a hassle-free manner. There are a few tricks for ensuring your library can handle any system, and there are also a few things your resource-packing system must be able to do in order to work well with this (or most any other) audio library. We'll be going over them all in this chapter.

The code listed in this chapter can be found in \Game_Audio\ audio_sdk\include\audiolib\IAudioStream.h\

Game_Audio\ audio_sdk\src\audiolib\, AudioStreamFactory.h, AudioStreamFactory.cpp, FileStream.h, FileStream.cpp, IAudioLoader.h.

RESOURCE PACKING EXPLAINED

Resource packing is simply the combining of many different files into a single larger file, typically while preserving the original filename and directory structure. In games, this is done for a number of reasons:

- It is simply more convenient to work with one or several large files than it is to work with hundreds, or even thousands of small files.
- Opening and reading data from a single file is more efficient than opening many small files, especially on NT-based operating systems (mostly due to the additional overhead of security requirements).
- It takes less space on the disk to store one file than it takes to store many files.

> ■ **BYTES AND BLOCKS**
>
> In case you're wondering how it could take less space to store one large file in-stead of the same data stored in separate files, the answer lies in the way data is stored on hard drives. Drives are separated into discrete data blocks typically ranging from 1 KB to 64 KB in size. Each of these blocks may contain data from only one file. As you might surmise from this, the average amount of data wasted on a hard drive will be approximately equal to one half the block size times the total number of files. Thus, if your game uses 1,000 files, your game may waste anywhere from 500 KB to 32 MB, depending on the block size of the user's hard drive.

ENCRYPTION AND SECURITY

Some people feel that packing resources also gives some additional mea-sure of security, but this is a flawed premise unless your packing system is actually encrypted using a secure algorithm. File formats are routinely re-verse-engineered, and simply packing your files together into an unknown file format will provide little real security—except from the most amateur-ish attempts at cracking. Even an encrypted system can be broken, because both the decryption algorithm and key must be stored locally in order to gain access to the system. Essentially, you must consider everything on a local user's hard drive as compromised data. Naturally, this is usually not an issue that audio systems must consider per se, but keep it in mind when making decisions in a larger context.

COMPRESSION CONSIDERATIONS

While many resource formats are uncompressed, it is also possible to com-bine resource packing with data compression in order to (potentially) speed up load time and reduce the size of your game's footprint on the user's hard drive. Of course, you should use general-purpose compression only when it will actually be able to compress the data. Many native file for-mats are already compressed about as much as they can be, such as Ogg Vorbis, PNG, or JPEG files. Attempting to recompress natively compressed data is a waste of computing resources. There are some additional benefits to keeping your resource files uncompressed, such as the ability to easily stream audio directly from the hard drive. If data is compressed (other than by a file format's native algorithms), it is much more difficult (or even impossible) to stream it directly from a resource file, depending on the compression method used.

IStream—A READY-MADE TEMPLATE

For our audio system, we have chosen to use the standard COM template file IStream as a pattern to model our file system on. While it may seem like this breaks our intended design goals of separation and abstraction from platform-specific components, it is important to remember that IStream is not necessarily a COM implementation, but simply an interface—a set of specifications to adhere to when creating our file system objects. If we were to port to a system that did not use COM, it would be a fairly simple matter to copy the IStream specifications to that platform as well, as it is little more than a couple of abstract interface classes.

IStream was chosen not only because it fulfills all of the potential requirements of a generic data-streaming solution, but using IStream-compliant interfaces in particular is a great benefit on DirectX and Win32 platforms, since several systems can directly use these objects instead of having to go through a more-clumsy and limited method of passing file-names or memory buffers. After all, memory buffers cannot be used for streaming audio (since we naturally must load the entire file into memory first, which defeats our purpose), and most custom file systems will not be able to work with an interface that only accepts filenames. As such, an IStream interface is often the only way that certain libraries, such as DirectMusic or Windows Media, will be able to stream audio resources from custom file systems.

THE IStream INTERFACE

IStream is derived from ISequentialStream, which in turn is derived from IUnknown. All methods from these classes must be implemented to some degree in order to compile a class derived from IStream. Let's first look at the list of functions to be implemented, which are shown in Listing 19.1.

LISTING 19.1

```
// IUnknown Interface
HRESULT __stdcall QueryInterface(
```

```
      const struct _GUID& guid,
      void** ppInterface);
ULONG __stdcall AddRef();
ULONG __stdcall Release();

// ISequentialStream Interface
HRESULT __stdcall Read(
    /* [length_is][size_is][out] */ void *pv,
    /* [in] */ ULONG cb,
    /* [out] */ ULONG *pcbRead);

HRESULT __stdcall Write(
    /* [size_is][in] */ const void *pv,
    /* [in] */ ULONG cb,
    /* [out] */ ULONG *pcbWritten);

// IStream Interface
HRESULT __stdcall Seek(
    /* [in] */ LARGE_INTEGER dlibMove,
    /* [in] */ DWORD dwOrigin,
    /* [out] */ ULARGE_INTEGER *plibNewPosition);

HRESULT __stdcall SetSize(
    /* [in] */ ULARGE_INTEGER libNewSize);

HRESULT __stdcall CopyTo(
    /* [unique][in] */ IStream *pstm,
    /* [in] */ ULARGE_INTEGER cb,
    /* [out] */ ULARGE_INTEGER *pcbRead,
    /* [out] */ ULARGE_INTEGER *pcbWritten);

HRESULT __stdcall Commit(
    /* [in] */ DWORD grfCommitFlags);

HRESULT __stdcall Revert(void);

HRESULT __stdcall LockRegion(
    /* [in] */ ULARGE_INTEGER libOffset,
    /* [in] */ ULARGE_INTEGER cb,
    /* [in] */ DWORD dwLockType);
```

```
HRESULT __stdcall UnlockRegion(
    /* [in] */ ULARGE_INTEGER libOffset,
    /* [in] */ ULARGE_INTEGER cb,
    /* [in] */ DWORD dwLockType);

HRESULT __stdcall Stat(
    /* [out] */ STATSTG *pstatstg,
    /* [in] */ DWORD grfStatFlag);

HRESULT __stdcall Clone(
    /* [out] */ IStream **ppstm);
```

The first three functions are based on IUnknown, the next two from ISequentialStream, and the rest are from IStream. The most important functions are the Read() and Seek() functions, as these are the primary mechanisms by which the stream functions. Certain functions, such as Write() and SetSize(), are obviously intended for writeable streams, which we will not be dealing with. As such, these functions (and a couple others that we'll see) can simply return the error code E_NOTIMPL, which indicates the function has not been implemented.

You may notice a rather obvious omission, though. There are no methods suitable for creating a stream. This is intentional; it allows a derived interface class to implement its own specific methods for opening a stream.

THE IAudioStream INTERFACE

In our case, we must create an additional abstract interface class, which we'll call IAudioStream. The only additional interface this class provides is a method to open a stream. Our audio system is based on the concept of identifying files using strings. Typically, you can assume this will mean filenames, but it is important to realize that this does not necessarily have to be the case. A custom file system could, in fact, use unique string keys as hash values for looking up files in a table, for instance. Or, it might even internally convert a string into a numerical identifier before using it to access a file. Regardless, the one restriction we do impose with our audio design is that the files are identified as a string. As such, we use a simple string to identify and open an IAudioStream object, as you can see in Listing 19.2.

LISTING 19.2

```
class IAudioStream : public IStream
{
public:
    virtual HRESULT __stdcall Open(
        std::string sFileName) = 0;
};
```

For consistency, we return an HRESULT to indicate success or failure rather than our typical bool value, since other members work in this way. We now have a complete IStream-based interface ready for implementation.

DEFAULT FileStream IMPLEMENTATION

Although we'll learn how custom IAudioStream interfaces can be used a bit later in this chapter, it is likely that many clients will simply want to use the basic files. As such, the audio system will internally use a default file-based implementation of IAudioStream, called FileStream. While file-based IStream interfaces can be created using standard Windows system calls, it is more practical for us to implement our own class for a couple of reasons. First, we wish to do a bit of manipulation of the current working directory when opening a file; and second, it provides an excellent template to follow if you wish to create your own, custom IAudioStream-based implementation for use with the audio system, or if you wish to learn how to implement any IStream-compliant class.

There is no need to list the entire FileStream header file, as it mostly repeats previously seen in the interfaces from which it is derived. However,

---

■ A SLIGHT DIFFERENCE

ON THE CD You may notice a slight difference between the IAudioStream implementation you see on these pages and the code on the CD-ROM. We've added some small file auto-caching to the implementation for use with a Direct-Sound buffer-caching scheme, which we'll discuss in Chapter 30—General Optimization Strategies. However, the file-based functionality remains identical to what you see here.

we will show you the implementation, minus most of the IStream and
IAudioStream interface functions, in order to illustrate some of the implementation details.

LISTING 19.3

```
#pragma pack(push,4)

class FileStream : public IAudioStream
{

DEFINE_POOL(FileStream);

public:
    FileStream();
    virtual ~FileStream();
    void Clear();

    HRESULT __stdcall Open(std::string sFileName);
    void Close();

    // IUnknown Interface
    // [snip]

    // ISequentialStream Interface
    // [snip]

    // IStream Interface
    // [snip]

private:

    int32       m_iRefCount;
    FILE*       m_pFile;
    uint32      m_nSize;
    std::string m_sFileName;
};

#pragma pack(pop,4)
```

The basic class structure looks similar to other classes we've created. The Open() and Close() functions control initiating and terminating access to the file or file-type resource, respectively, and the IStream interface provides the rest of the interface. It should be noted that the Close() function is actually not a part of the IAudioStream interface. Instead, it is implicitly called when the object's Release() is called, and when the reference count drops to zero.

The FileStream class keeps track of several members, including a reference count needed for IUnknown compatibility, a standard FILE pointer, the variable m_nSize that holds the size of the file, and the original filename, which is stored in the m_sFileName string. You may notice a couple of additional details as well. For starters, we force this header to compile with four-byte alignment within the structure. This is required because the m_iRefCount variable must be aligned on a 32-bit boundary, since the InterlockedIncrement() and InterlockedDecrement() functions that operate on it will otherwise fail on x86-multiprocessor systems. In case you are not familiar with these functions, they are simply thread-safe methods of incrementing or decrementing a variable, and are typically used in COM implementations to manage the reference count.

We use our DEFINE_POOL() macro, which is designed to improve the efficiency of allocation and deallocation of this object through the use of some specialized functions and an object-caching system, which we'll point out a bit later when examining the FileStream implementation details. (You can read more about this object-caching mechanism in Chapter 30.)

Let's now take a look at the actual file-based, IStream-derived class FileStream in Listing 19.4. In order to give you a clear view of which functions are required to be implemented and which are not, and how these functions are expected to behave, we're listing the implementation in its entirety.

LISTING 19.4

```
#include "FileStream.h"
#include "AudioMgr.h"

using namespace std;
using namespace Audio;

IMPLEMENT_POOL(FileStream);
```

```
FileStream::FileStream()
{
    Clear();
}

FileStream::~FileStream()
{
}

void FileStream::Clear()
{
    m_iRefCount = 1;
    m_pFile = 0;
    m_nSize = 0;
    m_sFileName.erase();
}

HRESULT FileStream::Open(std::string sFileName)
{
    m_sFileName = sFileName;
    m_pFile = fopen(sFileName.c_str(), "rb");
    if(!m_pFile)
    {
        _getcwd(DXAudioMgr()->GetCurrentWorkingPath(),
            MAX_PATH);
        chdir(DXAudioMgr()->GetAudioSystemPath());
        m_pFile = fopen(sFileName.c_str(), "rb");
        chdir(DXAudioMgr()->GetCurrentWorkingPath());
        if(!m_pFile)
            return E_FAIL;
    }
    fseek(m_pFile, 0, SEEK_END);
    m_nSize = ftell(m_pFile);
    fseek(m_pFile, 0, SEEK_SET);
    return S_OK;
}

void FileStream::Close()
{
    if(m_pFile)
    {
```

```
            fclose(m_pFile);
            m_pFile = 0;
            Clear();
    }
}

HRESULT FileStream::QueryInterface(
    const struct _GUID& guid,
    void** ppInterface)
{
    if (guid == IID_IStream)
        *ppInterface = (IStream*)this;
    else if (guid == IID_ISequentialStream)
        *ppInterface = (ISequentialStream*)this;
    else if (guid == IID_IUnknown)
        *ppInterface = (IUnknown*)this;
    else
        return E_NOTIMPL;
    ((IUnknown*)*ppInterface)->AddRef();
    return S_OK;
}

ULONG FileStream::AddRef()
{
    InterlockedIncrement(&m_iRefCount);
    return m_iRefCount;
}

ULONG FileStream::Release()
{
    int32 iPrev = InterlockedDecrement(&m_iRefCount);
    if(iPrev == 0)
    {
        Close();
        FileStream::DestroyObject(this);
    }
    assert(m_iRefCount >= 0);
    return m_iRefCount;
}

HRESULT FileStream::Read(
    /* [length_is][size_is][out] */ void *pv,
    /* [in] */ ULONG cb,
```

```
    /* [out] */ ULONG *pcbRead)
{
    if(!m_pFile)
        return E_FAIL;
    uint32 nRead = fread((uint8*)pv, 1, cb, m_pFile);
    if(pcbRead)
        *pcbRead = nRead;
    return S_OK;
}

HRESULT FileStream::Write(
    /* [size_is][in] */ const void *pv,
    /* [in] */ ULONG cb,
    /* [out] */ ULONG *pcbWritten)
{
    return E_NOTIMPL;
}

HRESULT FileStream::Seek(
    /* [in] */ LARGE_INTEGER dlibMove,
    /* [in] */ DWORD dwOrigin,
    /* [out] */ ULARGE_INTEGER *plibNewPosition)
{
    if(!m_pFile)
        return E_FAIL;
    uint32 nSeek = (uint32)dlibMove.QuadPart;
    if(fseek(m_pFile, nSeek, dwOrigin))
        return E_FAIL;
    if(plibNewPosition)
        plibNewPosition->QuadPart = ftell(m_pFile);
    return S_OK;
}


HRESULT FileStream::SetSize(
    /* [in] */ ULARGE_INTEGER libNewSize)
{
    return E_NOTIMPL;
}


HRESULT FileStream::CopyTo(
```

```
    /* [unique][in] */ IStream *pstm,
    /* [in] */ ULARGE_INTEGER cb,
    /* [out] */ ULARGE_INTEGER *pcbRead,
    /* [out] */ ULARGE_INTEGER *pcbWritten)
{
    return E_NOTIMPL;
}


HRESULT FileStream::Commit(
    /* [in] */ DWORD grfCommitFlags)
{
    return E_NOTIMPL;
}


HRESULT FileStream::Revert(void)
{
    return E_NOTIMPL;
}


HRESULT FileStream::LockRegion(
    /* [in] */ ULARGE_INTEGER libOffset,
    /* [in] */ ULARGE_INTEGER cb,
    /* [in] */ DWORD dwLockType)
{
    return E_NOTIMPL;
}


HRESULT FileStream::UnlockRegion(
    /* [in] */ ULARGE_INTEGER libOffset,
    /* [in] */ ULARGE_INTEGER cb,
    /* [in] */ DWORD dwLockType)
{
    return E_NOTIMPL;
}


HRESULT FileStream::Stat(
    /* [out] */ STATSTG *pstatstg,
```

```
    /* [in] */ DWORD grfStatFlag)
{
    if(!pstatstg)
        return E_INVALIDARG;

    pstatstg->pwcsName = 0;
    if(grfStatFlag == 1)
    {
        pstatstg->pwcsName =
            (WCHAR*)CoTaskMemAlloc(MAX_PATH *
            sizeof(WCHAR));
        ConvertAnsiStringToWide(
            pstatstg->pwcsName, m_sFileName.c_str());
    }
    else
        pstatstg->pwcsName = 0;
    pstatstg->type = STGTY_STREAM;
    pstatstg->cbSize.QuadPart = m_nSize;
    pstatstg->atime.dwHighDateTime = 0;
    pstatstg->atime.dwLowDateTime = 0;
    pstatstg->ctime.dwHighDateTime = 0;
    pstatstg->ctime.dwLowDateTime = 0;
    pstatstg->mtime.dwHighDateTime = 0;
    pstatstg->mtime.dwLowDateTime = 0;
    pstatstg->grfLocksSupported = 0;

    return S_OK;
}


HRESULT FileStream::Clone(
    /* [out] */ IStream **ppstm)
{

    IAudioStream* pStream;
    if(!AudioMgr()->CreateAudioStream(pStream))
        return E_FAIL;
    if(FAILED(pStream->Open(m_sFileName)))
    {
        pStream->Release();
        return E_FAIL;
    }
    LARGE_INTEGER liPos;
    liPos.QuadPart = ftell(m_pFile);
```

```
    pStream->Seek(liPos, SEEK_SET, 0);
    *ppstm = (IStream*)pStream;
    return S_OK;
}
```

As you can see, most of the IStream functions map fairly easily to standard C-file functions. But, there are a few things that might not be obvious upon first inspection, though, especially if you are not used to working with COM or IStream interfaces.

You may notice the prolific use of ULARGE_INTEGER and LARGE_INTEGER types throughout the interface, especially in the Seek() function. These are COM versions of 64-bit integers, which are defined as structures in order to provide multipart access to the high and low bits in case 64-bit integers are not supported by the compiler. In our case, we can simply use the Quadword member directly as a 64-bit integer. While it's appropriate for COM to allow streams greater than 4 GB, it's a bit of an annoyance for us to have to deal with these custom types, but not enough of a problem to avoid using IStream altogether. We'll typically cast these values to standard 32-bit integers, as we are not expecting to deal with single audio file streams greater than 4 GB any time in the near future.

In the Open() function, there is a small piece of code that is worth discussion, as well, which looks like the following:

```
    m_pFile = fopen(sFileName.c_str(), "rb");
    if(!m_pFile)
    {
        _getcwd(DXAudioMgr()->GetCurrentWorkingPath(),
            MAX_PATH);
        chdir(DXAudioMgr()->GetAudioSystemPath());
        m_pFile = fopen(sFileName.c_str(), "rb");
        chdir(DXAudioMgr()->GetCurrentWorkingPath());
        if(!m_pFile)
            return E_FAIL;
    }
```

This code is designed to attempt to open a file first based on a combination of the file's path (if it is relative) and the current working directly. If the file could not be found, the system first saves a temporary copy of the current working directory, sets the new current working directory to one the client can specify when initializing the audio manager, and then attempts to open the file again. It then sets the current working directory back to the original directory.

This mechanism is handy if you prefer to store all filenames relative to a different directory instead of your primary working directory. For instance, you may have your game stored at C:\Program Files\YourGame, which you set as the current working directory for your game and all file operations. However, all of your audio files are stored at C:\Program Files\ YourGame\Data\Audio. Typically, in order to reference any file in this directory, such as in a script, you would have to refer to each file in the following manner:

```
"/Data/Audio/Music/SomeSong.ogg"
```

If you set the audio manager's local working directory as /Data/Audio, you could instead simply list any file as relative to this directory, like this:

```
"/Music/SomeSong.ogg"
```

In this manner, the audio system can always find its required files, regardless of where a program may point to as the current working directory. This is especially critical because of the audio system's dynamic load-on-demand mechanisms, which means that unloading and reloading of data could take place at any time.

This finishes our coverage of IStream implementations. You can read more-specific information about any of the basic IUnknown, ISequential-Stream, or IStream function specifications either in your local MSDN help files or at *http://msdn.microsoft.com.*

ABSTRACT STREAM FACTORY

We're not quite finished implementing a generic IStream-based data system yet, though. While we've prepared an IAudioStream interface and have a method for loading these files, we have not yet devised a suitable method for creating the actual IAudioStream objects themselves.

The task is not as trivial as some of our other abstract interfaces, because in this particular case, we wish to either create our own default FileStream objects or, if a client wishes, we must instead be able to create customized IAudioStream-based objects. If we know nothing about the client's IAudioStream object, how can we possibly create these objects inside the audio manager? As a matter of fact, we actually can't—at least not directly—but we can enlist the aid of another object, itself based on an abstract interface, which can do this for us. This is known as an *abstract factory*, a common design pattern used to solve this sort of problem. We'll create another abstract interface class called `IAudioStreamFactory`, and its sole purpose is to create `IAudioStream`-based objects.

LISTING 19.5

```
class IAudioStreamFactory
{
public:
    virtual bool CreateAudioStream(
        IAudioStream*& pStream) = 0;
};
```

By delegating the creation of the `IAudioStream` objects to these factories, we can allow the user to create their own factory implementations. A pointer to an `IAudioStreamFactory` is provided to the audio manager on initialization, and this factory will then be used instead of the default factory, which creates `FileStream` objects. Figure 19.1 demonstrates the object hierarchies and their relationships to each other, including a hypothetical custom resource stream and related factory object.

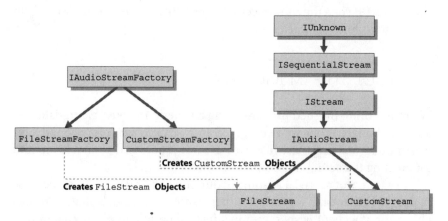

FIGURE 19.1   Abstract IStream-based file system and factory objects.

Now, the `AudioManager::CreateAudioStream()` function simply passes along the request to create a file to the factory object, as you can see in Listing 19.6.

LISTING 19.6

```
bool AudioManager::CreateAudioStream(
    IAudioStream*& pStream)
{
    CHECK_INIT();
    if(!m_pStreamFactory)
        return false;
    return m_pStreamFactory->CreateAudioStream(pStream);
}
```

The reason this function is provided at the audio manager interface level is to provide even higher-level libraries (such as our sample `AudioScript` add-on library) with the ability to use these same, customized stream objects—meaning that your entire audio system, as well as any additions you make to it, will use a consistent and robust file-handling system.

CONCLUSION

Using the standard COM interface `IStream` with our own library, we've created a powerful mechanism for handling any sort of file system, whether disk based or using a customized, resource-handling mechanism specific to your game engine.

In the next few chapters, we'll learn how to use this mechanism to help us create a set of file readers that are capable of decoding a number of different file formats, such as ADPCM wave files, Ogg Vorbis, WMA, and MP3 files.

CHAPTER 20

WINDOWS AUDIO COMPRESSION MANAGER SDK

Y ou may have noticed that there are a number of wave files that are not compatible with the wave reader we have written so far. In addition to plain PCM, Windows wave files can contain a number of types of compressed or otherwise altered data. However, DirectSound requires PCM data for its buffers. Is there a way to convert this data from its compressed format to raw PCM data? Fortunately, Windows also provides the solution to this problem with its Audio Compression Manager SDK, commonly referred to as "ACM."

 The code listed in this chapter can be found in \Game_Audio\ ON THE CD audio_sdk\src\audiolib\IAudioLoader.h, Wave.h, Wave.cpp.

ACM AND CODECS

Although wave files are often thought of as being containers for uncompressed PCM data, nearly any type of compression scheme (including MP3) can be implemented inside a wave file. In order to deal with these arbitrary data formats, Windows uses a standard library: the Audio Compression Manager. The ACM, in turn, manages any number of installed *codecs* on the user's system.

A codec is essentially a driver that understands how to "co"mpress and "dec"ompress (hence the name "codec") audio data using various encoding and compression algorithms. Typically, a user has anywhere from half a dozen to several dozen different codecs installed, depending on the software installed in the system and their particular audio-compression-codecs flavor.

Although applications may write and install their own custom codecs, we're more interested in some of the codecs common to all Windows machines. For instance, the Microsoft ADPCM codec comes standard on all Windows installations, and so is a good choice for lightly (and efficiently) compressed audio data. The ACM is designed to enable you to manage codecs in all sorts of ways, but we'll be utilizing it in a fairly straightforward manner: given a specific wave file format, find and load the codec best suited for decompressing or decoding the audio data to PCM format, and perform the conversion.

AN ACM-ENABLED WAVE FILE LOADER

Because the ACM technically only works with wave files, it makes sense to build this functionality right into our existing Wave class. Previously, this was left out for ease of understanding, as loading a wave is complicated enough without it. However, we're going to be finishing the class up in this chapter, ensuring that any wave file capable of being played in Windows can be loaded and decoded by your application.

CONCEPTUAL OVERVIEW

Let's start by reviewing portions of the basic Wave interface, which we're going to extend to support ACM decoding/decompression.

LISTING 20.1

```
class Wave : public IAudioLoader
{
public:
    Wave();
    virtual ~Wave();

    bool Open( std::string sFileName);
    bool Open( BYTE* pbData, uint32 dwDataSize);
    bool Close();
```

```
    bool Read( BYTE* pDestBuffer, uint32 dwSizeToRead,
        uint32* pdwSizeRead );

    bool Reset();
    WAVEFORMATEX* GetFormat()
    { return &m_DestFormat; }
    uint32 GetSize()
    { return m_dwSize; }
    bool IsEOF()
    { return m_bEOF; }

protected:
    bool OpenMMIO();
    bool ReadMMIO();
    bool PrepareACMBuffers(uint32& nDataIn,
        uint32& nStreamRead, uint32 dwSizeToRead);
    bool DecompressData(uint32 nDataIn, BYTE* pDestBuffer,
        uint32 dwSizeToRead, DWORD* pdwSizeRead)
private:
    WAVEFORMATEX  m_DestFormat;
    HMMIO         m_hmmio;
    MMCKINFO      m_ck;
    MMCKINFO      m_ckRiff;
    uint32        m_dwSize;
    uint32        m_nOffset;
    bool          m_bEOF;

    // ACM specific structures
    WAVEFORMATEX* m_pwfx;
    HACMSTREAM    m_hACMStream;
    uint8*        m_pCompressBuffer;
    uint32        m_nCompressBufferSize;
    uint8*        m_pDecompressBuffer;
    uint32        m_nDecompressStart;
    uint32        m_nDecompressEnd;
    uint32        m_nDecompressBufferSize;
    static uint32 s_nWaveCount;
};
```

If you compare this code to Listing 8.3, you will notice the only substantial difference is the addition of a number of new member data and internal functions, shown in the listing as bold text, which we'll explore in detail throughout this chapter.

Other than a new, dynamically allocated wave format structure (used for custom formats), there is one ACM-specific structure—a handle to a decompression stream. This will be used by the ACM initially when opening the file, and will then be stored to decompress audio either in a single `Wave::Read()` call, or over multiple calls, successively. The final additions are two memory buffers, along with members to help track information about them. The first is a compressed data buffer, along with its size member. The second is a decompression buffer, along with its size parameter, plus two pointers to mark the position of valid data inside the buffer.

You may be wondering why we have two additional buffers where one would seem to suffice, because we already have a destination buffer allocated by DirectSound to hold the amount of PCM data needed. Unfortunately, things are a bit more complicated than that when it comes to decompression. The ACM provides no simple means of determining the exact size of an output buffer given a specific input size, or vice versa. With many compression schemes, it is impossible to exactly predict the compression ratio. Instead, the system will err on the side of safety and estimate a larger buffer than you need. Even with fixed-ratio compression schemes such as ADPCM, the ACM still insists on providing a safety margin for us. If we were to simply use the ACM-recommended compressed data sizes given our decompression buffer, we would continuously be decompressing slightly less data than what we requested, given our buffer size. Our streaming routines are not tolerant of data starvation and will produce audible skipping and popping were this allowed to happen.

As a solution, we are forced to create our own double-buffering solution, so to speak. Each wave object has two buffers, a compressed data buffer and a decompressed data buffer. Both of these buffers are allowed to grow dynamically to any required size when requested. When determining how much to read from the original compressed wave data, we ask the ACM for a recommendation on the compressed buffer size, using a slightly larger amount of data than was actually requested. In this manner, we ensure that we will have slightly more decompressed data than we asked for. This may seem like just as bad a problem as having too little decompressed data; but in fact, this is what we are after. When we read data from the original file, we read first into the compressed data buffer, again asking for more than we really need. We now have a decompression buffer filled with slightly more data than we have room for in our output buffer. So, what do we do with this extra data? After we copy as much data as will fit into the final destination buffer, which is the pointer given to us by the `IDirect-SoundBuffer8::Lock()` function, we are left with a section of leftover, but still valid data that will likely be needed on the subsequent `Read()` function. Two pointers indicate where the valid data resides in the buffer by marking the beginning and end of the data section. The next time the `Read()` function is called, this valid data is moved to the front of the buffer. The size of this data is subtracted from the buffer calculations in the next cycle, and all the new decompressed data is copied just behind the valid data in the buffer that was left over from the previous `Read()`. For an overview of the data transmission path through the buffers, see Figure 20.1.

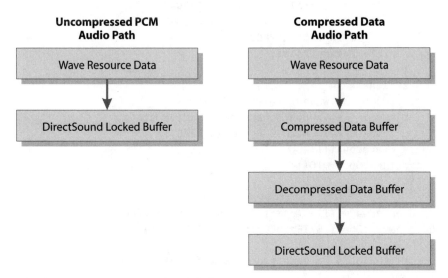

FIGURE 20.1   Data transmission through buffers.

This 'leftover-data-recycling' scheme also solves another thorny ACM problem: there usually are enforced minimum decompression buffer sizes, even when we want to decompress just a sliver of information to fill in the last portion of a circular buffer. Instead of having to deal with this in the streaming code, it make more sense to buffer the data in the reader object itself and provide exactly the amount of data to the stream that it requests—all the time, and with no restrictions on minimum size or other alignment issues.

The Decompression Code

We'll now examine the Wave::Open() functions, with new code added to automatically handle ACM-compressed wave files.

LISTING 20.2

```cpp
// Opens a wave file for reading from a file and offset
bool Wave::Open( string sFileName)
{
    if(!m_nWaveCount)
    {
        if(!mmioInstallIOProc(mmioFOURCC(
            'W', 'A', 'V', ' '), &CustomMMIOProc,
            MMIO_INSTALLPROC))
            return false;
    }
    sFileName += "+";
    // Open the wave file from disk
    m_hmmio = mmioOpen((char*)sFileName.c_str(),
        NULL, MMIO_ALLOCBUF | MMIO_READ);
    s_nWaveCount++;
    return OpenMMIO();
}

// Open a wave file format from a memory buffer
bool Wave::Open( BYTE* pbData, uint32 dwDataSize)
{
    // Indicate to read from a memory buffer
    MMIOINFO mmioInfo;
    ZeroMemory( &mmioInfo, sizeof(mmioInfo) );
    mmioInfo.fccIOProc = FOURCC_MEM;
    mmioInfo.cchBuffer = dwDataSize;
    mmioInfo.pchBuffer = (CHAR*) pbData;
    // Open the memory buffer
    m_hmmio = mmioOpen(NULL, &mmioInfo, MMIO_READ);
    return OpenMMIO();
}

bool Wave::OpenMMIO()
{
    // Read the wave header file
```

```
if(!ReadMMIO())
{
    // ReadMMIO will fail if it's not a wave file
    mmioClose(m_hmmio, 0);
    return Error::Handle("Wave Error: ReadMMIO");
}

// Reset the file to prepare for reading
if(!Reset())
{
    mmioClose(m_hmmio, 0);
    return Error::Handle("Wave Error: Reset");
}

// Set (or estimate) the size of the decompressed wave data
if(m_hACMStream)
{
    MMRESULT error = acmStreamSize(m_hACMStream,
    m_ck.cksize, &m_dwSize,
        ACM_STREAMSIZEF_SOURCE);
    if(error)
        return false;
}
else
{
    m_dwSize = m_ck.cksize;
}
return true;
}
```

You will notice that the listing looks almost identical to our original Wave reader from Listing 8.5, except for the bold sections. Let's begin by examining what has changed in the first Open() function. The changes made here were to enable the wave reader to decode from an IAudioStream-based system instead of just from a standard file. Two things must be done for this to happen. We call the function mmioInstallIOProc() if this is the first wave file created, and we add a "+" to the end of the filename, signaling that we should use the custom IO procedure when opening the file. We keep track of how many wave files are loaded using the static member s_nWaveCount. This allows us to know when to install and uninstall the custom IO procedure based on how many wave files currently exist.

You can see that we are passing in the address of a function, CustomIO-Proc(), to the IO installation function. Let's see what this function looks like in Listing 20.3.

LISTING 20.3

```
LRESULT CALLBACK CustomMMIOProc(
 LPSTR lpmmioinfo,
 UINT uMsg,
 LONG lParam1,
 LONG lParam2
)
{
    char cBuffer[MAX_PATH];
    LRESULT ret = 0;
    MMIOINFO* pMMIOINFO = (MMIOINFO*)lpmmioinfo;
    IAudioStream* pStream =
        (IAudioStream*)pMMIOINFO->adwInfo[0];

    switch(uMsg)
    {
    case MMIOM_OPEN:
    {
        strcpy(cBuffer, (char*)lParam1);
        cBuffer[strlen(cBuffer) - 1] = 0;
        if(!AudioMgr()->CreateAudioStream(pStream))
            return MMIOERR_CANNOTOPEN;
        if(FAILED(pStream->Open(cBuffer)))
            return MMIOERR_CANNOTOPEN;
        pMMIOINFO->adwInfo[0] = (DWORD)pStream;
    }
    break;
    case MMIOM_SEEK:
    {
        if(!pStream)
            return 0;
        ULARGE_INTEGER lnNewPos;
        LARGE_INTEGER liSeek;
        liSeek.QuadPart = lParam1;
        pStream->Seek(liSeek, lParam2, &lnNewPos);
        pMMIOINFO->lDiskOffset =
```

```
            (DWORD)lnNewPos.QuadPart;
        }
    break;
    case MMIOM_READ:
    {
        if(!pStream)
            return 0;
        uint32 nRead;
        pStream->Read((void*)lParam1, lParam2, &nRead);
        pMMIOINFO->lDiskOffset += nRead;
        return nRead;
    }
    case MMIOM_CLOSE:
    {
        pMMIOINFO->lDiskOffset = 0;
        pMMIOINFO->adwInfo[0] = 0;
        SAFE_RELEASE(pStream);
    }
    break;
    };
    return ret;
}
```

The Windows Multimedia routines use a single function as an entry point for all custom IO routines, meaning that you have to handle a number of different cases based on the parameters given to you. Our custom function handles four basic IO procedures: open, close, read, and seek—each designated by the uMsg parameter. One of the trickier aspects in creating this custom system was figuring out exactly where the custom file data goes. The lpmmioinfo parameter is cast to an MMIOINFO structure, and it turns out there are some fields that may be directly manipulated (and some that must be manipulated) by our IO procedures. The lDiskOffset data member must be adjusted during seek and read functions to help track the current read pointer. Additionally, there is array of three DWORD values (named "adwInfo") that can be used for any data storage needed by custom IO procedures. We store a pointer to a newly created IAudioStream object in one of these slots when we open a new file, and that's all we'll need for future IO operations.

The system is not too complicated once you figure out what messages you have to handle and which parameters mean what. Adding support for any custom file system should be a fairly simple matter now that you have an example to work from.

Now, let's examine the last portion of the OpenMMIO() function from the end of Listing 20.2. Here, we see the first of several switches on the m_hACM-Stream handle, which we'll use from now on to determine if we're dealing with raw PCM or a compressed wave format. In this function, we estimate the uncompressed final data size using the acmStreamSize() function. As mentioned earlier, there is a significant problem when using this function in that for safety's sake, it will always overestimate the final size of the buffer size you request. Unfortunately, for this reason, you should not expect a static buffer created with ACM-compressed waves to be able to loop precisely. You could work around this problem by forcing the wave object to read the entire buffer first, then create the DirectSound buffer based on the number of bytes actually read. This would be a more practical measure for smaller wave files if you cache the buffers in memory. However, the sample *GAP* library works on difference principles, and so we do not do this.

So where exactly did the ACM handle get set? You may recall in the ReadMMIO() function that there was already an if/else condition based on whether or not the wave file was a PCM file. We'll simply exploit this branch to create an ACM stream that is capable of decoding whatever non-PCM file was read. Let's look at the ReadMMIO() function now.

LISTING 20.4

```
// Verifies that this is a wave file, and allocates and
// fills out the wave format header structure.
bool Wave::ReadMMIO()
{
    // chunk info for general use.
    MMCKINFO        ckIn;
    // Temp PCM structure to load in.
    PCMWAVEFORMAT pcmWaveFormat;

    // Make sure this structure has been deallocated
    SAFE_DELETE_ARRAY(m_pwfx);

    if(mmioSeek(m_hmmio, m_nOffset, SEEK_SET ) == -1)
        return false;
```

```
if((0 != mmioDescend( m_hmmio, &m_ckRiff, NULL, 0)))
        return false;

// Check to make sure this is a valid wave file.
if((m_ckRiff.ckid != FOURCC_RIFF) ||
   (m_ckRiff.fccType !=
   mmioFOURCC('W', 'A', 'V', 'E')))
    return false;

// Search the input file for for the 'fmt ' chunk.
ckIn.ckid = mmioFOURCC('f', 'm', 't', ' ');
if(0 != mmioDescend( m_hmmio, &ckIn, &m_ckRiff,
   MMIO_FINDCHUNK))
    return false;

// Expect the 'fmt ' chunk to be at least as large
// as <PCMWAVEFORMAT>; if there are extra
// parameters at the end, we'll ignore them.
if(ckIn.cksize < (LONG) sizeof(PCMWAVEFORMAT))
    return false;

// Read the 'fmt ' chunk into <pcmWaveFormat>.
if(mmioRead(m_hmmio, (HPSTR) &pcmWaveFormat,
   sizeof(pcmWaveFormat)) != sizeof(pcmWaveFormat))
    return false;

// Allocate the WAVEFORMATEX, but if it's not PCM
// format, read the next word, and that's how many
// extra bytes to allocate.
if(pcmWaveFormat.wf.wFormatTag == WAVE_FORMAT_PCM)
{
    memcpy(&m_DestFormat,&pcmWaveFormat,sizeof(
        pcmWaveFormat));
    m_DestFormat.cbSize = 0;
}
else
{
    // Read in length of extra bytes.
    WORD cbExtraBytes = 0L;
    if( mmioRead( m_hmmio, (CHAR*)&cbExtraBytes,
        sizeof(WORD)) != sizeof(WORD) )
        return false;
```

```
    m_pwfx = (WAVEFORMATEX*)new
        CHAR[sizeof(WAVEFORMATEX) + cbExtraBytes];
    if( NULL == m_pwfx )
        return false;

    // Copy the bytes from the PCM structure to
    // the WAVEFORMATEX structure.
    memcpy( m_pwfx, &pcmWaveFormat,
        sizeof(pcmWaveFormat));
    m_pwfx->cbSize = cbExtraBytes;

    // Now, read those extra bytes into
    // the structure if cbExtraAlloc != 0.
    if( mmioRead( m_hmmio, (CHAR*)(((BYTE*)&
        (m_pwfx->cbSize))+sizeof(WORD)),
        cbExtraBytes ) != cbExtraBytes )
    {
        SAFE_DELETE( m_pwfx );
        return false;
    }

    // Since this is a non-PCM format, we must
    // retrieve an appropriate PCM format to
    // convert to.
    ZeroMemory(&m_DestFormat, sizeof(WAVEFORMATEX));
    m_DestFormat.wFormatTag = WAVE_FORMAT_PCM;

    MMRESULT error = acmFormatSuggest(NULL, m_pwfx,
        &m_DestFormat, 16,
        ACM_FORMATSUGGESTF_WFORMATTAG);
    if(error)
        return false;

    error = acmStreamOpen(&m_hACMStream, NULL,
        m_pwfx, &m_DestFormat, NULL, 0, 0, 0);
    if(error)
        return false;
}

// Ascend the input file out of the 'fmt ' chunk.
if( 0 != mmioAscend( m_hmmio, &ckIn, 0 ) )
```

```
    {
        SAFE_DELETE( m_pwfx );
        return false;
    }
    return true;
}
```

Because we are expecting non-PCM code, we now must allocate a WAVE-FORMATEX structure in a more-robust manner, using the proper size to dynamically create a structure of the proper (and potentially custom) size. Previously, we did a simple memory copy to a member data structure.

Next, we ask the ACM for an appropriate format to convert to, based on the wave header we've already extracted. This is the acmFormatSuggest() function, and it fills out m_DestFormat with a PCM format if the function succeeds. After this, we open an ACM stream using, logically enough, acmOpenStream(). This function is designed to open the most appropriate codec based on the wave information passed to it. If this function succeeds, we know that we will be able to proceed with decompressing the encoded wave data in the Read() function. Chronologically, this stream is opened just before the file size is estimated in the OpenMMIO() function.

DECOMPRESSING THE DATA

We now come to the Wave::Read() function. The function has stayed relatively unchanged because two decompression-related functions have been broken out into their own functions, and so the differences in the code for this particular function are quite minor.

LISTING 20.5

```
bool Wave::Read( BYTE* pDestBuffer, DWORD dwSizeToRead,
DWORD* pdwSizeRead )
{
    MMIOINFO mmioinfoIn; // current status of m_hmmio

    if (m_hmmio == NULL)
        return false;
    if (pDestBuffer == NULL || pdwSizeRead == NULL)
        return false;
```

```
if (pdwSizeRead != NULL)
    *pdwSizeRead = 0;

if (0 != mmioGetInfo(m_hmmio, & mmioinfoIn, 0))
    return Error::Handle("Wave Error: mmioGetInfo");

// Data member specifying how many bytes to actually
// read out of the wave file.
uint32 nDataIn = 0;
BYTE* pWaveBuffer = 0;
uint32 nStreamRead = 0;

// If we're decompressing this data...
if(m_hACMStream)
{
    // Prepare the ACM buffers for decompression.
    if(!PrepareACMBuffers(nDataIn, nStreamRead,
    dwSizeToRead))
        return false;

    // Use the oversized compression buffer to
    // read the source before sending it to the
    // decompression routines.
    pWaveBuffer = m_pCompressBuffer;
}
else
{
    // If we're not decompressing data, we can
    // directly use the buffer passed in to this
    // function.
    pWaveBuffer = pDestBuffer;
    nDataIn = dwSizeToRead;
}

// Begin reading from the actual wave data
if (nDataIn > m_ck.cksize)
    nDataIn = m_ck.cksize;
m_ck.cksize -= nDataIn;
uint32 nRead = 0;
uint32 nCopySize;
while(nRead < nDataIn)
```

```
{
    // Copy the bytes from the io to the buffer.
    if (0 != mmioAdvance(m_hmmio,
                & mmioinfoIn,
                MMIO_READ))
        return false;

    if (mmioinfoIn.pchNext ==
        mmioinfoIn.pchEndRead)
        return false;

    // Actual copy.
    nCopySize = mmioinfoIn.pchEndRead -
        mmioinfoIn.pchNext;
    nCopySize = ClampMax<uint32>(nCopySize,
        nDataIn - nRead);
    memcpy(pWaveBuffer + nRead, mmioinfoIn.pchNext,
        nCopySize);
    nRead += nCopySize;
    mmioinfoIn.pchNext += nCopySize;
}

if (0 != mmioSetInfo(m_hmmio, & mmioinfoIn, 0))
    return Error::Handle("Wave Error: mmioSetInfo");

// Report the number of bytes read.
if (pdwSizeRead != NULL)
    *pdwSizeRead = nDataIn;

// Check to see if we hit the end of the file.
if (m_ck.cksize == 0)
    m_bEOF = true;

// Convert to a PCM format if required
if(m_hACMStream)
{
    // Decompress the wave data stored in the
    // compressed buffer.
    if(!DecompressData(pWaveBuffer, nDataIn,
        dwSizeToRead, pDestBuffer, pdwSizeRead))
        return false;
}
```

```
    return true;
}
```

In this function, you can see that now instead of simply using the buffer passed into this function directly, we perform one of two actions based on the existence of the ACM stream handle.

If the handle exists, we call the PrepareACMBuffers() function, which will create (or expand as needed) a compressed data buffer and a decompressed data buffer, as well as preserving any data left over from the last Read() call. We'll examine this function a bit later. Instead of directly using the buffer passed to the function, in this case, the raw wave data is instead read into a dedicated compressed data buffer. If this is a PCM wave file, however, the new pointer is assigned to the originally passed-in buffer, so it should behave exactly as before.

Inside the PrepareACMBuffers() function, we start seeing some of the real work involved. Get ready for a bit of complex code. There's a lot going on here, but we'll break it down step by step so you will understand exactly how this works.

LISTING 20.6

```
bool Wave::PrepareACMBuffers(uint32& nDataIn,
    uint32& nStreamRead, uint32 dwSizeToRead)
{
    // This is where we overestimate by a specified
    // amount. Note that we reduce the overestimation
    // by the amount of valid data left over in the
    // decompression buffer from the last call to this
    // function.
    nStreamRead = dwSizeToRead +
        ACM_BUFFER_OVERESTIMATE -
        (m_nDecompressEnd - m_nDecompressStart);
    nStreamRead = ClampMin<int>(nStreamRead,
        ACM_BUFFER_OVERESTIMATE);

    // Use acmStreamSize to get a rough estimate of
    // how much data we should read from the wave file
    // to decompress to fill at least dwSizeToRead
    // bytes. cbDataIn should end up slightly
```

```
// more than dwSizeToRead.
MMRESULT error = acmStreamSize(m_hACMStream,
    nStreamRead, &nDataIn,
    ACM_STREAMSIZEF_DESTINATION);
int iErrorCount = 0;
while (error)
{
    // acmStreamSize cannot estimate below certain
    // minimum sizes, so we attempt to increase the
    // minimum estimation until we either succeed
    // or fail 10 times.
    nStreamRead += ACM_BUFFER_OVERESTIMATE;
    error = acmStreamSize(m_hACMStream,
        nStreamRead, &nDataIn,
        ACM_STREAMSIZEF_DESTINATION);
    iErrorCount++;
    if (iErrorCount > 10)
        return false;
}


// Check to see if we need to grow the conversion
// buffer
if (nStreamRead > m_nDecompressBufferSize)
{
    uint8* pTempBuffer = new BYTE[nStreamRead];
    // Copy any valid data into the beginning of
    // the new buffer if there is any valid
    // data there
    if (m_nDecompressStart != m_nDecompressEnd)
        memcpy(pTempBuffer, m_pDecompressBuffer +
            m_nDecompressStart, m_nDecompressEnd -
            m_nDecompressStart);
    m_nDecompressBufferSize = nStreamRead;
    SAFE_DELETE_ARRAY(m_pDecompressBuffer);
    m_pDecompressBuffer = pTempBuffer;
}
else
{
    // Otherwise, just move any "leftover" data
    // back to the beginning of the buffer
    memmove(m_pDecompressBuffer,
        m_pDecompressBuffer + m_nDecompressStart,
```

```
        m_nDecompressEnd - m_nDecompressStart);
}
// Reset the data markers
m_nDecompressEnd = m_nDecompressEnd -
    m_nDecompressStart;
m_nDecompressStart = 0;

// Now, if needed, create (or recreate) our
// compressed buffer, which is larger than the
// actual destination size
if (m_nCompressBufferSize < nDataIn)
{
    SAFE_DELETE_ARRAY(m_pCompressBuffer);
    m_pCompressBuffer = new uint8[nStreamRead];
    m_nCompressBufferSize = nDataIn;
}
return true;
}
```

This is some of the uglier code you'll be exposed to in this book—so grit your teeth, and let's plow through this. In a nutshell, the function is simply preparing two buffers: one for reading the compressed data, and one is a target for decompressed data. The buffers are designed to dynamically grow as needed. In addition, any valid data found in the existing decompression buffer from the last frame must have the data moved to the front of the buffer.

Believe it or not, that's all this function is doing. Most of the difficulty comes in trying to guess how much we should ask ACM to decompress for us *over* what it would normally tell us. This is not quite as simple as it may sound at first because of the finicky nature of the ACM system in how it deals with data and various decompression routines.

We're using the ACM function acmStreamSize() to retrieve the size of a compressed buffer based on the amount of data requested in the Read() function's parameter, dwDataToRead. The function will return an amount of *compressed* data that we should expect will translate into the *decompressed* size we have given it. We will then use this compressed-data amount to read from our raw wave data, and then pass this data to the decompression function. However, because of the conservative estimates of this function, we will always end up with slightly less data than we intended.

Instead, we wish to overestimate slightly, because it is better for us to have too much data. We can store this extra decompressed data, and use it in the next Read() call. So, we must come up with a formula to overestimate the size of our decompression buffer when asking the ACM to estimate the amount of compressed data to read. Let's examine this formula:

```
nStreamRead = dwSizeToRead + ACM_BUFFER_OVERESTIMATE -
    (m_nDecompressEnd - m_nDecompressStart);
nStreamRead = ClampMin<int>(nStreamRead,
    ACM_BUFFER_OVERESTIMATE);
```

We are going to pass the data nStreamRead into the acmStreamSize() function, and dwSizeToRead is the actual size of the buffer passed into the Read() function. Therefore, nStreamRead must be greater than dwSizeToRead by some amount.

The simplest solution would be to add a fixed amount to dwSizeToRead, and this is how the formula begins. ACM_BUFFER_OVERESTIMATE is defined as 2048, a good constant value by which to increase the estimated size. However, this would not work by itself. The reason is somewhat complicated: we must estimate our decompression buffer size in terms of free space, not in actual size, because we may have data left over from the previous function call. So, if we overestimated by a fixed amount every time without taking into account the amount of data we had accumulated, the buffer would continue to grow because of the overestimation on every Read() call, which is obviously untenable. So, we must subtract our leftover data from our fixed overestimation amount. The formula m_nDecompressEnd - m_nDecompressStart gives us the size of the valid data block in the decompression buffer, and so this amount is subtracted from the total.

The second line uses the ClampMin() template function to ensure that the total value of nStreamRead does not fall below ACM_BUFFER_OVERESTIMATE. This is important because the ACM decompression functions do not work when they are well below a minimum value of data. We now have a good [over]estimation of the amount of compressed data we must read from the wave in order to fulfill the requested read amount.

Unfortunately, it's not quite that easy. Each particular type of compressed wave format has a minimum block compression size, and so we attempt this a number of times, increasing the minimum size by the ACM_BUFFER_OVERESTIMATE every cycle, with a maximum of 10 tries before giving up.

```
int iErrorCount = 0;
while (error)
{
    // acmStreamSize cannot estimate below certain
    // minimum sizes, so we attempt to increase the
    // minimum estimation until we either succeed
    // or fail 10 times.
    nStreamRead += ACM_BUFFER_OVERESTIMATE;
    error = acmStreamSize(m_hACMStream,
        nStreamRead, &nDataIn,
        ACM_STREAMSIZEF_DESTINATION);
    iErrorCount++;
    if (iErrorCount > 10)
        return false;
}
```

Usually, this block of code is not needed; but some extremely high-compression codecs (such as voice-compression) may require a larger block than we have provided, and so we must increase the buffer size slightly. We now have the amount to read from the compressed wave data as well as the maximum size of our decompression buffer.

Next, the code checks to ensure that we have enough space in the decompression buffer. If not, it resizes the buffer, being careful to preserve the data there. The data is then shifted to the front of the buffer, and the decompressed buffer's data markers are appropriately repositioned.

```
// Check to see if we need to grow the conversion
// buffer
if (nStreamRead > m_nDecompressBufferSize)
{
    uint8* pTempBuffer = new BYTE[nStreamRead];
    // Copy any valid data into the beginning of
    // the new buffer if there is any valid
    // data there
    if (m_nDecompressStart != m_nDecompressEnd)
        memcpy(pTempBuffer, m_pDecompressBuffer +
            m_nDecompressStart, m_nDecompressEnd -
            m_nDecompressStart);
    m_nDecompressBufferSize = nStreamRead;
    SAFE_DELETE_ARRAY(m_pDecompressBuffer);
    m_pDecompressBuffer = pTempBuffer;
}
```

```
else
{
    // Otherwise, just move any "leftover" data
    // back to the beginning of the buffer
    memmove(m_pDecompressBuffer,
        m_pDecompressBuffer + m_nDecompressStart,
        m_nDecompressEnd - m_nDecompressStart);
}
// Reset the data markers
m_nDecompressEnd = m_nDecompressEnd -
    m_nDecompressStart;
m_nDecompressStart = 0;
```

If nStreamRead is greater than the current buffer size minus the amount of data that currently exists in it, we allocate a new buffer capable of holding that amount. If there is any data existing in the buffer, it is transferred to the newly allocated buffer before the old buffer is destroyed. In all likelihood, the buffer is not likely to grow after the initial allocation because the first Read() call to a streaming buffer extracts a full second of data, while all subsequent calls will generally extract approximately a quarter of a second of data or less. So, unless the code has a wildly fluctuating compression scheme, this should not be an issue; but the code is included for completeness' sake.

If the buffer does not need resizing, we call memmove() to transfer the existing data within the same buffer. Unlike memcpy(), it is safe to move data within a single buffer using memmove().

Finally, we set our data markers so they indicate the new position of any data existing in the decompression buffer. It is important that this data is marked so that the decompression routines can decompress the newly read data behind this existing data. In this manner, there will be no interruption in the decompressed data flow.

Now we have our buffers set up, and the Read() function will now extract the wave data into the compressed data buffer. Next, let's examine the function that decompresses this data and finally copies it to the buffer that was passed into the Read() function.

LISTING 20.7

```
bool Wave::DecompressData(uint32 nDataIn,
    BYTE* pDestBuffer, uint32 dwSizeToRead,
```

```
    DWORD* pdwSizeRead)
{
    // Prepare the conversion data
    ACMSTREAMHEADER StreamHeader;
    memset(&StreamHeader, 0, sizeof(ACMSTREAMHEADER));
    StreamHeader.cbStruct = sizeof(ACMSTREAMHEADER);
    StreamHeader.pbSrc = m_pCompressBuffer;
    StreamHeader.cbSrcLength = nDataIn;
    StreamHeader.pbDst = m_pDecompressBuffer +
        m_nDecompressEnd;
    StreamHeader.cbDstLength = m_nDecompressBufferSize -
        m_nDecompressEnd;
    MMRESULT error = acmStreamPrepareHeader(
        m_hACMStream, &StreamHeader, 0);
    if (error)
        // Signal an error, but go on anyway
        Error::Handle("Wave Conversion Error");

    // Do the actual non-PCM to PCM data conversion
    if (!error)
    {
        error = acmStreamConvert(m_hACMStream,
                    & StreamHeader,
                    ACM_STREAMCONVERTF_START |
                    ACM_STREAMCONVERTF_END |
                    ACM_STREAMCONVERTF_BLOCKALIGN);
        if (error)
            return false;
    }

    // Add the number of bytes read to the
    // "valid content" markers in the uncompressed
    // buffer
    m_nDecompressEnd += StreamHeader.cbDstLengthUsed;

    // Determine how much data we can actually copy
    uint32 nDataToCopy;
    if ((m_nDecompressEnd - m_nDecompressStart) <
        dwSizeToRead)
        nDataToCopy = m_nDecompressEnd -
            m_nDecompressStart;
    else
```

```
        nDataToCopy = dwSizeToRead;

    // Copy the decompressed data from our oversized
    // buffer to the final destination buffer
    memcpy(pDestBuffer, m_pDecompressBuffer,
        nDataToCopy);

    // Record how many bytes were actually read
    if (pdwSizeRead != NULL)
        *pdwSizeRead = nDataToCopy;

    // Advance the start of the valid data pointer
    // by the amount of data copied
    m_nDecompressStart += nDataToCopy;

    // Clean up any internal conversion data
    if (!error)
    {
        error = acmStreamUnprepareHeader(m_hACMStream,
            &StreamHeader, 0);
        if (error)
            return false;
    }
    return true;
}
```

The `Wave::DecompressData()` function is also a bit complex at first glance, so we'll go through it carefully, just like the previous function. The basic functionality works as follows: the compressed data is stored in `m_pCompressBuffer`, and the actual data in bytes is represented by `nDataIn`, which is passed to the function. The function must decompress the data to the `pDestBuffer`, copying `dwSizeToRead` bytes (or as many as possible), and fill in the `pdwSizeRead` variable with the actual number of bytes read. You should note that the last three parameters of this function correspond exactly with the `Read()` function's parameters.

ACM data decompression essentially happens in three stages once the codec has been identified and the stream has been opened. The decompression revolves around an `ACMSTREAMHEADER` structure, which is filled by both the client and the ACM structures to communicate information about the decompression process. This structure is first created, filled out, and then passed to the function acmStreamPrepareHeader(). The actual data conversion takes place in the acmStreamConvert() function and finishes up with the acmStreamUnprepareHeader() function.

Let's examine the first portion of this function.

```
// Prepare the conversion data
ACMSTREAMHEADER StreamHeader
memset(&StreamHeader, 0, sizeof(ACMSTREAMHEADER));
StreamHeader.cbStruct = sizeof(ACMSTREAMHEADER);
StreamHeader.pbSrc = m_pCompressBuffer;
StreamHeader.cbSrcLength = nDataIn;
StreamHeader.pbDst = m_pDecompressBuffer +
    m_nDecompressEnd;
StreamHeader.cbDstLength =
    m_nDecompressBufferSize - m_nDecompressEnd;
MMRESULT error = acmStreamPrepareHeader(m_hACMStream,
    &StreamHeader, 0);
if(error)
{ /* Signal an error, but go on anyway */ }
```

Here, we initialize and zero-out the StreamHeader structure, which will contain all of the data pertinent to the streaming process. The pbSrc member is pointed to our data source buffer, m_pCompressBuffer, and the data size is set as nDataIn, which was obtained while reading the actual file data. We also set the destination buffer at this time, pbDst, being careful to set the actual position just beyond the valid data already residing in the decompression buffer, m_pDecompressBuffer. Additionally, we tell the structure in its cbDstLength member how much free space actually exists in the destination buffer by subtracting the data end marker from the total size. We're now ready to begin the decompression process, so we call acmStreamPrepareHeader(), passing in the stream handle and the address of the StreamHeader structure. Note that we do not exit on a failure at this point, as we wish to continue processing information, even if this particular function fails. On a failure, we simply will not process any additional ACM functions.

Next, we are ready to do the actual conversion.

```
// Do the actual non-PCM to PCM data conversion
if(!error)
{
    error = acmStreamConvert(m_hACMStream,
```

```
    &StreamHeader,
    ACM_STREAMCONVERTF_START |
    ACM_STREAMCONVERTF_END |
    ACM_STREAMCONVERTF_BLOCKALIGN);
  if(error)
      return false;
}
```

For this, we call the acmStreamConvert() function, again passing in the stream handle and the address of the StreamHeader structure. This will decompress the wave data into our decompressed buffer. We now must determine exactly how much data was read, then copy this data to the actual destination buffer, as well as adjusting the decompressed buffer's pointers to reflect the updated content.

We first adjust the decompressed buffer's end marker by adding the amount of data decompressed, as reported by the StreamHeader structure.

```
m_nDecompressEnd += StreamHeader.cbDstLengthUsed;
```

After this, we must determine how much data we may actually copy into the destination buffer. By comparing the size of the requested data against how much data was *actually* decompressed, we can obtain a value that we store in nDataToCopy, which we will use later in the data-transfer process. Ideally, we should usually be decompressing more data than is actually requested—otherwise the streaming buffer will starve, and hiccups will occur in the playback. The exception is when the file runs out of data to decompress; but at this point, an end-of-file flag will be set, and the stream will handle this case by filling in the rest of the buffer with silence.

```
uint32 nDataToCopy;
if((m_nDecompressEnd - m_nDecompressStart) <
    dwSizeToRead)
    nDataToCopy = m_nDecompressEnd - m_nDecompressStart;
else
    nDataToCopy = dwSizeToRead;
```

After the amount to copy has been determined, we simply copy the data from the decompression buffer to the destination buffer.

```
memcpy(pDestBuffer, m_pDecompressBuffer, nDataToCopy);
```

When the data is copied, we record how much data was transferred in the pdwDataRead value, which will be read by the client, and then advance the 'start-data' pointer in the decompression buffer.

```
if( pdwSizeRead != NULL)
    *pdwSizeRead = nDataToCopy;

m_nDecompressStart += nDataToCopy;
```

If there was more data decompressed than was read, this will leave a small section of valid data in the middle of the decompression buffer. At the beginning of the next read function, this buffer will be moved to the beginning of the buffer, and the cycle will start over.

Finally, for good housekeeping measures, we call the acmStream-UnprepareHeader(), which finishes off the conversion process.

```
if(!error)
{
    error = acmStreamUnprepareHeader(
        m_hACMStream, &StreamHeader, 0);
    if(error)
        return false;
}
```

CONCLUSION

While a bit of work is involved to get the ACM working correctly with our file-reading system, it is handy to have the resources of Windows codecs at our disposal when decompressing wave files. Even better is the fact that the client does not have to perform any additional steps in order to play compressed files. In the next few chapters, we'll examine some alternative high-compression formats, such as MP3, Ogg Vorbis, and Windows Media Format, along with their corresponding SDKs.

CHAPTER 21

OGG VORBIS SDK

Ogg Vorbis, an open-source, high-compression audio format, is a bit of an anachronism in today's world of commercially patented and/or proprietary audio formats, but a very welcome one. While not as well known as the popular MP3 format, it nonetheless is making significant strides in many markets, including game development. Most PC-based audio players, such as WinAmp, now support Vorbis natively. As an open alternative and as a superior audio-compression format, Ogg Vorbis has many features to its credit. It actually out-performs MP3 and WMA in compression, quality, and efficiency; it is quite easy to use; and it is completely royalty- and license-free. In short, Vorbis might just be the perfect solution for high-quality streaming audio in games.

ON THE CD
The code listed in this chapter can be found in \Game_Audio\ audio_sdk\src\audiolib\IAudioLoader.h, Vorbis.h, Vorbis.cpp.

WHAT IS OGG VORBIS?

The Ogg project is an open-source-based attempt to provide an alternative to proprietary and patented codecs for digital media, such as audio and video. The Vorbis project, one of several ongoing Ogg projects, has designed a high-compression, lossy algorithm for encoding audio content. According to the official Ogg Web site (*http://www.vorbis.org/*):

> Ogg Vorbis is a fully Open, non-proprietary, patent-and-royalty-free, general-purpose compressed audio format for mid- to high-quality (8 kHz-48.0 kHz, 16+ bit, polyphonic) audio

and music at fixed and variable bitrates from 16 to 128 kbps/channel. This places Vorbis in the same competitive class as audio representations such as MPEG-4 (AAC), and similar to, but higher performance than MPEG-1/2 audio layer 3, MPEG-4 audio (TwinVQ), WMA and PAC.

As an added bonus, the variable-bit nature of the scheme means that you are not restricted to choosing a specific, fixed bit rate, and instead can encode based on a quality level (although advance settings allow you to specify bit rates if you wish to). The purpose of variable-bit-rate encoding is to allow the encoder to 'save' bits in easily encoded parts and use them in more-complex areas, preserving the average bit rate while vastly improving the overall quality.

All in all, the Vorbis format is superior in quality and comparable in performance to MP3, but without the licensing costs. Developers of jukebox and player software could certainly not afford to support only Vorbis at the exclusion of the popular MP3 format, but for most game developers this is no real concern, since games provide both the audio player and the content. The particular file format used makes no real difference, other than for reasons of efficiency and quality.

How Vorbis Can Be Used

Keep in mind that high-compression audio may not simply be limited to streaming music tracks in your game. Because of the general-purpose nature of our IAudioReader interface (which we covered in Chapter 8), Vorbis-encoded audio can be used both for soundtracks and general-purpose sound effects. Static buffers are only decoded once at load time, making their use practical for just about any audio source in your game, if you can afford the initial decompression time. Additionally, Vorbis also has some properties that make it attractive for decoding to static buffers, not the least of which is that the format knows exactly how many bytes will be required in a decompressed state—something which is difficult or even impossible to determine with some other compression schemes or SDKs, such as the Windows Audio Compression Manager (ACM).

You should determine for yourself what is the greater drain on resources—decompressing audio at load time or loading 10 to 20 times that amount in uncompressed data. In essence, you must decide whether the

CPU (decompression) or the hard-drive/CD-ROM/DVD (file reading) is the bottleneck in your data-loading pipeline, and adjust your file-compression strategy accordingly. There is no guaranteed answer, of course, but it is a simple matter to experiment, since both Ogg Vorbis and raw wave formats can be seamlessly supported without code changes. You can also mix and match source formats, as well. For instance, you may want to use Vorbis for all streaming and other large buffers, while leaving smaller samples as uncompressed PCM wave files.

So, if Ogg Vorbis is free and open, and technically as good as MP3, why would anyone want to actually use the MP3 format for games? One good reason might be due to the popularity of the MP3 format itself. Many users have created their own personal libraries of encoded MP3 music, and it may be desirable for your particular game to be able to play user's existing audio soundtracks.

XIPHOPHORUS' VORBIS SOFTWARE LIBRARIES

The examples demonstrated here use Xiphophorus's Vorbis libraries, and so are subject to the conditions of the business-friendly, BSD-like licensing of those libraries. Both open and closed source, commercial and freeware projects may use these libraries freely. Although you should read and verify the license agreement for yourself, it simply states that public acknowledgement must be given to Xiphophorus when using these libraries in whole or in part, which is not an uncommon licensing stipulation for many freely available libraries.

ON THE CD The Vorbis libraries on the CD-ROM are organized as shown in Figure 21.1. The arrangement is similar to other SDKs you have seen, including the Microsoft DirectX SDK. All relevant header files are included in the /include folder, static libraries are in the /lib folder, and dynamic dlls are located in the /redist folder. If you wish to use Vorbis in your application, you must set proper include and library paths in Visual Studio's path-searching options dialog. You can find this under the Tools | Options menu. In the Directories property tab, you can point to the appropriate directories, as shown in Figure 21.2.

There are four basic Vorbis-related libraries available for use: ogg, vorbis, vorbisenc, and vorbisfile. Each of these libraries has a statically linked version and a dynamically linked stub version (dll). The static libraries

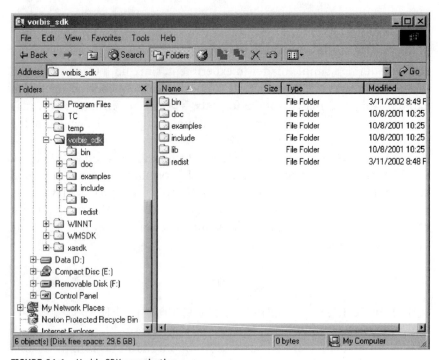

FIGURE 21.1 Vorbis SDK organization.

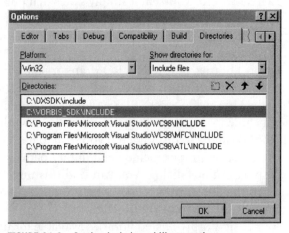

FIGURE 21.2 Setting include and library paths.

append "_static" to each library for easy identification. Each of these libraries also has both a release and debug version. All debug versions append "_d" to the library file. Essentially, there are four variations of each library, for a total of 16 libraries. Here's a quick overview of each library type and what it is used for:

TABLE 21.1   Ogg Vorbis Library Variations

ogg	Base library used for Ogg projects. Required library for any Vorbis application.
vorbis	Low-level Vorbis decoding library. Required library for any application reading Vorbis files or streams.
vorbisenc	Low-level Vorbis encoding library. Required library for any application writing Vorbis files or streams.
vorbisfile	High-level Vorbis file-reading library.

The sample audio library and example programs will statically link to the Vorbis libraries, using the following code located in a project header file:

LISTING 21.1

```
#ifdef USE_VORBIS
#ifdef _DEBUG
#pragma comment(lib, "ogg_static_d")
#pragma comment(lib, "vorbis_static_d")
#pragma comment(lib, "vorbisfile_static_d")
#else
#pragma comment(lib, "ogg_static")
#pragma comment(lib, "vorbis_static")
#pragma comment(lib, "vorbisfile_static")
#endif
#endif
```

Alternatively, you could place the Vorbis dlls into your project path and link with the dll stub libraries. Doing so would require you to redistribute the Vorbis dlls with your application. Note that we also conditionally compile Vorbis support based on a USE_VORBIS #define, allowing you to easily add or remove Vorbis support from the library. And of course, you also have the option of using the more traditional method of adding the library files directly to your project linker settings via the GUI or by using a makefile.

THE VORBIS READER

We'll now examine how to construct a Vorbis file reader. Like the wave file reader, the Vorbis class will be derived from the abstract interface class, IAudioLoader. By conforming to this interface, we guarantee compatibility with any class already capable of working with the Wave class. By choosing a file reader based on the extensions of the file, we ensure a large amount of flexibility in our audio library, allowing nearly any file to be used as long as we can write a reader capable of conforming to our abstract reader interface. (For a complete overview of the IAudioLoader interface, see Chapter 8—Basic Digital Audio Sample Playback, and examine the code in Listing 8.1.)

Let's examine the Vorbis class declaration, which is shown in Listing 21.2.

LISTING 21.2

```
#ifdef USE_VORBIS

#include "Audio.h"
#include "IAudioLoader.h"

#pragma pack(push,8)
#include <vorbis/codec.h>
#include <vorbis/vorbisfile.h>

namespace Audio
{
struct MemorySource
{
    MemorySource()
    {
        Clear();
    };
    void Clear()
```

```
    {
        m_pData = 0;
        m_nDataSize = 0;
        m_pReadPtr = 0;
    };
    char* m_pData;
    uint32 m_nDataSize;
    char* m_pReadPtr;
};

class Vorbis : public IAudioLoader
{
    DEFINE_POOL(Vorbis);
public:
    void Clear();

    bool Open(std::string sFileName);
    bool Open(BYTE* pbData, uint32 dwDataSize);
    bool Close();

    bool Read(BYTE* pBuffer, uint32 dwSizeToRead,
        uint32* pdwSizeRead);

    uint32 GetSize();
    bool Reset();
    WAVEFORMATEX* GetFormat();
    bool IsEOF();

    void Destroy();

protected:
    virtual ~Vorbis();
private:
    Vorbis();
    bool GetStreamInfo();

private:
    WAVEFORMATEX m_WaveFormatEx;

    bool m_bOpen;
    OggVorbis_File m_VorbisFile;
    vorbis_info* m_pVorbisInfo;
```

```
    uint8* m_pBufferPtr;
    uint8* m_pBuffer;
    uint32 m_nBufferSize;
    uint32 m_nNumSamples;

    bool m_bEOF;

public:
    // This has to be public so the callback functions
    // can access it
    MemorySource m_MemSrc;
    IAudioStream* m_pStreamSrc;
};
}; // namespace Audio

#pragma pack(pop,8)

#endif // USE_VORBIS
```

First, and most obviously, we see the Vorbis class is publicly inherited from IAudioLoader, ensuring that our Sound class will be able to use this class by calling only IAudioLoader virtual members. In this manner, the Sound class is well insulated from knowing about particular file formats. You can see back in Listing 8.2 how to write code to choose a reader based on the file extension—simply use the file extension to choose a loader.

There is one other structure that might catch your eye as well: the MemorySource struct. This is used in the Vorbis library's callback system to handle data transfer from a memory buffer to the Vorbis library. We'll examine how this works shortly.

IMPLEMENTING THE VORBIS READER

Before we examine the two Vorbis::Open() functions, we should first look at some function declarations found in Vorbis.cpp before the other functions are defined.

LISTING 21.3

```
// Memory callback function declarations
size_t read_func_mem(void* ptr, size_t size,
```

```
    size_t nmemb, void* datasource);
int seek_func_mem(void* datasource, ogg_int64_t offset,
    int whence);
int close_func_mem(void* datasource);
long tell_func_mem(void* datasource);

// Stream callback function declarations
size_t read_func_stream(void* ptr, size_t size,
    size_t nmemb, void* datasource);
int seek_func_stream(void* datasource,
    ogg_int64_t offset, int whence);
int close_func_stream(void* datasource);
long tell_func_stream(void* datasource);
```

Looking closely at these functions may give you a clue as to why we created the memory buffer structure to hold the source information. The Vorbis library provides callback functions that will be invoked when performing operations on the data stream. These callbacks allow us to substitute whatever source we wish in place of the internal, default file reader. Each function provides a single void pointer for the data source, meaning that we must use a single structure to represent our data source and perform operations on it. Because the IAudioStream source is already easily represented by a single pointer, there is no need to create an additional structure to hold this information. Let's look now at our Open() functions and see how we open a Vorbis file and set up the appropriate callback functions.

LISTING 21.4

```
// Use for IAudioStream-based source
bool Vorbis::Open(std::string sFileName)
{
    if (m_bOpen)
        return false;

    // Open the file
    if (!AudioMgr()->CreateAudioStream(m_pStreamSrc))
        return false;

    if (FAILED(m_pStreamSrc->Open(sFileName)))
        return false;
```

```
    // Set the proper callback functions
    ov_callbacks cb;
    cb.read_func = &read_func_stream;
    cb.seek_func = &seek_func_stream;
    cb.close_func = &close_func_stream;
    cb.tell_func = &tell_func_stream;

    // Open the Ogg bitstream
    if (ov_open_callbacks(m_pStreamSrc,
            &m_VorbisFile,
            NULL,
            0,
            cb) < 0)
        return false;

    m_bOpen = true;
    if (!GetStreamInfo())
        return false;

    return true;
}

// Used for loading direct from memory
bool Vorbis::Open(BYTE* pbData, uint32 dwDataSize)
{
    if (m_bOpen)
        return false;

    m_MemSrc.m_pData = (char *) pbData;
    m_MemSrc.m_nDataSize = dwDataSize;
    m_MemSrc.m_pReadPtr = (char *) pbData;

    // Set the proper callback functions
    ov_callbacks cb;
    cb.read_func = &read_func_mem;
    cb.seek_func = &seek_func_mem;
    cb.close_func = &close_func_mem;
    cb.tell_func = &tell_func_mem;

    if (ov_open_callbacks(&m_MemSrc,
            &m_VorbisFile,
```

```
            NULL,
            dwDataSize,
            cb) < 0)
        return false;

    if (!GetStreamInfo())
        return false;

    m_bOpen = true;
    return true;
}
```

Like all of our reader classes derived from IAudioReader, we have two Open() functions. One is designed to operate on IAudioStream-based files and will be used by the *GAP* audio library for both static and streaming buffers. The other Open() function is designed to read directly from a memory buffer. Typically, this is used as more of a one-shot loading method, although streaming from a memory buffer can theoretically work just as well. However, there is little gained from doing so, as the typical reasons for streaming are to save memory and load times. The *GAP* library does not actually use this particular version of the Open() function, but it is included as a way of demonstrating how the reader can be made to easily read from alternative sources, if desired.

We do not demonstrate using Vorbis in its default mode—simple disk file reading. This can be done by calling the ov_open() function and passing in a standard FILE pointer instead of the slightly more complex ov_open_callbacks() that we are using.

The first step in opening a file is to prepare our source and register the proper callback functions. Inside each Open() function, we set up the appropriate source parameters and pass these values via an ov_callbacks structure to the ov_open_callbacks() function. This function fills out m_VorbisFile, which is a OggVorbis_File structure. This structure is essentially a handle to an open Vorbis file, and it is passed to any subsequent Vorbis library functions.

After the file or memory buffer is readied and the Vorbis stream is initialized, we call GetStreamInfo() to determine what the output format of the decompressed PCM data will be.

LISTING 21.5

```
bool Vorbis::GetStreamInfo()
{
    if(!m_bOpen)
        return false;

    // Get Vorbis file information
    m_pVorbisInfo = ov_info(&m_VorbisFile,-1);

    // Get the number of PCM samples in this file
    m_nNumSamples = (long)ov_pcm_total(
        &m_VorbisFile, -1);

    // set up the WaveFormatEx structure
    m_WaveFormatEx.wFormatTag = WAVE_FORMAT_PCM;
    m_WaveFormatEx.nChannels = m_pVorbisInfo->channels;
    m_WaveFormatEx.nSamplesPerSec = m_pVorbisInfo->rate;
    m_WaveFormatEx.wBitsPerSample = 16;
    m_WaveFormatEx.nBlockAlign =
        m_WaveFormatEx.nChannels *
        m_WaveFormatEx.wBitsPerSample / 8;
    m_WaveFormatEx.nAvgBytesPerSec =
        m_WaveFormatEx.nSamplesPerSec *
        m_WaveFormatEx.nBlockAlign;
    m_WaveFormatEx.cbSize = 0;

    return true;
}
```

ON THE CD   A few extraneous bits of information have been trimmed out for clarity (you can see the entire function on the CD-ROM), but here is the essential information needed to fill out the m_WaveFormatEx structure, which will be used to construct the destination DirectSound buffer. Once the wave format structure is filled out, and now that we know the total number of samples in this file, we can determine the final size in bytes of the decompressed data in this file with the following function:

LISTING 21.6

```
uint32 Vorbis::GetSize()
{
```

```
    return m_nNumSamples * m_WaveFormatEx.nChannels *
        m_WaveFormatEx.wBitsPerSample / 8;
}
```

The Read() function is fairly straightforward. A buffer and the requested amount to read are passed as pBuffer and dwSizeToRead, and the number of bytes actually read is returned in pdwSizeRead. Listing 21.7 shows how the Read() function works.

LISTING 21.7

```
bool Vorbis::Read(BYTE* pBuffer, uint32 dwSizeToRead,
    uint32* pdwSizeRead )
{
    if(!m_bOpen)
        return false;

    char* pCurBuffer = (char*)pBuffer;
    uint32 nBytesRead = 0;
    int iSection = 0;
    while((nBytesRead < dwSizeToRead) && !m_bEOF)
    {
        int32 iRet = ov_read(&m_VorbisFile, pCurBuffer,
            dwSizeToRead - nBytesRead, 0, 2, 1,
            &iSection);
        if (iRet == 0 || iSection != 0)
            m_bEOF = true;
        else if (iRet < 0)
            return false;
        nBytesRead += iRet;
        pCurBuffer += iRet;
    }
    *pdwSizeRead = nBytesRead;
    return true;
}
```

The function first checks to see if the file has been properly opened. Next, it enters a loop, wherein the ov_read() function is called repeatedly until the correct amount of data is read or until the end of the file is reached.

It is necessary to loop in this manner because ov_read() decodes the Vorbis data in incremental chunks. The number of bytes read, as well as the current position in the destination buffer, are both based on how many bytes are reportedly read by the ov_read() function via the nBytesRead variable. When the loop exits, the total number of bytes is assigned to pdwSizeRead, to be passed back to the client.

When the file is finished and must be reset to be read again, the Reset() function is called.

LISTING 21.8

```
bool Vorbis::Reset()
{
    if(!m_bOpen)
        return false;
    // Seek to beginning of file to
    // begin reading it again
    m_bEOF = false;
    ov_pcm_seek(&m_VorbisFile, 0);
    return true;
}
```

After checking for a valid file, the Reset() function simply seeks to the beginning of the file. When finished with the Vorbis file, the Close() function is called. Listing 21.9 demonstrates how to shut down our Vorbis reader.

LISTING 21.9

```
bool Vorbis::Close()
{
    if(!m_bOpen)
        return false;

    // close out the Vorbis file bitstream
    ov_clear(&m_VorbisFile);

    Clear();
    return true;
}
```

IMPLEMENTING THE SOURCE CALLBACK FUNCTIONS

Now that we have the basic reader in place, we must implement our callback that will actually perform the work of seeking and transferring data from the data source to the Vorbis library's internal decompression buffers. As we saw earlier in Listing 21.3, there are four callback functions that must be implemented for each data source type: a *read* function, a *seek* function, a *tell* function, and a *close* function. Each of these essentially mimics the behavior of the corresponding C file functions fread(), fseek(), ftell(), and fclose().

With that in mind, let's first examine our file-wrapping functions, utilizing our pseudo-file structure to store and transmit the information between the functions.

LISTING 21.10

```
size_t read_func_stream(void* ptr, size_t size,
    size_t nmemb, void* datasource)
{
    if (!size || !nmemb)
        return 0;

    IAudioStream* pSrc = (IAudioStream*) datasource;
    uint32 nBytesToRead = size* nmemb;

    uint32 nRead;
    if(FAILED(pSrc->Read(ptr, nBytesToRead, & nRead)))
        return 0;

    return nRead;
}

int seek_func_stream(void* datasource,
    ogg_int64_t offset, int whence)
{
    IAudioStream* pSrc = (IAudioStream*) datasource;
    LARGE_INTEGER liOffset;
    ULARGE_INTEGER lnNewPos;
    liOffset.QuadPart = offset;
    if(FAILED(pSrc->Seek(liOffset, whence, &lnNewPos)))
        return -1;
```

```
    return 0;
}

int close_func_stream(void* datasource)
{
    IAudioStream* pSrc = (IAudioStream*) datasource;
    SAFE_RELEASE(pSrc);
    return 0;
}

long tell_func_stream(void* datasource)
{
    IAudioStream* pSrc = (IAudioStream*) datasource;
    LARGE_INTEGER dlibMove;
    dlibMove.QuadPart = 0;
    ULARGE_INTEGER nNewPos;
    pSrc->Seek(dlibMove, SEEK_CUR, & nNewPos);
    return nNewPos.QuadPart;
}
```

In each of these functions, the IAudioStream class pSrc is first cast from the void pointer datasource. Now, all we must do is ensure proper C-file-compliant behavior. For instance, in the 'read' function, we must ensure that the correct number of actual read bytes is returned by the function. Because most of the work involved in doing this has been done (or, more accurately, is defined by the IStream interface), all we must do is to make equivalent function calls on the IAudioStream object.

For the memory reader, we simply manipulate the pointers and buffer as you might expect. A memory buffer along with a 'current seek' pointer can behave nearly identically to an open file, only requiring a bit more manual manipulation. We've chosen to implement the seek pointer as a true pointer into the buffer. An alternative method would have been to implement it as an integer offset value, performing a simple addition operation on the base pointer to reach its target. Either method works fine—it's just a matter of preference. Let's look at these functions now:

LISTING 21.11

```
size_t read_func_mem(void* ptr, size_t size,
    size_t nmemb, void* datasource)
```

```
{
    MemorySource* pSrc = (MemorySource*) datasource;
    uint32 nBytesToCopy = size* nmemb;
    uint32 nBytesRemaining = (pSrc->m_pData +
        pSrc->m_nDataSize) -
        pSrc->m_pReadPtr;
    if (nBytesToCopy > nBytesRemaining)
        nBytesToCopy = nBytesRemaining;
    memcpy(ptr, pSrc->m_pReadPtr, nBytesToCopy);
    pSrc->m_pReadPtr += nBytesToCopy;
    return nBytesToCopy;
}

int seek_func_mem(void* datasource, ogg_int64_t offset,
    int whence)
{
    MemorySource* pSrc = (MemorySource*) datasource;
    switch (whence)
    {
    case SEEK_SET:
        pSrc->m_pReadPtr = pSrc->m_pData + offset;
        break;
    case SEEK_CUR:
        pSrc->m_pReadPtr += offset;
        break;
    case SEEK_END:
        pSrc->m_pReadPtr = (pSrc->m_pData +
            pSrc->m_nDataSize) -
            offset;
        break;
    };

    // check for out-of-bounds seek pointer
    if (pSrc->m_pReadPtr < pSrc->m_pData)
    {
        pSrc->m_pReadPtr = pSrc->m_pData;
        return -1;
    }
    else if (pSrc->m_pReadPtr >
        (pSrc->m_pData + pSrc->m_nDataSize))
    {
        pSrc->m_pReadPtr = pSrc->m_pData +
            pSrc->m_nDataSize;
```

```
        return -1;
    }

    return 0;
}

int close_func_mem(void* datasource)
{
    MemorySource* pSrc = (MemorySource*) datasource;
    return 0;
}

long tell_func_mem(void* datasource)
{
    MemorySource* pSrc = (MemorySource*) datasource;
    return pSrc->m_pReadPtr - pSrc->m_pData;
}
```

For the most part, the C file functions have essentially been replaced with memory operation functions from the C library in the case of the 'read' function, or by simple pointer manipulation in the case of the 'seek' function.

With these simple callback functions added to the class reader, we now have an IAudioLoader-compatible Ogg Vorbis reader that is capable of reading from any type of custom file system or from memory buffers.

CONCLUSION

Adding Ogg Vorbis support to our library has been a snap, and considering the great performance and open nature of the format and accompanying libraries, it makes a lot of sense for game developers to give it serious consideration when deciding what type of high-compression audio formats to use for an audio engine. The general flexibility and robustness of the system is rather impressive, and we will likely be hearing much more about Ogg Vorbis in the future.

Next, we'll examine the Microsoft Windows Media SDK. This SDK gives us a single-code solution for decoding both MP3 and WMA formats, providing us with even more compressed-audio decoding options for our audio library.

CHAPTER 22

WINDOWS MEDIA FORMAT SDK

The Windows Media SDK provides programmers with a way of decoding both its native Windows Media Audio files as well as the popular MP3 format. The SDK is freely available from Microsoft, making it a tempting alternative to often very expensive or unwieldy MP3-decoder alternatives.

The bad news is that the Windows Media SDK was not designed primarily for low-level decoding, such as we need to do; so it requires a number of rather ugly programming tricks to force the system into behaving the way we need it to. Fortunately, we are here to walk you through the decoding process, and we will explain how and why the code design presented in this chapter was chosen.

 The code listed in this chapter can be found in \Game_Audio\ audio_sdk\src\audiolib\IAudioLoader.h, WMA.h, WMA.cpp.

INTRODUCTION TO THE WINDOWS MEDIA FORMAT SDK

Windows Media is the audio/video format commonly used across the Internet for streaming video and/or audio media files to end users, usually through the use of the Microsoft Windows Media Player. To encourage more widespread use of their format, Microsoft has released the Windows Media Format SDK, providing access to decoding libraries, among many other things. Although primarily used for streaming media across network connections in real-time, the Windows Media Format SDK can also be used equally well as stand-alone files, which is what games usually require. Because it is a general-purpose media decoder, it can handle both audio and video, either separately or as a combined package. For our purposes, we'll obviously be looking at an audio-only solutions.

WINDOWS MEDIA AUDIO

Windows Media Audio (WMA) is audio component of Windows Media (there is also a video component). It is a high-compression lossy format, capable of achieving compression rates of 11:1 (128 KB/sec.) while retaining near-CD-quality sound comparable to the popular MP3 format. As a more-recent format, though, WMA is arguably superior in audio quality/compression rate. In addition, unlike MP3, there are no potential royalty issues to deal with because Microsoft, while retaining control of the format, is not charging for the use of the WMA format.

MP3 FORMAT

The MP3 format is more accurately titled MPEG-1 layer 3. It is by far the most popular high-quality, high-compression audio format in use today. MP3 showed up first on personal computers and then on portable players. Now, nearly every media player on a computer supports MP3 by default. Even Microsoft's Windows Media format, while in some ways directly competing with the MP3 format, has acknowledged the massive popularity of the format by supporting MP3 with the exact same code path in their SDK used to decode WMA files.

Like Ogg Vorbis and WMA, MP3 is a high-quality, high-compression format, and good encoders can achieve near-CD quality at approximately 128 KB/sec. (and even lower to less-discriminating listeners). Because the format is somewhat older than Vorbis or Windows Media Audio, slightly higher bit rates are needed to achieve a similar quality as in those formats, although the difference is not huge.

However, the MP3 format has recently gotten a face-lift in the form of MP3-Pro. Thomson Multimedia claims to achieve 128 KB quality in a 64 KB stream, without sacrificing compatibility with existing MP3 players—although players not optimized for the new MP3-Pro format would not realize the full improved quality of the new format. Indeed, the new format achieves remarkable quality, even at compression rates as high as 20:1, making it an ideal format for designers who require extremely high compression rates while retaining high-quality audio. Unfortunately, Windows Media does not currently support MP3-Pro.

Any use of MP3 technology is subject to royalty payments for the use of Thomson and Franhofer patents. See Appendix C for more specific information about MP3 licensing.

ACQUIRING AND INSTALLING THE WINDOWS MEDIA FORMAT SDK

The latest version of the Windows Media Format SDK can be found at *http://msdn.microsoft.com*. After decompressing the downloaded file, you will notice a file called "wmstub.lib" in addition to the installation executable. This is a required digital-rights management stub file that you must link with to compile and run any Windows Media project. Projects using digital-rights management must acquire a special stub file from Microsoft before shipping a product, but since you are most likely not using the digital-rights management system, you may simply use the 'generic' stub file. For ease of use, you may wish to place this stub file into the /lib file created by the Windows Media installation program.

If the installation program does not automatically set proper include and library paths that point to the Windows Media Format SDK, you will have to set them yourself. Select Tool | Options in Visual Studio, and select the Directories tab in the Options dialog box. Then, fill in the appropriate paths to point to the /include and /lib directories.

In order to successfully link a project designed to play WMA and MP3 files using Windows Media, you must link with two libraries: wmstub.lib and wmvcore.lib. You may either link with these libraries in your application's

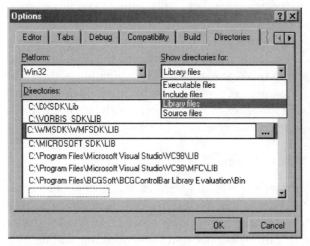

FIGURE 22.1   Setting Windows Media SDK include and library paths.

project settings or alternatively place the following in a library header file (this is what we've chosen to do in the *GAP* library):

```
#pragma comment(lib, "wmstub.lib")
#pragma comment(lib, "wmvcore.lib")
```

CREATING THE WINDOWS MEDIA READER OBJECT

As with all the file readers/decoders we have created and demonstrated in this book, we base the Windows Media reader on a common abstract interface, IAudioLoader, which will help to ensure the system will work seamlessly with our existing code. This interface has been documented in several other places in the book, including Chapter 8—Basic Digital Audio Sample Playback, as well as Chapter 21, which demonstrates the Ogg Vorbis SDK.

The Windows Media Format SDK is based on the concept of asynchronous decoding, meaning that all status and data will be handled on a different thread than the main interfaces. This presents somewhat of a challenge for us, as our audio system decoders are expected to be able to decode audio data on demand. The *GAP* library handles its own background loading and decoding. The Windows Media Format libraries work by utilizing a specially designed callback object, which is used to handle all messages and information retrieved from the decoding thread. We then must transfer this information to the primary decoding thread.

Typically, the primary thread will continue executing while the decoding takes place. However, we can force synchronous behavior by blocking the primary thread until the decoding thread is finished. After the primary thread is allowed to resume, we then block the decoding thread until it is needed again. In this manner, using a combination of thread blocking and signaling techniques, we can force the Windows Media Format SDK to behave as though it were decoding synchronously. It's not an elegant solution by any stretch of the imagination, but it does actually work.

WMA AND WMACallback CLASS DECLARATIONS

Our WMA reader will consist of two basic classes. The WMA class is derived from IAudioLoader, and is the primary loading class. Another class, WMACallback, is derived from IWMReaderCallback and IWMReaderCallbackAdvanced, and is designed to retrieve decoding and status information from the Windows Media decoding objects. Listing 22.1 shows the declarations of both of these classes.

LISTING 22.1

```
#ifdef USE_WMA


#include "Audio.h"
#include "IAudioLoader.h"
#include "WMSDK.h"


namespace Audio
{
class WMACallback : public IWMReaderCallback,
    public IWMReaderCallbackAdvanced
{
public:

    HRESULT __stdcall QueryInterface(
        const struct _GUID& guid,
        void** ppInterface);
    ULONG __stdcall AddRef();
    ULONG __stdcall Release();

    HRESULT __stdcall OnStatus(WMT_STATUS Status,
        HRESULT hr, WMT_ATTR_DATATYPE dwType,
        BYTE* pValue, void* pvContext);

    HRESULT __stdcall OnSample(DWORD dwOutputNum,
        QWORD cnsSampleTime, QWORD cnsSampleDuration,
        DWORD dwFlags, INSSBuffer* pSample,
        void* pvContext);

    HRESULT __stdcall OnStreamSample(WORD wStreamNum,
        QWORD cnsSampleTime, QWORD cnsSampleDuration,
        DWORD dwFlags, INSSBuffer __RPC_FAR* pSample,
        void __RPC_FAR* pvContext);

    HRESULT __stdcall OnTime(QWORD qwCurrentTime,
        void __RPC_FAR* pvContext);
```

```
    HRESULT __stdcall OnStreamSelection(
        WORD wStreamCount,
        WORD __RPC_FAR* pStreamNumbers,
        WMT_STREAM_SELECTION __RPC_FAR* pSelections,
        void __RPC_FAR* pvContext);

    HRESULT __stdcall OnOutputPropsChanged(
        DWORD dwOutputNum,
        WM_MEDIA_TYPE __RPC_FAR* pMediaType,
        void __RPC_FAR* pvContext);

    HRESULT __stdcall AllocateForOutput(
        DWORD dwOutputNum, DWORD cbBuffer,
        INSSBuffer __RPC_FAR* __RPC_FAR* ppBuffer,
        void __RPC_FAR* pvContext);

    HRESULT __stdcall AllocateForStream(
        WORD wStreamNum, DWORD cbBuffer,
        INSSBuffer __RPC_FAR* __RPC_FAR* ppBuffer,
        void __RPC_FAR* pvContext);
};


class WMA : public IAudioLoader
{
    DEFINE_POOL(WMA);
public:
    void Clear();

    // This Open function is used if the source is to be
    // streamed or read from IAudioStream objects
    bool Open(std::string sFileName);
    bool Open(BYTE* pbData, uint32 dwDataSize);
    bool Close();

    bool Read(uint8* pBuffer, uint32 dwSizeToRead,
        uint32* pdwSizeRead);

    uint32 GetSize();
    bool Reset();
```

```
    WAVEFORMATEX* GetFormat();
    bool IsEOF();

    void Destroy();

    friend class WMACallback;

protected:
    virtual ~WMA();
private:
    WMA();

    bool PreOpen();
    bool PostOpen();

    bool OpenReader();

    HRESULT OnStatus(WMT_STATUS Status, HRESULT hr,
        WMT_ATTR_DATATYPE dwType, BYTE* pValue);

    HRESULT OnSample(DWORD dwOutputNum,
        QWORD cnsSampleTime, QWORD cnsSampleDuration,
        DWORD dwFlags, INSSBuffer* pSample);

    HRESULT STDMETHODCALLTYPE OnTime(
        QWORD qwCurrentTime);
private:

    IWMReader* m_pReader;
    IWMReaderAdvanced* m_pReaderAdvanced;
    IWMReaderAdvanced2* m_pReaderAdvanced2;
    IWMHeaderInfo* m_pHeaderInfo;
    WAVEFORMATEX m_WaveFormatEx;
    WMACallback m_Callback;

    HANDLE m_hWaitEvent;
    HANDLE m_hRespondEvent;

    bool m_bOpen;

    HRESULT m_hrCallbackResult;
```

```
        uint32 m_nStreamSize;
        uint32 m_nBytesRead;

        bool m_bFirstRead;
        uint8* m_pBuffer;
        uint32 m_nBufferSize;
        uint32 m_nWritePtr;
        uint32 m_nTargetPtr;
        bool m_bEOF;
        uint64 m_qwTime;

        CRITICAL_SECTION m_csTerm;
};
}; // namespace Audio

#endif // USE_WMA
```

The WMACallback class is declared first and handles the work of retrieving status messages and decoded data from the WMA reader. In order to simplify the process of handling these messages, we've essentially mirrored the critical functions in the WMA class as well: OnStatus(), OnSample(), and OnTime(). This was done in order to simplify the process of handling data, since we would then have access to any member data or helper functions needed, instead of having to work through different objects. The WMA's object pointer was passed using a void pointer that is passed to all the callback functions.

WMACallback IMPLEMENTATION

Let's first examine how the WMACallback class is implemented. For now, don't worry if you don't understand the parameters and what all the functions do. Many of them are, in fact, not used at all for our purposes. We're only interested in how they pass along their information to the WMA class, allowing us to perform all our necessary decoding work in a single, convenient object.

LISTING 22.2

```
WMACallback::WMACallback()
{
    Clear();
```

```
}

WMACallback::~WMACallback()
{
    assert(!m_iRefCount);
}

void WMACallback::Clear()
{
    m_iRefCount = 0;
}

HRESULT WMACallback::QueryInterface(
    const struct _GUID& guid,
    void** ppInterface)
{
    if ( guid == IID_IWMReaderCallback )
        *ppInterface = ( IWMReaderCallback* )this;
    else if( guid == IID_IWMReaderCallbackAdvanced )
        *ppInterface =
            ( IWMReaderCallbackAdvanced* )this;
    else
        return E_NOINTERFACE;
    return S_OK;
}

ULONG WMACallback::AddRef()
{
    return 1;
}

ULONG WMACallback::Release()
{
    return 1;
}

HRESULT WMACallback::OnStatus(
    WMT_STATUS Status,
    HRESULT hr,
    WMT_ATTR_DATATYPE dwType,
    BYTE* pValue,
    void* pvContext)
```

```
{
    if(!pvContext)
        return E_FAIL;
    WMA* pWMA = static_cast<WMA*>(pvContext);
    return pWMA->OnStatus(Status, hr, dwType, pValue);
}

HRESULT WMACallback::OnSample(
    DWORD dwOutputNum,
    QWORD cnsSampleTime,
    QWORD cnsSampleDuration,
    DWORD dwFlags,
    INSSBuffer* pSample,
    void* pvContext)
{
    if(!pvContext)
        return E_FAIL;
    WMA* pWMA = static_cast<WMA*>(pvContext);
    return pWMA->OnSample(dwOutputNum, cnsSampleTime,
cnsSampleDuration, dwFlags, pSample);
}

HRESULT WMACallback::OnStreamSample(
    WORD wStreamNum,
    QWORD cnsSampleTime,
    QWORD cnsSampleDuration,
    DWORD dwFlags,
    INSSBuffer __RPC_FAR *pSample,
    void __RPC_FAR *pvContext)
{
    return E_NOTIMPL;
}

HRESULT WMACallback::OnTime(
    QWORD qwCurrentTime,
    void __RPC_FAR *pvContext)
{
    if(!pvContext)
        return E_FAIL;
    WMA* pWMA = static_cast<WMA*>(pvContext);
    return pWMA->OnTime(qwCurrentTime);
}
```

```
HRESULT WMACallback::OnStreamSelection(
    WORD wStreamCount,
    WORD __RPC_FAR *pStreamNumbers,
    WMT_STREAM_SELECTION __RPC_FAR *pSelections,
    void __RPC_FAR *pvContext)
{
    return S_OK;
}

HRESULT WMACallback::OnOutputPropsChanged(
    DWORD dwOutputNum,
    WM_MEDIA_TYPE __RPC_FAR *pMediaType,
    void __RPC_FAR *pvContext)
{
    return S_OK;
}

HRESULT WMACallback::AllocateForOutput(
    DWORD dwOutputNum,
    DWORD cbBuffer,
    INSSBuffer __RPC_FAR *__RPC_FAR *ppBuffer,
    void __RPC_FAR *pvContext)
{
    return E_NOTIMPL;
}

HRESULT WMACallback::AllocateForStream(
    WORD wStreamNum,
    DWORD cbBuffer,
    INSSBuffer __RPC_FAR *__RPC_FAR *ppBuffer,
    void __RPC_FAR *pvContext)
{
    return E_NOTIMPL;
}
```

As you can see, many of the functions are either not implemented at all or are trivial. The ones that are important simply cast a void pvContext pointer to a WMA object pointer, and then call its equivalent member function, passing on any appropriate data.

OPENING THE WMA READER

Let's now examine how we actually use the Windows Media Format SDK to do our audio decoding. As always, we have two ways of opening a file, either using our custom IAudioStream system or using a standard memory buffer. In each of the two functions, common functionality is further split off into two functions, PreOpen() and PostOpen(), which are called at the beginning and end of each Open() function. This helps to keep the code more readable and organized, as only the differences in code are stored in the two Open functions. Let's first examine the PreOpen() function shown in Listing 22.3, which creates a number of Windows Media interfaces that will be needed later.

LISTING 22.3

```
bool WMA::PreOpen()
{
    InitializeCriticalSection(&m_csTerm);

    m_hWaitEvent = CreateEvent(NULL, FALSE, FALSE,
        NULL);
    m_hRespondEvent = CreateEvent(NULL, FALSE,
        FALSE, NULL);

    HRESULT hr = WMCreateReader(0, 0, & m_pReader);
    if (FAILED(hr))
        return false;

    hr = m_pReader->QueryInterface(
        IID_IWMReaderAdvanced,
        (void**)&m_pReaderAdvanced);
    if (FAILED(hr))
        return false;

    hr = m_pReaderAdvanced->QueryInterface(
        IID_IWMReaderAdvanced2,
        (void**)&m_pReaderAdvanced2);
    if (FAILED(hr))
        return false;

    hr = m_pReader->QueryInterface(
```

```
        IID_IWMHeaderInfo,
        (void**)&m_pHeaderInfo);
    if (FAILED(hr))
        return false;

    return true;
}
```

In this function, we create a number of items, including a critical section used for shutting down the system safely, two events used to communicate between threads, and four Windows Media interfaces. Each WMReader interface exposes more advanced and low-level functionality. Because we are working at a fairly low level with the audio stream, we require the use of all three of them: IWMReader, IWMReaderAdvanced, and IWMReaderAdvanced2.

Let's look at the actual Open() functions next in Listing 22.4. In each case, notice that we create an IStream-compatible interface for use with the reader, although one is based on a memory buffer, and one is based on a file (or a custom file system supplied to the audio system). Additionally, you can see how the PreOpen() and PostOpen() functions are called from the Open() functions.

LISTING 22.4

```
bool WMA::Open(string sFileName)
{
    if (!PreOpen())
        return false;

    IAudioStream* pStream;
    CreateAudioStream cas(pStream);
    if (!pStream)
        return false;

    HRESULT hr = pStream->Open(sFileName);
    if (FAILED(hr))
        return false;

    hr = m_pReaderAdvanced2->OpenStream(pStream,
        &m_Callback, this);
```

```
    if (FAILED(hr))
        return false;

    if (!PostOpen())
        return false;

    return true;
}

bool WMA::Open(uint8* pbData, uint32 dwDataSize)
{
    if (!PreOpen())
        return false;

    HGLOBAL hMem;
    IStream* pStream;

    hMem = GlobalAlloc(GMEM_MOVEABLE |
        GMEM_NODISCARD | GMEM_SHARE, dwDataSize);

    LPVOID pMem = GlobalLock(hMem);
    CopyMemory(pMem, pbData, dwDataSize);
    GlobalUnlock(hMem);

    HRESULT hr = CreateStreamOnHGlobal(hMem,
        TRUE, &pStream);
    if (FAILED(hr))
        return false;

    hr = m_pReaderAdvanced2->OpenStream(pStream,
        &m_Callback, this);
    if (FAILED(hr))
        return false;

    if (!PostOpen())
        return false;

    return true;
}
```

In addition to opening the stream, the OpenStream() function also takes two additional parameters, a callback object and a user-defined variable.

Our m_Callback variable is the WMACallback class we created earlier, and is used to handle events signaled by the Windows Media libraries. The this pointer that we pass into the function is passed to every callback function in the class, allowing us to route the messages back to our WMA reader class for easier processing.

Next, we have some additional processing work to take care of in PostOpen(), which you can see in Listing 22.5.

LISTING 22.5

```
bool WMA::PostOpen()
{
    WaitForSingleObject(m_hRespondEvent, INFINITE);
    if (FAILED(m_hrCallbackResult))
        return false;

    uint32 nOutputCount;
    HRESULT hr = m_pReader->GetOutputCount(
                        &nOutputCount);
    if (FAILED(hr))
        return false;
    if (nOutputCount != 1)
        return false;

    uint32 nOutputFormatCount;
    hr = m_pReader->GetOutputFormatCount(0,
                        &nOutputFormatCount);
    if (FAILED(hr))
        return false;

    uint32 nFormatSize = 0;
    BYTE* pBuf = 0;
    IWMOutputMediaProps* pProps;
    for (uint32 j = 0; j < nOutputFormatCount; j++)
    {
        hr = m_pReader->GetOutputFormat(0, j, & pProps);
        if (FAILED(hr))
            continue;

        // Get the required size of the media type
        // structure
        uint32 nNewSize = 0;
```

```
hr = pProps->GetMediaType(NULL, & nNewSize);
if (FAILED(hr))
    continue;
if (nNewSize > nFormatSize)
{
    SAFE_DELETE_ARRAY(pBuf);
    nFormatSize = nNewSize;
    pBuf = new BYTE[nFormatSize];
}

WM_MEDIA_TYPE* pType = (WM_MEDIA_TYPE*) pBuf;
hr = pProps->GetMediaType(pType, & nFormatSize);
if (FAILED(hr))
    continue;

if (pType->formattype == WMFORMAT_WaveFormatEx)
{
    memcpy(&m_WaveFormatEx,
        pType->pbFormat,
        pType->cbFormat);
    if ((m_WaveFormatEx.nChannels == 2) &&
        (m_WaveFormatEx.wBitsPerSample ==
        DXAudioMgr()->GetOptimalSampleBits()) &&
        (m_WaveFormatEx.nSamplesPerSec ==
        DXAudioMgr()->GetOptimalSampleRate()))
    {
        break;
    }
}
SAFE_RELEASE(pProps);
}
SAFE_DELETE_ARRAY(pBuf);

// Now set the format we want
hr = m_pReader->SetOutputProps(0, pProps);
if (FAILED(hr))
    return false;

SAFE_RELEASE(pProps);

// Tell the reader to read as fast as possible
hr = m_pReaderAdvanced->SetUserProvidedClock(true);
```

```
if (FAILED(hr))
    return false;

// Determine the size of the opened file
WORD wStreamNum = 0;
WMT_ATTR_DATATYPE Type;
DWORD dwDuration = 0;
WORD wLength = 8;
hr = m_pHeaderInfo->GetAttributeByName(&wStreamNum,
    g_wszWMDuration, &Type,
    (unsigned char*)&dwDuration, &wLength);
if (FAILED(hr))
    return false;

// divide by 10 million to get seconds
double fTime = double(dwDuration) / 10000000.0f;

// Calculate the stream size
m_nStreamSize = fTime *
    m_WaveFormatEx.nAvgBytesPerSec;

// Create a default 1.5 second scratch
// buffer for decoding streams
m_pBuffer = new uint8[
    m_WaveFormatEx.nAvgBytesPerSec * 1.5];
m_nBufferSize =
    m_WaveFormatEx.nAvgBytesPerSec * 1.5;

m_nTargetPtr = 0;
m_nWritePtr = 0;

m_bOpen = true;

return true;}
```

The PostOpen() function handles quite a bit of setup work, so let's examine what's going on here, step by step.

The first thing we see in this function is that we're blocking the thread, waiting for an event to signal using the m_hRespondEvent handle. As we mentioned earlier, Windows Media is designed as a streaming system, and as such will respond to almost every major event (including opening a file) asynchronously, using the callback object we talked about earlier. This is obviously beneficial when working with a remote file stream to continue execution while the connection is made and streamed across the network; but in our case, it is simply a liability, since we are only working with local files and want to know immediately that the MP3 or WMA file is ready for processing. To do this, we block the WMA's thread and wait for the callback function to respond. Once the "Opened File" message has been successfully received, the WMA thread is allowed to continue. We'll examine this code later when we look at some of the message-handling functions.

Windows Media files may contain more than one stream of data, such as video and audio, but we enforce an audio-only system by ensuring that only files with a single stream of data are allowed. Later, a check for format type ensures that we're indeed working with a single stream of *audio*, since theoretically a single stream of video would also qualify in this check. We then proceed with determining what output format the WMA or MP3 format should be decoded to. Unlike the Vorbis decoder, which picks a decoding format for us, we are allowed to decode the audio stream into any legal format we choose; and so we simply pick the optimal format for our audio system by using the IWMOutputMediaProps interface in an iteration loop. Once the optimal format is found, this interface is then passed to the IWMReader::SetOutputProps() function, which actually sets the output format.

Next, we instruct the reader to decode as fast as possible with the function IWMReaderAdvanced::SetUserProvidedClock(), passing in a value of true. Normally, Windows Media decodes data at a constant, specified rate anywhere from 1 to 10 times the speed at which it would normally be output. Again for our purposes, we wish to handle the background processing ourselves, so we'll be decoding as fast as possible in short bursts for a streaming buffer or all at once to a static buffer.

Finally, we must perform some general housekeeping procedures for the WMA reader class. We must perform two tasks: determine the final output buffer size, and create a decoding buffer capable of holding the decoded data either for streaming or static buffers.

To determine the decoded length of the final output buffer, we retrieve the length of the audio stream in 100 nanosecond units using the GetAttributeByName() function. This is converted to seconds and then multiplied by the bytes per second of the final output format that we previously determined. We now have a fairly accurate idea of how many bytes are needed to fully decode this file.

Finally, we create a two-second decoding buffer used for streaming. Generally speaking, we expect this audio loader to be used primarily for streaming buffers, and so the system is optimized for this. However, we do allow the decoding buffer to grow to any size in order to accommodate large, one-shot decoding requests, if necessary.

CLOSING THE READER

Now the WMA reader is ready to begin processing a WMA- or MP3-encoded file. But before we look at the Read() function, let's briefly examine the code needed to shut down the reader in Listing 22.6.

LISTING 22.6

```
bool WMA::Close()
{
    m_bOpen = false;
    if (m_hWaitEvent)
    {
        if (m_pReader)
            m_pReader->Stop();

        SetEvent(m_hWaitEvent);
        EnterCriticalSection(&m_csTerm);
        LeaveCriticalSection(&m_csTerm);
        DeleteCriticalSection(&m_csTerm);
    }
    if (m_hWaitEvent)
    {
        CloseHandle(m_hWaitEvent);
        m_hWaitEvent = 0;
    }
    if (m_hRespondEvent)
    {
        CloseHandle(m_hRespondEvent);
        m_hRespondEvent = 0;
    }
    SAFE_RELEASE(m_pHeaderInfo);
    SAFE_RELEASE(m_pReaderAdvanced2);
    SAFE_RELEASE(m_pReaderAdvanced);
    SAFE_RELEASE(m_pReader);
```

```
        SAFE_DELETE_ARRAY(m_pBuffer);
        Clear();
        return true;
}
```

The WMA::Close() function must be careful in how it releases the reader interfaces, because we are once again dealing with multithreaded code. As such, we employ the use of a critical section to ensure that no multi-threaded code is active when we release the reader interfaces.

READING AND DECODING DATA

Now that the WMA reader is open and primed for reading, we must implement the WMA::Read() function, which is shown in its entirety in Listing 22.7.

LISTING 22.7

```
bool WMA::Read(uint8* pBuffer, uint32 dwSizeToRead,
    uint32* pdwSizeRead)
{
    if (!m_bOpen)
        return false;

    m_nTargetPtr = dwSizeToRead - m_nWritePtr;

    // First, we have to check to see if we have enough
    // extra data stored in the buffer to satisfy the
    // read without doing any decoding.
    if (dwSizeToRead > m_nWritePtr)
    {
        if (m_bFirstRead)
        {
            // Grow the decoding buffer if necessary
            if (dwSizeToRead >
                m_nBufferSize -
                DECODING_BUFFER_ERROR)
            {
                SAFE_DELETE(m_pBuffer);
                m_nBufferSize = dwSizeToRead;
```

```
                m_pBuffer = new uint8[m_nBufferSize +
                    DECODING_BUFFER_ERROR];
            }

            // Start decoding now
            HRESULT hr;
            hr = m_pReader->Start(0, 0, 1.0f, this);
            m_bFirstRead = false;
            if (FAILED(hr))
                return false;
        }
        else
        {
            // Release the decoding thread so decoding
            // continues
            SetEvent(m_hWaitEvent);
        }

        WaitForSingleObject(m_hRespondEvent, INFINITE);
        if (FAILED(m_hrCallbackResult))
            return false;
    }

    // Normally we should have more than enough data
    // in the buffer...
    if (m_nWritePtr >= dwSizeToRead)
    {
        memcpy(pBuffer, m_pBuffer, dwSizeToRead);
        *pdwSizeRead = dwSizeToRead;
        memmove(m_pBuffer,
            m_pBuffer + dwSizeToRead,
            m_nWritePtr - dwSizeToRead);
        m_nWritePtr -= dwSizeToRead;
    }
    // But if we're at the end of the file, we may have
    // less than requested
    else
    {
        memcpy(pBuffer, m_pBuffer, m_nWritePtr);
        *pdwSizeRead = m_nWritePtr;
        m_nWritePtr = 0;
    }
```

```
m_nBytesRead += *pdwSizeRead;

if (m_bEOF)
    m_pReader->Stop();

return true;
}
```

The way this function works is a bit odd if you don't know what is going on behind the scenes, so we'll explain the methodology. As you recall, actual decoding is done through the callback system on a separate thread. As such, the basic strategy for decoding is to simply block either the primary thread (the one that calls the Read() function) or the decoding thread, using signals to communicate back and forth when specific tasks are completed. This essentially turns a multithreaded, asynchronous system into a synchronous decoding function. While not easy to implement or to understand, the system actually does work. Let's look at the details.

The first thing the Read() function must do is determine if we have enough decoded data in our decompressed data buffer to satisfy the read request without having to actually decode any more data. If we do have enough, we skip straight to the section that copies the data from our temporary decompressing buffer to the buffer that was passed into the Read() function. It may seem a bit strange that we would have leftover data from a previous read, but the WMA reader, unlike the Vorbis libraries, enforces a minimum read amount. This amount may actually turn out to be more than the average read size of a streaming buffer, which means that we can actually skip decodes from time to time. If we did not do this, the decoding buffer would continuously grow—obviously not a good thing.

Next, we must differentiate between the very first read and subsequent reads. On the first read, several things happen. We initially check to see if we need to increase the decoding buffer. For a streaming buffer, this should never have to occur. Once the buffer size is known to be appropriate, the decoding process begins by calling IWMReader::Start(). If, on the other hand, we are on a subsequent read, we instead set a Win32 event, m_hWaitEvent.

Immediately after this, we wait for a responding event m_hRespondEvent from the decoding function. This will let us make sure the decoding process is finished before the function continues. After decoding is finished, we simply halt the decoding thread until the next Read() call is made. This is why we send an event on subsequent reads: to signal the decoding thread to continue. We'll see what that decoding function looks like when we examine the message-handling functions.

In case this description leaves you a bit confused, perhaps a timeline would help illustrate what happens on each thread through two complete reads. You can read this sequence of events from top to bottom, each column representing actions and behavior in each of the reader threads.

By carefully utilizing thread blocking and signaling techniques, we've effectively eliminated the concurrent behavior of the two threads, forcing the decoder to produce samples on demand instead of at its normal pace, as is required for our audio system.

TABLE 22.1 Windows Media SDK Thread Timeline

Main WMA Thread	Decoding Thread
Initial Read() call is made.	Thread does not exist yet...
IWMReader::Start() launches decoding thread, and waits for a signal that decoding is finished...	Thread does not exist yet...
Thread sleeps...	Thread is launched and decoding begins.
Thread sleeps...	Decoding ends, main thread is signaled, and decoding thread waits for a signal to resume decoding...
Main thread resumes, and copies decoded material to supplied buffer.	Thread sleeps...
Next Read() call is made.	Thread sleeps...
Decoding thread is signaled, and main thread waits for signal that decoding is finished...	Thread sleeps...
Thread sleeps...	Thread and decoding resume.
Thread sleeps...	Decoding ends, main thread is signaled, and decoding thread waits for a signal to resume decoding...
Main thread resumes and copies decoded material to supplied buffer.	Thread sleeps...
Et cetera...	Thread sleeps...

At the end of the Read() function, we carefully move any outstanding data to the front of the decoding buffer, tracking how much data is currently in m_pBuffer by using the m_nWritePtr member. Because the Read() function may request any amount of data, and the decoding process typically returns fixed-size decoded chunks of data, we must use a temporary buffer that slightly exceeds our requested buffer size. We will then typically end up with slightly too much decoded data. This extra data cannot simply be discarded; it must be saved for the next call. You may recall that we had to solve a similar problem in the Windows ACM wave reader (Chapter 20), in which we also had to use multiple decoding buffers.

CALLBACK IMPLEMENTAION

The second half of the reader consists of properly responding to the messages and data sent to the callback functions by the Windows Media system. There are actually three functions that must be implemented: OnStatus(), OnTime(), and OnSample(). The OnStatus() function responds to, logically enough, any and all status messages sent by the Windows Media system, such as "Open," "Close," "Started," "Stopped," or "Error."

We have to respond in specific ways to a number of these messages in order to keep the main thread advancing. For instance, you may recall how we blocked the main thread after opening the file. We'll now see how we respond by signaling the main thread to continue after the "Open" message is received. Listing 22.8 shows the OnStatus() messages we respond to.

LISTING 22.8

```
HRESULT WMA::OnStatus(WMT_STATUS Status, HRESULT hr,
    WMT_ATTR_DATATYPE dwType, BYTE* pValue)
{
    m_hrCallbackResult = hr;
    switch (Status)
    {
    case WMT_ERROR:
        SetEvent(m_hWaitEvent);
        SetEvent(m_hRespondEvent);
        DebugOut(1, "Status: WMT_ERROR");
        return E_FAIL;
    case WMT_OPENED:
        DebugOut(5, "Status: WMT_OPENED");
        SetEvent(m_hRespondEvent);
        break;
```

```
case WMT_END_OF_FILE:
    DebugOut(5, "Status: WMT_END_OF_FILE");
    m_bEOF = true;
    // Make sure no threads are kept waiting,
    // since no more reads will come
    SetEvent(m_hWaitEvent);
    SetEvent(m_hRespondEvent);
    break;
case WMT_STARTED:
    DebugOut(5, "Status: WMT_STARTED");
    DebugOut(5, "Advancing deliver time at start");
    m_qwTime += 1000000;
    if (m_pReaderAdvanced)
        m_pReaderAdvanced->DeliverTime(m_qwTime);
    break;
case WMT_STOPPED:
    DebugOut(5, "Status: WMT_STOPPED");
    SetEvent(m_hWaitEvent);
    SetEvent(m_hRespondEvent);
    break;
};

return S_OK;
}
```

While many of the messages are ignored (we've listed them all in the
source code for illustrative purposes), there are a few important messages
that must be handled properly. Most involve sending response messages of
some sort or another. One of the more unusual events and responses involves the WMT_STARTED message, in which we advance a time counter for
the user-defined clock we previously enabled. In addition to this initial
function call to DeliverTime(), we must also respond to a special callback
in order to manage the reader's clock. Listing 22.9 shows how we respond
to the OnTime() callback function.

LISTING 22.9

```
HRESULT WMA::OnTime(QWORD qwCurrentTime)
{
    // Keep asking for the specific duration of the
    // stream until EOF
```

```
    if (!m_bEOF)
    {
        m_qwTime += 1000000;
        if(m_pReaderAdvanced)
            m_pReaderAdvanced->DeliverTime(m_qwTime);
    }
    return S_OK;
}
```

By arbitrarily advancing the decoding target forward every time the current target is reached, at which point this function is called, we ensure the Windows Media reader decodes as fast as it can.

The final and perhaps most-critical function is the OnSample() callback function shown in Listing 22.10, which of course actually receives the decoded sample data and places it in the decode buffer.

LISTING 22.10

```
HRESULT WMA::OnSample(DWORD dwOutputNum,
    QWORD cnsSampleTime, QWORD cnsSampleDuration,
    DWORD dwFlags, INSSBuffer* pSample)
{
    if (!m_bOpen)
    {
        if (m_hRespondEvent)
            SetEvent(m_hRespondEvent);
        return S_OK;
    }

    if (m_bEOF)
    {
        SetEvent(m_hRespondEvent);
        return S_OK;
    }

    BYTE* pBuf;
    DWORD dwLen;
    if (!pSample)
        return E_FAIL;
```

```
HRESULT hr = pSample->GetBuffer(&pBuf);
if (FAILED(hr))
    return E_FAIL;
hr = pSample->GetLength(&dwLen);
if (FAILED(hr))
    return E_FAIL;

// Expand the decoding buffer if needed
if ((m_nWritePtr + dwLen) > m_nBufferSize)
{
    uint32 nNewBufferSize = m_nWritePtr +
        dwLen + DECODING_BUFFER_ERROR;
    uint8* pNewBuffer = new uint8[nNewBufferSize];
    memcpy(pNewBuffer, m_pBuffer, m_nWritePtr);
    SAFE_DELETE_ARRAY(m_pBuffer);
    m_pBuffer = pNewBuffer;
    m_nBufferSize = nNewBufferSize;
}

memcpy(m_pBuffer + m_nWritePtr, pBuf, dwLen);
m_nWritePtr += dwLen;

if (m_nWritePtr >= m_nTargetPtr)
{
    SetEvent(m_hRespondEvent);
    CRITICAL_FUNCTION(&m_csTerm);
    WaitForSingleObject(m_hWaitEvent, INFINITE);
}

return S_OK;}
```

The OnSample() function receives data via an INSSBuffer pointer, a specifically designed class that stores data and the length of a buffer. The length and data are extracted from this object and copied to our decoding buffer, which tracks the accumulation of data with the m_nWritePtr member. You may also notice that our buffer is allowed to grow in this function, as well; sometimes the pre-allocated buffer may not be quite enough, and a crash or lost data would occur if we did not reallocate at this point.

When it is detected that there is currently enough data to meet the demands of the latest read request, a Win32 event is triggered using the m_hRespondEvent handle. This will allow the main thread to continue executing, and the Read() function will finish. The function then enters a critical section using m_csTerm. You may recall that this critical object was also used in the Close() function in order to ensure that the function did not proceed until this function had completely exited. You can see why this is important, as it could potentially cause a crash if the Windows Media reader interfaces were all released while the callback function (which is called by the readers) was still executing. Finally, the callback thread is blocked using WaitForSingleObject() with the m_hWaitEvent handle. Again, this is the handle used when signaling that the Read() function wishes to begin decoding.

CONCLUSION

While forcing the Windows Media system to work in a synchronous manner can be a bit confusing, the end result is a combination decoder that can read either WMA or MP3 files just like any other audio file. The versatility, proliferation, and quality of these formats make this a welcome addition to our audio system.

This concludes Part IV, which has covered custom file readers and compressed-audio decoders. By adhering to common interface guidelines, both for our files and decoders, we enable a great deal of flexibility in our audio system.

In the next chapter, we begin our discussion of 3D audio technology, such as property sets like EAX and ZoomFX. We will also delve into some more-advanced and theoretical audio topics.

PART V

ADVANCED 3D TECHNIQUES

23

DIRECTSOUND HARDWARE EXTENSIONS

While the results from standard DirectSound programming can be quite impressive, one of the great features of DirectSound is its ability to provide direct access to modern hardware. This is done with a mechanism known as DirectSound property sets, and these will give you direct control over a number of very important hardware features, such as Creative Labs' EAX, as well as Sensaura's ZoomFX and MacroFX. We'll be looking specifically at these extensions in the next few chapters; but for now, we'll first learn how to use the property-set functions, as well as some strategies for managing property sets in a dynamic audio environment.

ON THE CD

The code listed in this chapter can be found in \Game_Audio\ audio_sdk\src\audiolib\Sound3D.cpp, PropertySet.h, Property-Set.cpp.

PROPERTY SETS INTRODUCED

In version 5.0, DirectSound introduced the concept of hardware *property sets*. Simply stated, a property set is a driver-specific set of data that can be associated with a particular hardware sound buffer. Functions are available for querying, reading, and writing any generic set of data to a particular buffer. Using the data passed to the buffer from the application, the driver is free to translate this into any desired hardware-specific function. As you can imagine, this gives an incredible amount of power to the audio programmer in just a few simple functions.

By providing a generic and neutral mechanism at the API level, Microsoft enabled hardware vendors to develop and adopt hardware-specific extensions—developers did not need to use custom APIs specific to each potentially supported vendor. As a result of this and other collaborations by a number of audio companies, several standards emerged for various types of property sets, ensuring a simpler means of supporting a large variety of hardware with minimal programming effort.

PREPARATION

Before we look at the actual hardware extension functions, we will first examine the steps required to ensure that these extensions will be available for use. The first two requirements are, unfortunately, out of your control as a developer.

First and most obvious, in order to make use of hardware extensions, the hardware must actually support these extensions. DirectSound does not emulate hardware properties in software, with the exception of I3DL2 reverb effects, and even this is done through a separate API. Despite the relative longevity of standards such as EAX and I3DL2, there are still a huge number of cards sold even today that do not support these extensions. Generally, these cards are found in low-end machines, laptops, or dedicated business or scientific computers that have no need for higher-end audio processing. Or, some computer manufacturers will save money by supplying a motherboard with a built-in sound card. Often, these combination motherboard/sound cards have no hardware acceleration of any sort, save a primary mixing buffer for output. We'll see later how to use the `IDirectSoundBuffer8::QuerySupport()` function to check for availability of a specific hardware property set.

Second, the user must have hardware acceleration enabled in Windows. Generally speaking, this is not a problem on Windows 9x platforms, as they support hardware acceleration as the default setting—meaning a user would have to explicitly turn it off before it didn't work. Unfortunately, Windows 2000 defaults to only basic hardware acceleration. You can see in Figure 23.1 what these settings look like.

Even if the user's sound card supports hardware extensions of a particular type, the program will not be able to use them unless the default Windows settings are changed. This dialog box can be found in the Windows control panel under "Sounds and Multimedia." Click on the Audio tab, and then click the Advanced button in the Playback section. The dialog box

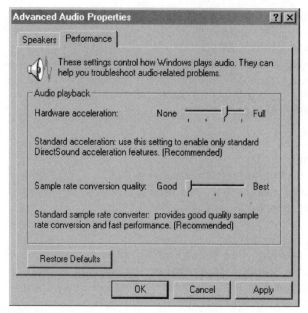

FIGURE 23.1   Default audio hardware acceleration settings for Windows 2000.

that pops up will allow the user to change both the speaker configuration and the hardware acceleration settings. Instructions on how to change these settings should be a standard part of any troubleshooting FAQ in a shipping product.

The third somewhat obvious requirement of using hardware extensions is that you must be using a hardware DirectSound buffer. You have the option of either forcing a buffer to be in hardware, letting it choose hardware on its own (although it may choose software if all the hardware buffers are used), or you can let the buffer choose hardware or software when it is first played (known as *deferred settings*). Of the three options, only one option is really suitable for reliably creating buffers for which hardware extensions must be used: forcing the buffer to use hardware. You can see how this is done in Listing 23.1.

LISTING 23.1

```
// Set the buffer creation flags, depending on user preferences
uint32 nFlags =
```

```
DSBCAPS_GETCURRENTPOSITION2 |
DSBCAPS_CTRLFREQUENCY |
DSBCAPS_CTRLVOLUME |
DSBCAPS_GLOBALFOCUS |
DSBCAPS_CTRL3D |
DSBCAPS_MUTE3DATMAXDISTANCE |
DSBCAPS_LOCHARDWARE;

// Create the actual sound buffer
HRESULT hr;
IDirectSoundBuffer* pDSBuffer;
DSBUFFERDESC desc;
ZeroMemory(&desc, sizeof(desc));
desc.dwSize = sizeof(desc);
desc.dwFlags = nFlags;
desc.lpwfxFormat = &m_WaveFormat;
desc.dwBufferBytes = nBufferSize;
hr = DXAudioMgr()->DirectSound()->CreateSoundBuffer(
    &desc, &pDSBuffer, NULL);
if(FAILED(hr))
{
    // First attempt failed. Remove a buffer then try again.
    if(!DXAudioMgr()->RemoveBuffer())
    {
        Unload();
        return false;
    }

    hr = DXAudioMgr()->DirectSound()->CreateSoundBuffer(
        &desc, &pDSBuffer, NULL);
    if FAILED(hr)
    {
        Unload();
        return false;
    }
}
```

In addition to simply forcing a hardware buffer, we also see one example of how to gracefully handle a failed creation (as shown by the bold text in Listing 23.1). By removing a lower-priority hardware buffer, the RemoveBuffer() function allows us to attempt another creation, which should then succeed under normal circumstances. This allows us to create any number of sounds as 'hardware' buffers, but only the highest-priority sounds will remain in hardware at one time. (You can find more details on this and other procedures for managing buffers in Chapter 11—Direct-Sound Buffer Management.)

If you are working with a 3D property set such as EAX, I3DL2, or MacroFX, you will also need to create a 3D buffer in the normal manner (see Chapter 10—3D Audio Basics). Once you have your hardware buffer created, you are then ready to retrieve and start using the IKsPropertySet interface.

THE IKsPropertySet INTERFACE

In Listing 23.2, you can see how to retrieve an IKsPropertySet interface from either a 2D or 3D DirectSound buffer interface. Once you have a valid interface, you can use it to set and retrieve data on a hardware buffer as long as that buffer remains valid, meaning until it is released.

LISTING 23.2

```
// Get the property set interface for this buffer. Note that we
// don't consider a failure on this function a fatal error.
// This function will always fail on a software 3D buffer.
IKsPropertySet* pPropertySet = 0;
hr = m_p3DBuffer->QueryInterface(IID_IKsPropertySet,
    (void**)&pPropertySet);
if FAILED(hr)
    // not a fatal error - just don't have property sets
```

There are three methods in the IKsPropertySet interface in addition to the standard three methods derived from IUnknown. These methods are named QuerySupport(), Get(), and Set(). The property-set functions work with GUIDs, integer-based identifiers, and chunks of generic data in order to pass information to and from hardware-based DirectSound buffers.

```
HRESULT QuerySupport(
    REFGUID rguidPropSet,
    ULONG ulId,
```

```
    PULONG pulTypeSupport
);
```

IKsPropertySet::QuerySupport() is used to determine whether a particular property set is supported in hardware. All property sets are defined by a specific GUID, which is defined by the hardware's manufacturer. In the case of standardized hardware extensions, all drivers/hardware will respond correctly to the published GUID identifier. Additionally, specific items within a given property set may be accessed using an integer ID. This allows a programmer to selectively set or retrieve a particular property within a larger set of data. Individual elements are always accessed consecutively, starting with an index of zero, and are always consistently given the same property set. This enables programmers to use a simple GUID and enumeration value to define any particular property. Many properties have a special index value that designates the selection "all properties" within the set for convenience, allowing entire property sets, usually defined as structures, to be set or retrieved in a single function call.

```
HRESULT Set(
    REFGUID rguidPropSet,
    ULONG ulId,
    LPVOID pInstanceData,
    ULONG ulInstanceLength,
    LPVOID pPropertyData,
    ULONG ulDataLength
);
```

The Set() function operates in a manner similar to QuerySupport(), but it has additional parameters to pass in arbitrarily sized and configured data. The first two parameters work exactly like QuerySupport(). The third and fourth parameters are used in case there are multiple objects (or property sets) than can be acted upon in a single buffer. In most cases, these parameters can simply be left at zero, since most buffers only have a single set of properties to operate on. The fifth and sixth parameters, pPropertyData and ulDataLength, allow any data structure to be passed in. The nature of this structure is highly specific to the property set being used. A structure will typically be provided to hold all the properties of a particular property set.

```
HRESULT Get(
    REFGUID rguidPropSet,
    ULONG ulId,
```

```
        LPVOID pInstanceData,
        ULONG ulInstanceLength,
        LPVOID pPropertyData,
        ULONG ulDataLength,
        PULONG pulBytesReturned
);
```

The Get() function has the same parameters as the Set() function, except for the last parameter, but the function operates in a different manner. Instead of setting the property data using the structure provided, this function instead fills out the structure passed to it. The last parameter, pulBytesReturned, is filled out with the number of bytes actually returned and can be used as an added validity- or information-check against the expected behavior of the function.

Let's see how this might look in code. In Listing 23.3, we are querying the audio hardware to see if it supports a hypothetical property set. Note that depending on the particular property set, it will either indicate support by returning a success HRESULT error code *or* by setting the supported flags, KSPROPERTY_SUPPORT_SET and KSPROPERTY_SUPPORT_GET. You will have to consult the documentation to see which method is specifically used for the property set you are querying.

LISTING 23.3

```
// pKsProp is a valid interface to an IKsPropertySet object.

// MADEUP_PROPERTY_SET is a hypothetical property set GUID.

// MADEUP_ALL_PROPERTIES is a hypothetical enumeration value
// designating that all properties of the set should be
// accessed.

// MadeupProps is a hypothetical structure containing all
// the data in the property set.

uint32 nSupport = 0;
HRESULT hr = PKsProp->QuerySupport(MADEUP_PROPERTY_SET,
    MADEUP_ALL_PROPERTIES,
    &nSupport);
if FAILED(hr)
```

```
    // property definitely not supported

// Next, we check for explicit set and get support. However,
// some property sets are supported even though they may not
// set these flags.

// The property may signal support via the nSupport param
if(nSupport & KSPROPERTY_SUPPORT_SET == KSPROPERTY_SUPPORT_SET)
    // property may be set
if(nSupport & KSPROPERTY_SUPPORT_GET == KSPROPERTY_SUPPORT_GET)
    // property may be retrieved

// Try setting the property set. All values in the struct
// MadeupProps will be passed to the hardware
hr = pKsProp->Set(MADEUP_PROPERTY_SET,
    MADEUP_ALL_PROPERTIES,
    0,
    0,
    &MadeupProps,
    sizeof(MadeupProps));
if FAILED(hr)
    // handle failure — is it actually supported?

// Now we retrieve the values we just set
uint32 nBytesReturned = 0;
hr = pKsProp->Set(MADEUP_PROPERTY_SET,
    MADEUP_ALL_PROPERTIES,
    0,
    0,
    &MadeupProps,
    sizeof(MadeupProps)
    &nBytesReturned);
if FAILED(hr)
    // handle failure — is it actually supported?
```

ADVANCED PROPERTY-SET MANAGEMENT

One of the great features of a dynamic audio system with built-in buffer management is that the client programmer is, to an extensive degree, freed from having to worry about tracking and monitoring the sound system and each sound buffer. However, being able to destroy and then recreate sound buffers at will imposes a degree of responsibility on the sound system. When a sound buffer is destroyed, it is expected that the sound object will preserve any sound buffer settings, such as the current position, volume, and so on, so that these values can be restored when the buffer is created again. This also enables the very handy ability to set a sound's properties even before it has been created for the first time.

■ **DIRECTSOUND BUFFER MANAGEMENT**

In addition to being useful for highly dynamic audio systems, the ability to save and restore property sets happens to be crucial when using DirectSound buffer management. This is because you are not guaranteed that a DirectSound buffer is actually connected to hardware at any point in time, meaning that you will have to manually acquire the hardware channel and then set the properties on the buffer before it is played. You can read more about this in Chapter 11—Direct-Sound Buffer Management.

The great news is that we're building a system that can easily handle this, as well as our own management routines. It would simply mean using them in slightly different places in the code.

This is no less true for property set data. All property-set information is lost when a sound buffer is released. In our sound API, this occurs when the `IAudioBase::Unload()` function is called, whether internally or externally. When `IAudioBase::Load()` is next called, the buffer should be recreated as before, the sound data must be reloaded from disk (or it could be pulled from a cache), and the sound buffer's properties should be set using the latest stored settings. To this end, we are in need of a method to store and retrieve an arbitrary number of property sets, each containing an arbitrary amount of generic data. We'll be examining a class called `Property-Set`, which is designed to do exactly that.

THE `PropertySet` CLASS

The `PropertySet` class is designed to store any number of property sets for use by the buffer, specifically when the buffer is unloaded (released, in fact) and subsequently loaded again (created with the same properties and attributes). It is impossible to know exactly how many property sets will be associated with each buffer, or in fact what size each of these property sets will be. Thus, we will create a container structure, called `GenericProperty`, to help track this data, and we will simply allocate any necessary data based on the sizes passed into the appropriate `Set()` and `Get()` functions. This structure is then used in a standard STL list, and the list object is wrapped inside of a class to make it more functional. From the standpoint of the audio class that uses the property set, it looks nearly identical to a standard `IKsPropertySet` interface—which is the entire point. The only real difference is the two hook functions, `OnLoad()` and `OnUnload()`. These are called, naturally enough, in the `Load()` and `Unload()` functions of the audio object, respectively. You can see the interface in its entirety in Listing 23.4.

LISTING 23.4

```
struct GenericProperty
{
    GenericProperty()
    {
        m_guid = GUID_NULL;
        m_nID = 0;
        m_pInstanceData = 0;
        m_nInstanceLength = 0;
        m_pPropData = 0;
        m_nPropLength = 0;
    }
    GUID m_guid;
    uint32 m_nID;
    uint8* m_pInstanceData;
    uint32 m_nInstanceLength;
    uint8* m_pPropData;
    uint32 m_nPropLength;
};

typedef std::list<GenericProperty> PropertyList;

class PropertySet
{
public:
    PropertySet();
    ~PropertySet();
    void Clear();
    void Term();
```

```
// Call when the associated DS buffer is
// loaded or unloaded
bool OnLoad(IUnknown* pUnknown);
bool OnUnload();

// Generic property support (for driver-specific
// extensions)
bool QuerySupport(const GUID& guid, uint32 nID,
    uint32* pTypeSupport);
bool Get(const GUID& guidProperty, uint32 nID,
    void* pInstanceData, uint32 nInstanceLength,
    void* pPropData, uint32 nPropLength,
    uint32* pBytesReturned);
bool Set(const GUID& guidProperty, uint32 nID,
    void* pInstanceData, uint32 nInstanceLength,
    void* pPropData, uint32 nPropLength,
    bool bStoreProperty);
private:

    IKsPropertySet* m_pPropertySet;
    PropertyList m_PropertyList;
};
```

Now, let's examine in detail how the class works. The constructor and destructor, and the Clear() and Term() functions are patterned exactly like many other classes in this book. Note in Listing 23.5 how the only dynamically allocated memory (other than the internal memory allocated by the list) is the m_pInstanceData and m_pPropData members of the GenericProperty structure. These are being safely deallocated in the Term() function.

LISTING 23.5

```
PropertySet::PropertySet()
{
    Clear();
}

PropertySet::~PropertySet()
{
```

```
    Term();
}

void PropertySet::Clear()
{
    m_pPropertySet = 0;
    m_PropertyList.clear();
}

void PropertySet::Term()
{
    PropertyList::iterator itr;
    for (itr = m_PropertyList.begin();
        itr != m_PropertyList.end();
        ++itr)
    {
        SAFE_DELETE_ARRAY((*itr).m_pInstanceData);
        SAFE_DELETE_ARRAY((*itr).m_pPropData);
    }
    Clear();
}
```

In Listing 23.6, we see the OnLoad() and OnUnload() hook functions. These are both placed in the Load() and Unload() functions of our Sound3D class. Technically speaking, we could in fact add support to the Sound class as well as the Segment class (or perhaps an Audiopath class would be more appropriate). However, because properties are most often set on 3D sound buffers, we have decided to only add support to these objects. Feel free to add similar support to other classes if you wish to.

LISTING 23.6

```
bool PropertySet::OnLoad(IUnknown* pUnknown)
{
    if (!pUnknown)
        return false;
    IKsPropertySet* pPropertySet;
    HRESULT hr = pUnknown->QueryInterface(
        IID_IKsPropertySet,
        (void**)&pPropertySet);
    if (FAILED(hr))
```

```
        return false;
    m_pPropertySet = pPropertySet;
    // Iterate through all the properties and
    // set them on the buffer
    PropertyList::iterator itr;
    for (itr = m_PropertyList.begin();
        itr != m_PropertyList.end();
        ++itr)
        m_pPropertySet->Set((*itr).m_guid,
                            (*itr).m_nID,
                            (*itr).m_pInstanceData,
                            (*itr).m_nInstanceLength,
                            (*itr).m_pPropData,
                            (*itr).m_nPropLength);
    return true;
}


bool PropertySet::OnUnload()
{
    if (!m_pPropertySet)
        return true;

    // Retrieve any buffer property sets
    PropertyList::iterator itr;
    for (itr = m_PropertyList.begin();
        itr != m_PropertyList.end();
        ++itr)
    {
        uint32 nBytesReturned;
        m_pPropertySet->Get((*itr).m_guid,
                            (*itr).m_nID,
                            (*itr).m_pInstanceData,
                            (*itr).m_nInstanceLength,
                            (*itr).m_pPropData,
                            (*itr).m_nPropLength,
                            & nBytesReturned);
    }

    SAFE_RELEASE(m_pPropertySet);
    return true;
}
```

The OnLoad() function expects an IUnknown interface pointer, from which it can extract the IKsPropertySet interface using the standard COM QueryInterface() method. Simply pass in the IDirectSoundBuffer8 interface pointer, or an IDirectSound3DBuffer8 interface pointer if you're working with a 3D sound buffer, and the function will retrieve the IKsPropertySet interface automatically.

Next, the function then loops through all the property sets, retrieving the data stored earlier in m_PropertyList (we'll see this a bit later when we examine the Set() function). In this manner, the moment a buffer is loaded (or reloaded), if any previous property sets had been associated with it, all the data will be immediately restored without the client having to keep track of all the data originally passed to it.

The OnUnload() function works in a similar manner, except in reverse. As it is unloaded, we cycle through the list of properties we are storing and retrieve all the parameters for each of them.

Next, we create wrapper functions that duplicate the IKsPropertySet interface functions QueryInterface(), Get(), and Set(). Let's examine the first function, QueryInterface(), in Listing 23.7.

LISTING 23.7

```
bool PropertySet::QuerySupport(const GUID& guid,
    uint32 nID, uint32* pTypeSupport)
{
    if (!m_pPropertySet)
        return false;
    HRESULT hr = m_pPropertySet->QuerySupport(guid,
                                    nID,
                                    pTypeSupport);
    if (FAILED(hr))
        return Error::Handle("Error = %s",
            DXGetErrorString(hr));
    return true;
}
```

This function is quite straightforward, as it is a simple wrapper for the actual IKsPropertySet interface function of the same name. As you can see, we are careful to ensure that the m_pPropertySet interface pointer is valid, which is another way of making sure the buffer is valid before proceeding. Obviously, there is no real way to return valid information from QuerySupport() if the hardware buffer does not currently exist.

However, with the next two functions, Get() and Set(), we will make an attempt to provide consistent behavior whether the buffer currently exists or not. We will do this by storing all of the data passed into the Set() function in a list of GenericProperty structs.

You should be aware that our property-set interface cannot possible operate with maximum efficiency on complex property sets such as EAX. This is because individual properties within a set can be altered individually, yet affect other values within the global property set. Obviously, because of this, there is no universal method of storing highly complex property sets, especially if the user makes a number of individual adjustments to the data members that end up altering the other properties. As such, we'll be learning later how important, standardized property sets, such as EAX and ZoomFX, are better off implemented in their own specialized wrapper classes. However, it is still worthwhile to have a generic property-set wrapper for future expandability or for extensions that are not worth building into the audio API itself.

Let's first examine how we set properties on a buffer. We have the proper interfaces at this point and can determine whether a property set is supported. Now we simply must pass the data along to the IKsProperty-Set interface while storing the data for later retrieval, if necessary. Listing 23.8 demonstrates how this is done. Notice how we allow the user to determine if they wish individual properties to be stored with a parameter, bStoreProperty.

LISTING 23.8

```
bool PropertySet::Set(const GUID& guidProperty,
    uint32 nID, void* pInstanceData,
    uint32 nInstanceLength, void* pPropData,
    uint32 nPropLength, bool bStoreProperty)
{
    FN("PropertySet::Set()");

    if (m_pPropertySet)
    {
        HRESULT hr = m_pPropertySet->Set(
            guidProperty, nID, pInstanceData,
```

```
                nInstanceLength, pPropData, nPropLength);
        if (FAILED(hr))
            // We still need to store the data, so don't
            // return an error
            Error::Handle("Error = %s",
                DXGetErrorString(hr));
    }


    // Don't bother continuing if the user doesn't wish
    // to store the property
    if (!bStoreProperty)
        return true;

    bool bFoundProperty = false;

    // Iterate through all the properties and set them
    // on the buffer
    PropertyList::iterator itr;
    for (itr = m_PropertyList.begin();
        itr != m_PropertyList.end();
        ++itr)
    {
        // Set the data if we have a match on the
        // property-set GUID and the ID
        if ((guidProperty == (*itr).m_guid) &&
            (nID == (*itr).m_nID))
        {
            uint32 nBytesReturned = 0;
            // Update instance data if needed
            if (pInstanceData)
            {
                memcpy((*itr).m_pInstanceData,
                    pInstanceData,
                    nInstanceLength);
                (*itr).m_nInstanceLength =
                    nInstanceLength;
            }
            // Update PropData if needed
            if (pPropData)
            {
                memcpy((*itr).m_pPropData,
                    pPropData,
```

```
                    nPropLength);
                (*itr).m_nPropLength = nPropLength;
            }
            bFoundProperty = true;
            break;
        }
    }

    // If we haven't found an existing property
    // (GUID + ID as key), allocate storage for the data
    // and create a new entry in the property list
    if (!bFoundProperty)
    {
        GenericProperty prop;
        prop.m_guid = guidProperty;
        prop.m_nID = nID;
        if (pInstanceData)
        {
            prop.m_pInstanceData = new
                uint8[nInstanceLength];
            memcpy(prop.m_pInstanceData,
                pInstanceData,
                nInstanceLength);
            prop.m_nInstanceLength = nInstanceLength;
        }
        if (pPropData)
        {
            prop.m_pPropData = new uint8[nPropLength];
            memcpy(prop.m_pPropData,
                pPropData,
                nPropLength);
            prop.m_nPropLength = nPropLength;
        }
        m_PropertyList.push_back(prop);
    }

    return true;
}
```

Although the function is a bit lengthy, it is fairly straightforward in what it actually does. The function simply iterates through the existing list of properties, looking for a unique combination of GUID and ID values. When it finds a match, it copies the data to the buffers contained in our existing property set list. Otherwise, we allocate the data buffers and add them to our property-set list at the end of the function.

The Get() function works in a somewhat similar manner to the Set() function, as shown in Listing 23.9.

LISTING 23.9

```
bool PropertySet::Get(const GUID& guidProperty,
    uint32 nID, void* pInstanceData,
    uint32 nInstanceLength, void* pPropData,
    uint32 nPropLength, uint32* pBytesReturned)
{
    FN("PropertySet::Get()");

    if (m_pPropertySet)
    {
        HRESULT hr = m_pPropertySet->Get(
            nID, pInstanceData, nInstanceLength,
            pPropData, nPropLength, pBytesReturned);
        if (FAILED(hr))
            return Error::Handle("Error = %s",
                    DXGetErrorString(hr));
        return true;
    }
    // If we can't retrieve the information from the
    // buffer, we'll retrieve it from our stored data.
    PropertyList::iterator itr;
    for (itr = m_PropertyList.begin();
        itr != m_PropertyList.end();
        ++itr)
    {
        // Set the data if we have an exact match on
        // both GUID and ID
        if ((guidProperty == (*itr).m_guid) &&
            (nID == (*itr).m_nID))
        {
            if (pInstanceData &&
                (nInstanceLength <=
```

```
                (*itr).m_nInstanceLength))
            memcpy(pInstanceData,
                (*itr).m_pInstanceData,
                (*itr).m_nInstanceLength);
        if (pPropData &&
            (nPropLength <= (*itr).m_nPropLength))
            memcpy(pPropData,
                (*itr).m_pPropData,
                (*itr).m_nPropLength);
        *pBytesReturned = (*itr).m_nPropLength;
        return true;
        }
    }

    return false;
}
```

In this function, we attempt to retrieve the data in one of two ways. If the `IksPropertySet` interface is available, we simply retrieve the requested data set from the hardware buffer itself. If the hardware buffer is not available (the buffer has been unloaded), then we essentially provide the value of the property at the time when the buffer was unloaded. In this manner, we can still view and manipulate properties, even when a buffer is unloaded, and it will reapply those settings (as long as we make the proper `OnLoad()` and `OnUnload()` calls from our Sound3D class) as needed.

CONCLUSION

Although storing and retrieving hardware buffer-specific property sets on demand is actually slightly more difficult than one would initially guess, the payoff is a vastly easier-to-use audio system. Game programmers will no longer be forced to keep track of a set of property data—or even multiple sets of data—for each buffer, making the prospect of more-advanced environmental effects programming just a little less daunting.

With a basic understanding of hardware buffer property sets, how to use them, and how to automatically manage them in a dynamic audio environment, we can now move on to specific hardware extensions you will

likely need to use, including several environmental reverberation extensions. Because of the popularity of these property sets (such as EAX),
though, you will see that it is easier in the long run to implement dedicated wrapper classes similar to the one presented in this chapter, but
specifically designed to work with the idiosyncrasies of the specific property-set extensions.

CHAPTER 24

ENVIRONMENTAL REVERBERATION— INTRODUCTION AND THEORY

Perhaps one of the biggest benefits of modern hardware-accelerated audio cards is the typical support for environmental reverberation effects that can be applied to 3D sounds. Environmental effects are almost as critical to a realistic aural environment as lighting is to 3D graphics. We'll explain exactly what environmental reverberation effects are and how they can best be used.

ENVIRONMENTAL EFFECTS DEFINED

While it is possible to use environmental effects at a somewhat primitive level without really understanding why certain settings sound correct in certain situations, it is helpful to have at least a slight understanding of how these effects occur in the real world. Computer games typically attempt to simulate the real world in some manner, and this is especially true of 3D graphics and sound. The closer we come to suspending disbelief via a believable simulation of real physical phenomenon (such as dynamic lighting or environmental reverberation), the greater the player's immersion into your game world and the more enjoyable their gaming experience.

THE NATURE OF SOUND PROPAGATION

Before we can understand environmental reverberation and echo, we must first understand the physical nature of sound waves. In Chapter 2, we learned a bit of how sound waves are transmitted through the air (or any compressible medium, like water or other gases). What we did not discuss, though, is how these sound waves interact with other objects. Much like a wave in a pool of water, a sound wave will tend to reflect off of other surfaces, creating a modified effect based on the original sound. In an enclosed area with highly reflective surfaces, a sound might, in fact, bounce around hundreds or thousands of times before eventually reaching the listener's ear.

When we speak of environmental effects, we are describing the natural phenomenons of *reverberation* and *echo*. These effects give sound its unique characteristics, helping the listener determine if a sound is being emitted in a stadium, a cave, a small living room, or a forest. Depending on our environment, sound waves emitted from a source might bounce off of various structural components before reaching our ears. In a game, this is simulated by a virtual microphone, and is usually tied to the camera position. Reverberation and echo, then, are the characteristic waves that bounce off of structures before those waves reach our ears, rather than waves that reach us directly from their source. The sound that reaches our ears without interference is often referred to as *direct path*. Figure 24.1 shows three distinct parts of a sound—direct path, echo, and reverberation—and how they reach a listener in an enclosed space.

Naturally, sound moves outward in concentric waves, not in rays as depicted; but this visual is useful to demonstrate one representative path of a sound. In reality, there are groups of initial echoes, and reverberation is not a single entity, but a series of reflections from all around the environment. These multiple reflections occur over a period of time, sometimes referred to as the "decay time," and give reverberation its characteristic fade-out effect.

You can perhaps get a better perspective by looking at a simulated sound sample that demonstrates the original sound, the echoes, and the reverberation decay at the end. Figure 24.2 shows what a sampling of our previous diagram might look like. Note that the effects have been highly exaggerated for easy identification.

Although real-world sound propagation and environmental effects are quite complicated and have many contributing factors, by far, the two greatest determining factors in overall sound characteristics are *environmental geometry* and *material composition*.

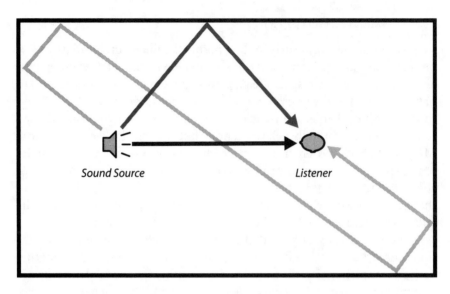

Direct Path ⟶
Echo ⟶
Reverberation ⟶

FIGURE 24.1 Demonstration of direct path, echo, and reverberation.

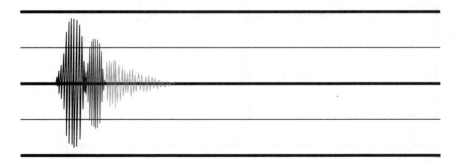

Direct Path ⟶
Echo ⟶
Reverberation ⟶

FIGURE 24.2 Graphical sampling of the sound in Figure 24.1.

ENVIRONMENTAL GEOMETRY

The nature of the world surrounding both the audio source and listener is perhaps the most obvious factor in shaping environmental reverberation and effects. Large open spaces (e.g., plains, grasslands, and forests) tend to have little echo or reverberation, mostly because there is little for a sound to reflect off of. Large, semi-enclosed areas, such as canyons and valleys, tend to have substantially delayed echoes, but typically little reverberation. Medium-size, closed environments with a lot of odd or arbitrary angles tend to produce very large, pronounced echoes. Very small, enclosed areas, such as a bathroom, tend to have short echo and reverberation times. All of these effects are largely due to the physical geometry and proximity of the structures surrounding both the sound source and the listener.

Not only can geometry affect the delay (*early reflections*) and reverberation (*late reflections*), but it can also drastically affect the sound by altering or even completely canceling out the direct path. Figure 24.3 demonstrates a sound source with a large obstacle between it and the listener.

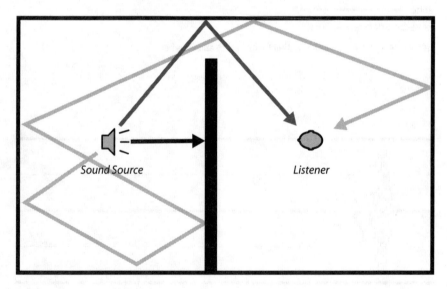

Direct Path ⟶

Echo ⟶

Reverberation ⟶

FIGURE 24.3   No direct path for sound.

Because a large obstacle is in the way, only the early and late reflections can get around the obstacle. Because the sound must bounce off of at least one wall before reaching the listener, it will tend to be slightly subdued. You can hear this effect for yourself by placing a sound source of any type in a different room. If you pass by the open door of this room, the sound should become noticeably brighter and louder.

If a sound source is moved far enough away, and multiple obstructions are placed in its way, it is possible that only late reflections can actually reach the listener from the sound source, as shown in Figure 24.4.

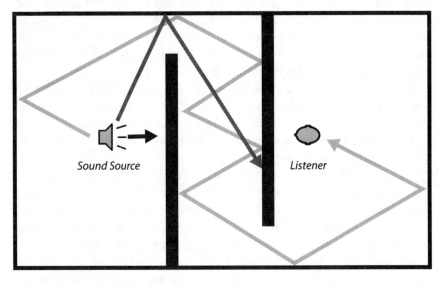

Direct Path

Echo

Reverberation

FIGURE 24.4   No direct path or early reflections path for sound.

In this case, the sound will appear to be even quieter; the sound's energy quickly dissipates due to the waves' bouncing around before reaching the listener's position.

Both Figure 24.3 and Figure 24.4 demonstrate a concept known as *obstruction*, which is the blocking of the direct path to the sound. In games, obstruction can be a complicated problem to solve, because any solution must involve path-finding or line-of-sight algorithms in order to determine the shortest open-air distance between two sound sources. (We'll discuss some ways of solving this problem when we cover acoustical modeling in Chapter 27.)

MATERIAL COMPOSITION

In addition to the shape of the physical objects that surround the sound and listener, the materials that compose and cover those objects also have a substantial impact on the reverberation effect. Each time a sound reflects off of a surface, a certain percentage of its energy is absorbed into the surface itself. This is why (other than air absorption) a sound will not reflect indefinitely, causing massive amounts of echo and reverberation in any enclosed environment. The amount of energy lost is dependent on the type material that the sound is reflecting off of.

In general, hard, solid, smooth surfaces will reflect a high amount of a sound's energy. Examples of highly reflective substances are tile, steel, stone, and wood. Other materials will tend to absorb much of the sound. Highly absorptive materials tend to be soft, porous, and light, such as curtains, carpeting, fabric, and fur.

Because of the differences in absorptive qualities, sound emitted in a large bathroom will sound very different than sound emitted a small study, even if the bathroom and the study are approximately the same size. The bathroom will likely contain highly reflective surfaces, such as tile, marble, ceramic, and glass, which makes it a mini echo-chamber. The study, on the other hand, is probably carpeted, has curtained windows, and rows of books covering the walls—all of which tend to be good at diffusing sounds. This prevents excessive reflections of sound waves off of the study's surfaces, emphasizing direct-path sounds with only a small amount of early reflections and no significant reverberation effects.

This brings up yet another effect of materials—*diffusion*. Instead of absorbing sounds, diffusion instead scatters the sound, causing a reduction in the overall energy of sound reflections and further reducing the effects of harsh echoes or long reverberations. Even hard surfaces can act as diffusion materials, such a wood, concrete, and steel. The amount of diffusion has more to do with the small-scale shape or surface complexity of a material than what it is made of. As an example, a stucco wall will tend to diffuse sound to a greater degree than a flat tile wall; or, a tree trunk is highly diffusive when compared to a polished hardwood floor. Diffusion can be thought of as 'the degree of absorption' when calculating how much echo and reverberation an area will produce, even though it works according to slightly different principles.

FREQUENCY EFFECTS

Yet another problem to consider when contending with environmental sound effects is the vastly different characteristics that sounds of different frequencies exhibit when confronted with exactly the same geometry. A common manifestation of this is *occlusion*—the transmission of sound through another material that completely separates the sound source from the listener. Figure 24.5 demonstrates occlusion.

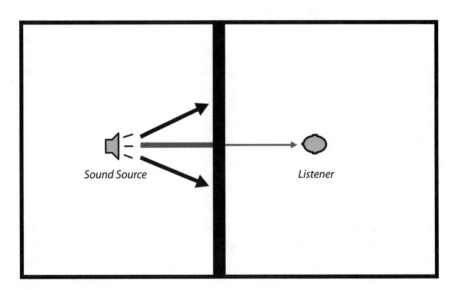

High Frequencies ──────▶
Low Frequencies ──────▶
FIGURE 24.5   Effect of occlusion on different frequencies.

You can see that the high frequencies do not penetrate the wall, but the lower frequencies, although attenuated to some degree, can pass through. This effect is similar to listening to music from a high-power stereo in another room; you hear the thumping bass, but little else. Most or all of the high frequencies are attenuated, but the lowest frequencies are transmitted right through the wall, only partially attenuated.

This might lead to the conclusion that reverberations are primarily composed of the highest frequencies, but this would be an incorrect assumption. Extremely high frequencies tend to be scattered and absorbed much more easily due to their short wavelengths, and so reverberations and echoes tend to be composed of middle-range frequencies for the most part. Most materials will simply absorb frequencies above a certain threshold. In general, you can assume that the higher the absorption ratio (or conversely, the lower the reflection ratio) of a material, the lower the high-frequency threshold will be.

TRANSMISSION-MEDIUM ABSORPTION

Although we have discussed loss of sound energy due to factors such as surface reflection/absorption, there are other factors that contribute to the decline in a sound's energy over time. The transmission medium (e.g., the air itself) also contributes to a loss of energy over time and distance. Sound will tend to attenuate at a slightly faster rate when there is more moisture in the air. Thus, dampening the sounds a tiny bit more when rendering a foggy evening more-accurately simulates reality.

CONCLUSION

Understanding the basic principles behind environmental reverberation in the real world will help when attempting to understand how and why environmental property sets such as EAX 2.0 are modeled as they are. Next, we'll examine the EAX 2.0 property set in detail and discuss how it works, how it should be implemented, and why this property set is still the number-one choice among extension support for today's games.

25

IMPLEMENTING EAX 2.0 PROPERTY SETS

The most widely supported and implemented of environmental reverberation sets is EAX 2.0. Initially pioneered and developed by Creative Labs, EAX is now an open-industry-standard set of properties that nearly all mid- to high-end consumer audio cards support in hardware. It provides robust support for a wide range of aural parameters and effects, giving audio designer and programmers an easy way to simulate extremely complex environments with little or no impact on run-time performance.

ON THE CD

The code listed in this chapter can be found in \Game_Audio\ audio_sdk\src\audiolib\Extensions.h, Extensions.cpp.

INTRODUCING EAX 2.0

EAX (Environmental Audio eXtensions) provides the programmer and sound designer with a *statistical reverberation engine* that can operate globally as well as apply specific parameters and filters to individual sound sources. By "statistical" reverberation, we mean that the engine does not dynamically create effects based on actual geometry, but instead uses a collection of numerical parameters to create customizable effects. There are two basic property sets: one for the listener and one for each individual sound. The listener's property set acts as a global effect and represents the overall environment in which a real listener might be located. The sound (buffer) property sets represent the unique characteristics of each sound and how the environment between it and the listener might affect the final sound.

ALTERNATIVE STANDARDS AND METHODOLOGIES

Since we are working with EAX version 2.0, you may be wondering about EAX 1.0, and whether you should support it as well. EAX 1.0-only support would be a very rare thing to find in modern hardware; and as such, there is little reason to support it directly. Most cards that were able to support the 1.0 property sets were actually also able to support the 2.0 property extensions with only driver updates; the basic reverberation engine is essentially the same. Version 2.0 simply exposes more-detailed parameters, allowing much finer-tuned controls.

Creative Labs has recently developed EAX version 3.0, also referred to as "EAX HD." At the moment, EAX 3.0 remains governed by an NDA (Non-Disclosure Agreement) agreement. As such, you must contact Creative Labs if you wish to learn about or support this updated version of EAX, since we will only be implementing EAX 2.0 property sets in this book. While we are prohibited from discussing the specifics of EAX 3.0, you can rest assured that the interfaces and techniques you learn in these chapters can be applied to future versions of EAX. Creative Labs strives to maintain a certain level of backward compatibility for obvious reasons.

■ **CREATIVE LABS' EAX UNIFIED LIBRARY**

If you install the Creative Labs EAX SDK, you will see a library called the "EAX Unified library." There are currently versions available for DirectSound 7 and DirectSound 8, and it is likely that a version supporting DirectSound 9 will be appearing shortly after DirectX 9 is released. This library provides automatic downward translation between several different versions of EAX, and even I3DL2 if EAX support is not found. For the widest-ranging support, the EAX Unified library is a great way of ensuring that some version of environmental reverberation will be played on nearly all hardware that can support it, and you are only responsible for supporting a single interface. This is an especially critical library to use if you choose to implement support for the latest version of EAX (version 3.0), because relatively few cards currently support 3.0. The EAX unified library is well-documented and very simple to use, so you should have little trouble integrating it into your audio system if you wish to.

A few years back, Aureal produced an innovative environmental reverberation standard based on real-time analysis of actual geometry, which they utilized in a combination of manufactured hardware chips and an API known as "A3D."

Performing dynamic geometry-based calculations did have some enormous benefits compared to statistical-based methods, such as EAX. For instance, calculating occlusion and obstruction is much simpler with a geometry-based reverb engine because the necessary data to check for these conditions is already available. And, because the reverberation settings were generated on the fly, the effect tended to be much more dynamic than with earlier implementations of EAX, which only allowed for static environmental settings that could not be smoothly interpolated. Even EAX 2.0 has problems interpolating between multiple environments unless you know a few tricks.

This type of approach, while seemingly a logical method of creating dynamic reverberation, also had a number of disadvantages. Because much of the work of processing the geometry was done in the drivers, not in the hardware, a large percentage of CPU time was required to model as few as 16 unique sound sources in a relatively simple 3D environment. With modern ultrahigh polycount environments and huge numbers of simultaneous sounds, a dynamic environment-based model would simply be a waste of processor time, unless it could be implemented entirely in hardware.

Aureal declared bankruptcy in 2000 and was subsequently acquired by Creative Labs, so A3D technology and its supported hardware effectively died as a viable platform for which to develop. On the positive side, having a single industry standard does help to simplify the lives of developers. And, over the long term, the statistical reverb model, while not quite as attractive as a geometry-based model, has proven much easier to implement and support for most developers.

Eventually, we may see a resurgence of geometry-based reverberation engines in the future as more processing tasks are increasingly off-loaded to dedicated video hardware. It is not too outrageous to foresee the day when entire graphical and audio 'scenes' are both stored and rendered by a unified graphics/audio (and maybe even physics, too) board with little effort required from the primary CPU, other than basic setup instructions and interaction commands. Such a unification of video and audio would make a lot of sense, as the same geometry used to render the scene could also be used to process environmental reverberation on sounds. But, we're still a long way off from that sort of integrated hardware system, and statistical reverberation models are what we'll be using into the foreseeable future.

I3DL2 (Interactive 3D Audio Rendering Guidelines, Level 2) was developed by IASIG (Interactive Audio Special Interest Group) as a competing standard to EAX 2.0. Although EAX 2.0 has been declared as an open standard, apparently some programmers felt more comfortable with a standard that was not controlled by a single company. Unfortunately, I3DL2 is really not well-implemented in many audio cards, if at all, unlike EAX 2.0. And, it really is a redundant standard; it provides no substantial advantages over EAX, even though it is a slightly cleaner and easier-to-understand API. While open community standards are a great thing, having too many standards ends up creating the same effect as having no standards—it tends to fragment developers' efforts, causing more time to be spent supporting multiple iterations of similar APIs for very few benefits. As a result, until I3DL2 is more effectively and widely supported by hardware, it is probably best to focus on support for EAX 2.0.

THE EAX 2.0 SPECIFICATION

This chapter does not describe in detail each individual property in the listener and buffer property sets. Instead, we will show you how to integrate the EAX 2.0 property sets into an extension API that makes using the property sets much easier and more practical.

There are authoritative references for EAX 2.0 that do a great job of explaining each parameter in great detail. Creative Labs provides a comprehensive, 88-page specification and tutorial document describing EAX 2.0 on their developer Web site (*http://developer.creative.com*). This tutorial covers topics ranging from using DirectSound property sets to detailed descriptions of every individual EAX 2.0 property. You should study this tutorial if you wish to understand how the individual settings of the property sets will affect sounds. It is recommended that you experiment with a program that can adjust and play sounds using the property sets, as well, such as the *GAP* library's sample program AudioTest, found on the CD-ROM, or perhaps by using Sensaura's Player3D program, which will be installed along with their SDK. The Sensaura SDK is found on the CD-ROM in the \extras\Sensaura\SDK1.0 folder.

IMPLEMENTING EAX 2.0

Our implementation of an EAX 2.0-compliant interface extension draws upon a couple of mechanisms that we've already seen. In order to provide a clean interface while still preserving our abstract interfaces in the API, we will be creating a two-tiered system consisting of an abstract base class, which will serve as the interface, and a concrete implementation class, which performs the actual work.

LISTENER INTERFACE AND IMPLEMENTATION

The more important of the two interfaces is the listener property set. This provides the core effect that is heard, while property-set extensions allow more subtle effects. A good general effect for most sounds can be obtained by simply setting a general preset effect on the listener.

> ■
>
> We'll learn in Chapter 27 why it may be a good idea to avoid using presets in EAX 2.0 if you wish to smoothly transition between effects. Creative Labs promotes EAX 3.0 as being able to perform smooth transitions between effects, but we'll learn how this can be done to a degree using version 2.0, as well.

ON THE CD The first thing we do for our API interface is to subclass the EAX listener property structure. This is defined in the file eax.h, which is included on the CD-ROM along with the *GAP* audio library. You can examine this code in Listing 25.1.

LISTING 25.1

```
struct EAXListenerProps : public _EAXLISTENERPROPERTIES
{
    // Default constructor calls the Clear() function.
    EAXListenerProps()
    {
        Clear();
    }
    // Sets all members to their default values
    // as defined in eax.h
    void Clear()
    {
        lRoom = EAXLISTENER_DEFAULTROOM;
        lRoomHF = EAXLISTENER_DEFAULTROOMHF;
        flRoomRolloffFactor =
            EAXLISTENER_DEFAULTROOMROLLOFFFACTOR;
```

```
        flDecayTime = EAXLISTENER_DEFAULTDECAYTIME;
        flDecayHFRatio =
            EAXLISTENER_DEFAULTDECAYHFRATIO;
        lReflections = EAXLISTENER_DEFAULTREFLECTIONS;
        flReflectionsDelay =
            EAXLISTENER_DEFAULTREFLECTIONSDELAY;
        lReverb = EAXLISTENER_DEFAULTREVERB;
        flReverbDelay = EAXLISTENER_DEFAULTREVERBDELAY;
        dwEnvironment = EAXLISTENER_DEFAULTENVIRONMENT;
        flEnvironmentSize =
            EAXLISTENER_DEFAULTENVIRONMENTSIZE;
        flEnvironmentDiffusion =
            EAXLISTENER_DEFAULTENVIRONMENTDIFFUSION;
        flAirAbsorptionHF =
            EAXLISTENER_DEFAULTAIRABSORPTIONHF;
        dwFlags = EAXLISTENER_DEFAULTFLAGS;
    }
};
```

Using this subclassed structure helps to ensure that appropriate default values can easily be used via the Clear() function or when the structure is first created.

The actual EAX listener API is more or less a direct reflection of the individual parameters that can be set, along with members to set and retrieve the entire property set at once. We have not provided member functions to retrieve individual properties, as this was considered less likely to be needed than individual member sets. Listing 25.2 shows the IEAXListener interface.

LISTING 25.2

```
class IEAXListener
{
public:

    virtual void SetRoom(int32 iRoom) = 0;
    virtual void SetRoomHF(int32 iRoomHF) = 0;
    virtual void SetRoomRolloffFactor(
        float fRoomRolloffFactor) = 0;
```

```
virtual void SetDecayTime(float fDecayTime) = 0;
virtual void SetDecayHFRatio(
    float fDecayHFRatio) = 0;
virtual void SetReflections(int32 iReflections) = 0;
virtual void SetReflectionsDelay(
    float fReflectionsDelay) = 0;
virtual void SetReverb(int32 iReverb) = 0;
virtual void SetReverbDelay(float fReverbDelay) = 0;
virtual void SetEnvironment(
    uint32 nEnvironment) = 0;
virtual void SetEnvironmentSize(
    float fEnvironmentSize) = 0;
virtual void SetEnvironmentDiffusion(
    float fEnvironmentDiffusion) = 0;
virtual void SetAirAbsorptionHF(
    float fAirAbsorption) = 0;
virtual void SetFlags(uint32 nFlags) = 0;
virtual void SetProperties(
    const EAXListenerProps& props) = 0;
virtual void GetProperties(
    EAXListenerProps& props) = 0;
};
```

This provides our `IListener` interface class with a clean extension API to use. The `IListener` class provides a function, `EAX()`, which retrieves an object derived from this class, and so it becomes quite easy to use. Listing 25.3 demonstrates how this interface is used.

LISTING 25.3

```
if(!AudioMgr()->GetListener(pListener))
    return false;

EAXListenerProps props;
pListener->EAX()->GetProperties(props);

// adjust property values

pListner->EAX()->SetProperties(props);
```

This is so much easier than having to deal directly with the IKsProperty-Set interface, as you'll soon see, so it seems worth the trouble of creating a dedicated API for the EAX properties.

Now, let's take a look at the concrete implementation class derived from IEAXListener. This class, EAXListener, will actually do all the low-level work needed to manage property sets. Listing 25.4 shows the class declaration.

LISTING 25.4

```
class EAXListener : public IEAXListener
{
public:
    void SetRoom(int32 iRoom);
    void SetRoomHF(int32 iRoomHF);
    void SetRoomRolloffFactor(
        float fRoomRolloffFactor);
    void SetDecayTime(float fDecayTime);
    void SetDecayHFRatio(float fDecayHFRatio);
    void SetReflections(int32 iReflections);
    void SetReflectionsDelay(
        float fReflectionsDelay);
    void SetReverb(int32 iReverb);
    void SetReverbDelay(float fReverbDelay);
    void SetEnvironment(uint32 nEnvironment);
    void SetEnvironmentSize(float fEnvironmentSize);
    void SetEnvironmentDiffusion(
        float fEnvironmentDiffusion);
    void SetAirAbsorptionHF(float fAirAbsorption);
    void SetFlags(uint32 nFlags);
    void SetProperties(const EAXListenerProps& props);
    void GetProperties(EAXListenerProps& props);

public:
    EAXListener();
    bool OnLoad(IUnknown* pUnknown);
    bool OnUnload();
    void Term();

private:
    IKsPropertySet* m_pPropertySet;
};
```

Naturally, the Set and Get functions match what we've already seen in the abstract interface that this class is derived from. What are of more interest to us, however, are the functions and data members specific to this class. The class uses two functions, OnLoad() and OnUnload(), which are called when the listener is created and destroyed, respectively. Because the listener object and the corresponding buffer used to set these interfaces are expected to remain valid throughout the life of the application, we do not have to worry about preserving the EAX settings if the buffer is destroyed and later recreated. This is a problem we must deal with when creating the buffer property-set implementation (as you'll see in the Chapter 26).

The class acts as a simple wrapper for an IKsPropertySet interface, so this will be a great introduction to how vanilla DirectSound in combination with EAX code looks. Listing 25.5 shows some selected functions from the object's code definition. There is no need to list the entire class, as most of the functions look identical, except for changed EAX parameters.

LISTING 25.5

```
EAXListener::EAXListener()
{
    m_pPropertySet = 0;
}

bool EAXListener::OnLoad(IUnknown* pUnknown)
{
    if (!DXAudioMgr()->GetInit()->m_bUseEAX)
        return true;
    if (!pUnknown)
        return false;
    HRESULT hr = pUnknown->QueryInterface(
        IID_IKsPropertySet, (void**)&m_pPropertySet);
    if (FAILED(hr))
        return false;

    uint32 nSupport = 0;
    hr = m_pPropertySet->QuerySupport(
        DSPROPSETID_EAX20_ListenerProperties,
        DSPROPERTY_EAXLISTENER_ALLPARAMETERS,
        &nSupport);
    if((nSupport != (KSPROPERTY_SUPPORT_GET |
```

```
            KSPROPERTY_SUPPORT_SET)))
    {
        SAFE_RELEASE(m_pPropertySet);
        return false;
    }

    EAXListenerProps props;
    hr = m_pPropertySet->Set(
        DSPROPSETID_EAX20_ListenerProperties,
        DSPROPERTY_EAXLISTENER_ALLPARAMETERS,
        0,
        0,
        (void*)&props,
        sizeof(EAXListenerProps));
    if(FAILED(hr))
    {
        SAFE_RELEASE(m_pPropertySet);
        return false;
    }
    return true;
}


bool EAXListener::OnUnload()
{
    SAFE_RELEASE(m_pPropertySet);
    return true;
}


void EAXListener::Term()
{
    SAFE_RELEASE(m_pPropertySet);
}


void EAXListener::SetRoom(int32 iRoom)
{
    if (!m_pPropertySet)
        return;
    m_pPropertySet->Set(
        DSPROPSETID_EAX20_ListenerProperties,
        DSPROPERTY_EAXLISTENER_ROOM,
        0,
        0,
```

```
        &iRoom,
        sizeof(int32));
}

void EAXListener::SetRoomHF(int32 iRoomHF)
{
    if (!m_pPropertySet)
        return;
    m_pPropertySet->Set(
        DSPROPSETID_EAX20_ListenerProperties,
        DSPROPERTY_EAXLISTENER_ROOMHF,
        0,
        0,
        &iRoomHF,
        sizeof(int32));
}

// snip...

void EAXListener::SetProperties(const EAXListenerProps& props)
{
    if (!m_pPropertySet)
        return;
    m_pPropertySet->Set(
        DSPROPSETID_EAX20_ListenerProperties,
        DSPROPERTY_EAXLISTENER_ALLPARAMETERS,
        0,
        0,
        (void*)&props,
        sizeof(EAXListenerProps));
}

void EAXListener::GetProperties(EAXListenerProps& props)
{
    if (!m_pPropertySet)
        return;
    uint32 nSize;
    m_pPropertySet->Get(
        DSPROPSETID_EAX20_ListenerProperties,
        DSPROPERTY_EAXLISTENER_ALLPARAMETERS,
        0,
        0,
```

```
            &props,
            sizeof(EAXListenerProps),
            &nSize);
}
```

The `OnLoad()` function is the primary initialization function for this class. All that is needed is an `IUnknown` interface to retrieve the `IKsProperty-Set` interface. Using `IUnknown` instead of a specific DirectSound buffer interface helps to avoid any dependency on a specific interface version. After retrieving the `IKsPropertySet` interface, we use the `QuerySupport()` function to ensure that the hardware supports the requested property set. You will note that we are careful to release the property-set interface, ensuring that all future calls to the EAX listener interface will simply be no-ops.

When the `Listener` object is shut down or unloaded, the `UnLoad()` function is called, at which point the `IKsPropertySet` interface is release.

All other functions in the class simply pass the function-name-appropriate property ID, along with the value passed to the function. No other manipulation or clamping is done. It is the client programmer's responsibility to ensure all values are valid and in range.

BUFFER INTERFACE AND IMPLEMENTATION

Like the listener interface, we first create a subclassed structure based on the original buffer property structure. Listing 25.6 shows what this looks like.

LISTING 25.6

```
struct EAXBufferProps : public _EAXBUFFERPROPERTIES
{
    // Default constructor calls the Clear() function.
    EAXBufferProps()
    {
        Clear();
    }
    // Sets all members to their default values
    // as defined in eax.h
    void Clear()
```

```
    {
        lDirect = EAXBUFFER_DEFAULTDIRECT;
        lDirectHF = EAXBUFFER_DEFAULTDIRECTHF;
        lRoom = EAXBUFFER_DEFAULTROOM;
        lRoomHF = EAXBUFFER_DEFAULTROOMHF;
        flRoomRolloffFactor =
            EAXBUFFER_DEFAULTROOMROLLOFFFACTOR;
        lObstruction = EAXBUFFER_DEFAULTOBSTRUCTION;
        flObstructionLFRatio =
            EAXBUFFER_DEFAULTOBSTRUCTIONLFRATIO;
        lOcclusion = EAXBUFFER_DEFAULTOCCLUSION;
        flOcclusionLFRatio =
            EAXBUFFER_DEFAULTOCCLUSIONLFRATIO;
        flOcclusionRoomRatio =
            EAXBUFFER_DEFAULTOCCLUSIONROOMRATIO;
        lOutsideVolumeHF =
            EAXBUFFER_DEFAULTOUTSIDEVOLUMEHF;
        flAirAbsorptionFactor =
            EAXBUFFER_DEFAULTAIRABSORPTIONFACTOR;
        dwFlags = EAXBUFFER_DEFAULTFLAGS;
    }
};
```

The IEAXBuffer interface is very similar to the IEAXListener interface. Each of the members of the EAXBufferProps structure is represented by a Set() function, and there are two functions to set and get the entire set of buffer properties at once. Listing 25.7 shows the entire IEAXBuffer interface class.

LISTING 25.7

```
class IEAXBuffer
{
public:
    virtual void SetDirect(int32 iDirect) = 0;
    virtual void SetDirectHF(int32 iDirectHF) = 0;
    virtual void SetRoom(int32 iRoom) = 0;
    virtual void SetRoomHF(int32 iRoomHF) = 0;
    virtual void SetRoomRolloffFactor(
        float fRoomRolloffFactor) = 0;
```

```
    virtual void SetObstruction(int32 iObstruction) = 0;
    virtual void SetObstructionLFRatio(
        float fObstructionLFRatio) = 0;
    virtual void SetOcclusion(int32 iOcclusion) = 0;
    virtual void SetOcclusionLFRatio(
        float fOcclusionLFRatio) = 0;
    virtual void SetOcclusionRoomRatio(
        float fOcclusionRoomRatio) = 0;
    virtual void SetOutsideVolumeHF(
        int32 iOutsideVolumeHF) = 0;
    virtual void SetAirAbsorptionFactor(
        float fAirAbsorptionFactor) = 0;
    virtual void SetFlags(uint32 nFlags) = 0;
    virtual void SetProperties(
        const EAXBufferProps& props) = 0;
    virtual void GetProperties(
        EAXBufferProps& props) = 0;
};
```

Again, like the property-set interface, we create a similar concrete class derived from this abstract interface class. Listing 25.8 shows the EAXBuffer class declaration.

LISTING 25.8

```
class EAXBuffer : public IEAXBuffer
{
public:
    void SetDirect(int32 iDirect);
    void SetDirectHF(int32 iDirectHF);
    void SetRoom(int32 iRoom);
    void SetRoomHF(int32 iRoomHF);
    void SetRoomRolloffFactor(float fRoomRolloffFactor);
    void SetObstruction(int32 iObstruction);
    void SetObstructionLFRatio(
        float fObstructionLFRatio);
    void SetOcclusion(int32 iOcclusion);
    void SetOcclusionLFRatio(float fOcclusionLFRatio);
    void SetOcclusionRoomRatio(
        float fOcclusionRoomRatio);
```

```
    void SetOutsideVolumeHF(int32 iOutsideVolumeHF);
    void SetAirAbsorptionFactor(
        float fAirAbsorptionFactor);
    void SetFlags(uint32 nFlags);
    void SetProperties(const EAXBufferProps& props);
    void GetProperties(EAXBufferProps& props);

public:
    EAXBuffer();
    void Clear();
    bool OnLoad(IUnknown* pUnknown);
    bool OnUnload();
    void Term();

private:
    IKsPropertySet* m_pPropertySet;
    EAXBufferProps m_Props;
};
```

The only difference between this class and the EAXListener concrete class (other than in parameters) is the EAXBufferProps structure that is used to store the properties of the buffer when the sound buffer is unloaded. It will then attempt to restore these properties when the buffer is reloaded. Let's examine the Load() and Unload() functions in Listing 25.9 to see how this was done.

LISTING 25.9

```
bool EAXBuffer::OnLoad(IUnknown* pUnknown)
{
    if (!pUnknown)
        return false;
    HRESULT hr = pUnknown->QueryInterface(
        IID_IKsPropertySet, (void**)&m_pPropertySet);
    if (FAILED(hr))
        return false;

    uint32 nSupport = 0;
    hr = m_pPropertySet->QuerySupport(
        DSPROPSETID_EAX20_BufferProperties,
```

```
        DSPROPERTY_EAXBUFFER_ALLPARAMETERS,
        &nSupport);
    if ((nSupport !=
        (KSPROPERTY_SUPPORT_GET |
        KSPROPERTY_SUPPORT_SET)))
    {
        SAFE_RELEASE(m_pPropertySet);
        return false;
    }

    hr = m_pPropertySet->Set(
        DSPROPSETID_EAX20_BufferProperties,
        DSPROPERTY_EAXBUFFER_ALLPARAMETERS,
        0,
        0,
        (void*)
        (&m_Props),
        sizeof(EAXBufferProps));
    if (FAILED(hr))
    {
        SAFE_RELEASE(m_pPropertySet);
        return false;
    }
    return true;
}

bool EAXBuffer::OnUnload()
{
    if (!m_pPropertySet)
        return false;

    uint32 nSize;
    m_pPropertySet->Get(
        DSPROPSETID_EAX20_BufferProperties,
        DSPROPERTY_EAXBUFFER_ALLPARAMETERS,
        0,
        0,
        &m_Props,
        sizeof(EAXBufferProps),
        &nSize);

    SAFE_RELEASE(m_pPropertySet);
```

```
    return true;
}
```

The `EAXBuffer::OnLoad()` function works similarly to the `EAX-Listener::OnLoad()` function. It checks to see if the EAX 2.0 property set is supported and sets the buffer's properties using the member function `m_Props`. Because this class does not get destroyed when the DirectSound buffer is destroyed in our `Sound3D` class, we ensure that the sound buffer will be restored with exactly the same buffer parameters as it had when the buffer was unloaded. This is done by retrieving all the parameters in the `EAXBuffer::OnUnload()` function. All the code has to do is make sure this function is called before the sound buffer is actually released.

USING THE EAX PROPERTY CLASSES

Although we've described the basic use of the `EAXListener` and `EAXBuffer` classes to some degree, it may help to describe exactly how they are used in the *GAP* library's `Listener` and `Sound3D` classes, even though it is fairly trivial to do so. Obviously, the `EAXListener` object is associated with the `Listener` class, and the `EAXBuffer` is associated with the `Sound3D` class.

The EAX objects are simply declared as private member data of their respective container classes, ensuring that they will remain valid for the lives of their container objects. When their respective DirectSound buffers are created or destroyed, the appropriate `OnLoad()` and `OnUnload()` functions are called. In the case of the `Listener` object, this only happens in the `Init()` and `Term()` function. In the `Sound3D` object, these functions are called from the `DoLoad()` and `Unload()` functions, since this is where the actual creation and destruction of the DirectSound buffers take place.

CONCLUSION

By creating an easy-to-use API and interface for the EAX 2.0 property set, we greatly reduce the volume and difficulty of code required to set and alter listener and buffer parameters. More importantly, by properly preserving buffer properties between unloading and subsequent reloading of a sound, we ensure a simpler and more-consistent interface, and we can focus our attention on the logical implementation of a practical reverberation system, rather than on the details of how to get specific properties to particular buffers.

Next, we'll learn about Sensaura's ZoomFX and MacroFX property sets, and how to implement a similar API for them.

CHAPTER 26

IMPLEMENTING SENSAURA'S ZOOMFX AND MACROFX EXTENSIONS

Environmental reverberation is not the only type of hardware extension available on modern audio cards. Some manufacturers have created specific extensions for their hardware, as Sensaura has done. Unless an audio card is a SoundBlaster series or uses hardware from the now-defunct Aureal, there is a good chance it has hardware from Sensaura in it. ZoomFX™ and MacroFX™ are two property sets designed to enhance sounds in unique ways. In this chapter, we'll describe these effects and how to implement the property sets.

ON THE CD The code listed in this chapter can be found in \Game_Audio\ audio_sdk\src\audiolib\Extensions.h, Extensions.cpp.

ZOOMFX DESCRIBED

DirectSound 3D positional audio represents all sound sources as points in three-dimensional space. While this obviously makes for a cleaner mathematical model and API, it unfortunately bears little resemblance to the real world in many regards. While smaller objects such as chirping birds, whizzing bullets/rockets, or even people (e.g., dialog samples at a person's head or footsteps at their feet) can be fairly accurately modeled as point sources, other sounds might not sound quite right when placed inside a single point in 3D space. A roaring waterfall, a cheering crowd, and a huge, rumbling truck are not well-represented as point sources.

While it might be possible to split sound effects into multiple components and assign them to different positions within the object itself, the ZoomFX property allows a much more straightforward approach. By creating a bounding box around the object, you give the Sensaura hardware the necessary information it needs to automatically apply spatial-enhancing algorithms to the sound. The effect will be that of a sound emanating from a larger area, rather than from a single point source. Figure 26.1 shows a large truck with a bounding box around it. The front and top vectors are used to define the orientation of the bounding box.

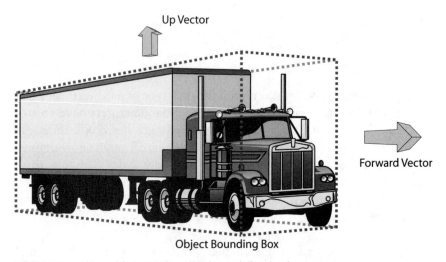

FIGURE 26.1   Object with ZoomFX bounding box and directional vectors.

Naturally, since only Sensaura hardware will have the ability to expose this property, you should be careful to use it only as a general enhancement; don't rely on this effect to provide key information that would otherwise make your game sound less than optimal. For instance, in a racing or sports game, you may wish to place a series of crowd sounds in the stands to provide proper spatial coverage, but only use the ZoomFX property to extend the coverage more evenly and provide a slightly more realistic effect.

MacroFX Described

MacroFX is another Sensaura-specific property set. Technically, however, it is actually exposed as part of the ZoomFX property set extension, although it is generally referred to as a unique effect. Simply put, it is a method of providing enhanced, close-proximity sound simulation.

In standard DirectSound 3D models, there are three zones of audio, which can be visualized as concentric circles around the listener. Each sound has a far zone in which a sound remains constant (or is cut off completely), a far zone in which sound is attenuated at the standard $1/R^n$ rate, and a 'near' zone in which the sound is clamped at a maximum volume to prevent skyrocketing volume levels as the sound approaches the listener's position. Because this near zone clamps the maximum volume at a constant level, in effect, it forces all sounds to appear as though they are at least one meter away.

The MacroFX algorithm instead divides this near zone into no less than four unique subzones, each with specific algorithms tuned to provide optimal-sounding results for a given position. In this way, very realistic sounds seem to emanate very close to the listener's ears, or even inside the listener's head. Best of all, the MacroFX algorithm makes use of the positional information already contained in the 3D sound data provided to DirectSound3D, and so no additional work is required. However, the actual effect of the algorithm can be fine-tuned though the ZoomFX property set, allowing a designer to enhance or reduce the effect of the MacroFX algorithms on a particular sound.

Using ZoomFX and MacroFX

The ZoomFX (along with MacroFX) property set is very straightforward to use. In order to set the ZoomFX property on a DirectSound buffer, set the bounding box ranges (which consist of two vectors defining the coordinate boundaries) to any *non-zero* values. Setting the bounding box range to zero will turn off the ZoomFX property on the buffer.

Once the buffer dimensions have been established as an axis-aligned box, you may freely rotate this box in 3D space using the orientation properties. ZoomFX uses a pair of `DirectSound3DListener`-style orientation vectors—one defining the 'up' vector and another defining the 'forward' vector.

The only other parameter is a percentage value used by MacroFX to scale the algorithm's effect on the final sound, and this value can range from 0% to 200%.

■ AVOIDING A ZOOMFX DRIVER BUG

Certain ZoomFX-capable cards may exhibit an odd behavior that is likely due to a driver bug: all EAX listener effects are canceled out when a ZoomFX property set is applied to a buffer for the first time, even if you are doing nothing more than setting the ZoomFX property to zero (turning it off). There is a simple solution, though. Before we apply the first EAX listener property that is set on the hardware buffer associated with the listener object, we first set a null ZoomFX property on this buffer. After this is done, ZoomFX property sets will work properly with EAX effects. Because there will likely be a number of buggy drivers out there for years to come, it is highly recommended that you implement this fix, even if your own system does not exhibit this behavior.

IMPLEMENTING ZOOMFX AND MACROFX

Implementing the ZoomFX and MacroFX property sets is done in much the same way as implementing the EAX property sets, although we are only dealing with buffer properties (no listener properties). Both algorithms are controlled using a single property set, and as such, we are providing a single interface called IZoomFX. Before we examine this interface, though, let's look at the structures used for the ZoomFX algorithm. Again, like with the EAX interface, we have derived new algorithms from the ones declared in the zoomfx.h header in order to ensure the structures have proper default values. Listing 26.1 shows all of the new structures we've derived from the original ZoomFX structures.

LISTING 26.1

```
struct ZoomFXBox : public ZOOMFX_BOX
{
    ZoomFXBox()
    {
        Clear();
    }
    void Clear()
```

```
    {
        vMin.x = 0.0f;
        vMin.y = 0.0f;
        vMin.z = 0.0f;
        vMax.x = 0.0f;
        vMax.y = 0.0f;
        vMax.z = 0.0f;
    }
};

struct ZoomFXOrientation : public ZOOMFX_ORIENTATION
{
    ZoomFXOrientation()
    {
        Clear();
    }
    void Clear()
    {
        vFront.x = 0.0f;
        vFront.y = 0.0f;
        vFront.z = 1.0f;
        vTop.x = 0.0f;
        vTop.y = 1.0f;
        vTop.z = 0.0f;
    }
};

struct ZoomFXProps : public ZOOMFX_BUFFERPROPERTIES
{
    void Clear()
    {
        box.vMin.x = 0.0f;
        box.vMin.y = 0.0f;
        box.vMin.z = 0.0f;
        box.vMax.x = 0.0f;
        box.vMax.y = 0.0f;
        box.vMax.z = 0.0f;
        orientation.vFront.x = 0.0f;
        orientation.vFront.y = 0.0f;
        orientation.vFront.z = 1.0f;
        orientation.vTop.x = 0.0f;
        orientation.vTop.y = 1.0f;
        orientation.vTop.z = 0.0f;
```

```
                lMacroFx = ZOOMFXBUFFER_MACROFX_DEFAULT;
        }
};
```

Three structures are used for the ZoomFX (and MacroFX) system. The ZoomFXBox provides the bounding box for the sound container, which is shown in Figure 26.1. Two 3D vectors define the upper and lower limits of the box on the *x, y,* and *z* axes. Remember that this only defines the size of the box, which can be rotated in any direction using the next structure, ZoomFXOrientation. Again, this structure uses two 3D vectors, but in a different manner. These work in a fashion similar to the DirectSound3D listener orientation, utilizing an up and a forward vector to define orientation in 3D space. The last structure, ZoomFXProps, is a combination of the first two structures, as well as the individual parameter lMacroFX, which defines the percentage of MacroFX effect to apply to the sound. The default effect to be applied is 100%; this can be reduced to 0% effect or scaled all the way up to an exaggerated 200% effect.

These structures are all used in the IZoomFX interface, as shown in Listing 26.2.

LISTING 26.2

```
class IZoomFX
{
public:
    virtual void SetBox(const ZoomFXBox& box) = 0;
    virtual void SetOrientation(
        const ZoomFXOrientation& orientation) = 0;
    virtual void SetMacroFX(uint32 nMacroFX) = 0;
    virtual void SetProperties(
        const ZoomFXProps& props) = 0;
    virtual void GetProperties(ZoomFXProps& props) = 0;
};
```

The IZoomFX class allows a client to set individual properties and allows the retrieving of all properties at once, similar to the EAX interfaces.

The concrete ZoomFx class is shown in Listing 26.3. By the way: in case you're wondering why the class name is ZoomFx instead of ZoomFX, we wished to leave the identifier ZoomFX available as a member function of the Sound3D class to retrieve the interface.

LISTING 26.3

```
class ZoomFx : public IZoomFX
{
public:
    void SetBox(const ZoomFXBox& box);
    void SetOrientation(
        const ZoomFXOrientation& orientation);
    void SetMacroFX(uint32 nMacroFX);
    void SetProperties(const ZoomFXProps& props);
    void GetProperties(ZoomFXProps& props);
public:
    ZoomFx();
    void Clear();
    bool OnLoad(IUnknown* pUnknown);
    bool OnUnload();
    void Term();

private:
    IKsPropertySet* m_pPropertySet;
    ZoomFXProps m_Props;
};
```

The ZoomFx class consists of inherited Set and Get members, OnLoad() and OnUnload() functions to be used in the Sound3D DoLoad() and OnUn-load() members, and the structure ZoomFXProps as member data, allowing the class to retain data even when the property-set interface has been destroyed.

The implementation of ZoomFx looks very similar to that of the EAX, but we'll list it in its entirety, since it is a bit shorter and gives you a chance to see a complete class listing.

LISTING 26.4

```
ZoomFx::ZoomFx()
{
```

```
    Clear();
}

void ZoomFx::Clear()
{
    m_pPropertySet = 0;
    m_Props.Clear();
}

bool ZoomFx::OnLoad(IUnknown* pUnknown)
{
    if (!DXAudioMgr()->GetInit()->m_bUseZoomFX)
        return true;
    if (!pUnknown)
        return false;
    HRESULT hr = pUnknown->QueryInterface(
        IID_IKsPropertySet, (void**)&m_pPropertySet);
    if (FAILED(hr))
        return false;

    uint32 nSupport = 0;
    hr = m_pPropertySet->QuerySupport(
        DSPROPSETID_ZOOMFX_BufferProperties,
        DSPROPERTY_ZOOMFXBUFFER_ALL,
        &nSupport);
    if ((nSupport != (KSPROPERTY_SUPPORT_GET |
        KSPROPERTY_SUPPORT_SET)))
    {
        SAFE_RELEASE(m_pPropertySet);
        return false;
    }

    ZoomFXProps props;
    hr = m_pPropertySet->Set(
        DSPROPSETID_ZOOMFX_BufferProperties,
        DSPROPERTY_ZOOMFXBUFFER_ALL,
        0,
        0,
        (void*)&props,
        sizeof(ZoomFXProps));
    if (FAILED(hr))
    {
```

```
        SAFE_RELEASE(m_pPropertySet);
        return false;
    }
    return true;
}

bool ZoomFx::OnUnload()
{
    if (!m_pPropertySet)
        return false;

    uint32 nSize;
    m_pPropertySet->Get(
        DSPROPSETID_ZOOMFX_BufferProperties,
        DSPROPERTY_ZOOMFXBUFFER_ALL,
        0,
        0,
        &m_Props,
        sizeof(ZoomFXProps),
        &nSize);

    SAFE_RELEASE(m_pPropertySet);
    return true;
}

void ZoomFx::Term()
{
    SAFE_RELEASE(m_pPropertySet);
}


void ZoomFx::SetBox(const ZoomFXBox& box)
{
    m_Props.box = box;
    if (!m_pPropertySet)
        return;
    m_pPropertySet->Set(
        DSPROPSETID_ZOOMFX_BufferProperties,
        DSPROPERTY_ZOOMFXBUFFER_BOX,
        0,
        0,
        (void*)&box,
```

```
        sizeof(ZoomFXBox));
}

void ZoomFx::SetOrientation(const ZoomFXOrientation&
orientation)
{
    m_Props.orientation = orientation;
    if (!m_pPropertySet)
        return;
    m_pPropertySet->Set(
        DSPROPSETID_ZOOMFX_BufferProperties,
        DSPROPERTY_ZOOMFXBUFFER_ORIENTATION,
        0,
        0,
        (void*)&orientation,
        sizeof(ZoomFXOrientation));
}

void ZoomFx::SetMacroFX(uint32 nMacroFX)
{
    m_Props.lMacroFx = nMacroFX;
    if (!m_pPropertySet)
        return;
    m_pPropertySet->Set(
        DSPROPSETID_ZOOMFX_BufferProperties,
        DSPROPERTY_ZOOMFXBUFFER_MACROFX_EFFECT,
        0,
        0,
        &nMacroFX,
        sizeof(uint32));
}

void ZoomFx::SetProperties(const ZoomFXProps& props)
{
    m_Props = props;
    if (!m_pPropertySet)
        return;
    m_pPropertySet->Set(
        DSPROPSETID_ZOOMFX_BufferProperties,
        DSPROPERTY_ZOOMFXBUFFER_ALL,
        0,
        0,
        (void*)&props,
```

```
          sizeof(ZoomFXProps));
}

void ZoomFx::GetProperties(ZoomFXProps& props)
{
    props = m_Props;
    if (!m_pPropertySet)
        return;
    uint32 nSize;
    m_pPropertySet->Get(
        DSPROPSETID_ZOOMFX_BufferProperties,
        DSPROPERTY_ZOOMFXBUFFER_ALL,
        0,
        0,
        &m_Props,
        sizeof(ZoomFXProps),
        &nSize);
}
```

The OnLoad() function really performs two tasks at once. First, it retrieves the IKsPropertySet interface from whatever object is passed to it (here, this will be an IDirectSound3DBuffer8 object) and ensures the ZoomFX/MacroFX properties are supported. Second, it uses its m_Props data member to re-initialize the property set. When an object is first created, the m_Props member, which is a ZoomFXProps structure that encapsulates all the property data, contains a default null property set value, meaning that the property set is turned off by default.

However, if the client programmer sets the bounding box to any nonzero value, these settings will be preserved when this data set is retrieved in the OnUnload() function, which is called from the Sound3D object right before the buffer is released. If the sound object is reloaded, the OnLoad() member will be called, and the previously set property data will be fully restored, preventing the client from having to worry about continuously restoring the property-set data.

CONCLUSION

ZoomFX and MacroFX are wonderful extensions to take advantage of, especially since they are implemented in hardware and can enhance a user's sound experience with no additional drain on CPU resources. And the fact that they are so simple to use leaves you with little excuse not to implement a simple property-set wrapper API for your sound system.

In the next chapter, we'll once again return to the topic of environmental reverberation; but this time, we'll be discussing more-abstract and game-specific issues, such as automated environment generation, customized storage solutions, and some inventive ways in which you can store real-time, dynamic occlusion data without causing your audio designers or level designers undo anguish.

CHAPTER 27

ACOUSTICAL MODELING AND ENVIRONMENTAL EFFECTS RUN-TIME DATA STORAGE

One of the most challenging aspects of modern audio development for games is the problem of how to effectively store, retrieve, and calculate the required information necessary to reproduce all the wonderful environmental effects heard within the virtual world. As with visual rendering, it is impossible to equivocally state that one specific data structure, algorithm, or methodology is the most optimal approach for all types of games. Different games typically require different, specifically optimized data structures designed to store world data, both on disk and in memory—and game audio is no exception.

Moreover, as game worlds become bigger and more complex, developers must find ways of streamlining the content-creation process. Forcing audio designers to hand-model and tweak each unique environment will soon prove to be an impossible task; vast worlds of hundreds or even thousands of square miles, and containing a staggering number of unique indoor and outdoor environments, will soon become commonplace.

DEFINING THE PROBLEM

Before we begin discussing data-storage structures and search algorithms, we should first take a moment to precisely define the problem we are trying to solve.

■ NO EASY SOLUTIONS (YET)

The job of determining how to effectively store audio reverberation and occlusion data is not simply a matter of whipping up some sample code and describing a simple, well-known algorithm. There is still much ongoing research into the most effective and realistic methods of modeling the acoustic and reverberation parameters of various types of environments. We'll be discussing some techniques that have practical applications, such as in Creative Labs' EAGLE, and some techniques that, so far at least, remain in the theoretical realm. While the EAGLE tool is impressive, our goal in this chapter is to investigate better methods of automating the acoustical modeling process, ideally reaching a point where minimal designer involvement is necessary in order to obtain convincing and effective results.

Only at this point will we see the widespread application and full potential of the EAX property set, beyond the simple and often primitive preset effects applied so often in today's applications. Most developers simply do not have the luxury of time, money, or personnel to allow designers to acoustically model each environment in the game world (beyond the simple application of preset effects or static effects, at least), especially as worlds grow ever larger in size and complexity.

Unfortunately, we're only now reaching the point of thinking about developing such tools. Moreover, such tools tend to be highly dependent upon the particular 3D engine in which they have been developed—and we're not exactly capable of providing this much in the way of demo material. As such, there will be no code in this chapter, just some fundamental data structures, a few illustrations, a couple of algorithms, and several ideas on which to build. The rest will be up to you.

REVERBERATION EFFECTS STORAGE

The most fundamental of environmental storage requirements is to associate basic global environmental (listener) settings with a particular area or environment. The simplest possible solution is to activate one of the environmental presets at key points in the level, such as transitions between indoor and outdoor environments. Or, at a slightly more-complicated level, a level designer may partition the level into various zones, probably defined by simple axis-aligned bounding boxes. In each of these zones, a particular EAX setting is stored. It is a simple enough matter to store either preset or custom settings with these bounding areas. Whenever the player (or, more typically, the camera) enters one of these zones, the appropriate effect is set on the listener object. Figure 27.1 demonstrates this concept, showing how a level map might be organized into various zones.

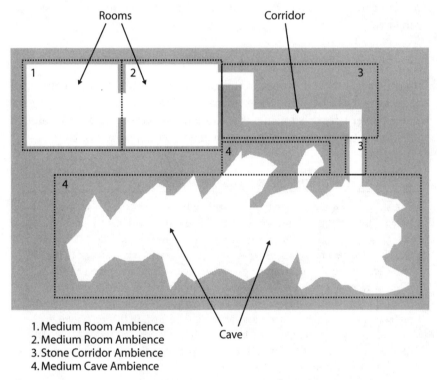

1. Medium Room Ambience
2. Medium Room Ambience
3. Stone Corridor Ambience
4. Medium Cave Ambience

FIGURE 27.1   Simple EAX 'zones' in a top-down view of a game environment.

Naturally, this is not a terribly sophisticated approach. As the world increases in size and complexity, it become apparent that searching through these various bounding boxes will be a linearly complex algorithm—not exactly ideal, since it must be performed fairly often (between 10 to 20 times per second, similar to the rate at which the DirectSound listener object commits its settings).

This leads us to the problem of efficient run-time storage. The basic problem is to retrieve a predefined set of environmental reverberation settings, given x, y, and z coordinate values. This category of algorithm is known sometimes as *spatial sorting* or *spatial subdivision*, and graphics programmers are well familiar with a number of them. These typically take the form of a tree of some sort, such as binary space partition trees, octrees, and axis-aligned bounding-box trees. We'll discuss some of these structures later in the chapter when looking at feasible solutions to our storage problems.

REAL-TIME REVERBERATION AND EFFECTS TRANSITIONS

It may be acceptable in some circumstances to instantly switch from effect to effect, such as when rendering a high-speed race car entering a tunnel, or when a player teleports to a new location; but often we prefer to be able to transition between effects smoothly over a specified period of time.

■ **REAL-TIME BLENDING USING EAX 2.0 OR I3DL2**

EAX 3.0 is advertised as having the capability to perform smooth transitions between different effects, and this is possible because all internal parameters used for calculating reverberation are exposed in the interface. In EAX 2.0, selecting various preset environments will cause internal parameters not exposed to the API to be adjusted, which obviously prevents any chance of a smooth blend. Thus, it is highly recommended that you avoid using presets if at all possible in EAX 2.0 or I3DL2. In fact, most environments can be decently modeled using only the generic preset and adjusting only exposed parameters as needed. In this way, you can ensure the ability to smoothly blend between any two environments.

You can actually use the presets to signal to your engine that it should not attempt a blend. For instance, a game character that jumps into water should trigger the underwater preset, and because the transition is instantaneous, a blend is not desired (nor possible).

You can perform the actual blend by interpolating between individual settings of EAX properties (source property and destination property), and scaling by the distance ratio. Because many of the values in the EAX property sets are logarithmic by nature, you may wish to experiment to see if logarithmic blending sounds better to you than a simple linear blend. (Actually, you may wish to have your sound designer's ear listening in on this.)

The mechanism for blending property sets is fairly easy, but determining exactly when and how the blends occur in the game can be a bit trickier. There are several approaches to look at.

Perhaps the simplest approach would be an automatic blend over a preset span of time whenever a new environment is entered. This has the advantage of implementation simplicity and requires no additional storage or heavy CPU requirement. This approach could in fact work quite well if the environmental storage system provides a reasonably fine-grained mapping of environments, meaning that transitions are typically not huge jumps from one environmental setting to another. This type of mapping is more typical of automatically generated environment maps than manually created ones, though, unless the designers take pains to place 'transition' zones between large jumps in reverberation settings. A gradual blending of settings over approximately one second or so should typically suffice without causing too many odd artifacts.

Alternatively, we could dispense with 'areas' altogether and utilize a weighted point system. Instead of storing areas, we store 3D points that reference EAX properties. A listener determines relative proximity to the three closest points (two might work as well), and a custom EAX property set is created, based on a weighted interpolation of these three property sets. Unfortunately, the effort required to locate the three closest points requires some sort of spatial subdivision, making the original goal of eliminating this sort of mechanism a moot point. Additionally, unless each point contains a map of local nodes that can be used in conjunction with it, the algorithm might tend to choose points on the other side of solid objects, creating bogus effects. Or, each zone might contain these connection maps, making the storage requirements a bit less daunting.

Despite the potential pitfalls, the approach of weighted, distance-based interpolation remains intriguing, as it would provide the most-accurate and smoothest transitioning effects. If the cost of storing both area-subdivision information as well as point sample data is not too great for your application, you could combine these to create very compelling environments with continuous and smooth transitions/blends. However, it remains extremely difficult to envision a simple algorithm that will not break under specific circumstances.

All in all, because accurate environment blending is a less-important criterion than creating accurate primary effects with efficient data structures and operating algorithms, it is perhaps best to concentrate first on the effects-storage system; later on, we can devise the best method of effectively blending environments, given the system used.

ACOUSTICAL DATA CREATION/GENERATION

Obviously, we must determine some method of actually creating specific effects data for various areas of our virtual world. This can range from dedicated tools, such the EAGLE editor, to custom tags and structures in proprietary or commercial world-building/modeling programs. However, the ultimate goal of programmers should always be to minimize the intrusiveness of the art path while still retaining a high degree of flexibility and functionality. Figure 27.2 shows a typical art path through which world data must travel in order to reach the state of run-time game data.

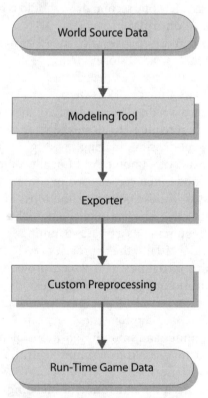

FIGURE 27.2   Typical art path for world data, from creation to game.

Often, the exporter is combined with a preprocessing step, or is otherwise automated to an even further degree. Using a third-party tool such as EAGLE results in a separate processing stage, such as the 'custom preprocessing stage.' Ultimately, the best scenario is to have as few interruptions as possible in the data flow between the raw data source and the final runtime data output. A streamlined data flow encourages experimentation and frequent checks to ensure the world is looking (sounding) the way it should—resulting in higher-quality work as well as the more-obvious benefit of time savings in the long run.

There are two basic tasks required for generating environmental reverberation data, and there are two approaches to performing each of these tasks. First, in order to define an environmental effect for an area, we must first define what the 'area' is. Second, we must decide what type of environmental effect to assign to this area. You must also decide whether you are going to create tools to perform each of these tasks manually or instead create algorithms to do it automatically. Bear in mind that either way, you will be required to write supporting code (either in the form of algorithms or user interfaces/tools). If your world happens to be already predivided into subsections, and you can make use of this information (such as in a portal-based engine), consider yourself lucky—the first task is already finished, and you can then just focus on environmental generation for these zones.

■ AUTOMATED TOOLS AND WORK INTERRUPTIONS

It may seem as though computationally expensive, automated processing phases would tend to discourage frequent updates and modifications to the final world data, and this is certainly true to a degree. This is why it is important to ensure that a level designer/world artist is not forced to endure lengthy audio-processing runs when simply checking the placement of a new texture. Levels of detail settings in the audio-processing phase can ensure that a designer can either opt out of audio processing altogether (perhaps even reusing the last processed data) or performing a light processing run and save the full, high-detail processing for periodic checks and the final product. Even better, if you design your tools to offload this sort of processing to a separate machine, you ensure that the artist or designer does not have to relegate full processing to a once-a-day procedure before leaving for the evening.

A bit later in the chapter, we'll be examining methods that can be used to automatically generate environmental and acoustical data without human intervention, and how to pair this with user-defined portals for dynamically generating sound occlusion data.

PVS VS. PAS

In most game engines, there is a concept of some sort of PVS (Potentially Visible Set) optimized data storage to help speed rendering times. The PVS assists the renderer by giving it only the data that can potentially be seen from any one particular point in the 3D world. Figure 27.3 shows what a typical PVS might look like when viewing a sample set of rooms. The darkened areas represent the data stored in the PVS data system, based on viewer's current position.

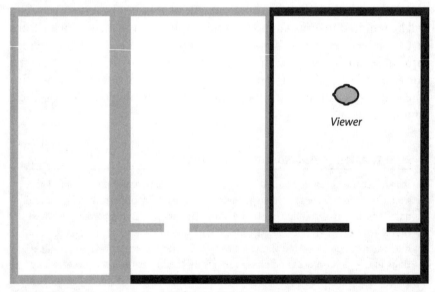

FIGURE 27.3   PVS representation of a point in the game world.

Unfortunately, you can plainly see that the PVS is not an effective method for culling out potentially audible sounds. Figure 27.4 demonstrates that a sound can be heard through the walls of the rooms. If the PVS were used to cull out the object making this sound, this subtle and effective sound would be lost. Instead, what is required is a PAS (Potentially Audible Set) of data.

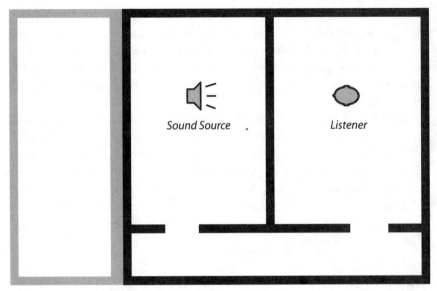

FIGURE 27.4   PAS representation of a point in the game world.

The PAS represents a reasonable approximation of where sounds can possibly be heard from. Naturally, in real life, a loud-enough sound can generally be heard in all but the most soundproof of environments. As such, you must determine a reasonable level of sound from which to base these calculations. We therefore call it a 'reasonable' approximation of potential sounds.

■ **NEED WE SAY IT?**

Although many games do use such a system, employing a simple radius test around the player does *not* make a very effective PAS algorithm. While this will work to a certain extent, it obviously breaks down when dealing with principles such as occlusion. Nothing is more frustrating than having an enemy character hear something which you, as a player, intuitively know the enemy should not be able to hear, especially given your relative positions. One way that a radius test *can* be effectively used, however, is in conjunction with our zone structures. Each zone can store a maximum radius at which enemies may potentially hear (or be heard), allowing for more efficient culling of irrelevant, algorithmic audio-search paths, which we'll discuss in a bit.

You should, of course, allow this 'calculation distance' to be adjusted; the range at which a designer wishes a sound to be heard could vary greatly from game to game. A traditional FPS might only care about what is in the next room or two, but a tactical shooter might want the sounds of a gun firing to travel clear across a large building, echoing realistically through all the corridors.

As with a PVS structure, the PAS is used as a method of quickly discarding irrelevant data and can be used to manage 3D sounds. For instance, if a monster that creates unique sounds enters the PAS, those particular sounds that are not already in memory can be cached, ensuring they are ready for playback. More importantly, though, it is used as a threshold test when performing more-expensive audio calculations, such as real-time occlusion path-finding, ensuring that algorithms do not exceed reasonable bounds.

REAL-TIME OCCLUSION AND OBSTRUCTION CALCULATIONS

Among the trickier problems to solve are those of occlusion and obstruction calculations. As you recall, occlusion is the muffling of sound that passes through walls when no open-air path exists, and obstruction is the blocking of the direct-path sound by a large obstacle, allowing only early or even late reflections to reach the listener. The basic problem to be solved is this: from any 3D point in the world, what is the unique occlusion and obstruction value to any other 3D point in the world? This type of problem is a programmer's nightmare, requiring exponentially increasing data-storage as the size of the working set increases. Note that one of the critical requirements of the PAS is to minimize the size of this working set in order to help offset problems of data-storage size. Otherwise, as the size of the map increases, the data requirements for this information alone soon spirals out of control.

Keep in mind that while the PAS represents a threshold at which audio calculations should be considered, the real beauty of the system appears when this information is paired with the dynamic occlusion and obstruction calculations (which we'll discuss later on in this chapter). This turns into an abstract system that can answer the question, "From point A on a map, how loud will a sound of x volume seem when played from point B, taking into account all the physical geometry of the map between A and B?" When you consider the ramifications of this, you can understand why this sort of system might be of considerable interest to AI programmers and game designers as well. Imagine that it actually makes a difference in your game world that a player shuts a heavy wooden door before smashing a window, ensuring that the guards in a room at the other end of the hall cannot hear the window smash. Typically, this sort of behavior is found in somewhat annoying, one-time scripted sequences, and tends to destroy believability in the world because the feat can only be performed once and only in special circumstances.

CREATIVE LABS' EAGLE—A PREPACKAGED SOLUTION

Now that you actually understand how complex this problem is (count how many pages were spent in describing it) you can see why many developers have chosen to use Creative Labs' EAGLE tool. We won't be giving a full tutorial on how to use it, but we'll present a basic overview on how EAGLE works, as well as some of its pros and cons.

EAGLE is designed to give developers a prepackaged solution, allowing them to more effectively integrate EAX into their applications. It is a multipart system, consisting both of a stand-alone authoring environment and a run-time system component that can be integrated into your game. Developers must write an importer that allows EAGLE to extract geometry data in specific chunks (i.e., the environment must be divided into 'rooms'), and EAGLE will then generate environmental reverberation data for each room or area imported, and allow manual tweaking of environments. Once the data set is generated, the EAGLE run-time component is called from the game, supplying the listener position and providing EAX parameters in return.

EAGLE, like any prepackaged solution to a very complex problem, has its pros and cons. Its biggest advantage is that it is an existing, viable solution with proven workability. Unfortunately, it does have a few significant drawbacks. First and foremost, EAGLE requires significant user intervention in setting up the final environmental data—it is by no means an automatic process. Each room or area must be manually extracted and imported into the tool, which would require a significant investment in time and effort for a very large, complex world. And, because it is a separate, stand-alone tool, it is by nature one more step in the data path, which means additional processing time and complexity. It is possible that the time saved in development costs by using EAGLE over a proprietary system might be lost in actually performing the work of splitting up all the world data, importing it into EAGLE, applying obstacles, and level/audio designers' hand-tweaking the environments.

Additionally, EAGLE relies on geometry to perform its area calculations, which it eventually turns into a BSP structure that closely matches the original geometry. This data structure is well suited to earlier 3D shooter-style games, as poly-counts were limited and geometry was somewhat basic and constrained in nature. As hardware capabilities and world geometry increase at nearly exponential rates, storing actual world geometry in order to bound and define audio data becomes less optimal a solution.

Finally, EAGLE is a proprietary, closed tool and library set developed by Creative Labs, and this may make it less attractive to some developers, especially those interested in cross-platform solutions. Closed products and libraries, such as DirectSound, are typically less of a problem, being fairly low-level in nature. High-level tools and libraries, on the other hand, might give pause to developers if they have no intentions of modifying the code for their needs or porting the run-time environment to other platforms.

Nonetheless and despite these issues, EAGLE still remains the *only* viable solution on the market, aside from developing your own custom tools. And, as such, it is worth looking into if you are serious about dramatically improving the quality and realism of your audio environments.

STORAGE SOLUTIONS DISCUSSED

The most basic problem in organizing and retrieving world-environment EAX data is how to store the data. In defining 'data-storage' structures, we are in fact talking about two types of storage systems. Hierarchical (tree-based) or patterned (grid) structures are used to subdivide or partition the world into searchable components, allowing a specific data structure to be located quickly, based upon a set of 3D coordinates. Other types of structures are used as geometric representations, perhaps encapsulating an area more efficiently than a sorting (searching) would.

These two types of storage structures are often combined. For instance, an octree structure might contain pointers to lists of oriented bounding-box structures that represent the actual area. The octree is used to quickly cull the potential number of oriented bounding boxes to search, while the bounding boxes themselves represent the actual room geometry. By effectively using complementary combinations of structures, we can maximize their strengths and minimize their weaknesses.

Before you even consider manipulating sound-specific data structures, you should thoroughly understand your 3D game engine's existing world-storage system. Debate exists over whether it is more efficient to pack all required world data into a unified data structure (this has often been done with BSP structures) or to split data apart into dedicated and highly optimized storage solutions. While a case could theoretically have been made for unified data structures a few years ago when world poly-counts were reasonably low, with today's highly detailed worlds, it makes less sense to tie area-based audio data to actual world geometry. We can instead use massively simplified volumetric representations and save a great deal of storage space. One exception to this might be if the global world representation is subdivided or tiered in such a manner as to be conducive to storing audio data—for instance, a world structure that naturally divides a world by rooms or specific areas is ideal for storing environmental reverberation data.

Additionally, the type of game your engine supports is another huge factor in deciding how to store audio data. What is an optimal storage system for a team-based FPS game with its limited, enclosed environments might be completely inappropriate for an adventure game or RPG with vast outdoor areas and varied dungeons/caverns. Other factors should be considered, such as whether your engine is strictly level-based, requiring loading discrete data sets as a player moves from area to area, or if it supports a seamless world paradigm in which data is continuously and transparently loaded. In cases like seamless worlds, attention must be paid to ensuring that the engine is capable of loading specific areas dynamically.

We will examine a number of data structures next and discuss their strengths, weaknesses, and how they can be applied to store environmental reverberation data. Keep in mind that this is a far-from-exhaustive list of data structures. It is likely that there are a number of viable alternatives to what is mentioned here—alternatives that can perform similarly well in different circumstances.

GRID

A regular grid is perhaps the simplest of spatial-organizing structures. Although you may not have even considered a grid when considering data structures, it has a number of obvious advantages over traditional tree-based methods. The most obvious benefit is that a grid allows constant-time access to any of its nodes. Because of its predictable structure, it is also well suited as a means of indexing other, more-efficient data structures stored on disk.

Naturally, a grid would have to be paired with additional structures that would be used to augment the inherent lack of fine resolution in a grid structure. Although you would not wish to use a grid to represent small-scale data, using it to perform large, initial subdivisions can actually be very useful, especially for seamless worlds; here they are very useful because it is easy to predict which grid location must be loaded next. Figure 27.5 shows how such a dynamic loading system might work. Obviously, with this sort of design criteria, it is highly improbable that this sort of design would be handled solely by the audio system. Instead, the audio system would most likely be responsible for loading specific data blocks when called upon to do so by a global loading mechanism in the game engine.

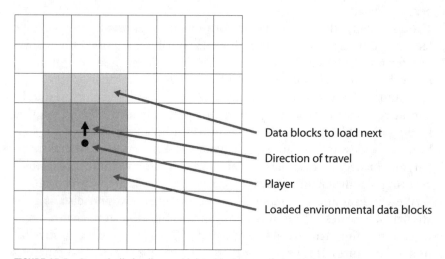

FIGURE 27.5   Dynamically loading world data blocks are called as a player moves.

BSP TREES

One well-known method of subdividing three-dimensional space is known as a *BSP (Binary Space Partitioning)* tree. The basic mechanism works by subdividing areas, using planes that are defined by the world polygons. The world is recursively split into smaller and smaller subdivisions, until each surface has been accounted for. This creates a perfectly fitting shape that matches the environment, allowing us to ensure that no matter where the player is located, we can identify a discrete node and return a specific EAX effect for that area.

The biggest problem with BSP structures is that as the world detail increases, so too does the representative BSP structure. You can see in Figure 27.6 how our original demonstration world has been subdivided into a BSP-compatible structure. Note that the BSP structure is highly efficient in the rooms, a low-poly environment; but in the higher-poly caves, the structure grows tremendously.

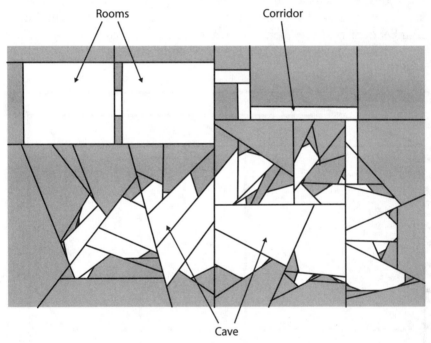

FIGURE 27.6   Subdividing a world using a BSP tree.

There is really only one good way to solve this problem, and that is to simplify the area's geometry in some fashion. This can be done either by creating a separate geometry set exclusively for generating the BSP, or perhaps by marking certain world objects as 'detail' objects. Either way will still require a large amount of work, though, and make a BSP less suitable for use on large-scale worlds unless effective and efficient ways can be found to reduce the geometric complexity prior to processing.

Nonetheless, the BSP's tight geometric alignment makes it an attractive option, despite these shortcomings. Looser structures, such as octrees or axis-aligned bounding-boxes trees have problems that BSP structures do not have to deal with, especially in certain worst-case scenarios.

OCTREES

Octrees are structures well suited to area-based spatial subdivision. In an octree, a cube that represents 3D space is subdivided equally into eight partitions, each smaller cube defined as a child of the larger cube. Recursion continues until a specific criterion is reached, such as a minimum number of distinct reverberation areas occurring in each node. Figure 27.7 shows a sample octree with two layers of subdivision.

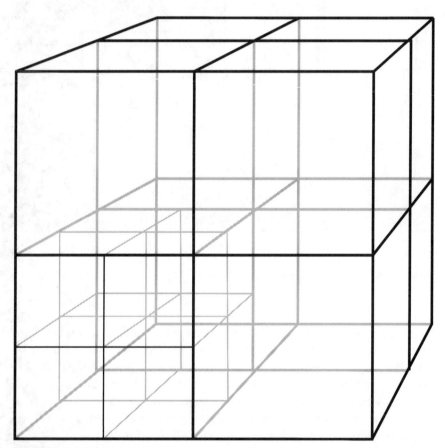

FIGURE 27.7   An octree structure.

The octree structure is somewhat unique in that it is a regular structure that can also provide a fine level of detail. This makes it extremely well suited for storing node-adjacency information, which we'll see can also be important for occlusion calculations. Often, octrees are paired with other structures that may be stored at the lowest nodes, such as oriented bounding boxes, although this does not necessarily have to be the case. Figure 27.8 demonstrates how our sample level might be subdivided by an octree. Of course, on the printed page, we only show a two-dimensional subdivision, which is in fact known as a *quadtree*, for clarity.

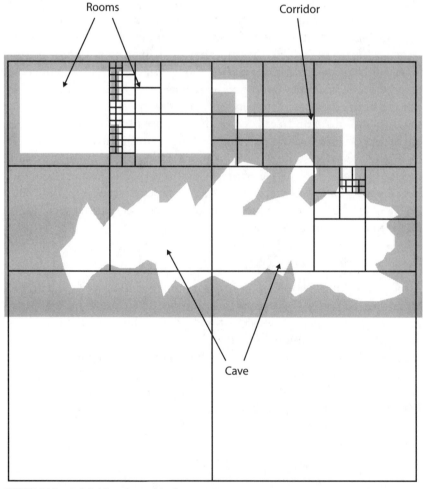

FIGURE 27.8   Subdividing the world using an octree.

In *Game Programming Gems* (Charles River Media, Inc., 2000), Dan Ginsburg wrote an article, "Octree Construction," which describes the basic principles of creating geometry-based octrees. There are also many resources available both in books and online that describe the basic principles of octrees, and you should not have too much trouble even finding sample code to peruse.

AABB TREES

AABB (Axis-Aligned Bounding Box) trees are recursively subdivided bounding boxes that are designed to contain half the number of unique elements as their parent nodes. Each subdivision contains exactly two smaller divisions, split among the longest axis. The bounding boxes may overlap to any extent necessary in order to completely encapsulate the objects that are being divided (they are, after all, defined as 'bounding boxes').

AABB trees are a viable alternative to octrees as top-level containers for reverberation data. They have some advantages over octrees in that they are not constrained by having to perform subdivisions in equal divisions. One practical use of AABB trees is when they are used to contain lists of axis-aligned or oriented bounding boxes that define individual regions.

If you are interested in learning more about AABB trees, check out Miguel Gomez's informative article, "Compressed Axis-Aligned Bounding Box Trees" [*Game Programming Gems 2*, Charles River Media, Inc., 2001, pp. 388–393]. In it, he describes how data storage requirements can be reduced to only 11 bytes per node.

ROOMS-BASED SUBDIVISIONS

Although technically not a data structure or algorithm, world data representations that already are divided into room-size chunks have an enormous advantage in storage calculations. One of the biggest challenges in automatically determining where and how to place EAX settings in 3D space is in how 'rooms' are defined in the first place. If your engine (or perhaps the level designer's) already performs the task of dividing the world into discreet areas or rooms, you can simply take advantage of this information when organizing your own data storage.

AUTOMATED ACOUSTICAL DATA GENERATION

One of the more-interesting challenges that most audio programmers are still waiting for is the preprocessor that can scan an entire world and automatically generate appropriate environmental reverberation, occlusion, and obstruction data, without human intervention. Quite frankly, until this sort of processing tool is developed and refined to a reliable degree, adding statistical-based environmental reverberation data to worlds will remain a tedious and time-consuming process. It is difficult to justify the expense of having designers fine-tune environmental reverberation for each specific room in every single structure in your game, but it is far less daunting to have a computer algorithm perform this same sort of work. After all, environmental reverberation is based on physical properties of sound waves; and given enough information, it should be possible for a computer to perform such calculations, similar to the way a computer can generate light maps or automatically split levels into BSP trees.

DEFINING REVERBERATION AREAS

One of the first tasks that must be accomplished is to determine what the boundaries of each environmental zone are. Locating logical boundaries is a key step in being able to effectively partition a world. Let's look at our theoretical mini-world again and determine where logical zones lie.

Back in Figure 27.1, we manually divided our level into four zones, representing the four discreet areas of the level. Creating an algorithm to perform such as task (that is deceptively easy for a human) can prove to be somewhat daunting. We have two basic tasks: first, we must create divisions along any boundary where a drastic change in reverberation takes place. The boundaries between sections two, three, and four are all characteristic of this type of division. By performing sampling analysis inside the level, we can determine exactly where the reverberation will change. Essentially, we must then simply bound all of the similar-sounding sample points in common areas.

Determining the boundaries between sections one and two, though, can prove to be slightly more difficult. One way of helping to define areas is to perform concavity tests and loosely base areas on geometry that demonstrates a high degree of concavity. Such a test may end up breaking up sections three and four into smaller sections, but this would not necessarily be a bad thing, either, as long as they can still be represented reasonably efficiently.

Another test could be to calculate connectivity between sample points and to measure the percentage of connectivity between large, adjacent sections of connected nodes. In this case, the algorithm would detect two large blocks of connected nodes with a small bridge of connectivity between them. Because of the difference in the size of the overall connection between the sections, the algorithm would know to subdivide the two zones.

ROOM REVERBERATION CALCULATIONS

Calculating reverberation data can be done in a number of ways, but since we are working with a statistical reverberation engine, we might as well take advantage of this fact. At a very basic level, most reverberation properties result from answers to the following three questions:

1. What is the shape of the room?
2. What is the size of the room?
3. What is the absorption rate of materials in this room?

The essence of calculating the reverberation data for the room seems, then, to depend on the answers to these three questions.

Perhaps the simplest method to determine the basic shape of a room is to combine statistical sampling using raycasting to determine intersection positions and fundamental geometry. This same method can also help to determine the overall size. Figure 27.9 shows a number of sample points and the raycasting used to determine the closest intersecting polygon in a given direction.

By casting in a number of directions, an algorithm can easily determine the basic shape of a room. For instance, at point A, the rays are all of approximately equal length, with the exception of the eastbound ray—thus, indicating a relatively square room. The mean lengths of the rays help to determine the overall size of the room and the material information collected from the polygons that the rays intersected. With enough sample points to ensure consistent coverage of the room, we gain a very clear picture of the overall shape and size, as well as the materials within. Naturally, we would be casting rays in all directions, not just along a single, horizontal plane.

For a sample like that at point C, it can easily be determined that we are in a hallway or other narrow corridor because of the relative narrowness of

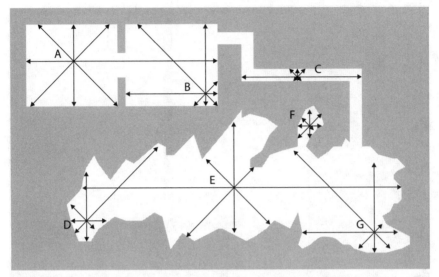

FIGURE 27.9   Point-sample raycasting to determine shape, size, and material.

the space, except for one or two directions, and we can adjust the reverberations accordingly.

Points D, E, and G all provide information about a spacious environment covered by rock, and so we will set the reverberations to match these parameters. Interestingly, at point F, we enter a narrow subcavern; and because the rays do not exit easily into the larger cavern, the reverberation in this area should be adjusted accordingly to render a realistic effect.

STORING CONNECTIVITY INFORMATION AS OCCLUSION HINTS

One way of solving the occlusion problem is to utilize a connectivity map. This type of system would work well with either hand-placed effect node markers or by an automated scan that stores data in an octree or similar structure. By storing a simple graph of adjacent areas along with corresponding occlusion rates, the occlusion value between any two adjacent areas can be determined in constant time, with little in the way of additional storage requirements. Figure 27.10 demonstrates what this looks like.

This type of adjacency information can be determined by performing dual-direction raycasts from various sampling points inside each room. The thickness of the wall and the materials from which it is constructed are

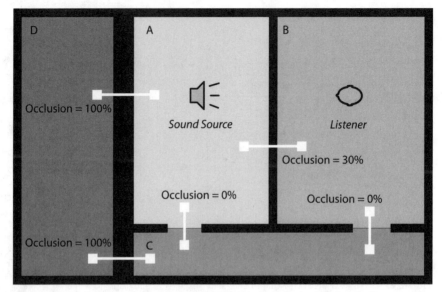

FIGURE 27.10 Utilizing adjacent occlusion information for a simple occlusion check.

stored, and the smallest occlusion value that is found (meaning the thinnest or weakest point in the wall) is used as the occlusion value between the rooms. A light, wooden door will produce a marginal amount of occlusion, a standard wood-frame and plaster wall will produce substantial occlusion, and a double-thick concrete block wall will produce complete occlusion between the rooms.

What about sounds from areas that are not adjacent to the room that the listener is in? In this case, the problem turns into a basic path-finding problem; we must search along nodes that do not completely block occlusion until either no reasonable path is found or a maximum distance is covered. In this way, the search path is always limited, preventing extremely long and fruitless searches, and helping to cap CPU usage. Listing 27.11 demonstrates what such a search might look like.

We can see that the path of least occlusion is D–A–C–B, and this adds up to a total occlusion value of 55%. However, the shortest distance path is D–A–B, with an occlusion value of 70%. A fitness function in the search should attempt to balance distance with scale. The exact formula to be used is, at this point, a matter of speculation, but a bit of experimentation should result in a good formula that balances occlusion and distance. You will need to store the center position of each environment zone, and you

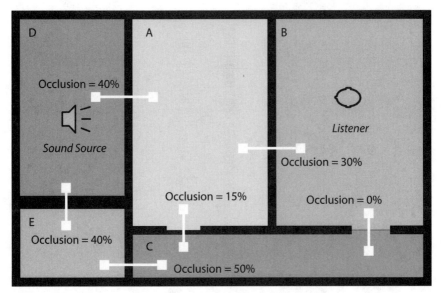

FIGURE 27.11 Utilizing adjacent occlusion information to perform a multiroom sound-path search.

might also want to store the distance between center points of adjacent nodes, as well as the occlusion data between them; this will save you the cost of having to calculate the distance between each node when searching.

DEFINING AND STORING DYNAMIC OCCLUSION HINTS

When referring to 'dynamic occlusion hints,' what we are basically describing a simple door, but we could also be talking about a window (which could either be broken or open), a breakable wall, or some other geometry that moves in a manner that can potentially cause the obstruction of sound transmissions.

These types of items must be marked in a way that is recognizable in the preprocessing phase, especially when attempting to determine occlusion hints in adjacency maps. When a scanning ray intersects a door or other dynamic occluder, it knows to register and query this object as special when attempting to determine the occlusion value. In this way, you can set an occlusion value for a door, reduce the occlusion when it opens, and raise the occlusion it when shuts. Figure 27.12 demonstrates a door in action and acting as a dynamic occlusion modifier.

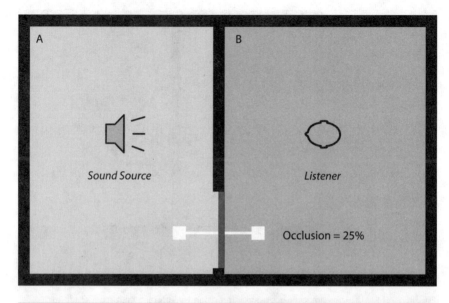

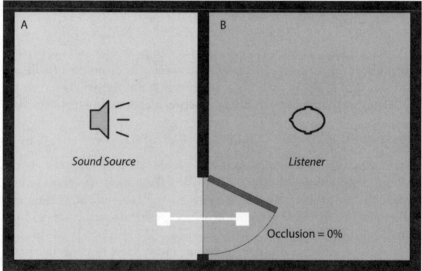

FIGURE 27.12   Occlusion data that is dynamically affected by a door.

OPTIMIZING SAMPLING PATTERNS AND CALCULATIONS

Obviously, the sampling rate that is required to accurately determine proper environmental settings inside a dungeon will be much different than those for a barren desert, even though these two environments might be part of the same map. The trick in using sampling is to ensure that high-density sampling is only applied where needed, otherwise the time required to scan and sample an entire map grows exponentially as the map gets larger.

As such, we must use different sampling rates and techniques when rendering outdoors versus closed environments. However, we don't want to simply abandon our sampling when we move to an outside environment. On the contrary, actually hearing a clanking sword's echo when inside a rock-faced canyon would be impressive, especially when noticed consistently throughout a large, outdoor environment.

One method of determining if the algorithm is scanning outside is to simply check the upward scan. If we consistently see no ceiling ("consistently" being the key word here, as we don't want to switch to an outdoor environment simply because of one small skylight), we know that we are scanning outdoors, and we can adjust accordingly. Another method might simply be to use large-scale bounding volumes as global terrain hints, or perhaps marker nodes to help the scanner ensure it does not miss a small building in an otherwise barren outdoor environment.

Regardless of how it is determined, you must somehow ensure you scan using tight sampling points when indoors and revert to large-scale sampling and raycasting when outside, or the automatic-generation algorithms will bog down to the point of being unusable.

ACOUSTICAL DATA STORAGE AND RUN-TIME RETRIEVAL

Obviously, the data-storage structures you choose to implement have an enormous impact on what sort of queries can be performed as well as how efficiently that data will be stored. Although we've hinted at how certain data systems might be arranged, let's review one example of how we might wish to implement this sort of environmental reverberation data-storage and retrieval system.

OCTREE-BASED STORAGE

For our example, we'll be demonstrating the use of an octree as the principle spatial subdivision structure. This sort of system allows us to reach a resolution of 0.25 meter when starting from an area of over 128 kilometers in just 20 iterations. An octree has the benefit of working completely independently from stored geometrical data, once the data structures have been established. Although we could actually choose to store alternate structures at each node, for this example we will be representing geometric areas with the octree node bounding boxes themselves, similar to Figure 27.8.

Each environmental reverberation zone is actually made up of a number of nodes, which are stored in an internal list. Additionally, each end node of the octree structure contains a pointer to its designated zone, ensuring the zone structure can be reached from a location-based query through the octree.

In addition to containing a list to octree nodes that define its shape, a zone also contains reciprocal links to special data structures that contain occlusion and distance data (and possibly other information, as well), helping to define links between adjacent nodes. A unique key must define each of these link structures, and the run-time environment must match these link structures with doors and other objects that can alter occlusion properties between zones. Figure 27.13 shows these data structures and how they could be linked together.

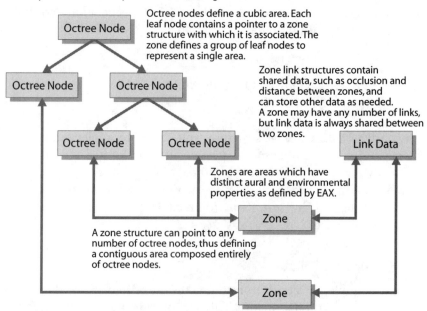

FIGURE 27.13 Internal organization of storage structures.

OCTREE OPTIMIZATIONS

One of the major problems in defining areas with octrees concerns the worst-case scenario in which a number of angled zones are packed tightly together. Figure 27.14 demonstrates this type of situation and shows how it can cause an enormous waste of storage resources.

In Figure 27.14, every single subdivision is required to fit entirely inside one and only one zone. Any box straddling two zones must be subdivided and checked again. This can cause a tremendous amount of subdivision and might lead to the assumption that octrees are a horribly inefficient algorithm for representing odd-shaped areas. However, this is working

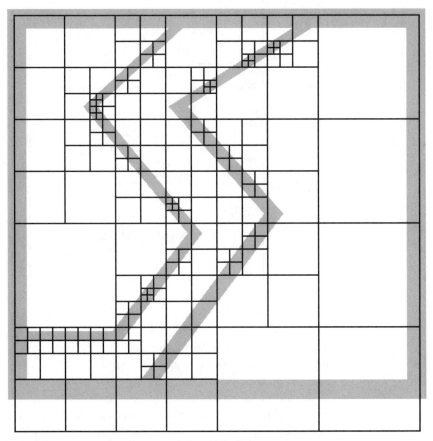

FIGURE 27.14   Worst-case data scenario for a tight-fitting octree.

under the false impression that our octree structure must actually match the world geometry precisely, something it will never be good at.

Let's briefly examine the worst trouble spots in our previous diagram. In Figure 27.15, the map areas that need an inordinate amount of subdivision to accurately represent the world zones have been shaded.

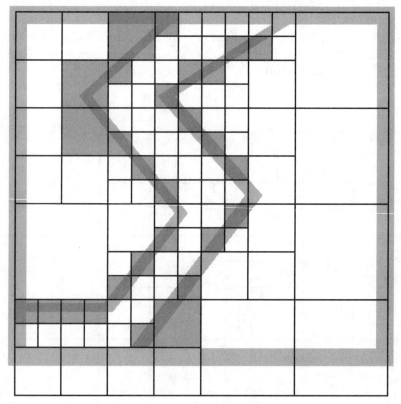

FIGURE 27.15 Worst-case areas have been shaded.

You can see that without these areas, the octree still represents a reasonable approximation of the geometry in a reasonable number of subdivisions. Best of all, no matter how complex the shapes, the octree representation will remain at approximately the same complexity. (Imagine, for example, that these are curved surfaces instead of angular ones—or that the walls contain extremely complex or detailed geometry, which is not uncommon in today's (and especially tomorrow's) games.) But how can we simply discard these problem areas?

Believe it or not, the answer is almost as simple as the question. Those nodes are simply considered null data, and the real key lies in how that data is interpreted. Our basic assumption is that the listener cannot move through walls; and therefore, they must always cross a node, which contains valid data, before they actually enter one of these 'null' zones. When a null node is entered, the EAX data that is fed to the listener does not change; instead, it relies on the previously calculated settings. Thus, any node straddling two or more zone boundaries may simply be discarded. Naturally, we should ensure, by using heuristics, that null nodes are appropriate to the overall size of the zone, and that these heuristics tighten up when a player can freely travel between zones (e.g., at crossable boundaries). In this manner, we ensure accurate results and an acceptably sized data-storage system that is free from any reasonable geometric constraints.

An octree will always tend to fare worse in tightly packed areas with odd angles and very thin walls between zones; but then again, most storage systems tend to fare poorly in these circumstances. The real benefits of octrees will be seen in true amortized performance—meaning that they can take into account all types of terrain, not just tightly packed, indoor environments. However, by keeping in mind that acoustical data storage can be a much 'looser' process than when storing visual data, we can take a lot of shortcuts and drastically increase the overall storage efficiency.

CONCLUSION

We have provided some basic information and ideas to get you started in creating your own engine's environmental reverberation, auto-generation and mapping system. However, there is still much research and testing to be done, as few developers have embarked on such advanced projects, let alone completed and packaged any into a shipped product. The Creative Labs EAGLE tool is a great start, but a fully automated process would provide such an advantage in time and resources that it is difficult to ignore the challenge of such a project.

Next, we will discuss the various Dolby technologies and what they mean to you as an audio programmer and game developer.

CHAPTER 28

UNDERSTANDING DOLBY TECHNOLOGIES

Dolby has been a household name for nearly a generation now—not only for audio professionals, but for consumers as well. Beginning with noise-reduction audio equipment and later pioneering the encoding of multichannel surround sound onto stereo tracks, Dolby has most recently advanced the digital multichannel technology that is currently used in today's high-end home theater systems. We'll discuss several Dolby technologies, current hardware compatible with Dolby technologies, and what you as a developer must do to take advantage of this technology.

WHAT ABOUT DOLBY TECHNOLOGIES?

Because Dolby is such a well-known name that is synonymous with high-quality audio, it behooves you as a developer to understand how this technology works, what it can and can't do for you, and how you can use it. Surprisingly, although nearly everyone knows the Dolby name, there is a lot of confusion about what the different technologies are and how they are used—and not just among consumers, either. When a game developer states that they are building an audio engine that complies with Dolby® Digital technology, most audio programmers and designers scratch their heads, trying to figure out what exactly this means. There is also a lot of potential confusion regarding consumer products and their support for the various Dolby products.

DOLBY TECHNOLOGIES

There are two distinct Dolby technologies that you as a game developer might be using: Dolby Digital 5.1 and Dolby Pro Logic®. We'll explain and discuss these two formats.

DOLBY DIGITAL 5.1

Dolby Digital (also known as AC-3) is a high-compression digital audio codec designed specifically to encode the six discrete channels required to reproduce theater-quality soundtracks. It is similar in principle to modern *psychoacoustic* audio compression codecs, such as Ogg Vorbis, MP3, and WMA. Psychoacoustic audio compression means that data is compressed using advanced algorithms that discard audio information that the human ear is unlikely to be able to hear, resulting in dramatically less data while retaining a very high-quality reproduction.

Unlike other general-purpose audio codecs, Dolby Digital was specifically designed for only one purpose: reproducing six-channel, high-quality movie soundtracks, making it remarkably good at what it does. Many hardware receivers, both in consumer and theater products, are equipped with Dolby Digital decoders, making this one of the most widely supported digital audio formats on the market today. It is a safe bet that any new surround-sound receiver will support Dolby Digital 5.1. Movies, both in the theater and now on DVD, are currently the primary users of Dolby Digital data. However, you should expect that the new generation (and all future generations) of game console and PC audio hardware will try to take advantage of the digital decoding hardware in home-theater systems, and they will have their hand at encoding real-time Dolby Digital streams for superior, theater-like sound reproduction.

The Dolby Digital format, although closely tied to positional audio, is not a true 3D audio format, as it contains no positional sound information. Rather, it is a compressed, multichannel audio format that is encoded and decoded using dedicated hardware. These channels are, of course, used to represent spatial information at times, but this is a subtle distinction that is important to make, and we'll discuss why later in the chapter.

DOLBY SURROUND AND PRO LOGIC II

Dolby Pro Logic II, and the older Dolby Surround, are somewhat different technologies that were designed to solve a different problem from Dolby

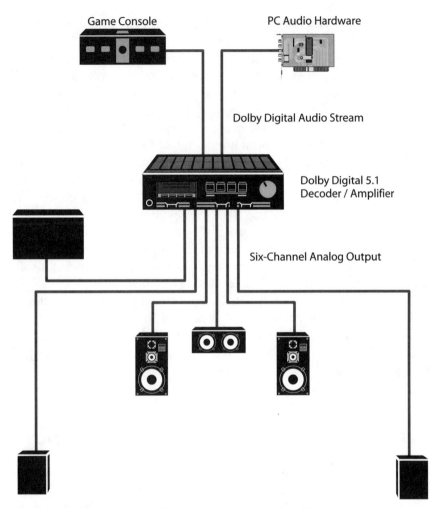

FIGURE 28.1   Game console and PC hardware connected to a Dolby Digital decoder.

Digital. Dolby Surround encoding allows four channels (left, right, center, and surround) to be encoded into two standard stereo tracks, using heuristics that take advantage of slight differences in phase and amplitude between the two stereo tracks to determine how to direct the sound. Dolby Surround encoding makes use of Pro Logic decoding to reproduce the original four channels from the two stereo tracks.

The more-advanced Pro Logic II allows five channels to be encoded, enabling stereo differentiation in the surround channel. In this case, the encode and decode processes are both called Dolby Pro Logic II, in order to simplify the signal path for consumers.

Unlike Dolby Digital's six discrete channels, tracks encoded in Dolby Surround and Pro Logic II may only steer a single dominant positional source at any one time. Thus, if you have three positional sound sources to represent in a Dolby Surround mix, only the loudest (most dominant) of the three sources will be represented as positional audio.

Despite some of the technical limitations of Dolby Surround and Pro Logic II technologies, they are still the best for situations in which Dolby Digital encoding is not available, such as game consoles without dedicated Dolby Digital encoding hardware. Because stereo channels encoded in Dolby Surround and Pro Logic II are compatible with normal stereo or monaural playback, they can be used as a graceful fallback for systems not equipped with digital playback and decoder systems.

Dolby Surround and Dolby Pro Logic II are also good choices for software-encoding solutions in consoles lacking a dedicated Dolby Digital encoder, such as the algorithms needed to apply the stereo-stream amplitude and phase shifts in the Nintendo Gamecube and Sony Playstation 2. On the PC, the Miles Sound System provides a software-based encoder that will encode a Dolby Surround signal in real time based on currently playing 3D positional sounds.

HARDWARE COMPATIBLE WITH DOLBY TECHNOLOGY

When looking at PC audio cards, it is sometimes difficult to know what card manufactures mean when they label their cards as "Dolby Digital 5.1 enabled" or "Supporting Dolby Digital." Generally speaking, most cards on the market today are actually not, in fact, capable of creating a real-time Dolby Digital data-stream mix from true-3D sound sources, such as those found in DirectSound3D. In other words, these cards do not actually contain a Dolby Digital *encoder*.

Instead, they might support Dolby Digital coding in a number of other different ways. Some are capable of decoding a pre-encoded Dolby Digital source from a DVD movie to a virtual multichannel or stereo source on your PC (in fact, this is often done by the CPU, rather than by the video card using bundled software). Or, the card might pass the signal through to an external decoder unchanged if you are using an external desktop decoder/amplifier or a home-theater system.

While this may be of some use in static-cut scenes, it's of no use to game developers, who by nature are typically working with dynamic 3D positional audio. For this, a hardware-based Dolby Digital encoder is required in order to digitally compress and mix the audio stream in real time. At the time of this writing, only one console on the market, the Xbox, actually supports real-time Dolby Digital encoding from interactive 3D sources.

The PC, surprisingly, does not fare much better in regards to supporting true, real-time Dolby Digital encoding. There are currently very few audio cards or products that support real-time encoding, and these are not yet widely adopted in the marketplace. You should contact Dolby Laboratories if you wish to find out which cards currently support hardware-based Dolby Digital encoding. However, now that the initial development work has been done, you can expect Dolby Digital encoder systems to become increasingly commonplace.

DEVELOPMENT USING DOLBY TECHNOLOGIES

While Dolby Digital technology is most obviously beneficial to console developers because of the proliferation of hardware-based amplifiers that decode Dolby technology, you should expect to see some advances in personal computers, as well. Computers are becoming more integrated into households, and they still occupy a significant role as entertainment systems. This means that gamers are willing to invest in high-quality, mini-theater-like systems for the desktop, and they will expect high-quality digital audio from their PC hardware in order to take full advantage of these systems.

However, it should be made clear that Dolby technology encoding is a hardware problem, not a software problem. As such, you as a developer need not attempt to write real-time Dolby Digital encoders or decoders. (In fact, doing so will probably get you into trouble.) Instead, you should simply ensure that your game's audio is optimized for high-quality, Dolby Digital 5.1 channel output. For PC and Xbox developers, this just means using DirectSound3D as always, and let the hardware provide behind-the-scenes encoding into the Dolby Digital format where appropriate.

In fact, the most important thing you must do as a developer is to make sure your audio is developed and tested on a Dolby Digital 5.1 multichannel audio system, or you won't really be able to tell how it will sound. Additionally, there is one more reason why you should pay attention to Dolby Digital compatibility, which we'll discuss next.

DOLBY LOGO PROGRAM

Dolby Laboratories is in the business of selling Dolby technology for use in hardware, but they are also interested in software developers who make a concerted effort to maximize the sound quality of a game title, which includes making sure it sounds correct on Dolby hardware. As such, Dolby allows developers to use the Dolby logo as a way of letting consumers know that they can expect high-quality audio from a title.

You should be sure to contact Dolby (games@dolby.com) to discuss the logo program and find out what you can do to ensure your game sounds as good as it can. Their Web site (*www.dolby.com*) should provide you with the information and contacts to get started. We have also included some technical information on the CD-ROM that accompanies this book. Look in the /extras/Dolby folder.

ON THE CD

CONCLUSION

Adding Dolby Digital support is out of your hands as a software developer, but that doesn't mean you can't benefit from Dolby technology, resources, and marketing. As digital technologies become cheaper and more prolific for the PC, you can expect to see more Dolby Digital equipment in the desktops, and you should be prepared to understand and optimize both your sound engine and content for this technology.

This concludes the advanced 3D techniques part of *Game Audio Programming*. In Part VI—Miscellaneous, we'll deal with a few leftover topics, such as how to play redbook CD format (standard CD audio). We will then discuss various optimization strategies and techniques.

PART VI

MISCELLANEOUS

CHAPTER 29

REDBOOK AUDIO PLAYBACK FOR WINDOWS

O ne of the simplest ways to implement high-quality music playback on the Win32 platform is to use the audio playback capabilities of the computer's CD-ROM drive. These days, all computers come with either a DVD-ROM or CD-ROM as standard hardware, and either should be capable of reading Redbook audio-format CDs.

ON THE CD The code listed in this chapter can be found in \Game_Audio\ audio_sdk\include\audiolib\CDPlayer.h\Game_Audio\audio_sdk\ src\audiolib\, CDPlayer.cpp.

ADVANTAGES AND DISADVANTAGES OF REDBOOK AUDIO

The compact-disk, Redbook audio format (i.e., standard music CD format) provides a simple method of storing audio and can be considered analogous to storing digital audio in an uncompressed, 16-bit stereo, 44.1 kHz wave file. Playing the audio directly from the CD in Redbook format also has the distinct advantage of taking almost no CPU time away from the game. The CD-ROM drive and the sound card's mixer do nearly all the work of actually playing the audio. This makes it an attractive option for some types of CD-ROM-based games, but there are a few disadvantages to note.

The first and perhaps most significant disadvantage is that Redbook audio stores data in an uncompressed format, meaning that if you have a significant amount of audio data to store, the majority of the disk space could be monopolized by audio. For larger commercial games, this usually means that there is not enough space for Redbook audio unless you provide the game audio on a CD that is separate from the game disk. But this might be an attractive option if you want to give your players the option of listening to their own CDs while the game is in progress. Programmatically, it's a relatively simple matter with Windows multimedia functions in control, and since all computers now come with CD-ROM drives that also can function as CD audio players, it's worthwhile to know how to write a basic CD player.

WINDOWS MCI FUNCTIONS

Windows MCI (Media Control Interface) functions provide a convenient, device-independent method for controlling a computer's CD-ROM device, or nearly any other multimedia device found on a PC. Since most forms of media have a common concept of opening/closing a device, as well as loading, playing, stopping, pausing, resuming, and seeking media, a common set of functions (with a plethora of options) serve a number of device types, such as audio and video streams—and, of course, CD players. These functions can always be identified by their `mci` prefix, such as `mciOpen()`.

There are two classes of functions in the MCI family—the *command message interface* and the *command string interface*. The command message interface uses numerical flags and structures to communicate to the MCI functions what the parameters of a function should be, which is much easier and more efficient in C or C++. In the command string interface, all MCI commands and return values are string-based. While this is obviously handy for a text-based environment, such as a command-line interpreter, the command message interface is easier to work with and more efficient in code, so this is what we will be working with.

CDPlayer CLASS DESIGN

We are not interested in creating a fully featured CD player, so our class will reflect more modest goals. Here is what our CDPlay class looks like:

LISTING 29.1

```
class CDPlay
{
```

```cpp
private:
enum CD_STATUS_TYPE
{
    CDSTATUS_STOPPED,
    CDSTATUS_PAUSED,
    CDSTATUS_PLAY,
};
public:
    CDPlay();
    virtual ~CDPlay();

    void Clear();

    bool Init(HWND hWindow, const char* pDrive = NULL);
    void Term();

    bool Play();
    bool Pause();
    bool Stop();

    bool OnMCINotify(WPARAM wParam, LPARAM lParam);

    void SetLooping(bool loop)
    { m_bLoop = loop; }
    UINT GetCurrentTrack()
    { return m_nCurrentTrack; }
    void SetCurrentTrack(UINT track)
    { m_nCurrentTrack = track; }
    bool IsPlaying()
    { return (m_Status == CDSTATUS_PLAY) ?
        true : false; }
    bool IsPaused()
    { return (m_Status == CDSTATUS_PAUSED) ?
        true : false; }

private:
    // Window handle is required for the
    // callback function
    HWND m_hWindow;
    // The MCI functions require this device ID
    MCIDEVICEID m_iDeviceID;
    // The currently playing or selected track
    uint32 m_nCurrentTrack;
```

```
    // Indicates whether the CD player should loop
    // the tracks
    bool m_bLoop;
    // Current status of the CD player
    CD_STATUS_TYPE m_Status;
    // CD player is initialized
    bool m_bInitialized;
};

static CDPlay* CDPlayer()
{ static CDPlay cdplyr; return &cdplyr; }
```

Our basic CDPlay class gives us all the basic functions needed for a computer game's CD player, including the ability to play, pause, and stop individual tracks. Easy, singleton-like access is provided via the CDPlayer() function, allowing notation such as CDPlayer()->Play() from anywhere in the code where the header file is included. You will note that we did not bother with creating an abstract interface for this class. For those creating a true platform-independent system, however, it would be a simple matter to add an abstract ICDPlayer interface to the system and use a factory to create the concrete object in the same manner as the other audio classes.

OPENING AND CLOSING THE DEVICE

The CD player device is 'opened' in the Init() function and 'closed' in the Term() function—not to be confused, of course, with literally opening and closing the CD drive tray; although that's technically possible too, using some other functions. In this case, mciOpen() simply prepares the device for playback and mciClose() shuts it down. Let's examine what happens in our startup and shutdown code, Init() and Term(), respectively.

LISTING 29.2

```
// The open function prepares the CD player for
// playing and checks to see if it is ready
bool CDPlay::Init(HWND hWindow, const char* pDrive)
{
    if (m_bInitialized)
        return false;
```

```
// This tells which window should receive the
// MCI messages
m_hWindow = hWindow;

// Open the MCI cdaudio device
MCI_OPEN_PARMS OpenParms;
OpenParms.lpstrDeviceType = "cdaudio";
DWORD dwFlags = MCI_OPEN_TYPE | MCI_WAIT;
// If a user has specified a drive letter, then try
// to initialize that device by name
if (pDrive)
{
    TCHAR szElementName[4];
    if ((strlen(pDrive) > 1) && (pDrive[1] == ':'))
        wsprintf(szElementName, TEXT("%s"),
            pDrive);
    else
        wsprintf(szElementName, TEXT("%s:"),
            pDrive);
    OpenParms.lpstrElementName = szElementName;
    dwFlags |= MCI_OPEN_ELEMENT;
}
MCIERROR error = mciSendCommand(0,
                    MCI_OPEN,
                    dwFlags,
                    (DWORD) (LPVOID) & OpenParms);
if (error)
    return false;

// Store this value for later comparison when
// checking MCI Windows messages
m_iDeviceID = OpenParms.wDeviceID;

// Set the proper time format
MCI_SET_PARMS SetParms;
SetParms.dwTimeFormat = MCI_FORMAT_TMSF;
error = mciSendCommand(m_iDeviceID,
            MCI_SET,
            MCI_SET_TIME_FORMAT,
            (DWORD) (LPVOID) & SetParms);
if (error)
    return false;
```

```
    m_bInitialized = true;

    return true;
}


// Closes the CD audio device. Make sure this function
// is called before the program exits, or it may leave
// the device in limbo.
void CDPlay::Term()
{
    // Make sure the CD stops before closing it
    if(IsPlaying())
        Stop();
    mciSendCommand(m_iDeviceID, MCI_CLOSE, 0, NULL);
    Clear();
}
```

The CDPlay::Init() function takes a handle to a window and a character string as an argument. The window handle acts as a callback parameter for some of the operation functions, using the MM_MCINOTIFY and the device ID obtained during the mciOpen() function to identify relevant messages. We will later examine what we can do with these messages. The character string allows the program to specify which drive should be activated. This is important, because many users have more than one CD audio-capable drive, especially with the popularization of DVD and CDR drives in recent years. A string format of either "[drive letter]" or "[drive letter]:" is acceptable.

The mciSendCommand() function is defined as follows:

```
MCIERROR WINAPI mciSendCommand(
    MCIDEVICEID mciId,
    UINT uMsg,
    DWORD dwParam1,
    DWORD dwParam2);
```

The mciID argument represents the device returned from the initial Open function, and is henceforth used to identify the device that is being controlled. The uMsg contains the basic type of message to send to the device.

Some common messages used in our code are: MCI_OPEN, MCI_CLOSE, MCI_PLAY, MCI_PAUSE, MCI_RESUME, and MCI_STOP. The dwParam1 is typically used as a set of message-specific flags, used to further qualify the command being sent to the device. If no additional flags need be set, you should set this value to zero. And dwParam2 is typically used to hold a message-specific structure containing any additional information required. We will examine these structures as they are used throughout the code.

Let's now examine the specific parameters and operation of the mciSendCommand() functions found in CDPlay::Init() and CDPlay::Term(), and we'll see exactly what they accomplish.

As always with defensive coding, we protect against the CD device from being opened more than once, and we set the window handle for later use in our functions.

```
if(m_bInitialized)
    return false;

// This tells which window should receive the
// MCI messages
m_hWindow = hWindow;
```

We next see the first of our custom message structures, MCI_OPEN_PARMS, and properly fill it out with the required values.

```
// Open the MCI cdaudio device
MCI_OPEN_PARMS OpenParms;
OpenParms.lpstrDeviceType = "cdaudio";
OpenParms.lpstrAlias = szAliasName;
DWORD dwFlags = MCI_OPEN_TYPE;
// If a user has specified a drive letter, then try
// to initialize that device by name.
if(pDrive)
{
    TCHAR    szElementName[4];
    if((strlen(pDrive) > 1) && (pDrive[1] == ':'))
        wsprintf(szElementName, TEXT("%s"), pDrive);
    else
        wsprintf(szElementName, TEXT("%s:"), pDrive);
    OpenParms.lpstrElementName = szElementName;
    dwFlags |= MCI_OPEN_ELEMENT;
}
```

The device type we wish to open is identified with the string "cdaudio." The MCI_OPEN_TYPE indicates we are identifying the device to open in this manner. Next, we check the drive parameter. If a drive string is not specified, the Open command will look for the most appropriate CD audio-capable device. For most games that have a CD audio track to play, it is likely that the game code will know which drive the CD disk resides in. This information should be passed to this function so the wrong drive is not accessed. If this field is used, MCI_OPEN_ELEMENT is added to dwFlags.

Next, the mciSendCommand() function is called with the appropriate parameter values. Note how we must cast the address of the MCI_OPEN_PARMS structure to a VOID pointer and then to a DWORD value.

```
MCIERROR error = mciSendCommand(0, MCI_OPEN, dwFlags,
    (DWORD)(LPVOID)&OpenParms);
if(error)
    return false;

// Store this value for later comparison when checking
// MCI Windows messages.
m_iDeviceID = OpenParms.wDeviceID;
```

MCI functions return an error of type MCIERROR, which is really a type-def'd unsigned long. A zero value indicates success. If the MCI_OPEN command fails, we exit the function and return false. If the function succeeds, we have successfully opened the CD audio device, and the device ID is stored in the wDeviceID field of the MCI_OPEN_PARMS structure. This value is stored for later use in all future mciSendCommand() functions and represents a handle to the open CD player device.

After the device is opened, we must set the proper time format for the device and then set our m_bInitialized flag to true. The CDPlay::Init() function returns true at this point.

```
// Set the proper time format
MCI_SET_PARMS SetParms;
SetParms.dwTimeFormat = MCI_FORMAT_TMSF;
error = mciSendCommand(m_iDeviceID, MCI_SET,
    MCI_SET_TIME_FORMAT,
    (DWORD)(LPVOID)&SetParms);
if(error)
    return false;
```

```
m_bInitialized = true;
```

Closing the device, as you might expect, is straightforward.

```
// make sure the CD stops before closing it.
if(IsPlaying())
    Stop();
mciSendCommand(m_iDeviceID, MCI_CLOSE, 0, NULL);
Clear();
```

We stop the player if necessary, send an MCI_CLOSE command to the device, and then clear the internal class variables. Now we'll look now at the CDPlay::Play() function.

LISTING 29.3

```
// This function plays a single track. If the
// looping variable is set, then it will play this track
// repeatedly.
bool CDPlay::Play()
{
    if (!m_bInitialized)
        return false;
    MCIERROR error;
    // Depending on whether we're paused or not,
    // either send a RESUME or a PLAY command to
    // the CD device.
    if (IsPaused())
    {
        MCI_GENERIC_PARMS DefaultParms;
        DefaultParms.dwCallback =
            MAKELONG(m_hWindow, 0);
        error = mciSendCommand(m_iDeviceID,
                    MCI_RESUME,
                    0,
                    (DWORD) (LPVOID) & DefaultParms);
    }
    else
    {
        MCI_PLAY_PARMS PlayParms;
```

```
        PlayParms.dwFrom = m_nCurrentTrack;
        PlayParms.dwTo = m_nCurrentTrack + 1;
        PlayParms.dwCallback = DWORD(m_hWindow);
        error = mciSendCommand(m_iDeviceID,
                    MCI_PLAY,
                    MCI_FROM | MCI_TO | MCI_NOTIFY,
                    (DWORD) (LPVOID) & PlayParms);
    }
    if (error)
    {
        m_Status = CDSTATUS_STOPPED;
        return false;
    }
    m_Status = CDSTATUS_PLAY;
    return true;
}
```

When using MCI devices, 'play' and 'resume' are two different functions. We have made the design decision with our library to simplify this into a single function, CDPlay::Play(), which always works by playing from the current 'play cursor,' much in the same way a physical audio player works. As such, we must detect the current paused status of the player and send either an MCI_PLAY or an MCI_RESUME command, as appropriate.

You will notice that one of the common parameters passed to both commands is the window handle. By giving the function this handle along with setting the MCI_NOTIFY flag, we tell the function to notify us via the Windows MM_MCINOTIFY message that the function has finished.

In the MCI_PLAY_PARMS structure, you will notice we set both dwFrom and dwTo fields to the current track value and the current track value plus one, respectively. Additionally, we indicate the usage of these values by passing MCI_FROM and MCI_TO to the dwParam1 parameter. By default, this will play a single track before stopping and sending the notification message. Although this is not standard CD-player behavior, it was deemed more useful for game programming in which a single track is typically looped for a given level or situation. If you wish to modify this behavior, there are several alternatives. First, you could set only the dwFrom field and pass its corresponding flag, which would cause the player to play from that position to the end of the CD. Alternatively, you could handle the notification messages yourself by detecting the end of the Play() function, incrementing the current track, and then calling `Play()` again. Because of the open nature of the Windows messages, either the `CDPlay` class or game code could perform this task.

Here is the code required to pause the player:

LISTING 29.4

```
bool CDPlay::Pause()
{
    if(!m_bInitialized)
        return false;
    MCIERROR error;
    MCI_GENERIC_PARMS DefaultParms;
    DefaultParms.dwCallback = MAKELONG(m_hWindow, 0);
    error = mciSendCommand(m_iDeviceID, MCI_PAUSE,
        MCI_NOTIFY, (DWORD)(LPVOID)&DefaultParms);
    if(error)
        return false;
    m_Status = CDSTATUS_PAUSED;
    return true;
}
```

The code undoubtedly looks familiar to you at this point. You will notice that we again set the Windows handle as the callback parameter. However, this command is intended to interrupt another command. As such, the message received will be slightly different after this command is sent. We'll examine this in more detail when we look at the `OnMCINotify()` function.

The `Stop()` function looks nearly identical, except for a different command and the value we set to `m_Status`.

LISTING 29.5

```
bool CDPlay::Stop()
{
    if(!m_bInitialized)
        return false;
    MCIERROR error;
    MCI_GENERIC_PARMS DefaultParms;
    DefaultParms.dwCallback = MAKELONG(m_hWindow, 0);
```

```
    error = mciSendCommand(m_iDeviceID, MCI_STOP,
        0, (DWORD)(LPVOID)&DefaultParms);
    if(error)
        return false;
    m_Status = CDSTATUS_STOPPED;
    return true;
}
```

Our next function to examine is OnMCINotify(). This function is a Windows handler function, designed to be placed in the main window-handling function of whatever window is passed to the Init() function. Here is how that might look in a typical program:

LISTING 29.6

```
long WINAPI WindowProc(HWND window, UINT message,
    UINT wParam, LONG lParam)
{
    switch (message)
    {
    case MM_MCINOTIFY:
        CDPlayer()->OnMCINotify(wParam, lParam);
        break;
    }
}
```

Placing this function here allows the player object to respond to MCI events, such as the end of a playing track. More specifically, this allows our loop functionality to determine that the track is done and to restart it. As was mentioned earlier, it could also be used to auto-increment tracks as they play, as well, or shuffle tracks, or any such functionality.

LISTING 29.7

```
bool CDPlay::OnMCINotify(WPARAM wParam, LPARAM lParam)
{
    if (!m_bInitialized)
        return false;
```

```
if (long(lParam) == m_iDeviceID)
{
    switch (wParam)
    {
        // An MCI command has successfully completed
    case MCI_NOTIFY_SUCCESSFUL:
        switch (m_Status)
        {
        case CDSTATUS_STOPPED:
            break;
        case CDSTATUS_PLAY:
            if (m_bLoop)
            {
                if (!Play())
                    return false;
            }
            else
                m_Status = CDSTATUS_STOPPED;
            break;
        };
        // An MCI command has superceded a
        // previously executed command
    case MCI_NOTIFY_SUPERSEDED:
        break;
    };
}
return true;
}
```

The function first checks to see if the CD player has been initialized and if lParam matches our device ID value. If both are true, we can check the wParam parameter for one of two messages: MCI_NOTIFY_SUCCESSFUL or MCI_NOTIFY_SUPERSEDED. The former value is sent when a function has successfully completed, such as when a track has finished playing. In this case, we only need to handle this particular message. The looping flag is checked, and if it is set, we play the current track again.

The MCI_NOTIFY_SUPERSEDED message is passed when one command, such as the MCI_PLAY command, is superseded by another command, such as MCI_PAUSE or MCI_STOP. We currently do not require handling these situations, but it is worthwhile to know that the options exist.

CONCLUSION

Although Redbook audio format playback is not as popular as it once was for games, it remains a viable option for some types of games, and it worth knowing how to add this basic functionality to your audio library's repertoire.

Next, we will look at a number of various optimizations we have made to the *GAP* audio library. We'll discuss how and why these were implemented, and what else you might want to do in order to improve the performance or memory efficiency of your audio system.

CHAPTER 30

GENERAL OPTIMIZATIONS STRATEGIES

Although audio programming does not require an extreme amount of low-level code optimization when the high-level systems and SDKs that we've covered in this book are used, we must always be aware that audio has the potential to become an extreme memory and CPU hog, simply because we're dealing with such a large set of physical resources. Time is better spent on optimizations at an algorithmic level. For instance, resource management issues typically deal with large-scale usage patterns, and great gains in optimization can be obtained by effectively predicting which resources are likely to be used most often and by ensuring that these resources remain in readily accessible memory caches, instead of having to load them from the hard disk each time they are used. After all, to paraphrase a common quote, "the most optimized file-loading function is the one that never gets called." Using this methodology, along with some careful spot-optimization and some practical guidelines, we can derail most performance issues before they actually become serious problems.

 The code listed in this chapter can be found in \Game_Audio\ audio_sdk\src\audiolib\BufferCache.h, BufferCache.cpp. Game_Audio\audio_sdk\include\audiolib\ObjectPool.h

AUDIO RESOLUTION CONSIDERATIONS

One of the old cardinal rules in audio programming is to ensure all audio source formats are matched, and this is still important today, although some details have slightly changed. Mixers must still convert audio samples to a common format before any mixing is possible, and this conversion still takes CPU time in many cases. While hardware mixing is more common than ever, there are still many cards on the market with minimal mixing capabilities, and this additional format conversion simply takes time away from an already-strained CPU.

One thing to keep in mind with modern Windows-based systems is that the old rule of matching all formats to the primary buffer no longer holds. Instead, Windows uses a system-level component, KMixer, to perform all mixing functions, and the final mixed format can only be indirectly controlled.

KMixer determines the final output mix, not the format of the primary buffer you set. In fact, the 'primary buffer' that you create and set the format on is really just an abstraction of the KMixer subsystem. This is very important, as one single 44.1 kHz sound might cause all other playing sounds to be up-sampled to this rate, instead of the single high-quality sound being mixed down. The KMixer specification is vague as to when format shifts in the primary mixing buffer occur, but there is no guarantee that the format will again drop while any audio is still playing, even if the higher-quality sample ends.

As computers have acquired more memory, disk space, and CPU horsepower, the de facto standard for audio quality has finally made the leap from 22.05 kHz, 16-bit samples to 44.10 kHz, 16-bit samples. Moreover, this quality level is now more practical than ever because most modern high-compression formats are optimized for these higher sampling rates; and as CPU power keeps increasing, it is becoming more practical to decompress a larger audio sample either at load time or on the fly.

It is unlikely that quality will rise much above this level, as there is very little to be gained from the user's perspective from further increases in sound quality. Samples at 48 kHz, or even 96 kHz and 24-bit audio are primarily used at the authoring stage because these sampling rates and bit depths are less susceptible to artifacts when processed by digital filters and mixing stages.

As such, 44.1 kHz, 16-bit samples can be considered a relatively stable, high-end target for audio quality, and you will definitely want to distribute your game's audio at this quality level, especially considering the high-end audio systems many gamers now have connected to their computers. Fortunately, newer high-compression audio codecs (and even older codecs, such as ADPCM) will allow these large amounts of data to be highly compressed while retaining a high-quality sound. Naturally, disk-based streaming can also reduce memory requirements, as well.

DEFERRED EXECUTION OF BATCH PARAMETERS

When changing 3D sound buffer parameters using DirectSound3D, you will likely have noticed that each function has an option to either mix the changes immediately or to wait and remix all the changed sound parameters at once. Obviously, you should be using deferred mixing in nearly all circumstances, especially for audio systems where there might be a large number of individual changes occurring on a significant number of 3D sounds.

Keep in mind that this even applies to most hardware property sets, as well, such as EAX. You will notice that the EAX header files include flags for choosing deferred or immediate settings. Again, unless you have a specific reason not to do so, you should always choose deferred settings for optimal performance.

Because positional audio does not require as high a frame rate as graphics, it is feasible to simply update the listener at a lower frame rate than the primary rendering loop, such as 15 or 20 times per second. Actual mixing will not occur until the listener's `CommitDeferredSettings()` function is called, even if individual sounds are updated much more often (usually corresponding to the frame rate). This simple trick can save even more CPU cycles. Depending on the type of game and how quickly objects move, you may want to adjust the rate of updates. The *GAP* library updates the listener approximately 20 times per second, which has been found to be adequate for most games. If you find it to be inadequate, you can simply adjust the timer in the code.

AVOID DYNAMIC RUN-TIME ALLOCATION WHERE POSSIBLE

One of the general rules of game programming is to avoid excessive run-time allocation and deallocation, as it tends to be very slow and can lead to worsening performance due to memory fragmentation. Various companies have different solutions for solving this problem. Some require the use of a central memory manager and allocator, which helps to finely tune allocations and run-time performance. Others simply ban run-time allocations altogether and require pre-allocation of all objects. This is a tricky problem to handle with an audio library, especially when our original design goal is to facilitate run-time, load-on-demand behavior.

Instead of attempting to pre-allocate everything we might possibly use—which is both wasteful as well as an impossible challenge with a general-purpose audio library—we've opted to utilize an allocate, cache, and reuse policy in regard to dynamic object and memory blocks. Quite simply put, our object and memory pool is allowed to grow to whatever size is required in order to accommodate the objects we wish to load. This is not quite as drastic or wasteful as it sounds, since there are other limiting factors at work. For instance, the number of active sound objects are restricted by the number of available sound buffers, which can be limited either by hardware or by a user-defined setting.

However, most of our objects are only allocated once and not technically deleted until the audio manager's Term() function is called. Again, this is not as memory-extravagant as it sounds. Most sound objects only require a couple of hundred bytes each, at most, when the sound data is unloaded. It would be rare for the total number of individual sounds in a game to exceed several thousand, meaning that even if all the sound objects were created at once, the game would not likely exceed a couple of hundred kilobytes, at most, to store all these objects concurrently in memory. In addition, if each of these objects is initialized, any object can be played on demand, as the audio system will load a sound on a background thread before playing it, if required.

There are undoubtedly places in the *GAP* audio library that could benefit from additional memory optimization and management strategies. One of the first of these places to come to mind is the somewhat extravagant use of memory buffers by some of the compressed file readers. These readers, in some circumstances, must allocate two buffers that are equal or larger in size than the largest single section of data that is decompressed at any one time. Instead of having to continuously allocate and deallocate these buffers, it would be far better to maintain a memory pool containing a large pool of these allocated buffers.

One effective strategy would be to create a manager of memory buffers designed to retrieve the smallest possible buffer among a collection of recycled buffers that have been allocated by previous readers. Because these buffers only need be concerned with a minimum size, this sort of system could work extremely well in reducing the overall number of deallocations and reallocations of similar-size buffers, helping to eliminate memory fragmentation.

Let's examine an even simpler solution that only works with an 'object-caching scheme,' which we'll learn about in the next section. Because our reader objects are not actually destroyed, we can actually preserve the largest of their memory buffers between their 'destruction,' which does not actually occur, and their 'recreation.' When these file readers are released, the objects are not destroyed, but are released to the care of an object pool, which waits for another request for one of these object types, at which point it is reused. Most of our prolific objects in the *GAP* library use this pool-management scheme (including all of the audio objects and readers)—meaning that any allocation done inside these objects can actually be preserved for the next use of that same object, instead of having to deallocate and reallocate a similar buffer during its next use.

The obvious downside to this system is that we must be careful not to extravagantly allocate memory inside these objects, as it will never be freed. This would be the case with the wave and WMA file readers, for instance. In other words, you should be careful not to read a 50 MB static buffer with either of these readers, as this memory will not be released until the audio manager is shut down. We could install some checks to ensure that extremely large buffers are deallocated when the object is no longer in use, but it is difficult to discern what 'extremely large' exactly is. It is probably best to simply avoid these silly allocations in the first place and stick to streaming large sound files, as should be done, anyhow.

The *GAP* library has implemented this basic memory-caching system in both the wave and WMA readers, although was not shown in the previous chapters in order to preserve the listings' clarity. Both the wave and WMA readers use large buffers to decompress their data, and can greatly benefit from this sort of system.

OBJECT POOL-CACHING SYSTEM

Because the *GAP* audio library uses a large number of dynamically allocated objects that might come and go, an object-caching and reuse system was devised to prevent excessive deallocation and reallocation, which can lead to degraded memory cohesion and decreased overall game-performance.

The object pool class has two parts. A rather complex macro, DEFINE_POOL(), adds a number of members and data to a class when it is included in a class declaration. A second macro, IMPLEMENT_POOL(), finishes implementing a static object as part of a class definition and is designed to be placed in the class's corresponding .cpp file.

The second part of the pool is the template-based class ObjectPool, which does all the work of actually allocating, distributing, and tracking the objects themselves. Let's take a look at all of this in Listing 30.1.

LISTING 30.1

```
#define DEFINE_POOL(ClassName) \
    public: \
    void SetPoolIndex(int32 iIndex) \
    { m_iPoolIndex = iIndex; } \
    int32 GetPoolIndex() \
    { return m_iPoolIndex; } \
    static bool ReservePool(uint32 nNumObjs) \
    { return s_ObjPool.Reserve(nNumObjs); } \
    static ClassName* CreateObject() \
    { return s_ObjPool.CreateObject(); } \
    static void DestroyObject(ClassName* pObj) \
    { s_ObjPool.DestroyObject(pObj); } \
    static void TermPool() \
    { s_ObjPool.Term(); } \
    friend class ObjectPool<ClassName>;\
    private: \
    int32 m_iPoolIndex; \
    static ObjectPool<ClassName> s_ObjPool;

#define IMPLEMENT_POOL(ClassName) \
    ObjectPool<ClassName> ClassName::s_ObjPool;

namespace Audio
{

template<class T>
class ObjectPool
{
public:
    ObjectPool()
    {}
    ~ObjectPool()
    { Term(); }

    bool Reserve(uint32 nNumObjs);
    void Term();

    T* CreateObject();
    void DestroyObject(T*);
    void DestroyAllObjects();
```

```cpp
private:
    std::vector<T*> m_aPool;
    std::vector<int32> m_aFree;
};

template<class T>
bool ObjectPool<T>::Reserve(uint32 nNumObjs)
{
    T* pT;
    m_aPool.reserve(nNumObjs);
    m_aFree.reserve(nNumObjs);
    int iPoolStart = m_aPool.size();
    for (int i = 0; i < nNumObjs; i++)
    {
        pT = new T;
        if (!pT)
            return false;
        pT->SetPoolIndex(-1);
        m_aPool.push_back(pT);
        m_aFree.push_back(iPoolStart + i);
    }
    return true;
}

template<class T>
void ObjectPool<T>::Term()
{
    for (int i = 0; i < m_aPool.size(); i++)
        delete m_aPool[i];
    m_aPool.clear();
    m_aFree.clear();
}

template<class T>
T* ObjectPool<T>::CreateObject()
{
    if (!m_aFree.size())
        Reserve(m_aPool.size() * 2 + 1);
    int32 iIndex = m_aFree.back();
    m_aFree.pop_back();
    T* pObj = m_aPool[iIndex];
    assert(pObj->GetPoolIndex() == -1);
```

```
    pObj->SetPoolIndex(iIndex);
    return pObj;
}

template<class T>
void ObjectPool<T>::DestroyObject(T* pObj)
{
    assert(pObj->GetPoolIndex() != -1);
    m_aFree.push_back(pObj->GetPoolIndex());
    pObj->SetPoolIndex(-1);
}

}; // namespace Audio
```

Without understanding what the intent of the object pool is, it might be slightly difficult to discern exactly what is going on. Let's begin by examining what happens in the two macros, DEFINE_POOL() and IMPLEMENT_POOL().

THE ObjectPool MACROS

Using these macros, a number of functions are added to the class in which we are using the pool-caching system. Two of the most important functions are CreateObject() and DestroyObject(). These are static functions that belong to the class and are designed as replacements for traditional allocation and deallocation methods, such as new or delete. Technically, it would be possible to overload the new and delete operators to perform these actions, but it seemed beneficial to make it obvious that nonstandard allocation was being performed.

There are other functions, ReservePool() and TermPool(), which are used to initially allocate objects and to delete all allocated objects. These would typically be called when the audio system is being initialized or shut down. Although the use of ReservePool() is optional, any class wishing to use object pool management must eventually call TermPool() in order to delete all of its objects, or they will leak.

Two data members are defined: a static ObjectPool object, the actual object manager, with the name of the class used as the template argument; and a single-integer m_iPoolIndex, used for management purposes by the ObjectPool class, which we'll discuss in a bit. Several related member functions help set and retrieve the integer data as well—SetPoolIndex() and GetPoolIndex().

THE ObjectPool CLASS

Now let's see what is happening in the ObjectPool class itself. Because we have instantiated this class' object with the macro, using the name of the class itself as the template argument, we are able to create and manage objects of any type, as long as the object has a default constructor. Moreover, the constructor and destructor can actually be private or protected, and this is encouraged, because this means there is no way to create the object except through the object pool. The macro declares the ObjectPool member as a friend of the class, allowing it unlimited access, including access to private constructors and destructors.

The ObjectPool class maintains two vectors, m_aPool and m_aFree, and it is crucial to understand the purpose of these two vectors before you can understand the basic operation of the object pool system.

The m_aPool member is a vector of class object pointers, and it is simply the repository for all allocated objects. The pool never shrinks—it only grows in response to demand for more objects. Allocated objects are created in batches and inserted into the back of the vector.

The m_aFree member is a vector of integers. Its purpose is to allow the manager to determine which objects are currently not in use. By simply pointing to the index of each free object, it gives the manager an $O(1)$ (constant time) algorithm for determining which object can be used next.

Let's see how this works in practice. The first function we must examine is the Reserve() function.

```
template<class T>
bool ObjectPool<T>::Reserve(uint32 nNumObjs)
{
    T* pT;
    m_aPool.reserve(nNumObjs);
    m_aFree.reserve(nNumObjs);
    int iPoolStart = m_aPool.size();
    for (int i = 0; i < nNumObjs; i++)
    {
        pT = new T;
        if (!pT)
            return false;
```

```
            pT->SetPoolIndex(-1);
            m_aPool.push_back(pT);
            m_aFree.push_back(iPoolStart + i);
        }
        return true;
    }
```

The object pool is allowed to allocate any number of objects and add them to the available pool. You can see that as the function adds these objects to the pool, the index at which they are stored in the pool vector is stored in the free vector. This will help us to quickly determine where, or if, a new free object can be found in the pool in our CreateObject() function. In fact, let's examine CreateObject() now.

```
template<class T>
T* ObjectPool<T>::CreateObject()
{
    if (!m_aFree.size())
        Reserve(m_aPool.size() * 2 + 1);
    int32 iIndex = m_aFree.back();
    m_aFree.pop_back();
    T* pObj = m_aPool[iIndex];
    assert(pObj->GetPoolIndex() == -1);
    pObj->SetPoolIndex(iIndex);
    return pObj;
}
```

The first thing this function does is to determine if there are any currently free objects by checking the size of the free index list. If no free objects can be found, the size of the object pool is doubled plus one. Now, with guaranteed free objects, we look to the free list and pop the back index off the list, which we then use to obtain an object. We then set the index of this object in the pool list, using the SetPoolIndex() function. Why set the index in the object itself? Let's look at the DestroyObject() to answer that question.

```
template<class T>
void ObjectPool<T>::DestroyObject(T* pObj)
{
    assert(pObj->GetPoolIndex() != -1);
    m_aFree.push_back(pObj->GetPoolIndex());
```

```
    pObj->SetPoolIndex(-1);
}
```

Because the object itself understands where it is located in the object pool, we can simply push this value onto the back of the free index vector to mark this object as free for use again. Additionally, by setting the object's index value to a negative number when unused, and by setting it to zero or greater when used, we gain an additional safety check, ensuring that objects are not being used multiple times or deleted more than once.

CACHING STREAMING DIRECTSOUND BUFFERS

One of the principle methods for optimizing a system is to avoid dynamic allocations where possible. Indeed, this has been the primary focus of our optimization discussion so far. However, one of the largest culprits of dynamic memory allocation has not been addressed: DirectSound itself. Well, unfortunately, we really can't do anything about the large buffers that must be continuously allocated and deallocated, can we?

You may be surprised to learn that it is actually possible to avoid having to dynamically create and destroy large numbers of DirectSound buffers. The basic strategy is simple—every buffer should become a streaming buffer. How does this solve our problem? Because we can now create buffers of uniform size, and we can freely reuse and redistribute them instead of having to destroy and reallocate large numbers of custom-size static buffers. This is essentially the same strategy that (we presume) DirectMusic uses under the hood to stream multiple segments into a single buffer.

Unfortunately, there is one problem with this approach. Extremely small sounds (smaller than the standard size of the streaming buffer) do not work well with our streaming mechanism. While we can get away with placing smaller sounds in the streaming buffers and filling the back end with silence, we cannot do this with small, looping sounds. To solve this, we simply allow small, looping buffers to have their own uniquely created DirectSound buffers. All other buffers will use standardized one-second buffers.

Next, you may be wondering about the different types of buffers. Not every buffer is created with the same options and parameters. For instance, there are stereo buffers, 2D mono buffers, and 3D mono buffers, to name a few. Additionally, some buffers might be created with different frequency characteristics than others.

We solve this problem by using the DSBUFFERDESC structure as a defining type. Each parameter and option means a different type of buffer, and so by defining a simple comparison function (equals operator), we match a requested buffer to one that already exists in the buffer cache—in other words, a buffer will only be matched up if the buffer description structure exactly matches one that is already stored. Otherwise, a new buffer will be created.

Let's examine our buffer-management system now in Listing 30.2.

LISTING 30.2

```
struct BufferInfo
{
    IDirectSoundBuffer8* m_pBuffer;
    DSBUFFERDESC m_Desc;
    WAVEFORMATEX m_Format;
};

typedef std::vector<BufferInfo*> BufferInfoVector;

class BufferCache
{
public:
    BufferCache();
    ~BufferCache();
    void Clear();

    void Init();
    void Term();

    bool Acquire(const DSBUFFERDESC& desc,
        IDirectSoundBuffer8*& pBuffer,
        bool bUseCache = true);
    void Free(IDirectSoundBuffer8* pBuffer);

private:

    BufferInfoVector m_Free;
```

```
    BufferInfoVector m_Used;
};
```

The basic component of the buffer cache is the BufferInfo struct. This contains a DirectSound buffer pointer, a buffer description structure, and a wave format structure. These three items make up a complete buffer definition.

These structures are stored in a pair of vectors, m_Free and m_Used, which are obviously used to determine which DirectSound buffers are currently free and which ones are in use.

Other than initializing and shutting down the manager, there are only two functions to deal with: Acquire() and Free(). These functions, as you might have guessed, are used to either acquire (or create) a buffer, or free it to be reused again later by another sound. Let's first take a peek at the Acquire() function in Listing 30.3.

LISTING 30.3

```
bool BufferCache::Acquire(const DSBUFFERDESC& desc,
    IDirectSoundBuffer8*& pBuffer, bool bUseCache)
{
    // If buffer caching is enabled, try to find a
    // buffer with a matching description structure
    if (DXAudioMgr()->GetInit()->m_bCacheBuffers &&
        bUseCache)
    {
        BufferInfoVector::iterator itr;
        for (itr = m_Free.begin();
            itr != m_Free.end();
            ++itr)
        {
            if ((*itr)->m_Desc == desc)
            {
                pBuffer = (*itr)->m_pBuffer;
                pBuffer->SetCurrentPosition(0);
                pBuffer->AddRef();
                m_Used.push_back(*itr);
                m_Free.erase(itr);
                return true;
```

```
            }
        }
    }

    // Create a buffer normally
    IDirectSoundBuffer* pDSBuffer;
    HRESULT hr =
    DXAudioMgr()->DirectSound()->CreateSoundBuffer(
        &desc, &pDSBuffer, NULL);
    if (FAILED(hr))
    {
        if (desc.dwFlags & DSBCAPS_CTRL3D)
        {
            DXAudioMgr()->ResetSound3DLimit();
            if (!DXAudioMgr()->RemoveSound3D(0))
                return false);
        }
        else
        {
            DXAudioMgr()->ResetSoundLimit();
            if (!DXAudioMgr()->RemoveSound(0))
                return false;
        }
        hr =
        DXAudioMgr()->DirectSound()->CreateSoundBuffer(
            &desc, &pDSBuffer, NULL);
        if (FAILED(hr))
            return false);
    }

    // Get the IDirectSoundBuffer8 interface
    hr = pDSBuffer->QueryInterface(
        IID_IDirectSoundBuffer8, (void**)&pBuffer);
    if (FAILED(hr))
        return false;

    // Release the temporary DirectSoundBuffer interface
    pDSBuffer->Release();

    // If buffer caching is enabled,
    if (DXAudioMgr()->GetInit()->m_bCacheBuffers &&
```

```
            bUseCache)
    {

        BufferInfo* pInfo = new BufferInfo;
        pInfo->m_pBuffer = pBuffer;
        pInfo->m_pBuffer->AddRef();
        memcpy(&pInfo->m_Format,
                desc.lpwfxFormat,
                sizeof(WAVEFORMATEX));
        memcpy(&pInfo->m_Desc,
                & desc,
                sizeof(DSBUFFERDESC));
        pInfo->m_Desc.lpwfxFormat = &pInfo->m_Format;
        m_Used.push_back(pInfo);
    }
    return true;
}
```

The mechanism for finding a buffer is straightforward. We simply iterate through a list of free buffers until we find one that exactly matches our specification. Although we are performing a linear search, we are not too concerned with this, as we will only be dealing with a small number of buffers.

If a matching DirectSound buffer is not found, we then proceed with the actual buffer creation. You may notice that the middle of this function looks suspiciously familiar. In fact, we've lifted it right from our Sound class and moved it into the buffer-caching class. This code attempts to create a DirectSound buffer; and if it fails, it releases one buffer before attempting to create another one.

However, you can read about this code in more detail in Chapter 11— DirectSound Buffer Management. What is of more interest to us here is the code listed before and after this buffer-creation code. Note that both of these sections of code may be bypassed by setting bUseCache to false. Likewise, there are global settings in the audio manager that can disable the caching system as well.

After a buffer is created, we must insert it into the m_Used vector. This involves a couple of memory copies and a pointer reassignment to ensure the buffer description and wave description are correct.

Next, we will examine how a buffer is freed back into the pool of usable buffers. Listing 30.4 shows how this is done.

LISTING 30.4

```
void BufferCache::Free(IDirectSoundBuffer8* pBuffer)
{
    if (pBuffer &&
        DXAudioMgr()->GetInit()->m_bCacheBuffers)
    {
        BufferInfoVector::iterator itr;
        for (itr = m_Used.begin(); itr != m_Used.end();)
        {
            BufferInfo* pInfo = (*itr);
            if (pInfo->m_pBuffer == pBuffer)
            {
                m_Free.push_back(*itr);
                itr = m_Used.erase(itr);
                return;
            }
            else
                ++itr;
        }
    }
}
```

Again, a very simple approach is taken. We perform a linear search through the list, looking for the buffer passed into the function as its only argument. When the structure containing this buffer is found, the buffer is moved from the Used list to the Free list, and the function exits.

In order to see this buffer management system in action, you can examine the *GAP* library in more detail, particularly the Sound class. You must explicitly set two flags, m_bAutoStream and m_bCacheBuffers, in the audio manager's initialization structures. It is likely that a highly dynamic audio system could save itself a considerable amount of memory fragmentation by activating this caching system.

However, you must keep in mind that you forgo some benefits of the library as well, such as the ability to decompress high-compression files (e.g., Ogg, WMA, or MP3 files) to static buffers. Because all sounds longer than one second are now streaming, your CPU overhead will increase if you use a large number of compressed sounds. As such, you will likely have to choose either PCM wave files or lightly compressed ADPCM waves for most sound effects in order to minimize the CPU impact. Because the ramifications of using this caching scheme are not as immediately obvious, it is turned off by default in the *GAP* library.

CONCLUSION

By focusing our programming energy on areas involving highly dynamic object use, memory allocation, and CPU-intensive procedures, we can considerably improve the performance of our audio library both in terms of CPU usage and memory consumption. Audio will always be a memory hog to some degree, simply because of the extremely large resources we must work with. However, an audio system does not have to drag a system to its knees in order to be highly dynamic and reasonably simple to use.

ABOUT THE CD-ROM

Game Audio Programming comes with a number of libraries, sample sources, and sample programs on the CD-ROM that accompanies the book. Here is a description of what can be found on the CD-ROM.

GAP MATERIALS

The *Game Audio Programming (GAP)* sample library source, samples, and reference documentation are all provided in the /game_audio folder. For a complete description of this library and its terms of use and distribution, see Appendix B.

Location	Description
audio_sdk\doc	Compressed HTML reference documentation on the GAP audio library.
audio_sdk\include	All header files needed to use the GAP libraries are contained in this and various subdirectories.
audio_sdk\lib	Pre-compiled libraries for the GAP audio library. Any new libraries compiled by the user will be placed in this directory.
audio_sdk\src	All source code other than header files for the GAP library are in two subfolders under this folder, AudioLib and AudioScript. AudioLib contains all the core source library files as detailed in the DirectX Audio and DirectSound3D chapters, and AudioScript contains the high-level scripting and manager code.

(continues)

Table Continued

Location	Description
AudioTest	The AudioTest project is what you should use when browsing through all the source code from the CD-ROM. It compiles and links to both the AudioLib and AudioScript in order to give you a clear picture of how the audio system work and is organized.
Data	The data folder contains some source material, including compressed and non-compressed waves for streaming and static tests, DirectMusic source, high-level sounds scripts, and other such material. We'll list some of the specific folders and what can be found in them next.
Data\dmscript	This folder contains Voice Script.spt, a DirectMusic script file containing sample data used by the ScriptTest sample program, described later in this table.
Data\music scripts	This contains two music scripts which can be loaded and played by the AudioTest sample program.
Data\segments	This contains run-time DirectMusic segments referenced by the music scripts described in the previous table entry.
Data\sound scripts	This contains three soundscapes that can be loaded and played by the AudioTest sample program.
Data\sounds	A number of wave samples referenced by the soundscapes script files described in the previous table entry.
Data\streaming	Contains various compressed and uncompressed data formats all encoded from a single song source, which can be used to test both decompression and streaming methods in the audio library.
ScriptTest	A sample application that tests the DirectMusic scripting capabilities in the GAP audio library. The sample is hard-coded to use the data\dmscript data described earlier in this table.
Voice Script	This is the DirectMusic project source of the data used in the TestScript application. The project and authoring data is provided for you to see how the data was created.

OTHER MATERIALS

All other materials may be found in the /extras folder. These include the following:

Location	Description
/DirectX 8.1	The Microsoft DirectX 8.1 SDK. Check *http://www.msdn.microsoft.com* for updated versions.
/Dolby	Contains Dolby's DISK 2 demo, which describes their technologies, as well as several documents of interest.
/Ogg Vorbis	Contains the Ogg Vorbis SDK and an encoder that can be used to convert wave files into Vorbis-encoded (*.ogg) files. The latest version can be found at *http://www.vorbis.org*.
/Sensaura	The Sensaura SDK contains sample code, programs, libraries, and a lot of great and informative reading material, some of which is extracted in the /docs folder. Visit *http://www.sensaura.com* or *http://www.sensauradeveloper.com* for more information about Sensaura products, including their latest GameCODA audio library at *http://www.gamecoda.com*.
/SourceStyler	Demo of a program used to format C/C++ in nearly any conceivable style. This demo was a great help in formatting source for this book. Visit *http://www.ochre.com* for more information and the latest version.

ABOUT THE *GAP* AUDIO LIBRARY

One of the benefits of this book, beyond the textual descriptions and in-structions, is the fully featured and professionally designed audio library that comes with it. The *GAP* audio library features a full set of HTML doc-umentation on the CD-ROM and full source code, ready for you to com-pile, use, or to dissect for learning. Or, you may decide to use it as a starting point for creating your own audio system.

LIBRARY FEATURES

The *GAP* audio library features:

- A clean, object-oriented interface designed for ease-of-use and effi-cient coding.
- Full HTML-help documentation explaining every interface, func-tion, and parameter.
- Low-level support for all essential 2D and 3D DirectSound buffer operations.
- Low-level DirectMusic segment queuing and playback.
- One initialization parameter, which enables automatic audio streaming for 2D or 3D sounds of any format.
- Supported formats, including wave files (both PCM and any ACM compressed format), Ogg Vorbis, MP3, and Windows Media Audio format, as well as any native DirectMusic file format.

- System-wide IStream-based loaders, which allow custom file systems.
- Audio objects that can be optionally loaded asynchronously, helping to avoiding frame-rate hiccups, and enabling more-dynamic management of sounds and music.
- Management of 2D and 3D sound buffers and segments based on available hardware resources or user-defined ranges.
- Initialized sound and music objects, which can be dynamically loaded and unloaded, and which will automatically preserve all settings, including volume, positional settings, and even hardware properties.
- Interfaces and support for specific property sets, including EAX 2.0 and ZoomFX, as well as generic property-set interfaces for future expansion.
- Global functions for volume control, as well as the ability to pause, resume, and stop all currently playing sounds with a single function call.
- Automatic cleanup of all audio objects, reducing the chances for memory leaks.

In addition, a high-level *GAP* scripting library is provided, which provides a number of valuable features and systems, including:

- A complete XML-like language specification and parsing system, including both high-level and low-level interfaces for internal use and further expansion.
- A 2D and 3D sound script definition system, allowing sounds to be created using string-based aliases.
- A multisound playback system, allowing multiple iterations of a sound to be created, distributed, and appropriately recycled for maximum efficiency.
- A high-level 'soundscape' object that enables audio designers to render complex audio background environments, using a simple, text-based scripting system with single-interface control for the entire batch of sounds.
- A scripted, segment-based interactive music system using the concept of 'themes' and 'interludes,' along with complex transition maps to achieve nearly any sequence of segment playback desired.

GAP LIBRARY USAGE TERMS

For a sample library, the *GAP* audio library contains a fairly significant feature set, and as such, there may be those who wish to use the library as is and/or modify it in some manner to suit their requirements. Here are the library's usage terms:

- The purchase of a copy of *Game Audio Programming* grants you the right to use, modified, and distribute the *GAP* library and sample code found in this book in any software product, commercial or otherwise.
- The *GAP* library and sample source code may be freely distributed with any software project, so long as it retains its original copyright notice and license terms.

The basic idea is that the source is yours to use freely, as long as you have paid for a copy of *Game Audio Programming*. We don't want there to be any concerns for anyone wishing to use the library in a software project. That would be completely counter-productive and negate the entire point of this book. Open-source developers are welcomed and encouraged to use this library as long as one of the developers has purchased a copy of the book, and thereby has purchased the right to use the library in their projects.

Please note that the sample content provided on the CD-ROM is not covered by this license. This content is copyrighted by James Boer and may not be reused or redistributed without the author's express written permission.

Also, remember that third-party libraries/SDKs are copyrighted by their respective owners and may be subject to additional use/distribution restrictions. The rights granted in this section for the *Game Audio Programming* libraries do not supercede any individual licensing agreements for other libraries used. See the documentation for each library or SDK you wish to use for specific details. And finally, the obligatory legal disclaimer in capital type:

THIS SOFTWARE IS PROVIDED BY THE COPYRIGHT HOLDERS AND CONTRIBUTORS "AS IS" AND ANY EXPRESS OR IMPLIED WARRANTIES, INCLUDING, BUT NOT LIMITED TO, THE IMPLIED WARRANTIES OF MERCHANTABILITY AND FITNESS FOR A

MP3 LICENSING

If you want to decode and/or distribute MP3 files with your game, you are required to pay a royalty to Franhofer and Thomson, the two companies that hold a number of joint patents that effectively give them rights to any program using the MP3 format.

As of August 2002, the royalty rates for a game using the MP3 format will cost $2,500 per title for any title selling over 5,000 copies. Use of the MP3-Pro format costs $3,750 for any title selling over 5,000 copies.

However, you should always first check the Thomson Multimedia Web site, which is dedicated to MP3 licensing, to ensure you have the latest information. For current licensing information and answers to specific questions, visit them at *http://www.mp3licensing.com*.

OGG VORBIS

Ogg Vorbis is free, open-source software. As such, you may use and distribute the Vorbis SDK and any software in accordance with the Vorbis license agreement. All Vorbis software, SDKs, and information can be found at *http://www.vorbis.com*. For more information about the Ogg project, of which Vorbis is only one component, visit their Web site at *http://www.vorbis.org*.

If you wish to support the development of high-quality open-source software, you may choose to contribute to Xiph.org (the development team responsible for Ogg Vorbis) via PayPal (*http://www.paypal.com*). The value of an open, patent-free, and high-quality code such as Vorbis is of great value to the game development community. When you help support this team, you also help ensure that products such as Vorbis continue to be developed.

AUDIO AND PROGRAMMING RESOURCES

BOOKS—AUDIO PROGRAMMING

Game Programming Gems 2, Mark DeLoura, ed., et al., Charles River Media, Inc., 2001.

Game Programming Gems 3, Dante Treglia, ed., et al., Charles River Media, Inc., 2002.

A Programmer's Guide to Sound, Tim Kientzle, Addison Wesley Longman, Inc., 1998.

BOOKS—ACOUSTICS AND AUDIO, GENERAL

Acoustics and Psychoacoustics, 2nd ed., Howard and Angus, Focal Press, 2001.

Master Handbook of Acoustics, 4th ed., F. Alton Everest, McGraw Hill, 2001.

Infinite Game Universe: Level Design, Terrain, and Sound, Guy W. Lecky-Thompson, Charles River Media, Inc., 2002.

BOOKS—PROGRAMMING

Game Programming Gems, Mark DeLoura, ed., et al., Charles River Media, Inc., 2000.

Effective C++, 2nd ed., Scott Meyers, Addison Wesley Longman, Inc., 1998.

More Effective C++, Scott Meyers, Addison Wesley Longman, Inc., 1996.

Design Patterns: Elements of Reusable Object-Oriented Software, Gamma, et al., Addison Wesley Longman, Inc., 1994.

The C++ Standard Library, Nicolai M. Josuttis, Addison Wesley Longman, Inc., 1999.

The C++ Programming Language, 3rd ed., Bjarne Stroustrup, Addison Wesley Longman, Inc., 1997.

Real Time Rendering, Möller and Haines, A K Peters, Ltd., 1999.

ONLINE RESOURCES

http://www.gameaudioprogramming.com: This book's information and update site.

http://msdn.microsoft.com: Microsoft online developers' resource site.

http://developer.creative.com: The Creative Labs developers site.

http://www.sensauradeveloper.com: The Sensaura developers site.

http://www.dolby.com: Dolby Laboratories online.

http://www.vorbis.com: Ogg Vorbis site.

http://www.gamasutra.com: General game-programming site.

http://www.iasig.org/: Interactive Audio Special Interest Group site.

http://www.borg.com/~jglatt/: Informative MIDI and wave format site.

http://www.3dsoundsurge.com/: Audio hardware-related site.

http://www.mp3licensing.com/: Thomson MP3-licensing site.

http://www.radgametools.com/: Makers of the Miles sound system.

http://www.gamecoda.com/: Sensaura GameCODA sound system site.

http://www.fmod.org/: FMOD sound system site.

INDEX